Fighting Their Own Battles

BRIAN D. BEHNKEN

Fighting Their

Own Battles

Mexican Americans,
African Americans,
and the
Struggle for
Civil Rights in Texas

■ ■ ■

The University of
North Carolina Press
Chapel Hill

Publication of this book was supported by a grant from the Iowa State University Publication Subvention Fund.

Designed by Jacquline Johnson. Set in Minion with Champion display by Tseng Information Systems, Inc. Manufactured in the United States of America.

The paper in this book meets the guidelines for permanence and durability of the Committee on Production Guidelines for Book Longevity of the Council on Library Resources.

The University of North Carolina Press has been a member of the Green Press Initiative since 2003.

Library of Congress Cataloging-in-Publication Data
Behnken, Brian D.
Fighting their own battles : Mexican Americans, African Americans, and the struggle for civil rights in Texas / Brian D. Behnken.
p. cm.
Includes bibliographical references and index.
ISBN 978-0-8078-3478-7 (cloth : alk. paper)
1. Mexican Americans—Civil rights—Texas—History—20th century. 2. African Americans—Civil rights—Texas—History—20th century. 3. Civil rights movements—Texas—History—20th century. 4. School integration—Texas—History—20th century. 5. African Americans—Relations with Mexican Americans—History—20th century. 6. Texas—Race relations—History—20th century. 7. Texas—Ethnic relations—History—20th century. I. Title.
F395.M5B56 2011
305.8009764—dc22
2010047529

15 14 13 12 11 5 4 3 2 1

Contents

Illustrations

good meals and beers made a difference in the character of this project. They include Lauren Araiza, Mark Brilliant, Randolph Campbell, David Chappell, Chris Danielson, Harland Hagler, José Angel Hernández, Theresa Jach, Max Krochmal, Gordon Mantler, Todd Moye, Brooke Newman, Stephen Prewitt, Lisa Ramos, Deb Reid, Mary Rollinson, Mark Schultz, Beth Slutsky, Greg Smithers, Simon Wendt, and numerous other friends and colleagues.

For financial assistance I am grateful to the History Department at UCD; timely research grants on two separate occasions made this project a reality. In addition, I received the Moody Research Grant from the Lyndon Baines Johnson (LBJ) Foundation for research at the LBJ Presidential Library. This very generous stipend allowed me to conduct more than a week's worth of research in the papers of President Johnson and Texas governor John Connally. I have fond memories of my time there, although thoughts of the animatronic joke-telling LBJ still freak me out. Finally, a Littleton-Griswold Grant for Research in American Legal History from the American Historical Association permitted me to tie up several loose ends at the concluding stages of this project.

Without the assistance of numerous research librarians and archivists, I would never have completed this study. I extend my heartfelt thanks to the head archivist and library director at the Texas/Dallas History and Archives Division of the Dallas Public Library, Carol Roark, the best archivist in the state of Texas. I also thank her wonderful staff, especially Rachel Howe and Adrianne Pierce. Also in the Dallas/Fort Worth area, special thanks go to Clair Galloway, Ben Huseman, and Cathy Spitzenberger at the University of Texas, Arlington, Special Collections. To Tom Kellam at the Fort Worth Public Library, many thanks. In Austin, I am profoundly grateful to the staff of the Nettie Lee Benson Latin American Collection at the University of Texas. Michael Hironymous is not only a master of sources at the "Nettie" but also wonderfully generous with his time. Michael, Robert Esparza, and Christian Kelleher all helped me find some nice illustrations at the last minute. My special thanks as well to the staff at the LBJ Presidential Library, especially Allen Fischer and Margaret Harman. For the very enjoyable time at the Austin History Center, I thank Ben Grillot and Daniel Alonzo. I am also grateful to the staff of the Dolph Briscoe Center for American History at UT, especially Aryn Glazier. Thanks go to the staff at the Houston Metropolitan Resource Center (HMRC) of the Houston Public Library and the archivists in Special Collections at UH. The HMRC's Joel Draut, a wonderful photo curator, also deserves my thanks. I very much enjoyed my time at the Robert J. Terry Library on the campus of Texas Southern University; thanks to Bernard Forrester for his assistance. The staff of the Southwestern Collection at Texas Tech University was also very helpful, especially Jenny Spurrier. In San Antonio, I benefited from the services of Frank Faulkner, Matt de Waelsche, and Clarissa Chevira at the Texana/Genealogy Department of the San Antonio Public Library as well as of Gerri Schaad, Traci Drummond, and Javier Garza at the Special Collections of UT, San Antonio. The Institute of Texas Cultures Library is another exceptional resource in San Antonio; I give thanks to Patrick Lemelle and Tom Shelton. One of my most enjoyable visits was to Corpus Christi and the Special Collections and Archives Division at the Bell Library at Texas A&M University. Many thanks to Grace Charles and Tom Kreneck for their help at the Island University. When I visited Grace and Tom during the holidays, they invited me, a lowly grad student researcher, to join them for the library's annual Christmas party—now that's good ole Texas hospitality. I give gracious thanks to Darlene Mott at the Texas State Library and Archives Commission's Sam Houston Regional Library and Research Center. Finally, I would like to thank photographer Jay Dickman for working hard to provide me with a brilliant cover image and another wonderful image for the interior of the book. The length of this paragraph alone demonstrates the importance of librarians and archivists to researchers. Again, thank you all.

In addition, I benefited immensely from the insights of movement participants who kindly agreed to speak to me about their experiences: Reverend Dr. Earl Allen, Thelma Scott Bryant, Pansy Burtis, L. Clifford Davis, Ovide Duncantell, Charles "Boko" Freeman, Reverend Marvin C. Griffin, Dr. José Angel Gutiérrez, Reverend Peter Johnson, Reverend William Lawson, Ernest McMillan, Mario Salas, Carol B. Sherman, Father Sherrill Smith, Dr. Darrell Vines, and Mary Vines. I also gratefully acknowledge the hundreds of interviews Dr. Gutiérrez conducted for his own research on Mexican American politics in Texas. Many of these interviews have been made available on the UT, Arlington's webpage, "Tejano Voices." This is a wonderful and unique source pool, and Dr. Gutiérrez is to be commended for making the interviews easily accessible to researchers. I also thank Dr. Gutiérrez for the personal images he shared with me and the tube of memorabilia he sent me in Iowa. Unfortunately, many of the most prominent African American and Mexican American participants in the civil rights movement of the 1940s and 1950s are no longer with us. While others did interview them, and those interviews served me well, their loss is a blow to scholars who rely on voices from the past to help us tell their stories.

For their thorough evaluations of my book, I wish to recognize the two readers who reviewed the manuscript for the University of North Carolina Press: Mario T. García and Amilcar Shabazz. They offered a combination of praise, thoughtful criticism, and outright disagreement. Their appraisals were right on the money; thanks to them, this is now a much stronger book. My editor at the University of North Carolina Press, Chuck Grench, showed a keen interest in my work going back to when I was a first-year grad student. I thank Chuck for shepherding me through what turned out to be a rather lengthy and cumbersome review process, and I thank others at the press who helped me, including Beth Lassiter, Ron Maner, Stevie Champion, and Jacquline Johnson.

Finally, I must thank my most intimate supporters: the members of my family. My parents, Tom and Mary Behnken, not only sustained me with love and curiosity about the project, they also gave me a place to stay for a month when I conducted research in Houston. They always had a hot meal for me at night, a welcome blessing. My Aunt Jan and Uncle Wayne McCollum did the same in Dallas on more than one occasion. In San Antonio, Uncle Jim and Aunt Gerry Rackley gave me a place to lay my head and a warm meal almost every night of a more than monthlong stay in the Alamo City. My cousin John O'Banion and his wife Laura also put up with me for a month in Austin. Meme watched the kids while I put the finishing touches on the manuscript. Thanks to you all for your hospitality and help.

My most encouraging supporter has always been my wife, Monic. Her patience, warmth, kindness, positivity, strength, and love have sustained me over the many years it has taken to bring this project to a conclusion. While I write and teach, she is busy changing the world, exploring the intersections of the law and psychology to improve the lives of children across the country. Despite her hectic schedule, Monic never grew tired of hearing my stories and anecdotes about civil rights politics and race relations in Texas. Indeed, conversations with her significantly influenced the final character of this book. I owe her more than words can say. I also owe my children. My late son Brandis taught me more about life and death than anyone else ever has. He gave me strength and willpower, and enabled me to persevere when I did not think it possible. Through Brandis, I found my finest self. I still miss him so. My daughter Elleka daily keeps me going with her smiles, laughter, and ever-increasing list of questions about the world. What a joy it is to see her grow. She gives me an energy and a love that is boundless. My third (and last!) child, Aven, entered the world at the final stages of this project. He is a wonderfully sweet little boy who has a smile and a laugh that lights up the darkest room and warms my heart. He's a fun-loving toddler who just wants to be included—in *everything* we do. Monic says Aven must be like me when I was a kid (God, I hope not!). My wife and children give me daily reassurance that our world is a good one and that my life is pretty sweet. This book is dedicated to them.

Acronyms and Abbreviations

ACLU	American Civil Liberties Union
Ad Hoc Committee	Mexican-American Ad Hoc Committee on Equal Employment Opportunity
ANMA	Asociación Nacional México-Americana (National Mexican American Association)
ARMAS	Advocating Rights for Mexican-American Students
BBC	Black and Brown Coalition
BPP	Black Panther Party
CAA	Community Action Agency
CAC	Civic Action Committee
CAP	Community Action Program
CASAA	Citizens Association Serving All Americans
CCBG	Citizens Committee for Better Government
CORE	Congress of Racial Equality
CRC	Citizens Relations Committee
DCC	Dallas Community Committee
DCCAC	Dallas County Community Action Committee
DCCCR	Dallas Coordinating Committee on Civil Rights
DISD	Dallas Independent School District
ECSC	Ecumenical Council on Social Concerns
EEOC	Equal Employment Opportunity Commission
EF	Ecumenical Fellowship
El Congreso	El Congreso del Pueblo de Habla Española (Congress of Spanish-Speaking Peoples)
EODC	Economic Opportunities Development Cooperation

FBI	Federal Bureau of Investigation
FWISD	Fort Worth Independent School District
G.I. Forum, Forum	American G.I. Forum
HA-YOU	Huntsville Action for You
H.B.	House Bill
HCCO	Harris County Council of Organizations
HCHR	Houston Council on Human Relations
HEW	Department of Health, Education, and Welfare
HISD	Houston Independent School District
HPD	Houston Police Department
ICMAA	Interagency Committee on Mexican American Affairs
INS	Immigration and Naturalization Services
INSA	Immigration and Nationality Services Act
IRCA	Immigration Reform and Control Act
ISD	independent school district
JBRL	John Brown Revolutionary League
LAC Project	Latin American Channel Project
La Liga	La Liga Pro-defensa Escolar (School Improvement League)
LCCR	Leadership Conference on Civil Rights
LDF	Legal Defense Fund of the NAACP
LISD	Lubbock Independent School District
LULAC	League of United Latin American Citizens
MAEC	Mexican American Education Council
MALDEF	Mexican American Legal Defense and Education Fund
MAPA	Mexican American Political Association
MAYO	Mexican American Youth Organization
MBGC	Missionary Baptist General Convention
Mine Mill	International Union of Mine, Mill, and Smelter Workers
MM	Minority Mobilization
NAACP	National Association for the Advancement of Colored People
NFWA	National Farm Workers Association
OEO	Office of Economic Opportunity
PASO	Political Association of Spanish-Speaking Organizations

PP2	Peoples Party II
PPC	Poor People's Campaign
Project FREE	Family, Rehabilitation, Education, Employment Project
PUSH	People for Upgraded Schools in Houston
PVL	Democratic Progressive Voters League
PYA	Progressive Youth Association
RUP	La Raza Unida Party
SCLC	Southern Christian Leadership Conference
SDA	Students for Direct Action
SDS	Students for a Democratic Society
SER	Operation SER
SMU	Southern Methodist University, Dallas
SNCC	Student Nonviolent Coordinating Committee
SSB	Social Security Board
TEA	Texas Education Agency
TGNC	Texas Good Neighbor Commission
TSU	Texas Southern University, Houston
TSUN	Texas State University for Negroes, Houston
UT	University of Texas
UTMB	University of Texas Medical Branch
VISTA	Volunteers in Service to America

Introduction

In 1957 Texas legislators drafted a plethora of segregationist legislation designed to circumvent the *Brown v. Board of Education* decision outlawing school segregation. Mexican American and African American civil rights activists quickly organized to prevent these bills from passing.* But when a few Mexican Americans associated with the League of United Latin American Citizens (LULAC) suggested working with blacks in the National Association for the Advancement of Colored People (NAACP), LULAC national president Felix Tijerina sternly reprimanded his colleagues, saying: "Let the Negro fight his own battles. His problems are not mine. I don't want to ally with him." Over the next two decades, such sentiments intensified as the school desegregation battles continued. In 1970, for instance, the school district in Houston implemented a desegregation plan that combined only black and Mexican American schools. Angered by this decision, Mexican Americans boycotted classes and formed *huelga* or strike schools. Some also appealed to black activist and NAACP official Reverend D. Leon Everett, the lone African American on the school board, for assistance. But at a school board meeting, an unnamed Mexican American youth yelled to Everett: "We don't want to

---

A note on terminology and translations. Throughout this book "black" and "African American" are used interchangeably to represent this community. In some places, "Negro" denotes specific references where the word is commonly used (e.g., the Negro press). For the Mexican-origin community, I use the terms "Mexican American," "Mexican-descent," "Mexican-origin," and, where chronologically and politically acceptable, "Chicano/a," "Latino/a," and "Hispanic." Persons of European ancestry are referred to as "white," "Anglo," and "Anglo American." For names and phrases in Spanish, I follow the usage of diacritical markings, especially the accent mark, as preferred by the historical actors using such markings. In conformance with convention, diacritical marks have been omitted in the names of legal cases. Unless otherwise noted, all translations are my own.

1

go to school with the Blacks because they are dirty!" Reverend Everett was incensed. "As a Black man I will join any group of oppressed people," he stated, "but when that group employs the same form of discrimination that I have been up against all these years, I will cut them loose." Everett then repeated Felix Tijerina's rebuke: "Let them fight their own battles."[1]

Although the circumstances clearly differed, Tijerina and Everett both ultimately responded negatively to the concept of Mexican American and African American unity. Their reactions encapsulated the tense nature of black and Mexican American relations during the civil rights era in Texas. From the 1940s to the 1970s, both groups fought numerous battles—in the courts, at the ballot box, in schools, and on the street—in an effort to eradicate state-imposed racism and de jure and de facto segregation. Indeed, Mexican Americans and blacks had a long history of civil rights activism in Texas and the Southwest. They won many significant victories during the civil rights era. But unification largely eluded these groups. Instead, two separate civil rights struggles occurred simultaneously. Despite repeated calls for cooperation and a number of examples of interethnic alliances, African Americans and Mexican Americans ultimately "fought their own battles." This book examines the history of both civil rights struggles.

Studies of the civil rights movement continue to capture the attention of scholars and the lay public. African Americans initiated the modern civil rights movement in the early twentieth century with lawsuits that challenged Jim Crow segregation. Blacks began to resort to more confrontational tactics during World War II, specifically in the Double Victory campaign, which sought to win a war in favor of democracy but also to secure liberty at home. In the late 1940s and into the 1950s, the movement gained momentum. Blacks won important lawsuits such as *Smith v. Allwright*, which destroyed the white primary; *Sweatt v. Painter*, which outlawed segregation in postsecondary educational facilities in Texas; and *Brown v. Board of Education*, which overturned the 1896 *Plessy v. Ferguson* decision that had served as the foundation for segregation. By the late 1950s and the early 1960s, African Americans organized grassroots, locally led, and nonviolent direct action demonstrations, including sit-ins, marches, pickets, and boycotts, to force southern governments to eradicate Jim Crow. After the passage of the Civil Rights Act of 1964 and the Voting Rights Act of 1965, many African Americans took part in the more aggressive Black Power movement. Black Power sought not only civil rights, but also economic and political equality, an end to discrimination in the labor force, the cessation of police brutality, and community control, among other things. The most intense period of protest activism ultimately came to an end in the 1970s.[2]

Much like their African American counterparts, Mexican American civil rights activists focused on military service and lawsuits to challenge the segregation of Mexican-origin people. During World War II, Mexican Americans served in the armed forces in great numbers and hoped that their service would win rights at home. Their hopes were misplaced. So Mexican American civic groups began to more forcefully push for rights. They won several important legal victories in their fight against Jim Crow. These included the 1947 *Mendez v. Westminster* and 1948 *Delgado v. Bastrop ISD* rulings, both of which began the process of school integration in the Southwest. In 1954 Mexican Americans won the *Pete Hernandez v. Texas* case, which barred the exclusion of Mexican-origin people from juries in the United States. In the next decade Mexican Americans also engaged in a great deal of political activism, creating groups like the "Viva Kennedy" clubs and the Political Association of Spanish-Speaking Organizations (PASO), which helped elect Mexican American candidates to local, state, and national offices. At the same time, the labor movement gained momentum when Cesar Chavez founded the National Farm Workers Association (NFWA). The NFWA conducted strikes across the nation. The political and labor activism of the 1960s pushed the Mexican American struggle into more radical territory. The militant Chicano or Brown Power movement focused on an aggressive agenda of community uplift, antipolice brutality, political activism, and antipoverty. The headiest days of Mexican American activism came to an end in the 1970s.[3]

American historians typically characterize the "civil rights movement" as a southern, black/white phenomenon. However, this book demonstrates that there was no single civil rights movement in the United States. Rather, almost every ethnic group—blacks, Latino/as, Asian Americans, Native Americans—engaged in their own civil rights battles. But the Mexican American and African American movements remain the two most influential, and longest lasting, freedom struggles. This book, an exercise in comparative civil rights history, bridges the fields of black and Mexican American history.[4] While comparative history has generally addressed questions of colonialism, nation building, and empire, a comparative theoretical framework can offer many new insights on American race relations and civil rights scholarship.[5] For example, this book reveals not only the major events of each movement, the principal players, and the tactics used, but also how events, leaders, and tactics differed. A comparative focus shows the ways in which the two movements intersected and diverged throughout the period and the reasons for that convergence and divergence. Additionally, a comparison of the two movements permits a sustained discussion regarding the divisive power of race, the nature of racial formation, and the concomitant racial transformations that both civil rights movements wrought. By exploring the shifting and contested boundaries of race, this study demonstrates not only how blacks and Mexican Americans challenged the racial caste system in Texas, but also how such challenges strained relations between these two groups, fragmented attempts at coalition building, and bifurcated both civil rights movements. In short, a comparative examination sheds light on the causes of Mexican American and African American disunity.

The Lone Star State offers a unique case study for such a comparative examination. Texas was the only southern state with a large Mexican American population and the only southwestern state with a significant black population. Out of nearly 10 million in 1950, blacks constituted approximately 13 percent, or 977,458 people. In 1960 the total number of blacks climbed to 1,187,125, although their percentage of the total population dropped to 12.4. In 1970 the population had reached 1,395,853, or 12.5 percent. The Mexican American community is more difficult to tabulate because the U.S. Bureau of the Census counted persons of Latin American heritage as white. Still, a rough estimate is available based on census figures taken in 1940 and 1970. In those years, the Mexican-origin population stood at 736,433 (or 11.5 percent) and 1,981,861 (or 17.7 percent), respectively. In other words, blacks and Mexican Americans had substantial and relatively equal numbers during the civil rights period.[6]

Texas also recommends itself for comparative study because of the incredible amount of civil rights activism witnessed throughout the era. For African Americans nationwide, the state served as the front line of the early movement and black legal victories such as *Smith v. Allwright* (1944) and *Sweatt v. Painter* (1950) inspired the national civil rights struggle. But, as in the rest of the South, the battle against Jim Crow was a local phenomenon. It included lawsuits, sit-ins, stand-ins, pickets, boycotts, marches, and other forms of direct action against segregated public and private facilities, against police brutality, and against racism more generally. Mexican Americans also struggled for rights in Texas. Much of the early movement involved Mexican Americans pushing for legal and political recognition as whites. Throughout U.S. history, race has operated as a binary, with whites on one side and blacks on the other. While Mexican-descent people did not easily fit into this binary, to gain rights they argued for status as white people. Activists also engaged in walkouts, boycotts, strikes, marches, and political campaigns to win equal rights in the 1950s, 1960s, and 1970s.

Mexican Americans and African Americans sought to overcome a similar type of segregation. Texas had, in both effect and practice, a dual Jim Crow system. Blacks and Mexican Americans fought to destroy a rigid system of de jure racial separation as well as de facto segregation. For blacks, the Jim Crow system was sacrosanct. As historian C. Vann Woodward observed more than four decades ago, "The Jim Crow laws applied to *all* Negroes. . . . The Jim Crow laws put the authority of the state or city in the voice of the street-car conductor, the railway brakeman, the bus driver, the theater usher, and also in the voice of the hoodlum of the public parks and playgrounds. They gave free rein and the majesty of the law to mass aggressions that might otherwise have been curbed, blunted, or deflected."[7] Mexican-descent people also encountered persistent discrimination in public accommodations, in schools, and at the ballot box. Indeed, Gilbert González, Ruben Donato, and others have shown that the segregation of Mexican-origin children in schools constituted a virulent form of de jure segregation.[8] But everyday circumstances and skin color allowed some Mexican Americans to avoid the most stultifying aspects of racial segregation. As David Montejano has pointed out, "'Jim Crow' may appear to be an odd description of the situation of Mexicans in Texas. There was no constitutionally sanctioned 'separate but equal' provision for Mexicans as there was for blacks. . . . But in political and sociological terms, blacks and Mexicans were basically seen as different aspects of the same race problem."[9] Anglo racial sentiments resulted in two segregation systems in Texas, a practice replicated in part throughout the Southwest.

The double Jim Crow system had many commonalities for both groups. Texas had five state-mandated segregation laws. The state's 1876 constitution legally segregated schools. The legislature also ensured the segregation of Mexican-descent children by making English the exclusive language used in schools.[10] In 1891, state law segregated the races in passenger cars on all rail lines and mandated separate railroad waiting facilities (the legislature eventually extended both laws to cover bus travel). Jim Crow statutes also separated water fountains and other public facilities. A poll tax instituted in 1902 and the establishment of the white primary in 1923 easily disenfranchised African American, Mexican American, and poor white voters. Additionally, a political boss system in South and Southwest Texas guaranteed that Mexicans and Mexican Americans either did not vote or voted for the candidate chosen by their employer. An antimiscegenation law rounded out the state's Jim Crow laws.[11]

Furthermore, various cities enacted statutes that prevented interracial contact. Houston city ordinances segregated streetcars in 1903; additional legal measures segregated hotels, restaurants, and theaters in 1907. A 1922 city code mandated "white only" and "black only" parks and forbade black/white cohabitation. And local customs forced nonwhites into certain parts of the city, mainly the Second, Third, Fourth, and Fifth wards.[12] Although Dallas and San Antonio had no laws that segregated restaurants, stores, and neighborhoods, local custom and economics ensured separation. Blacks and Mexican Americans were relegated to different neighborhoods, forced into low-paying jobs, and generally disregarded by local governments. Austin had a number of customs that divided blacks and whites in stores and neighborhoods, at the central library, and in the main hospital.[13] Besides state and local law, white Texans buttressed Jim Crow with lynch violence. "More than other Americans," historians William Carrigan and Clive Webb argue, "blacks and Mexicans lived with the threat of lynching throughout the second half of the nineteenth and the first half of the twentieth century."[14] Since local conventions formed the basis of much of this system, Mexican Americans frequently suffered the burden of racial segregation, discrimination, and lynching—hence two Jim Crows.

In addition to the Jim Crow system, Anglo Americans tended to regard African Americans and Mexican Americans as racially inferior and degenerate. Perceptions of white superiority and black/Mexican American inferiority allowed whites to bolster segregation with an understanding of racial difference that seemed natural, genetic, and immutable. A challenge to the segregation order thus disturbed a vaguely defined collection of racial, social, and moral beliefs.[15] In the battle for civil rights, blacks and Mexican Americans not only confronted Jim Crow, they also challenged this array of racist assumptions about nonwhite people. As both groups discovered, integrating restaurants and securing government aid proved far easier than eradicating the racist views that many white people continued to hold.

Both the Mexican American and African American civil rights movements attempted to eradicate the Lone Star State's entrenched system of racial segregation. Ironically, Jim Crow actually contributed to the emergence of two separate freedom movements. Because segregated spaces were designated for blacks, whites, and Mexicans, Jim Crow not only separated blacks and Mexican Americans from whites, but also from each other. From the outset of the civil rights movement, then, both groups saw themselves as separated by Jim Crow. The racial geography of Texas contributed to this perception. Since the majority of African Americans lived in the eastern part of the state—the so-called Black Belt—and the majority of Mexican Americans lived to the south and west, both groups were separated not only by Jim Crow but also by miles of space. While many civil rights leaders argued that black people and Mexican-origin people had much in common, distance meant their assertions often fell on deaf ears.

Mexican American white racialization contributed to disunity with black Texans. A number of immigrant groups—Jews, the Irish, eastern Europeans—all fought (and won) recognition as white people.[16] William Edward Burghardt Du Bois posited that white workers in the late nineteenth century received "a public and psychological wage" in compensation for low real wages, a terminology reframed by David Roediger as "the wages of whiteness."[17] Matthew Frye Jacobson has further contended that in order to maintain these "wages of whiteness" and to establish a stronger racial bulwark against blacks, "racial differences *within* the white community lost their salience." In other words, more "whites" meant better resistance to black rights.[18] Mexican Americans also fought to become white. They challenged discrimination by insisting that segregation should not apply to them since they were white, not black. Patrick Carroll has observed that in their struggle for equality, Mexican Americans "thought the first and most important step involved recognition by everyone of Mexican Americans' whiteness."[19] Indeed, the focus and debate on whiteness as a strategy of uplift was wide-ranging throughout this period. As a number of Mexican American leaders pragmatically understood, the whiteness strategy could provide Mexican-origin people a measure of safety on the white side of the Jim Crow system. These leaders made numerous appeals to local, state, and federal authorities for classification as white. Additionally, in many legal cases attorneys argued that segregation violated the rights of Mexican Americans because they were white. Historians Neil Foley, Thomas Guglielmo, Steven Wilson, Clare Sheridan, and Michael Phillips have all noted that whiteness had the potential to grant Mexican Americans rights.[20]

Mexican racial ideologies influenced Mexican American attitudes toward African Americans. Mexico had a racial makeup similar to that of the United States. Mexico's racial hierarchy positioned white Mexicans at the top of the socioeconomic ladder and mixed-race or dark-skinned Mexicans at the bottom. White racial privilege and antiblack racism in Mexico proved just as virulent as racism in the United States. Moreover, the Mexican government periodically banned the immigration of blacks, which sent a clear message to Mexicans about how they should regard persons of African descent. When Mexicans emigrated to the United States, they transported their own racial ideals and found an analogous system in the American racial binary and in

Jim Crow.[21] Consequently, to secure civil rights some Mexicans and Mexican Americans attempted to distance themselves from their nonwhite lineage. Whiteness proved a natural choice for many Mexicans—later Mexican Americans—because they already understood its value.

Mexican American white racialization as a strategy of uplift proved to be a complex phenomenon. For example, some Mexican Americans who fought for recognition as white people were phenotypically white. Consequently, whiteness made sense to them because they had white skin. The majority of the Mexican-descent population, however, came from a mixed-race or mestizo stock.[22] Some of these individuals pushed for a white identity even though they were not phenotypically white. Hence, they used whiteness strategically to gain rights, although many probably did not realistically think of themselves as Caucasian. Some Mexican Americans equated whiteness with first-class citizenship. Thus, white racial positioning had less to do with race and more to do with their hopes for status as citizens and the rights that came with citizenship. Finally, and importantly, whiteness crossed class lines. Elites did not solely advocate for the whiteness strategy. Rather, individual Mexicans Americans at all class levels argued in favor of white rights. In sum, whiteness presented Mexican Americans with a useful tool in their civil rights movement, but it also posed a significant dilemma for Mexican-origin people, especially in their interactions with black people.[23]

Mexican Americans' focus on whiteness ultimately damaged their relations with African Americans. By arguing for whiteness, Mexican Americans attempted to destroy Jim Crow as it applied to Mexican-origin people. Since blacks battled to end segregation altogether, Mexican American white racial formation ran counter to African American aims. Moreover, in fighting for white rights, some Mexican Americans practiced antiblack racism and conscientiously resisted black civil rights. Of course, not all Mexican Americans engaged in white racial formation. Equally important, not all Mexican Americans who fought for white rights were unfriendly toward blacks. Indeed, the concept of Mexican American/African American unity and whiteness caused considerable controversy within Mexican American leadership circles. As will be shown, white racialization and the idea of interethnic cooperation strained relations within groups like LULAC and the American G.I. Forum. These groups and others like them had a conservative wing that pushed the whiteness strategy and distanced Mexican Americans from black people, but also a liberal wing that either did not advocate whiteness or that promoted whiteness in a way that was not antagonistic toward blacks. Whiteness, therefore, had the potential to win rights, but it also divided blacks and

Mexican Americans while simultaneously causing rifts within the Mexican American movement. Obviously the whiteness strategy was only one tactic in the broader quest for Mexican American rights. And, according to the racial binary, the only alternative to fighting for white rights was fighting for black rights. Since the black community remained segregated and since American racism relegated blacks to second-class citizenship, for Mexican Americans, fighting for black rights hardly made sense.

The black response to the whiteness strategy varied. Some blacks interpreted white racial formation negatively. They saw it as proof that Mexican Americans, like racist Anglos, opposed the black movement. This made Mexican Americans adversaries of black civil rights. For these African Americans, whiteness signaled a great hostility to the black freedom struggle. "It's like having a brother violate some right of yours," noted activist Reverend Claude Black. "You can hate the brother much more than you would the outsider because you expected more from the brother." Others chose to ignore the Mexican American movement because of the whiteness strategy. And some simply did not care about whiteness, preferring to work with Mexican Americans sympathetic to blacks and disregarding those unsympathetic to the black struggle.[24]

African Americans often expressed their own prejudicial sentiments about Mexican Americans. Although they were more discreet when airing discriminatory attitudes, blacks often copied the opinions of whites regarding Mexican Americans. Some African Americans tended to regard Mexican Americans as foreigners who took jobs from the native born. Additionally, some blacks viewed Mexican Americans who fought for rights as simply imitating the black freedom struggle. As legal scholar George Martínez has cogently observed, blacks felt that "Mexican-Americans have been free riders. African-Americans fight for civil rights; Mexican-Americans ride their coat tails and share in the benefits."[25] These sentiments certainly did not win many Mexican American friends. Despite such attitudes, African Americans watched jealously as Mexican Americans won a number of civil rights battles. In the 1940s and 1950s, for instance, Mexican Americans secured the support of a number of local, state, and national white leaders. African Americans found only massive resistance from Anglo leaders, and they coveted the success of the Mexican American community. Blacks came to regard Mexican Americans as competitors who took political power away from African Americans and monopolized government aid programs. Such attitudes prevented a close working relationship between blacks and Mexican Americans.[26]

In the late 1960s some Mexican Americans began to distance themselves from whiteness during the more radical Chicano movement. Chicanos argued that individuals of Mexican heritage were an identifiable minority—they were brown, not white. As a distinct minority, Chicanos could more easily utilize the Equal Protection clause of the Fourteenth Amendment to the U.S. Constitution. They could also more easily become the allies of blacks. Despite this effort at racial repositioning, African Americans continued to have problematic relations with Mexican Americans. The move away from whiteness did not end racism; some Chicanos continued to air racist opinions about black people.[27] Moreover, some blacks found the brownness strategy disingenuous. Mexican Americans, these black activists argued, had fought for white rights for decades. Why had they suddenly changed tactics? For African Americans, the answer to this question lay in the success that the black freedom struggle enjoyed in the 1960s and that Mexican Americans coveted. In fact, Mexican Americans envied the success of the black movement in the same way that blacks had been envious of Mexican American victories in the 1940s and 1950s. Black victories not only made the Mexican American movement appear stagnant, they also destroyed Jim Crow and eliminated some of the potential benefits granted by whiteness. African American successes had forced Chicanos to change tactics. Blacks interpreted Chicano racial repositioning in a negative light and saw brownness as a reactionary tactic.[28]

More opportunities for cooperation existed during the Brown Power/Black Power era than in any period before, primarily because of the ethnic and class focuses of militant blacks and Chicanos. But each group still experienced problems uniting. For instance, African American anger toward Mexican Americans intensified at this time. As a minority, Chicanos competed with blacks for local government aid and national War on Poverty programs. African Americans lashed out violently at Mexican Americans on several occasions. This violence further contributed to the degradation of relations between blacks and browns. So too did the cultural nationalism that both the Black Power and Chicano Power movements adopted. Some movement participants embraced the ideal that black culture and Chicano culture had to be explored to counter negative stereotypes about black and brown people. But part of this exploration involved separating each group in order to more fully examine black or brown cultural dynamics. Cultural nationalism, then, led to the separation of black and brown people.[29]

Much of the rhetoric coming from African American and Mexican American leaders further damaged efforts at coalition building. For instance, while blacks issued calls for unity, they rarely followed through with concrete action.

Their verbal endorsement of unification was ultimately one-sided and insincere. Some of the discourse of Mexican American leaders equally damaged cooperation. For instance, in the 1960s, as blacks won numerous civil rights victories, Mexican Americans began to say that Mexican-origin people had suffered more than blacks and therefore deserved more state support. For black people, such an argument was offensive. In short, ill-conceived and tactless rhetoric damaged efforts aimed at unity.

A unified movement might have had greater success than the two individual struggles. Examples of black/brown unity bear this point out. In the fifties and sixties, blacks and Mexican Americans in San Antonio banded together to elect Henry B. Gonzalez to the Texas Senate and the U.S. House. Similarly, Black Power and Brown Power advocates developed several successful, albeit short-lived, coalitions to challenge racist local governments and combat police brutality. The labor movement, which tended to view social problems as based on economics rather than race, also witnessed cooperation between blacks and Mexican Americans. Moreover, when Mexican Americans and blacks joined forces to battle school segregation in Corpus Christi in 1970, their combined numbers forced the district to integrate schools fairly. Alas, these examples proved atypical. Instead, blacks fought for their community, while Mexican Americans fought for theirs. Of course, there is nothing to say that blacks and Mexican Americans should have united. Certainly different groups experience racism and discrimination differently, and they develop divergent methods to redress wrongs. But the fact that both groups tried to unite demonstrates that cooperative ventures could serve as effective weapons in the battle against Jim Crow. Be that as it may, throughout the civil rights period little unity occurred.

This book explores the history of both civil rights movements. Each chapter treats the African American and Mexican American movements independently before moving on to a comparison of the two undertakings and areas of interracial conflict and cooperation. Until now, no scholar has detailed the broad history of the Mexican American and black civil rights battles in Texas; I hope this book will fill a significant hole in the literature. I ultimately demonstrate that cultural dissimilarities, class tensions, organizational and tactical differences, and geographic distance reduced the potential for cooperative ventures between blacks and Mexican Americans. But my principal argument focuses on how racial prejudices hampered attempts to build a united movement. Of all the factors contributing to disunity, race and racism caused the most problems and dealt coalition building its most devastating blow. Racial animosities substantially reduced cooperation between these groups and divided the black and Mexican American struggles. The racial sentiments and prejudices of both Mexican Americans and blacks undercut the chances for a concerted, united, and cooperative civil rights movement. As Felix Tijerina and D. Leon Everett stated, both groups fought their own battles.

Advancing the Cause of Democracy

The Origins of Protest in the Long Civil Rights Movement

On a warm Monday night in May 1950, a handful of dynamite easily destroyed Robert and Marie Shelton's American dream. The bomb ripped through the African American couple's newly purchased home in South Dallas, demolishing their front porch, knocking the house off its foundation, and leaving behind a large hole in the ground. Robert received cuts and gashes about his face from flying debris, while Marie was uninjured. Roughly one month later, a bundle of dynamite exploded along the side of taxi driver Dennis Huffman's recently purchased home, also in South Dallas. The unoccupied house received only slight damage, but the next day a massive bomb obliterated Johnnie Staton's new home. Staton had not yet moved into the house, and no one sustained injuries from the explosion.[1]

The black citizens of South Dallas suffered more than fifteen racially motivated bombings in 1950 before the attacks ended. Like bombings in Birmingham, Alabama, and other southern cities, the terrorist acts in Dallas stemmed from the migration of blacks out of overcrowded segregated neighborhoods and into areas zoned for white use.[2] But in South Dallas, two of the main suspects were Mexican American men who felt threatened by the encroachment of African American families into white neighborhoods. One of these individuals, Pete Garcia, later admitted that he had painted "For Whites Only" signs in the neighborhood, threatened black home buyers with a knife, and chased two African American real estate agents out of the area. Several blacks had spotted Garcia near a home shortly before a bomb exploded. Dallas police arrested Garcia for the bombings. At his trial, despite his admitted abhorrence of African Americans and close proximity to a bombed house, an all-white jury refused to convict Garcia.[3]

Incidents like the South Dallas bombings divided Mexican Americans and blacks. Because at least two of the accused bombers were of Mexican descent, these episodes confirmed for some black Dallasites that Mexican Americans shared not only the racist attitudes of Anglos but also the violent proclivities that accompanied such racism. Of course, the Dallas bombings were the exception—few Mexican Americans disliked black people so much that they threw bombs. But as Michael Phillips has observed, "African American gains could only mean loss for Mexican Americans while oppression of his [Garcia's] black neighbors provided a quick route to whiteness."[4]

The early to mid-twentieth century witnessed the development of the African American and Mexican American freedom struggles, what Jacquelyn Dowd Hall has termed "the long civil rights movement."[5] Both groups experienced obstacles that blocked their paths to political, social, and economic uplift. The development of the dual Jim Crow system limited black and Mexican American options in fighting for rights. Moreover, the racist perceptions of whites that Mexican Americans and African Americans constituted racially degenerate and inferior groups further circumscribed their efforts. When fighting for civil rights, African Americans primarily focused on winning legal battles to eradicate some of the most offensive aspects of Jim Crow segregation, concentrating, for example, on removing obstacles to suffrage and black access to higher educational facilities. Indeed, Texas saw some of the earliest and most important legal victories in the national civil rights movement. Mexican Americans primarily fought for rights by positioning themselves as members of the white race in order to avoid Jim Crow. Mexican American leaders had a number of successes in obtaining recognition as white people from the state government. But the whiteness strategy frustrated a close working relationship with black Texans. In this time frame, African Americans and Mexican Americans rarely discussed forming coalitions, something they would each debate in the 1950s, 1960s, and 1970s. Instead, both movements traveled on parallel tracks as each group fought its own battles.

African Americans in Texas fought for civil rights long before a "civil rights movement" existed. In the early twentieth century, much of the freedom struggle occurred on the local level and took place spontaneously. Jim Crow ruled the day, which seriously curtailed efforts aimed at uplift. Segregation also meant that blacks had to establish a separate community with its own infrastructure. This helped to insulate African Americans while simultaneously giving them a concrete goal for which to fight. Businesspeople, attorneys, teachers, and members of the clergy all participated in the early struggle. Many of these individuals would come to form the backbone of the civil rights movement in the fifties and sixties. Moreover, since black preachers earned their livelihood via the church, religious and business concerns frequently merged. In addition to business and the ministry, blacks also began to more forcefully push for rights after the emergence of the NAACP.

As a segregated community, black Texans needed their own business establishments. Fighting for black-owned businesses contributed to the broader struggle for civil rights. In Houston, Dallas, San Antonio, and most other cities, the Negro press actively promoted the development of the black business sector. For example, in 1921 Clifton Richardson, the longtime editor of the weekly *Houston Informer*, argued: "Have we no race pride? no self-respect? . . . Are we content to forever serve in the 'Sambo,' 'Uncle Ned,' 'Aunt Dinah,' and 'Sally Ann' role both from a political, commercial and civic viewpoint?" Richardson wanted African Americans to develop a system of black capitalism as a way not only of generating "race pride," but also of overcoming the hardships of segregation. Business ventures, he maintained, could serve as a way to circumvent the most uncomfortable aspects of Jim Crow.[6]

Public transportation emerged as one area where African American businesspeople challenged racism. Reminiscent of big cities today, taxicabs often refused service to blacks. As a result, African Americans established an independent type of taxi service called a "jitney." Jitneys became a fixture in black communities such as Houston and Dallas, and some jitney drivers eventually transformed themselves into legitimate taxi services. But the jitneys also took profits from white businesses, which caused a backlash against them. In 1923 the Houston City Council banned jitney transportation after several white-owned businesses complained about lost profits. But the jitney drivers refused to halt their service and banded together to force the city to conduct a referendum to decide the jitney issue. Alas, the jitneys lost this vote by a two-to-one margin, which brought jitney service to an end.[7]

Dallas, Houston, and other cities served as distinct sites of African American culture and nightlife, another important aspect of community development. In particular, Dallas's Deep Ellum rivaled blues centers in Memphis, Harlem, and elsewhere. Blacks originally settled the area as part of "freedmen's town" after the Civil War. In the early twentieth century, Deep Ellum emerged as a business district with several restaurants, dance halls, bars, nightclubs, pawnshops, and domino parlors. But music was key. Deep Ellum became a way station for blues travelers en route to gigs in Tennessee, Louisiana, New York, or on the West Coast. Huddie "Leadbelly" Ledbetter and "Blind" Lemon Jefferson, who sang together, had their careers take off in Dallas. Robert Johnson and Bessie Smith also frequently performed in Deep Ellum. The music and festive atmosphere proved a balm to black Texans, while at the same time Deep Ellum afforded black entrepreneurs the opportunity to expand their business interests. As authors Alan Govenar and Jay Brakefield have written, Deep Ellum "was a crossroads, a nexus, where peoples and cultures could interact and influence each other in relative freedom." Unfortunately, integration killed the distinctiveness of Deep Ellum, although it reemerged in the twentieth century as a tourist trap much like Beale Street in Memphis.[8]

Education provided another area of African American employment, one that black leaders hoped would lead to equality. Since segregated black schools and colleges needed teachers, these facilities gave many local people much-needed jobs. But education also fit in well with the broader freedom struggle since teachers instructed students about their rights. Some African American educators encouraged their faculty to join groups like the NAACP. Matthew Dogan, the president of Wiley College in Marshall, actively promoted the NAACP. At Tillotson College in Austin, Mary Branch, the first woman of color to serve as a college president in Texas, also encouraged membership in the association. This support produced some amazing results. For instance, James Farmer was born in Marshall and in 1938 received a bachelor's degree from Wiley College. In 1942 Farmer went on to found the Congress of Racial Equality (CORE), one of the most important civil rights organizations in American history.[9] Lulu White, Moses Leonard Price, Eldrewey Stearns, Earl Allen, and many other civil rights leaders received their higher educations at Texas's historically black colleges.

Black ministers contributed to the educational and spiritual uplift of black Texans as well as to the broader struggle for rights. Those who promoted civil rights also advocated education for African Americans. They understood the value of colleges in cultivating a future generation of leaders. Additionally, black ministerial organizations like the Missionary Baptist General Convention (MBGC) stridently supported education and civil rights. MBGC president Reverend Albert A. Lucas, for example, drew on the power of Baptist churches in Texas to financially assist three colleges; Mary Allen College in Crockett, Union Seminary in Houston, and Guadalupe College in Seguin. He also helped the NAACP in the *Smith v. Allwright* case. When Reverend Moses L. Price succeeded Lucas as president of the MBGC, he continued many of Lucas's educational initiatives. Price consolidated the schools the MBGC financed. He brought Bishop College, one of the premier black educational institutions in the state, under the financial control of the MBGC and made Mary Allen College, Union Seminary, and Guadalupe College satellites of Bishop College. Price attempted to found a new black Baptist university in Texas but was unsuccessful.[10]

Black ministers supported the movement by preaching the message of civil rights. This enabled them to safely participate in the struggle without getting physically involved in demonstrations. Many prominent ministers who helped lead the movement in the 1950s and 1960s got their start preaching civil rights in previous decades—among them, Ernest Estell of Dallas, Claude Black of San Antonio, and Lee H. Simpson and M. L. Price of Houston. Reverend Simpson, for example, made frequent references to social justice and "social life" in his sermons. In the 1940s he began to encourage his congregation to fight for rights. "Social life," Simpson contended, "means society functioning in all of its varied aspects for the good of the whole." Since the United States failed to support all people, it fell to African Americans to make society work "for the good of the whole." "Living in a dynamic society which is in a period of transition," he argued, "we are challenged as to the meaning and purpose of social life."[11] The term "social life," which Simpson and others used repeatedly, became a code word for "civil rights." By the fifties and sixties many black ministers began to use the terms interchangeably. From the pulpit in 1965, Reverend Price observed: "To go forth into New Frontiers in Social Life is not so easy. . . . Different standards of living based upon race, creed and color have no place in Society. . . . Residential districts should not be restricted. . . . Schools should be for *people* because learning is for people. Eating places should be open to all people."[12] Ministers like Simpson and Price offered a discourse on the spiritual and the secular, on religion and rights. David Chappell asserts that ministerial leaders convinced movement participants "that God was on their side. . . . This conviction often came to participants in ritualistic expressions of religious ecstasy. Experiencing and witnessing such expressions gave participants confidence." Preachers in Texas did exactly this; they encouraged African Americans to fight for rights. A minister's words carried great meaning to the congregation and broader society. Their endorsement of a particular tactic prodded blacks to action.[13]

The military gave African Americans another avenue of uplift. Both world wars allowed them to prove their patriotism as a way to secure rights. They responded by enlisting in large numbers. During World War I, blacks provided 25 percent of all troops from Texas. Yet African American soldiers found no real appreciation for the role they played in the war. On the contrary, white Texans were particularly hostile to the idea of blacks in uniform. This enmity came to a head before and after the war. In 1906, for instance, the army assigned the 25th Infantry to guard duty in Brownsville. Local whites constantly harassed these black troops, and in response a group of twenty soldiers marched on the town and killed one man. This Brownsville Affray provoked such anger from whites that President Theodore Roosevelt discharged the entire infantry without honor. The bloodiest of the World War I riots occurred in Houston, where black soldiers mutinied in 1917 after Houston police beat a popular black officer. They marched on downtown and killed five police officers and ten other whites in several skirmishes. The troops eventually returned to camp voluntarily. The Army court-martialed 120 soldiers, 19 of whom received the death penalty and were hanged.[14]

The racism blacks experienced on a daily basis, and the instances of discrimination within the military, facilitated the growth of civil rights activism in Texas. The most important civil rights organization in Texas was the NAACP, formed by a group of blacks and whites in New York City in 1909. African Americans in Texas founded the Lone Star State's first NAACP chapter in El Paso in 1915.[15] The Dallas chapter, which would become the state's most powerful, was organized in 1917.[16] The Houston Riot led to the formation of the NAACP chapter in the Bayou City, which began operations during the trial of the black soldiers in 1918. By 1919 the NAACP had thirty-one branches and over seven thousand members in Texas.[17] Association leaders came primarily from the legal profession and the ministry, including attorneys George Flemmings, L. Clifford Davis, Crawford Bunkley, and William Durham, and ministers Ernest Estell, Claude Black, H. Rhett James, and Moses Price. In addition, A. Maceo Smith, Clarence Laws, Juanita Craft, and Lulu White volunteered their time to association work.

The NAACP was committed to challenging racism throughout the United States. In Texas, this translated into a quest for voting rights, educational equality, the prohibition of lynching, and, eventually, protests. But local racists and the state government constantly threatened to expel the NAACP from the state. These threats went along with the reemergence of the Ku Klux Klan in the 1920s. When the Klan in Longview invaded the black section of town and burned several homes, the state government blamed the NAACP for the Longview Race Riot. To intimidate black Texans, the state subpoenaed the NAACP's membership records. When the association's national secretary, John Shillady, traveled to Austin to complain, as historian Michael Gillette writes, "A gang comprised of local officials brutally beat him."[18]

The NAACP persevered through these trying times and won some of the most important U.S. Supreme Court cases in the twentieth century. African Americans first aimed their fire at limits on the franchise. In 1923 Texas adopted the statewide all-white Democratic primary. The Democratic Party barred blacks from membership and voting in the primary, which meant that, in a one-party state like Texas, segregationists almost always held the reins of power.[19] About a year later Dr. Lawrence A. Nixon, an African American, was denied a ballot in El Paso's Democratic primary. Nixon, with the NAACP acting as counsel, filed suit against elections judge Charles C. Herndon. The case made it to the Supreme Court in 1927. In *Nixon v. Herndon*, Justice Oliver Wendell Holmes declared: "States may do a good deal of classifying that it is difficult to believe rational, but there are limits, and it is too clear for extended argument that color cannot be made the basis of a statutory classification affecting the right set up in this case." Holmes reversed the lower courts and handed Nixon a victory.[20] The state party quickly passed a new resolution that, instead of barring blacks, allowed only whites to join. In other words, the party simply changed the language that kept African Americans from voting.

Lawrence Nixon tried again in 1932. In *Nixon v. Condon*, the Supreme Court again ruled for Nixon. The Court asserted: "The pith of the matter is simply this, that, when those agencies [the Democratic Party] are invested with an authority independent of the will of the association in whose name they undertake to speak, they become to that extent the organs of the state itself, the repositories of official power." Therefore, "delegates of the State's power have discharged their official functions in such a way as to discriminate invidiously between white citizens and black."[21] As before, however, loopholes remained in the wording of Texas's voting laws and the Democratic Party passed a hastily written resolution that barred African Americans from the party's nominating convention. The white primary survived.[22]

The NAACP tried to eliminate the all-white primary again in 1934 and 1943. This attempt to bring a new case in the middle of both the Great Depression and World War II might have generated a good deal of controversy but for the capable and determined leadership of a core group of black women. A number of women — among them, Lulu White, Juanita Craft, Minnie Flanagan, and Christia V. Adair — held prominent positions in the NAACP prior to the 1960s. Women played important roles in the NAACP precisely because of their sex. While black men may have appeared intimidating to white Texans, women did not. They made good leaders because they occupied a social space that seemed nonthreatening. Hence opponents of the movement left women alone to plan for a new voting case. As Juanita Craft said, "I got by with murder because I was a woman."[23] Women like Lulu White simply refused to accept the racial order of the day. Historian Merline Pitre has accurately characterized White as "an acid-tongued individual who was not afraid to speak her mind to powerful whites and to differing black factions."[24] The temerity of such women produced some amazing results.

In 1934 the NAACP in Houston instigated the *Grovey v. Townsend* case. Spearheaded by Lulu White, Carter Wesley, the owner of the *Houston Informer*, and Richard Randolph Grovey, a barber and the president of a militant voting league in one of Houston's poorest ghettos, the *Grovey* suit once again challenged the all-white primary. Like many other African American leaders, Grovey received his education at the historically black Tillotson College in Austin. He practiced a type of radical leadership akin to Black Power. "I intend to fight to my dying day in order that the Negroes' fight to be a man shall not be curtailed," Grovey declared. When the NAACP approached him to initiate a new white primary suit, he jumped at the opportunity. In 1934 Grovey requested a ballot from County Clerk Albert Townsend for primary elections in Houston. Townsend refused and Grovey sued. Grovey and his attorney then attempted to do something that white Texans had done for decades—they tried to make the law work for them. Texas law prohibited appeals to state courts when legal damages did not exceed twenty dollars. Grovey sued for ten dollars, and when he lost, barred from appealing to the state courts, his case automatically went to the Supreme Court of the United States.[25]

Before the Court the NAACP argued that since Texas law mandated primary elections, the state through the Democratic Party had disenfranchised African Americans. Justice Owen Roberts stated: "The charge is that respondent [Townsend], a state officer, in refusing to furnish petitioner a ballot, obeyed the law of Texas, and the consequent denial of petitioner's right to vote in the primary election because of his race and color was state action forbidden by the Federal Constitution." But the Court rejected this argument. Instead, it decided that elected officials like Townsend did not serve as state officers and that the Democratic Party operated as a voluntary organization akin to a private club. Grovey had confused "the privilege of membership in a party with the right to vote for one who is to hold a public office." As a club, the party could decide whom to include as members. The white primary survived once more.[26]

After the failure of *Grovey*, black Texans found another suit in Dr. Lonnie E. Smith—a member of Albert Lucas's Houston church—championed by Lulu White as the next test case of the NAACP. In 1940 Smith was denied a ballot when he attempted to vote in the Democratic primary in Houston. Filing suit in 1941, Smith was represented by a new NAACP attorney named Thurgood Marshall.[27] After losing in the local courts, the case made its way to the Supreme Court. Justice Stanley Reed appeared somewhat shocked that another Texas white primary case had reached the Court. Reed cut to the heart of the matter—that the *Grovey* case had erroneously considered the all-white primary a private club. Specifically overruling *Grovey*, Reed finally determined that the white primary served as the mechanism for the "selection of party nominees for inclusion on the general election ballot" and that this "makes the party which is required to follow these legislative directions an agency of the state."[28] Because the party acted as a state agency, it could not exclude blacks.

The *Smith* decision was probably the most important civil rights victory for blacks in the 1940s. It signaled that the United States would extend democracy to all Americans. But this was not the only triumph. The cases of Herman A. Barnett and Heman Sweatt proved even more significant for blacks in Texas. African Americans had begun preparing to challenge segregation in post-secondary schools in the late nineteenth century. The momentum of this campaign, referred to simply as the Texas University Movement, increased dramatically after the defeat of the white primary.[29] But before the more famous *Sweatt* decision, black Texans won the now largely forgotten integration of medical education with Herman A. Barnett. A uniquely gifted individual, Barnett had graduated with honors from Samuel Huston College in Austin. He then applied for medical school at the University of Texas Medical Branch (UTMB) in Galveston. UT president Theophilus Painter maintained that Barnett had the necessary qualifications for graduate study, but that he would have to attend medical school at the Texas State University for Negroes (TSUN) in Houston. TSUN, alas, had no medical school. So Barnett agreed to become the next NAACP education test case and planned to file suit against the university. Apprehensive about both Barnett's and Sweatt's planned legal actions, President Painter quietly wrote Herman Barnett that UTMB had accepted him as a new medical student. Painter circumvented segregation laws by admitting Barnett as a TSUN student who would attend classes at UTMB. Since Painter had not directly admitted Barnett to a white school, he saved face. "The vagaries associated with his status as a TSUN student who would matriculate at UT *by contract*," Amilcar Shabazz writes, "did not damper the NAACP's enthusiasm or jubilation." UTMB adopted a policy of in-house segregation and forced Barnett to sit outside of classrooms for his education, but Barnett persisted and received his medical degree in 1953.[30]

Like Herman Barnett, Heman Sweatt hoped to attend graduate school. Sweatt, a Houston postal clerk, had graduated from Wiley College in 1934. After hearing Lulu White speak at an NAACP meeting, he agreed to attempt to enroll at the UT Law School. Sweatt was a family friend of the Whites, and Lulu White accompanied him to UT when he filed his application. The school rejected him. So, with the NAACP again acting as counsel, Heman Sweatt brought suit in 1946.[31] UT officials attempted to assuage him by offering informal courses in a basement and by creating a new black law school at TSUN in Houston. Sweatt refused these offers. When the case made it to the Supreme Court in 1950, Attorney General Price Daniel, a leading defender of segregation and later one of the architect of Texas's massive resistance movement, oversaw the proceedings for the state. Daniel blamed the case on outside agitators. He also argued that segregation served as a kind of police power that prevented violent conflicts between the races: "If the states are shorn of this police power . . . the states are left with no alternative but to close their schools to prevent violence."[32]

Sweatt's lawyers refused to engage Daniel's legal argument that segregation helped maintain interracial harmony. Thurgood Marshall and William J. Durham, a well-known Dallas attorney and NAACP official, argued instead that segregation in higher education denied blacks the equal protection guaranteed by the Fourteenth Amendment. The Court refused to strike down *Plessy v. Ferguson*. Instead, Chief Justice Fred M. Vinson stated that the inferior classes offered in UT's basement and at TSUN marked segregation as unequal.[33] Vinson declared that "whether the University of Texas Law School is compared with the original or the new law school for Negroes, we cannot find substantial equality in the educational opportunities offered white and Negro law students by the State." The Court ruled that Sweatt must be admitted to UT's law school. The justices delayed overturning *Plessy*, stating they need not "reach petitioner's contention that *Plessy v. Ferguson* should be reexamined in the light of contemporary knowledge respecting the purposes of the Fourteenth Amendment and the effects of racial segregation."[34]

Sweatt v. Painter touched on a number of issues pertaining to segregation. First, it acknowledged that separate was not equal. Second, the case had implications in laying out the psychological arguments in *Brown v. Board of Education*. Third, by shedding light on a highly specialized profession, the case brought to light some of the uncomfortable aspects of Jim Crow. Segregation denied equality to well-educated and capable black professionals. Finally, the *Sweatt* case illustrated the Court's willingness to address segregation. As

Bishop College president Joseph Rhoads noted, *Sweatt* was "advancing the cause of democracy in education."[35]

Besides winning court decisions, blacks attempted to vote and in many cases successfully did so in local elections. As Alwyn Barr has shown, "Negroes consistently fought disfranchisement in Texas through the Republican and third parties and by appeals for federal action in Congress or the courts."[36] While the poll tax and white primary restricted both Mexican American and African American voting in state and national elections, most local governments did not disenfranchise these groups. This meant that minorities did have some advantages in big cities like Dallas, Houston, and San Antonio. Throughout the early twentieth century, black voting leagues in Dallas proved crucial in local elections. Women's voting groups also forcefully pushed for universal suffrage.[37] The formation of the all-black Democratic Progressive Voters League (PVL) in 1936 greatly facilitated voting efforts. Formed in Dallas, the league expanded rapidly and by the early 1940s operated statewide. The PVL encouraged the payment of the poll tax and supported legal challenges like the *Smith* case. The Dallas chapter of the PVL still exists.[38] In San Antonio, black and Mexican American voting groups helped elect Henry B. Gonzalez to the city council in 1953.

Blacks had a remarkable number of successes in the early civil rights period. African Americans showed a resiliency in the face of Jim Crow. The evolution of a core group of black business and religious leaders contributed to community development. As the community grew, blacks extended their energies to other areas like education and politics. They also began to protest discrimination by funding lawsuits. Legal victories in Texas had national significance — these legal challenges secured rights for African Americans across the United States. Indeed, from the 1920s to the 1950s Texas stood at the center of black civil rights activism. Because of the *Sweatt* decision, blacks in Oklahoma, Mississippi, and other states won their own victories.[39]

■ ■ ■

The Mexican American community also experienced a great deal of political and civic activism at this time. Like African Americans, Mexican-origin people faced discrimination and segregation. In places like El Paso and San Antonio, sites of original Spanish settlement, Mexicans and Mexicans Americans had mature communities. While the Mexican American Jim Crow existed here, the Spanish/Mexican composition of the city softened the harshness of segregation. In Houston, Dallas, and many of the other cities founded by Anglo migrants, Mexicans had to carve out their own niches and establish communities much the same as black Texans. Mexican Americans predominated in Houston's Segundo Barrio and in Dallas's Little Mexico. These segregated ethnic enclaves allowed for the maintenance of traditional Mexican culture and, over time, the flowering of distinct Mexican American cultural traditions. In Little Mexico and Segundo Barrio, Mexicans and Mexican Americans found shelter from the onerousness of Jim Crow in their own homes, restaurants, and churches.[40]

Mexican Americans had a host of civic groups that helped to combat some of the uncomfortable aspects of segregated Texas. Groups like LULAC and the American G.I. Forum began to vigorously fight for Mexican American advancement. These groups and individuals pushed the state government to treat Mexican-origin people fairly. They also attempted to position Mexican Americans as part of the white race as a method for securing rights. Since Americans viewed the racial caste system in the United States as based on a black/white binary, segregation applied only to black people. Therefore, as whites, other white Texans could not discriminate against Mexican Americans.

For Mexican-origin people, whiteness and citizenship were inextricably bound. These issues went back to 1848 and the signing of the Treaty of Guadalupe Hidalgo, which ended the Mexican American War. The treaty attempted to do two things of importance for the approximately 100,000 Mexicans living in the Southwest at the end of the war. It guaranteed Mexicans citizenship as Americans and protected their property rights. Alas, most found these stipulations a fiction.[41] Anglos forcibly dispossessed Mexican-descent people of their land, and most Mexicans who remained in the United States found the citizenship aspects of the treaty virtually worthless.[42]

Without the citizenship granted by the Treaty of Guadalupe Hidalgo, Mexican-descent individuals found they had few options. Some looked to become naturalized citizens via the 1790 Naturalization Act. But, according to this law, only whites could become citizens.[43] Since many Americans were unwilling to look upon non-Europeans as white, Mexican Americans could not become citizens. The Fourteenth Amendment also granted citizenship, but the amendment was aimed at blacks. This left immigrants with one recourse: the courts. In what came to be known as the "racial prerequisite cases," non-European immigrants used the courts in an attempt to become white for citizenship purposes. In almost every case, the court found individuals who were not of European origin "not white" and hence ineligible for citizenship.[44]

Then came Ricardo Rodríguez. He had emigrated from Mexico to San

Antonio in 1883 and a decade later filed naturalization papers to become a U.S. citizen. In 1896 he appeared before Judge Thomas Maxey for approval of his paperwork.[45] When considering Rodríguez's race, the judge said that should the "strict scientific classification of the anthropologist be adopted [then Rodríguez] would probably not be classified as white."[46] Maxey seemed uncomfortable with Rodríguez's racial appearance since he did not fit into the black/white binary. But Judge Maxey, citing the Treaty of Guadalupe Hidalgo, acknowledged that he should be granted citizenship. In *In re Rodriguez*, Maxey argued: "When all the foregoing laws, treaties, and constitutional provisions are considered, the conclusion forces itself upon the mind that citizens of Mexico are eligible to American citizenship."[47] As Neil Foley has noted, "By ruling that Mexicans were eligible for citizenship, the court was in effect ruling that Mexicans were to be naturalized as if they were 'whites.'"[48]

In re Rodriguez enshrined Mexican American whiteness in the canon of law. Partly as a result of this decision, many of the most important civil rights groups adopted positioning Mexican Americans as whites to acquire citizenship and avoid Jim Crow segregation.[49] For example, LULAC, which developed in 1929, served as the most prominent Mexican American civic group throughout much of the twentieth century. The league focused on the civic betterment of Mexican Americans, promoted cultural pluralism while simultaneously encouraging assimilation into American society, and railed against segregated Mexican schooling and educational inequalities. Chapters quickly appeared in San Antonio, Corpus Christi, Houston, El Paso, Laredo, and Dallas.[50] The league used the whiteness strategy as one of its primary methods of eradicating Jim Crow. For many LULACers, white racial positioning was both a racial and a political tactic. It spoke to their desire for first-class citizenship and social and political inclusion, though some phenotypically white league members probably pushed whiteness because they viewed themselves as racially white.

White racialization and education came to form the core of LULAC's civil rights work in the early twentieth century. For instance, in 1930 LULAC took issue with the U.S. Census Bureau for classifying Mexican Americans as "Mexican," which would have made them nonwhite. When designating a racial category, LULAC declared, Mexican Americans desired classification as "white," not "Mexican." The Census Bureau eventually relented and allowed Mexican-origin people to categorize themselves as white.[51] Two years later, the *LULAC News* extolled the virtues of Mexican American whiteness, noting that "Latin-Americans (Mexicans) . . . were the first white race to inhabit this vast empire of ours."[52] But in 1936 the league once again had problems with census classification. The Social Security Board (ssb) attempted to categorize Mexicans as "other than white" for statistical purposes. The ssb listed possible "other" races as "Mexican, Chinese, Indian, Filipino," to which the Latin American Club, the precursor to Houston's lulac chapter, replied: "We are not a 'yellow' race, and we protest being classified as such." lulac itself engaged in a letter-writing campaign to change the new racial classifications. After this pressure, the ssb agreed to classify Mexican Americans as white.[53]

Similar issues arose in regard to census data gathered from medical professionals. In the 1930s state health officials attempted to restructure racial classifications used on birth and death certificates and on hospital/medical forms in an effort to track the spread of communicable diseases. In 1936, Dr. T. J. McCamant of El Paso's city health office and city registrar Alex Powell tried to classify Mexican American newborns as "colored" on birth and death certificates. Many local groups demanded their resignations. A local Spanish teacher, Tomas Chavez, exclaimed: "The word 'colored' as used and accepted in the United States means African or an admixture of African blood," not Mexican-descent stock. Disavowing any possibility for the existence of Indian or African heritage in the Mexican American population, Chavez concluded: "To call a person of European stock 'colored' is a decided insult in the United States."[54] Similarly, lulac leaders in El Paso and League national president Frank Galvan faulted Dr. McCamant for following the new guidelines for racial classification. Indeed, the *LULAC News* praised the doctor backhandedly for bringing to light what the paper called a "'nigger in the woodpile.'" McCamant had exposed a problem, the paper reported, and now lulac could fix it.[55] The league and many Mexican Americans came to abhor any association, perceived or otherwise, with blackness. Classification as "nonwhite," the *LULAC News* stated, makes "our blood boil."[56] Local officials and city and state health offices eventually called this affair an "error" and agreed to reclassify Mexicans and Mexican Americans as white on the medical forms.

Despite lulac's protests, the Census Bureau continued to categorize Mexican Americans as "Mexican," "colored," and/or "nonwhite." This provoked another angry response in 1940. According to the *LULAC News*, "The result inevitably has been that, through this erroneous application and classification of 'Mexican' as separate from the 'Whites,' the . . . Census Bureau has been . . . casting an aspersion against all other groups included within the Mexican extraction, by giving the name of their origin the connotation of a serf-like condition." The paper went on to say that if Mexican Americans were "not 'White' as classified, they must be something less." If the Census Bureau did not regard Mexican Americans as white, then they might appear closer to the "Negro" racial category, something the league hoped to avoid. LULAC's insistence on whiteness had very little to do with classification as "Mexican." Rather, it had more to do with being viewed as "colored" and *not* being classified as white. After another letter-writing campaign, the Census Bureau once again agreed to classify Mexican Americans as "white."[57]

LULAC's general squeamishness regarding race meant that any mention of the words "Negro" and "Mexican" in the same sentence provoked a furious response. When Texas superintendent of public instruction L. A. Woods issued a survey that asked a question about "tuberculosis and syphilis among the Negro and Mexican peoples," LULAC leaders responded acidly. National president Ezequiel Salinas protested "the unnecessary[,] unfair and arbitrary manner and exceedingly poor taste of offending Americans of Mexican extraction." Salinas explained to Governor W. Lee "Pappy" O'Daniel why the question had offended: "We protest not against the use of the name Mexican, but against the very stupid phraseology used in the question since . . . it joins the Negro and Mexican peoples and differentiates them from the White people."[58] Hence, using "Negro" and "Mexican" simultaneously was the real problem. Phraseology also became an issue in city directories. For example, the Corpus Christi city directory listed "m" for "Mexican" and "em" for "English Speaking Mexican" next to Spanish-surnamed individuals and businesses. LULACers argued that Spanish surnamed people should "be classified the same as any other names pertaining to the white race." The writers of the city directory agreed to eliminate both the "m" and the "em" classifications. This left only two others; "Am—American" and "c—colored."[59]

Attempts to eradicate segregated schools benefited from the whiteness strategy. Mexican American civic groups first attacked Mexican schools in Texas in the 1930s. In most cases, lawyers relied on what became known as the "other white" racial argument. This legal technique acknowledged a level of ethnic otherness for Mexican Americans while also recognizing their whiteness. Mexican Americans were white but not Anglo—hence "other white," a thinly disguised contention that they were not black. This technique would help them assert that whites (Anglos) could act prejudicially toward other whites (Mexican Americans).[60] Lawyers first used this line of argument in *Del Rio Independent School District v. Salvatierra* (1930). The parents of Jesús Salvatierra and several other families initiated a lawsuit after the Del Rio district began planning to build new white schools and expand the two-room Mexican school. Their attorneys asserted that the district intended to "affect [and] accomplish the complete segregation of the school children of Mexican and Spanish descent from the school children of all other white races in the same grades."[61] The judge ruled in Salvatierra's favor, but the Texas Court of Appeals overturned the decision. When the U.S. Supreme Court refused to hear the case, the segregation of Mexican-descent children became legal.

Although the *Salvatierra* case failed, Mexican American leaders continued to appeal to the wages of whiteness. They also relied on their Anglo political allies. Wartime exigencies helped in this regard. Like blacks, Mexican Americans took part in great numbers in both world wars. The extent of the participation of Mexican-origin people in World War I remains a matter of some conjecture, but scholars estimate that approximately 10,000 served.[62] Service in World War II proved even more important to Mexican American civil rights efforts, with more than 300,000 Mexican-descent people participating.[63] It necessitated the recruitment of soldiers, as well as eased immigration of Mexican workers into the United States. The U.S. Congress facilitated immigration by establishing a guest worker plan called the "Bracero Program" to help meet wartime labor demands. The program fueled calls for expanded rights for braceros, or those working under the mandates of the program, and for Mexican Americans generally. But the program frustrated many Americans because it allowed Mexicans to immigrate legally and did nothing to halt illegal immigration. Numerous conservative individuals came to view immigration in a negative light. As they stereotypically saw it, immigration resulted in a flood of indigent Mexicans pouring into the United States, and these immigrants took jobs away from the native born and contributed to the erosion of American culture in the Southwest. Some Mexican Americans opposed the Bracero Program on similar grounds, fearing that guest workers and illegal immigrants lowered the standing of Mexican Americans and impeded their ability to claim U.S. citizenship. Others, however, detested the gross exploitation the braceros experienced and the wretched conditions in which most of them lived and worked.[64]

The Mexican American Jim Crow also threatened to undermine the Bracero Program. Indeed, due to segregation the Mexican government banned braceros from working in Texas. In an attempt to reassure the Mexican government that its citizens would not face discrimination, Texas governor Coke R. Stevenson issued two significant and far-reaching declarations. The first and most important was known simply as the "Caucasian Race Resolution." This resolution of 1943 proffered whiteness to Mexicans and, by unstated extension, Mexican Americans. It argued that all nations in the Americas had "banded together in an effort to stamp out Nazism and preserve democracy." Since Latin America aided the United States, Texas had to refrain from segregating Mexicans. "All persons of the Caucasian race within the jurisdiction of this state," the document began, "are entitled to the full and equal accommodations, advantages, facilities, and privileges of all public places of business and amusement." Moreover, "whoever denies to any person the full advantages . . . enumerated in the previous paragraph . . . shall be considered as violating the good neighbor policy of our state." A duplicate resolution, Texas House Concurrent Resolution 105, followed a short time later. These resolutions show the importance the state placed on guest workers. It needed laborers from Mexico and was willing to grant whiteness as a way of satisfying the Mexican government.[65]

In June 1943, roughly two months after issuing the Caucasian Race Resolution, Governor Stevenson announced the state's Good Neighbor Policy. Based on the Franklin Roosevelt administration's Good Neighbor Policy, Stevenson's proclamation created the Texas Good Neighbor Commission (TGNC). The governor vowed to create a "'bridge of understanding'" to facilitate "cordial relations." He also reminded Texans of the tenets of the Caucasian Race Resolution and further declared that "the Good Neighbor Policy is the public policy of Texas."[66] The six-member TGNC largely grew out of World War II fears that Mexican Americans in the Southwest might succumb to fascism or communism due to segregation in the region. The commission readily adopted the strategy that many Mexican American civic organizations had already established as the prime mechanism for ending racism. In short, they embraced Mexican American "sameness" by pushing for their inclusion in the white race.[67]

The TGNC assisted Mexican Americans in a number of ways. For example, in a 1948 speech in Mission, state Board of Control officer Ben Warden expounded on racial differences between Mexicans and whites. This provoked an angry letter-writing campaign in area newspapers. Efraín Domínguez Jr., a local accountant and Mexican consular official, explained that "Latin-Americans . . . are considered White in spite of the different hues of their skins." Calling Warden's characterization "a slap in our face," Domínguez warned: "So long as there are people among the Anglo-Saxons who unjustly clasiffy [sic] the Latin-Americans as indigent, ignorant riff-raff, so long shall there be Latin-Americans who will refuse to cooperate with you in civic affairs."[68] Hugo Dominguez, a dentist, had a similar reaction: "Incidents such as this only fan the fires of race prejudice and discrimination . . . and they tend to discourage the mutual cooperation which is necessary to our well-being."[69] TGNC director Thomas Sutherland wrote Warden a terse letter to remind him that Mexican Americans were white.[70]

Anti–Mexican American racism eventually resulted in the formation of the TGNC's Sub-Committee A in 1949 to address problems relating to discrimination and racial classification.[71] The work of Sub-Committee A exposed many problems that Mexican Americans faced in Texas. Meeting notes indicate that segregation of Mexican-descent people in public places, discrimination in housing, disenfranchisement, and the segregation of schoolchildren remained pervasive. Sub-Committee A attempted to deal with these issues in a variety of ways: by contacting businesses that segregated Mexican Americans and demanding that they end their discriminatory practices, by approaching school districts with the same goal, and by encouraging a close working relationship between the state and Mexican American civic groups. Tactically, the subcommittee primarily used the whiteness strategy.[72]

In the 1950s Sub-Committee A became increasingly concerned with the discrimination Mexican Americans faced at medical facilities. Former LULAC president Albert Armendariz, a prominent attorney in El Paso, wrote to state health officials and the TGNC in 1954 to protest the racial categories listed on hospital forms. LULAC "feels very strongly that . . . Texas citizens are entitled to the same rights and privileges as all others and therefore we are very concerned when we see your forms designating under the heading 'color' the possibilities of choices of white, mexican and colored," he stated. Armendariz wanted the "Mexican" classification removed.[73] After pressure from Sub-Committee A, the state Department of Health agreed that all forms would designate Mexican Americans as white.[74] TGNC executive director Glenn E. Garrett noted that other state agencies would use similar racial designations on their forms.[75]

LULAC took this debate over nomenclature to extremes. For instance, LULACers had reacted angrily when health officials refused to make changes on their forms. Luciano Santoscoy, another well-known El Paso attorney and league official, demanded that health forms allow Mexican Americans to classify themselves as white. State health officer Henry A. Holle argued that doctors needed racial/national origin data to improve the health of Mexican Americans. "Your organization is primarily concerned with the welfare of our Latin American citizens," Holle stated, "yet, the requested revision of our public health report forms might have a reverse effect and actually hamper our efforts to further lower the morbidity and mortality rates."[76] Santoscoy continued to pressure the government, which prompted action from the TGNC and Sub-Committee A. They pressured one of Holle's subordinates to write to various state hospitals and explain that "neither 'Mexican' nor 'Latin American' is a proper entry. . . . 'Mexican' and 'Latin American' is [sic] classified as 'white.'"[77] Holle then told Santoscoy that his department would comply with LULAC's wishes on most health forms, but that death certificates needed a racial designation.[78] This situation repeated itself in 1957. Santoscoy again complained that health forms still required persons of Mexican descent to categorize themselves as either "White, Color[ed], [or] Mexican." Since no "Mexican race" existed, Santoscoy argued, the state needed to remove the "Mexican" category, which would leave only the "white" and "color" categories on the forms. Once again Henry Holle agreed to change the forms.[79]

The TGNC assisted Mexican Americans in other ways. When several Mexican Americans complained to commission chairman Neville Penrose about discrimination in Fort Worth in 1955, the TGNC helped form a Human Relations Commission to deal with discrimination. The TGNC hoped the group would "operate as a model for the entire state," pointing out that "Fort Worth is pioneering tonight." The Human Relations Commission operated like the biracial committees that would become popular in the 1960s except that it concentrated on promoting Mexican American whiteness.[80]

Efforts by individuals, local cities, and groups like LULAC corresponded nicely with state bodies such as the TGNC. While these agencies focused on how the state should classify Mexican-origin people, Sub-Committee A more forcefully addressed the segregation issue. At the same time, the emphasis of these groups on whiteness fit in well with LULAC's desire to promote rights via white racialization. But these efforts sometimes went into dangerous areas. Limiting racial classifications to "white" and "colored" on health forms would have obscured important data on Mexican Americans and perhaps endangered others in the state, something Henry Holle had warned against.

Similarly to LULAC, the G.I. Forum advocated for the rights of Mexican American veterans after World War II. Founded by Corpus Christi's Dr. Hector P. García in 1948, the Forum developed slowly until García learned that a funeral home in Three Rivers had refused to allow services for Private Felix Longoria, who died in combat in 1945. The funeral director denied the family use of the chapel because "the whites would not like it" and insisted that Longoria be buried in the "Mexican Cemetery," an unkempt section of the main cemetery that separated Mexican American dead with a barbed wire fence. García brought the power of the Forum to bear on the funeral home and succeeded in winning the support of Senator Lyndon B. Johnson. The freshman senator helped arrange Longoria's burial at Arlington National Cemetery in early 1949. This victory galvanized García's G.I. Forum. Thereafter, it expanded rapidly to become one of the state's most important civil rights groups, as well as one of the most prominent advocates of the whiteness strategy. Indeed, García continued to insist on Mexican American whiteness well into the 1970s.[81]

The G.I. Forum began fighting for Mexican American rights via whiteness beginning in about 1950. That year Dr. García complained to the Census Bureau when it attempted to classify Mexicans as nonwhite. In response, Census officials agreed to classify Mexican Americans as white; they directed census takers to "Report 'white' (W) for Mexicans unless they are definitely of Indian or other nonwhite race."[82] In 1951 García objected to racial classification on poll tax receipts. Instead of encouraging the payment of the poll tax, he protested that poll tax receipts recorded Mexican Americans as "Mexican." The TGNC's John Vancronkhite reported to García that "poll taxes issued to citizens of Latin-American extraction will be marked as 'white race.'"[83]

The Forum made numerous appeals for Mexican American inclusion in the white race. As a medical doctor, Hector García was frequently provoked by discrimination in the state pertaining to health care. When he learned that in some cities "the Mexican people and the Negroes" had to share rooms in medical clinics, he angrily denounced these facilities for "violating the law because the Mexican people are white."[84] Further, when Carlos I. Calderon, chairman of the Forum in Austin, informed him that hospitals throughout Texas classified all children born to Spanish-surnamed parents as "Mexican,"[85] García ordered Forum members with children to check birth certificates for incorrect racial classifications. "We want all of them to check on classification of race," García stated, adding "I believe you know what I am driving at."[86] The Forum's *News Bulletin* followed up on this matter by encouraging Forum members to check birth certificates and by reminding them that "the only proper classification for such children should be that of 'white.'"[87]

Not all Mexican American civic organizations engaged in white racial formation, and many groups ignored the whiteness issue altogether. Unlike LULAC and the G.I. Forum, an abundance of Mexican American organizations adopted a much more confrontational approach when dealing with discrimination and racism. Such groups, however, tended to be short-lived. The formation of mutual aid societies, or *mutualistas*, in the early twentieth century helped Mexican Americans deal with oppression. The *mutualistas* were designed to assist community members in times of need and to improve cultural awareness through the sponsorship of holiday parties and dances. In 1919, for example, Mexican Americans in Houston formed the Sociedad Mutualista Mexicana "Benito Juárez" (Mexican Mutual Aid Society "Benito Juárez"). The group provided burial relief and other "insurance" services; it also promoted a traditional, Mexicanist ideology and value system. As Guadalupe San Miguel pointed out, Mexican immigrants in the early twentieth century "tended to view themselves as *Mexico de a fuera* (Mexico from the outside) and hoped to return to *la patria* (the motherland) as soon as conditions allowed."[88] Though Benito Juárez reinforced Mexican identity, it folded during the Depression due to economic problems and its national focus. Another Houston *mutualista*, Club Cultural Recreativo "México Bello" ("Beautiful Mexico" Cultural Recreation Club), formed in 1924, sponsored recreational activities such as dances and fiestas. It too sought to promote Mexican values but also desired greater inclusion within the Anglo community. "There was a great deal of discrimination in those days and we wanted to do something to benefit the Mexican American community," one member remembered. "We wanted to present our culture and heritage to Anglo-Saxon society." As a result, México Bello reinforced Mexican culture while simultaneously encouraging integration. Unlike Benito Juárez, México Bello exists today.[89]

Some organizations assumed a more confrontational stance. El Congreso del Pueblo de Habla Española (El Congreso) developed in the controversial 1930s. Founded by labor organizer Luisa Moreno and led by activists Eduardo Quevedo and Josefina Fierro de Bright, the group adopted the ideology of the Mexican American left and pushed a more aggressive civil rights agenda. As Mario T. García has observed, "El Congreso as both a state and national organization aimed to improve the economic, social, moral, and cultural conditions of Spanish-speaking people in the United States in conformity with the U.S. Constitution." This meant support of the New Deal, increased wages for the underpaid, better education, and the destruction of racial discrimination. Aside from these goals, El Congreso had a much bolder agenda: to encourage unity with all groups—Mexicans, Mexican Americans, white liberals, African Americans—interested in the uplift of underrepresented people. As David Gutiérrez has shown, the group demanded the "development of transnational, Pan-American coalitions as a constitutive component of United States domestic politics *and* a relaxation of immigration, naturalization, and citizenship requirements." It viewed the border as a distinct site of Mexican and American nationalities, a nation within a nation. Hence it downplayed national differences in support of civil rights. El Congreso was damaged by red-baiting throughout the thirties. Its support of U.S. war efforts also hurt El Congreso's relationship with the left. The organization folded in 1942.[90]

With the establishment of the Asociación Nacional México-Americana (ANMA) in 1948, another radical group emerged. Organized primarily as the political action arm of the International Union of Mine, Mill, and Smelter

Workers (Mine Mill), ANMA attempted to unite Mexican Americans as a powerful voting bloc. As Zaragosa Vargas has shown, labor unionism among Mexicans and Mexican Americans reached a fever pitch in the mid-twentieth century. Indeed, the labor activism in ANMA was preceded by numerous strikes in Texas, most importantly the 1938 pecan sheller's strike in San Antonio led by Emma Tenayuca. ANMA developed in an effort to give labor a more sophisticated political voice. But ANMA was much more. The group advocated a procivil rights, antidiscrimination agenda that went far beyond its original conception as a political organization. Its leaders appealed to all minority groups as well as sympathetic whites, pushed for the equal treatment of women, and adopted a culturally pluralistic stance that denounced stereotypes of Mexican-origin people while promoting Mexican American cultural traditions. Like El Congreso, ANMA was short-lived. Labor's victories tended to affect only local communities associated with strikes, and their frequent spontaneity contributed to their impermanence.[91] More problematically, the Federal Bureau of Investigation (FBI) considered Mine Mill a left-led union and ANMA a communist front organization. This red-baiting doomed the organization, and ANMA did not exist more than a decade.[92]

Finally, Mexican Americans aggressively confronted school segregation. In 1938 Eleuterio Escobar formed La Liga Pro-defensa Escolar in San Antonio to promote integrated education; for a brief time he even joined forces with the NAACP. Whereas groups such as LULAC primarily addressed segregation through the courts, Escobar challenged the San Antonio School Board directly.[93] In the 1950s he and other league members went to school board meetings to expose the pitiable conditions in San Antonio's West Side schools. They encouraged the election of school board members sympathetic to the Mexican-origin community, demanded the district close unsafe schools and install cafeterias and bathrooms where they did not exist, and used radio programs, community newspapers, and large rallies to unite Mexican Americans around the issue of school improvement. The school board agreed to address many of the conditions La Liga exposed. Like ANMA and El Congreso, however, La Liga was short-lived and ceased to operate by 1956.[94]

Mexican Americans, then, engaged in a great deal of activity in the early twentieth century. Leaders successfully appealed to state officials and pressured the government to consider them white. Mexican Americans also supplied soldiers in both world wars. Despite their patriotism, many Anglos refused to acknowledge the Mexican American contribution to the war efforts. While the G.I. Bill gave veterans access to education, groups like the G.I. Forum promoted services for them as part of the battle for civil rights. Participation in the military, legal cases like *Salvatierra*, and the whiteness strategy all worked to advance Mexican American rights. More confrontational organizations like El Congreso and La Liga gave voice to those who opposed the accommodationist approach favored by LULAC and the G.I. Forum. This variety of activism shows that Mexican Americans fought for rights in much the same manner as African Americans in the early twentieth century. But they also had a strategy that blacks could not use; they could appeal to the wages of whiteness. Indeed, the short-lived nature of radical groups like El Congreso, ANMA, La Liga, and labor organizations magnifies the importance of the whiteness strategy, since it proved so long-lived. Court victories such as *In re Rodriguez* and the support of state leaders demonstrated to Mexican Americans the efficacy of pushing for rights by fighting for racial inclusion. Since discrimination and segregation intensified during this period as the state finalized its Jim Crow laws, Mexican Americans attempted to use whiteness to challenge racism.

■ ■ ■

While Mexican Americans and African Americans shared tactics like legal challenges and participation in the military, this did not cause them to unite in their early civil rights efforts. The existence of numerous parallel institutions offers one explanation for this disunity. Blacks and Mexican Americans each had their own civil rights groups. LULAC, the G.I. Forum, ANMA, the NAACP, the PVL, and numerous other groups formed in the early twentieth century to fight for each community. LULAC, for example, fought exclusively for Mexican Americans while the NAACP fought for black people. Perhaps each community did not need to join forces because both had a sufficient number of civic organizations supporting the advancement of each ethnic group.[95] A close reading of the available sources demonstrates that African Americans and Mexican Americans rarely discussed forging coalitions in the early to mid-twentieth century, something various leaders would promote in the 1950s, 1960s, and 1970s.

Unlike African Americans, Mexican Americans could appeal to organizations within the state government for the alleviation of discrimination and the acquisition of civil rights. The Caucasian Race Resolution and the formation of the TGNC had a significant impact on Mexican Americans in Texas, but this government aid did not benefit black Texans. The race resolution and the TGNC and its Sub-Committee A encouraged patriotism, citizenship, assimilation, and, most importantly, whiteness. But blacks also labored, fought, and died "to stamp out Nazism." Yet the government created neither a Negro Race

Resolution nor a Good Neighbor Commission for African Americans even though black Texans proved their patriotism in the war and war industries. While the state and federal governments viewed foreign-born workers from Latin America as vital to the American war machine and later to the national economy, they saw native-born African American laborers differently. The focus on a "Caucasian" race resolution explains why: blacks were not, and could not become, white. Hence, white leaders did not view them as productive, necessary, or desirable citizens. Indeed, Governor Stevenson allegedly stated one reason he agreed to form the TGNC: "Meskins is pretty good folks. If it was niggers, it'd be different."[96] Stevenson and other state officials gave Mexican American civic groups a weapon in their quest for equal rights. In some legal actions, the Caucasian Race Resolution even trumped the U.S. Constitution for Mexican American civil rights groups. They could use the resolution against the state to acquire civil rights.[97] Mexican Americans thus received an advantage over blacks in their quest for rights via government support. While government aid helped the Mexican American community, this assistance frustrated unity with African Americans.

For African Americans, the struggle for civil rights proved in some ways a simple battle. They had one overriding goal: end Jim Crow segregation. Blacks did not have to trouble themselves with the politics of Americanization or whiteness. Unlike Mexican Americans, most blacks had no internal debates about appealing to white officials (they could not), winning white political friends (they had few), or attempting to alter their racial position in the state (an impossibility). Instead, they fought for the removal of a system they found degrading and unfair. Since African Americans challenged segregation directly, the overall tactical focus of their movement differed from the Mexican American struggle. Blacks hoped to destroy segregation, whereas Mexican Americans wanted to eradicate the Mexican American Jim Crow. In other words, they wanted an end to segregation for themselves.

African Americans understood that segregation affected them singularly. In many ways, Mexican Americans got caught in the middle of the system. Neither regarded universally as white nor black, they fell somewhere in between. Mexican Americans certainly felt the sting of segregation and discrimination, and in some ways the less well codified, more amorphous version of segregation that they faced proved more difficult to overcome. Blacks had a concrete obstacle to overcome, while the Mexican American enemy seemed harder to define. Whiteness appeared to be an easier and perhaps more advantageous path to follow. Numerous other ethnic groups had fought and won recognition as white. Why not Mexican Americans? The whiteness strategy also crossed class lines. Economist Paul Taylor interviewed a Mexican cotton picker who told him: "It does not look right to see Mexicans and Negroes together. Their color is different. They are black and we are white." In short, the whiteness strategy was not the sole purview of Mexican American elites.[98] And, according to the American racial binary, the only alternative to whiteness was blackness. For the Mexican American community, fighting for black rights seemed a step in the wrong direction. Groups like LULAC and the Forum were at their base civil rights organizations. If their quest for inclusion in the white race seems less than progressive, they nonetheless fought and advocated for Mexican American civil rights.[99] As Craig Kaplowitz has observed, "It is easy to criticize LULAC for its members' class and racial bias; we need not ignore it to realize that in a difficult time (the 1930s and 1940s) and place (the Southwest, particularly Texas) for any challenge to the status quo, LULAC pressed for equality and against discrimination based solely on Mexican ethnicity."[100]

But whiteness was a strategy fraught with contradictions. In many cases, Mexican Americans could win recognition as white and still find their communities segregated. They could also be classified as white, win a modicum of integration, and discover a few years later that their white status and integration had vanished, as school segregation and the debate over classification on hospital forms had demonstrated. A number of historians have pointed out that civil rights victories during this period changed very little in the daily practice of Mexican American segregation, especially in schools. These historians, while correct, have largely ignored the whiteness strategy, which did have an impact in civil rights battles.[101] But it was an impact that often proved fleeting. Whiteness was, nevertheless, an important strategy. And when compared to the hostility blacks faced from local, state, and federal governments, the gains made via whiteness seem that much more profound.

Whiteness especially influenced Mexican American/African American relations, albeit negatively. Mexican American white racialization heightened barriers between African Americans and Mexican Americans. Some Mexican Americans combined whiteness with antiblack racial prejudices. As Neil Foley has stated, racist sentiments could provoke feelings of violence from Mexican Americans. In one instance, a LULAC council ousted a member when he married a black woman. Another member of this council argued that "an American mob would lynch him. But we are not given the same opportunity to form a mob and come clean." In other words, this person wanted to lynch the offending LULACer, in part to show his own American-ness and whiteness.[102] Perhaps the Dallas bombings show most clearly how the whiteness strategy could lead to violence. While the bombings caused only minor injuries and property damage, Pete Garcia and the other Mexican American involved in the incidents felt their whiteness threatened by the encroachment of black families into white neighborhoods. Michael Phillips has cogently observed that racial violence afforded Garcia "ethnic promotion." By showing his disdain for black people and his willingness to do violence for his own rights, Garcia forcefully communicated his sympathy with fellow whites, not blacks.[103] Certainly Garcia made an impression on black Dallasites, but they used the bombings to press for their own rights. They forced the local government to accelerate plans for a new housing development for middle-class blacks. This was a partial victory, but a victory nonetheless.[104]

Despite the best efforts of LULAC and the G.I. Forum, and their successes, Mexican Americans continued to face discrimination. The Mexican American Jim Crow lived on, in large part because the whiteness strategy proved inconsistent as a method of redressing wrongs. In 1947 UT professor George I. Sánchez, an expert on Mexican American education, commented that "'Mexicans' have customarily been looked upon as a race apart, and varying degrees of Jim Crowism are applied to them." While he also noted that "in law, all 'Mexicans' are 'white,'" Sánchez understood that Mexican American whiteness had accomplished relatively little.[105]

Whiteness, the government assistance granted to Mexican Americans, and black indifference all contributed to the failure in communication between African Americans and Mexican Americans. This led to disunity. When Mexican Americans promoted whiteness in letters and newspapers and in person, they clearly conveyed to black people that they could not look to the Mexican American community for support. Some African Americans came to view Mexican Americans as part of the opposition.[106] Mexican Americans came to regard blacks as competitors, not allies. As the court battles continued, and as each group grew more aggressive, they would continue to fight for rights on parallel tracks. In the 1950s the lines were drawn for protracted battles over school desegregation. Mexican Americans continued to receive positive, if token, action from the state. For blacks, the Texas government showed little sympathy. Indeed, in the 1950s the state began a program of massive resistance in defiance of the Supreme Court's *Brown* decision. The state would also attempt to destroy the NAACP in Texas. But in their quest for rights, African Americans found some new friends. These included several heretofore unknown state legislators, one of whom had the last name Gonzalez.

... 2 ...

Sleeping on Another Man's Wounds

The Battle for Integrated Schools in the 1950s

In the mid-1950s, G.I. Forum national chairman Hector García dispatched San Antonio county commissioner Albert Peña Jr. to investigate the operation of a segregated Mexican school in the small South Texas town of Lytle. When he arrived in Lytle, Peña asked a resident for directions to the school. Perhaps because of his skin color and slight accent, the person asked: "You mean the Mexican School?" Peña responded caustically, "I didn't know I was in Mexico." Stunned, the individual admitted that the Mexican school was across the street from the white school. At the school, Peña found sixty Mexican-descent students who spoke little English and a white teacher who spoke no Spanish. "The only semblance of bi-lingualism," he stated, "was a parrot they had who cussed both in English and Spanish." After his encounter with the bilingual class mascot, Peña approached school officials and threatened legal action if the school board refused to desegregate. The district integrated the schools.[1]

Similarly, in 1955 in Mansfield, a small town adjacent to Dallas, a group of African American parents represented by the NAACP sought the admission of three black teenagers to the white high school. The school's superintendent denied the request. When the NAACP filed suit, the district court ruled for the school district. The NAACP then appealed to the Fifth Circuit Court of Appeals in New Orleans. The circuit court reversed the district court and remanded the case back to Mansfield with instructions that the district develop a desegregation plan. The district court judge ordered the superintendent to integrate the town's high school. In response, a mob of segregationists—four hundred strong—marched on the school and prevented the students from enrolling, hung several effigies of African Americans, and threatened to kill NAACP leaders and destroy the black section of town. Fearing the crowd, blacks bought guns and guarded the homes of important NAACP officials. Governor Alan Shivers ultimately sent in the Texas Rangers to defend the segregated system. When President Dwight D. Eisenhower declined to intercede, the district returned to the status quo. Thus Texas's version of the Little Rock crisis, which occurred two years later, passed into history.[2]

While the African American parents followed Peña's model, their experience differed radically from the event that occurred in Lytle. Even after they won a court case, blacks could not convince local whites to integrate. These two disparate examples demonstrate how Mexican Americans and African Americans faced the dual Jim Crow system. Peña learned some important lessons in Lytle and the other schools he attempted to desegregate. "You have to force these things," he explained.[3] But African Americans could not force desegregation in the same manner—for a number of reasons. First, as a county commissioner, Peña held an important elected position, while blacks rarely held such political offices at this time. Similarly, white Texans in state and local government helped Mexican Americans desegregate schools. African Americans found they could not approach local officials and convince them to integrate. Finally, some Anglos—among them, Governor Price Daniel and James W. Edgar of the Texas Education Agency (TEA)—recognized Mexican American whiteness.[4] Since they constituted a group of whites, the state could assist them in obtaining equality. State officials did not regard blacks as deserving of equal treatment or, unsurprisingly, as white people.

In Texas in the 1950s, the battle for school integration stimulated a wide-ranging debate over voting rights, the desegregation of buses and movie theaters, and the accessibility of preschool English instruction. But Mexican Americans and African Americans continued to follow separate paths when fighting for rights. While leaders of both movements engaged in more dialogue in the 1950s than at any previous time, this discourse frequently was acrimonious. On most occasions, Mexican Americans and blacks found they could not work together.

School desegregation for Mexican American children deeply concerned many local people and the leaders of LULAC, the G.I. Forum, and other civic groups. But Mexican American leaders found themselves bifurcated by the contours of the integration movement of this period. Albert Peña, as noted above, had discerned that some pressure was necessary to compel Anglos to desegregate Mexican schools. Leaders such as George Sánchez, John J. Herrera, Pete Tijerina, and Henry B. Gonzalez, among others, shared this viewpoint. They saw nothing wrong with advocating whiteness, working with sympathetic African Americans, and more directly pushing the issue of school integration. But other, more rearguard Mexican American leaders continued to pursue an accommodationist approach to integration. Felix Tijerina, Hector García, Phil Montalbo, Pedro Ochoa, and others believed that promoting whiteness, working with Anglo American allies, and distancing Mexican Americans from black people were the most viable strategies for desegregating schools. These divisions were difficult to overcome, but despite disagreements Mexican Americans accomplished a great deal during this period.

Mexican Americans in Texas had brought no lawsuits against segregated educational facilities since the *Salvatierra* defeat in 1930. The next major case, and a victory, came not in Texas but in Orange County, California, where *Mendez v. Westminster School District* in 1946 desegregated Mexican schools. After their children were denied admittance to the elementary school near their home, Gonzalo and Felícitas Méndez, with the support of LULAC attorneys, filed suit. But unlike the pre-1970s Texas cases, *Mendez* did not rely on an argument that posited Mexican American whiteness as the reason for desegregation. Rather, the lawyers argued straightforwardly that segregation in Orange County schools violated the Fourteenth Amendment rights of Mexican Americans. Ruling in the family's favor, Judge Paul McCormick determined that segregation denied children of Mexican ancestry their constitutional rights. The NAACP supported LULAC's efforts in this case, and Thurgood Marshall coauthored an amicus curiae brief. Mexican Americans won the case, and districts throughout California began implementing desegregation plans.[5]

Mendez was one of the precursors to *Brown v. Board of Education*, but the effects of the case remained limited to the Golden State. George Sánchez, the premier expert on Mexican American education in Texas, noted that "the segregation that goes on in many Texas communities is infinitely more vicious than that found in any place in California that I am acquainted with." He further argued that "there is no connection" between *Mendez* and *Brown*.[6] Instead of promoting desegregation in Texas, *Mendez* prompted Attorney General Price Daniel to issue an advisory opinion that authorized segregation of Mexican-descent children only for English-language deficiencies.[7]

The most important Mexican American school desegregation case in Texas was *Delgado v. Bastrop ISD* in 1948.[8] The second legal challenge to segregated education following *Salvatierra*, *Delgado* pushed desegregation by promoting Mexican American whiteness. Minerva Delgado and twenty others brought suit against the Bastrop school district for segregating Mexican American children in a Mexican school.[9] Representing the plaintiffs were the legendary Mexican American jurists Gustavo C. "Gus" Garcia and Carlos C. Cadena from LULAC. The G.I. Forum provided much-needed funds for the suit. Garcia and Cadena tried the case on limited grounds. They attempted to desegregate the school for only Mexican American children by arguing that they were white. LULAC and the American Civil Liberties Union (ACLU) advocated this strategy and cautioned against proceeding as African Americans had with *Sweatt v. Painter*. The use of *Sweatt*, they said, might create an unintentional association with blacks, detract from the whiteness strategy, and alienate Anglo supporters. George Sánchez noted that "the Sweatt case has no bearing whatsoever on the segregation of 'Mexicans.'"[10] The ACLU and Sánchez argued that the attorneys should demand that Mexican Americans "be admitted to the white schools on the ground that Mexicans are Caucasians."[11] Further, they contended that Mexican American integration had no bearing, and would have no impact, on court cases that upheld the segregation of blacks because these cases "uphold segregation of a different race; Mexican Americans are of the Caucasian or Caucasoid race, the same as Anglo Americans."[12] LULAC's lawyers wholeheartedly adopted this strategy of white racial positioning and won the suit handily.[13]

Mexican Americans also continued to receive assistance in their desegregation efforts from state agencies like the TGNC and the TEA. While many school districts persisted in operating Mexican schools after the *Delgado* decision, the TEA proved at least moderately sympathetic to the plight of Mexican-origin children. Two individuals in particular worked to help them. James W. Edgar, the commissioner of education and head of the TEA, and L. A. Woods, superintendent of public instruction, both encouraged integration for Mexican Americans.[14] These officials adopted the viewpoint that Mexican Americans were white. Woods believed that segregation "applies only to people of Negro ancestry." "Reference to 'colored' children," he added "has been interpreted consistently by the Texas courts and the Texas legislature as including only members of the Negro race or persons of Negro ancestry." While Woods noted that schools could maintain separate classes to remedy language handicaps, which left a loophole for segregation to continue, his message was overwhelmingly positive for Mexican Americans.[15] Edgar acknowledged that local school boards had the responsibility to ensure compliance with *Delgado*, but

Three of the main leaders of the Mexican American civil rights struggle. From left to right, Dr. Hector P. García, George I. Sánchez, and Gustavo C. "Gus" Garcia in the late 1940s. These individuals would all play crucial roles in the litigation of anti–Mexican American discrimination cases in the 1940s and 1950s. (Dr. Hector P. García Papers, Special Collections and Archives, Texas A&M University, Corpus Christi, Bell Library)

the TEA would serve as arbitrator when school districts refused to comply.[16] The TEA advised districts that "the segregation of children of Latin-American descent from Anglo-American children in the public school program is contrary to law." The agency also authorized the commissioner of education to investigate noncompliant schools to force integration.[17]

Despite these efforts, segregation did not end for the Mexican American community.[18] While the *Delgado* victory and the assistance of state officials demonstrated the efficacy of pushing for white rights, this did not mean that integration had been achieved. Indeed, Mexican Americans could successfully win white rights but still fail to integrate schools. This proved to be one of the great contradictions of the whiteness strategy. For example, in 1950, only two years after *Delgado*, the G.I. Forum's executive secretary, Ed Idar Jr., found a segregated Mexican school in the Kyle school district near San Antonio. Idar and Hector García both felt a lawsuit might be warranted. Idar explained to Dr. García that "the nigger-in-the-woodpile here, however, is that it will require money—and perhaps a fund-raising effort on the part of the Forum." Given the desperately tight budgets of groups like the G.I. Forum and LULAC,

Idar and García preferred to work with state officials. After just over a year of negotiations with officials in the TEA and the TGNC, Gus Garcia and J. W. Edgar received written assurance from J. C. Hinsley, the Kyle district's attorney, that the district would no longer segregate Mexican American students.[19] In 1952, four years after *Delgado*, Houston attorney and LULAC national president John Herrera continued to find Mexican schools in operation. In fact, the Pecos school district in West Texas announced in 1952 that it planned to construct a new segregated Mexican school. Herrera eventually helped raise fifty thousand dollars to enjoin the district from building the school.[20] The same year Gus Garcia observed that "we have had overcrowding, half-day sessions, a scarcity of qualified teachers. . . . But lo and behold! We have the luxury of three schools—none of them adequate from any standpoint—one for Anglo-Americans, one for so-called Mexicans and one for Negroes." For Garcia, this was a "rare and stupid situation" given the problems in all three schools.[21]

Mexican Americans began prosecuting another aspect of segregation in 1954. In *Pete Hernandez v. Texas*, a team of LULAC lawyers including Gus Garcia, James de Anda, Carlos Cadena, and John Herrera attacked segregation on Texas juries. In 1951 Pete Hernandez had shot to death Joe Espinoza. An all-white jury convicted Hernandez of murder and sentenced him to life in prison. His lawyers ultimately appealed the conviction to the U.S. Supreme Court, contending that the trial violated Hernandez's constitutional right to a jury of his peers. The attorneys also asserted that the Fourteenth Amendment should apply to all ethnic groups. Because this argument implied that Mexican Americans considered themselves a racial minority akin to black people, the lawyers walked a fine line. Indeed, George Sánchez called it "a very ticklish argument." The attorneys negotiated this potential minefield by creating the "class apart" theory, a variation of the "other white" racial argument. They asserted that the Fourteenth Amendment applied to Mexican Americans as a recognized class of white people.[22] The Supreme Court agreed, concluding that exclusion of Mexican Americans as a "class deprived [Hernandez], as a member of this class, of the equal protection of the laws guaranteed by the Fourteenth Amendment of the Constitution."[23] Use of the term "class" instead of "race" kept the lawyers from professing that the discrimination resulted from racial biases. Once again the Court recognized Mexican American whiteness, although the justices deemed them "distinct from 'whites,'" which meant distinct from Anglos. This nullified the potential damage of using the Fourteenth Amendment. Additionally, the lawyers avoided citing *Sweatt* and other cases applicable to blacks because those cases involved racial segregation. Chief Justice Earl Warren declared: "It taxes our credulity to say that mere chance resulted in there being no members of this class among the over six thousand jurors called in the past 25 years. The result bespeaks discrimination." The Court reversed Hernandez's conviction, ruling that Mexican Americans as a "class" of white people could not be excluded from juries.[24]

Not long after the *Pete Hernandez* ruling, Mexican schools once again became a focal point in the state. In 1954 members of LULAC and the G.I. Forum found a type of in-house segregation operating in the Mathis school district. In addition to using a small frame house for a Mexican school, the Mathis district segregated Mexican-origin children within the Main Campus School, operating two elementary classes exclusively for whites and six for Mexican Americans. In 1955 Forum and LULAC officials reported an even more egregious form of segregation when they discovered that one of two Kingsville junior high schools was a Mexican school. This proved especially galling considering segregation beyond the first three grades had been ruled unconstitutional going back to *Salvatierra*. The Mexican American leaders and local people involved in the Mathis and Kingsville cases ultimately were the victors when they forced education commissioner J. W. Edgar to integrate the districts.[25] These examples of segregation demonstrated the continuation of Anglo racism toward Mexican-origin people after the *Delgado* suit. The integration that followed, however, once again showed Mexican American leaders the value of working with their white friends in government.

The most important school lawsuit after *Delgado* came from the Corpus Christi area in 1956, when Mexican Americans challenged segregated schooling in *Herminia Hernandez v. Driscoll Consolidated Independent School District*. Believing that Mexican-descent students could not speak English, the school district placed them in separate classes for the first three grades (or had them spend three years in the first grade). After three years, many parents grew disillusioned and withdrew their children from school, the desired result.[26] George Sánchez accurately surmised the situation when he noted that language segregation was a "subterfuge to keep these 'dirty little Mexicans' away from the 'lily white' children."[27] Testifying on behalf of the parents, Sánchez labeled the South Texas region as "one of the most backward areas in the United States in the field of education."[28] The district argued that the students needed segregation because they could only learn English in separate classes. As historian Mario García observed, this type of segregation operated as a self-fulfilling prophecy: "Mexican-American children remained segregated because they did not know English and they did not know English because they were segregated."[29] Gus Garcia, the plaintiff's attorney, argued simply that the district violated state law. Adopting language from *Pete Hernandez*, Judge James Allred stated that the segregation was "against all children of Latin-American extraction *as a class*." Allred ruled that the district had violated state education statutes. While language could impede learning, he argued, it was unreasonable to segregate Mexican American children beyond the first grade.[30]

Although these legal challenges resulted in victories for Mexican Americans, they did not end segregation in Texas. Pete Tijerina, a passionate community leader in San Antonio and LULAC's Texas regional governor, made light of this fact shortly after the *Pete Hernandez* and *Herminia Hernandez* decisions. Tijerina observed that discrimination persisted in many communities. "I regret to inform you," he said to LULAC national president Felix Tijerina (no relation), "that our people living in the smaller towns or communities are still being humiliated and frightened by persistent, unreasonable and unprovoked acts of racial discrimination, both social and economic." Similarly, Houston's LULAC chapter told Felix Tijerina in 1958 that Mexican American students in Pearland attended a Mexican school. Felix Tijerina had even dispatched an associate to investigate the situation.[31] Pete Tijerina and the Houston LULAC chapter demonstrated that districts continued to operate Mexican schools, that law enforcement abused Mexican Americans, and that facilities like movie theaters segregated Mexican American patrons. "These people look to LULAC for redress," Pete Tijerina stated. While lawsuits like *Pete Hernandez* and *Herminia Hernandez* helped, he argued, leaders needed to do more. LULAC national president Tijerina ignored these instances of segregation.[32]

Instead, Felix Tijerina launched his own civil rights initiative, an alternate educational plan called the "Little School of the 400." Tijerina understood the difficulty Mexican American children experienced if they could not speak English—he had dropped out of school at a young age for precisely that reason. Indeed, dropout rates for Mexican-descent children were phenomenally high due to this problem. George Sánchez surmised that only 2 percent of Mexican Americans students in Tijerina's hometown of Houston spoke fluent English in 1955.[33] Tijerina voiced his concerns, telling Mexican Americans "You are American citizens and English is the national language."[34] He believed that if children could learn a few words of English when young, they would have a fighting chance for an education as they progressed through grade school.[35] In 1957 Ganado teacher Isabel Verver began her own pro-

LULAC national president Felix Tijerina (in backseat) with Senator Lyndon B. Johnson, accompanied by Officer José Davila and Alfredo Garza, in a 1958 LULAC parade in Laredo. Mexican American leaders like Tijerina were able to cultivate close relationships with Anglo politicians, a significant advantage for the Mexican American movement. (Photograph by Alfredo G. Garza, LBJ Library)

gram, one that sought to teach Mexican American five-year-olds several hundred words of English. Tijerina liked her approach and agreed to finance her efforts. While her initial class size of 4 seemed unimpressive, the results were more substantial. After a demonstration of what the children had learned in the first week, her enrollment climbed to 40, and she began another class in Edna with 35 pupils. By the end of the summer she had an estimated enrollment of 150 students.[36]

To fund a LULAC version of Verver's program, Tijerina established the LULAC Educational Fund, Inc., a nonprofit corporation disassociated from the main LULAC governing body. In 1958 he officially launched the Little School of the 400 in the Houston area. The experiment was so successful that the following year Tijerina, with the support of his friend Governor Price Daniel, extended the Little Schools to other locales. The Texas legislature voted to fund the program with an annual budget of $1.3 million. The funding of the "Pre-school Instructional Program for Non-English Speaking Children," as the Little Schools were more bureaucratically christened, proved a boon to the efforts of LULAC and the goals of national president Felix Tijerina. This appropriation led to the flowering of the program and Tijerina's finest hour.[37] State officials vowed to assist in such a worthy project. Commissioner of Education J. W. Edgar, who served on the Little School's board of directors, called the program "one of the most important developments in Texas public education." He lauded Tijerina for making "a great contribution to public education in Texas."[38]

Not everyone approved of the pedagogy behind Felix Tijerina's program, however. John Herrera thoroughly disapproved of the project, labeled Tijerina an "appeaser," and called "'The Little Schools of the 400' a 'big step backward.'" After all the desegregation cases, Herrera declared, "now Tijerina turns around and starts a school which says, in effect, that the Latin-American child should be segregated."[39] George Sánchez concurred. At the 1959 LULAC convention, the nationally recognized education expert stated that it came with "especial shock and amazement to me that LULAC's name has been used to support legislation in Texas that endorses segregated treatment of little children solely because they speak only Spanish—and that LULAC officers are proud of their achievement to that end!" "Will our next step be that, if they do not know English at the age of ten," Sánchez asked sarcastically, "they may be herded off to gilded concentration camps where they may be purged of their sins?" In disagreeing with the pedagogy behind the Little Schools, he labeled Tijerina "woefully non-conversant" with current pedagogical techniques.[40] Despite its critics, the Little Schools project assisted thousands of Mexican American children across the state and was a precursor to the more well-known Head Start program. And while Herrera and Sánchez may have objected to the Little Schools, they offered no alternative of their own.[41]

Mexican Americans could claim substantial victories in the 1950s. They had remarkable successes in the *Mendez, Delgado*, and two *Hernandez* cases. As George Sánchez declared, the "*Hernández* decision was tops!"[42] These suits did force integration in some locales. But legal victories could not compel all school districts to cease segregative practices. Instead, Mexican American leaders like Albert Peña and John Herrera continued to push local districts to comply with the law. Despite the success of the whiteness strategy in generating a victory such as *Delgado*, this did not mean an end to segregation. This was the ultimate paradox of the whiteness strategy. As a result, Mexican

American leaders would have to continue fighting, and in some cases refight, civil rights battles. Much work remained to be done.

■ ■ ■

Meanwhile, the separate African American struggle progressed with equal intensity. Blacks secured their own legal victories in the 1950s. In 1954 the Supreme Court issued the *Brown* decision, overturning the 1896 *Plessy v. Ferguson* case that had legalized segregation. Probably the Court's most significant decision in twentieth-century American history, *Brown* went well beyond previous rulings like *Sweatt v. Painter*.[43] The Court ruled that separate, even when equal, hurt African Americans. Concluding that "in the field of public education the doctrine of 'separate but equal' has no place," the Court sounded what many hoped would be Jim Crow's death knell.[44] The Texas NAACP saw *Brown* as a victory engineered by black Texans.[45] African Americans were ecstatic. "J. Crow Schools Outlawed," proclaimed the *San Antonio Register*.[46] "'Separate but Equal' Doctrine Outlawed by Supreme Court," announced the *Dallas Express*. Many African Americans hoped that *Brown* would end segregation, but numerous problems remained.[47]

The state NAACP found that it had to continue fighting segregation after *Brown*. Black leaders in the NAACP had already pushed the *Smith, Sweatt*, and *Nixon* cases, and similar victories continued in the 1950s as the association initiated what they called their "knockout blow for [the] Jim Crow" campaign.[48] This plan had a number of components that primarily involved developing lawsuits to test segregation at the local level. In 1950 the NAACP filed a suit to integrate Dallas city parks. In 1953 and 1954 the San Antonio association sued to integrate professional boxing matches in the state. Black Texans won this case when the state supreme court pronounced segregated boxing illegal.[49] In 1953 the Fort Worth branch planned a boycott of parks, while the Dallas branch targeted department stores. Suits to integrate housing, equalize teacher's salaries, and poll tax drives continued across the state after May 1954. In 1955 the Alamo City NAACP sued to integrate local parks and swimming pools. The same year the Austin association sued to integrate buses after Mrs. Howellen Taylor, a local version of Rosa Parks, refused to vacate her seat on the bus driver's order.[50]

African Americans began to agitate more forcefully for change in the mid- and late 1950s; they adopted new protest strategies inspired by the Montgomery Bus Boycott. In Dallas in 1955, members of the NAACP Youth Council picketed the Melba Theater. The theater's owners were admitting blacks to the balcony for the first time and called this privilege "Negro Night." The teenagers picketed the theater to "dramatize segregation and leave the decision to attend up to the patrons."[51] This protest inspired the San Antonio NAACP to picket the Texas Theater for segregating African Americans in the balcony at showings of the musical *Carmen Jones*, which had an all-black cast and starred Dorothy Dandridge.[52]

Also in Dallas in 1955, NAACP youths targeted the annual Texas State Fair, which took place on the city's fairgrounds. Black people could attend the fair only on one day, called "Negro Achievement Day." Two years earlier the state had agreed to allow blacks entry to the fair on any day, while still holding Negro Day, but fair operators ignored the agreement. This prompted blacks to picket the 1955 fair, carrying signs that read "Today Is Negro Appeasement Day at the Fair, Stay Out!!" and "Don't Trade Your Pride for a Segregated Ride."[53] Although 1,300 people joined the demonstrations, fair leaders made no response. Dallas mayor Robert Thornton, the fair board's president, simply denied that the fair was segregated. He maintained that blacks could enjoy all rides but noted contradictorily that "due to . . . legal commitments the eating concessions would remain as they are [i.e., segregated]."[54] By the end of the year the students had amassed volunteers to stretch "picket lines around every gate leading into the fairgrounds."[55] Joining the picket were Juanita Craft, the director of the NAACP Youth Council, and Houstonian Lulu B. White, the state director of NAACP branches.[56] The state still refused to integrate the fair.

Elsewhere the NAACP forced desegregation by threatening demonstrations. The fear of protests drove Fort Worth to integrate city buses and railroad depots, and to start planning for school integration in 1956. San Antonio began desegregating schools in 1955; the next year it integrated swimming pools, buses, and railroad stations. El Paso started to integrate schools on a piecemeal basis in 1955 and 1956. Dallas desegregated its bus system in 1956. After events in Montgomery and pressure from black leaders, many Texas communities chose to willingly integrate some facilities in 1956.[57]

The state government quickly dashed any hope for a smooth desegregation process. Organized opposition to integration began almost as soon as the Supreme Court handed down the *Brown* decision. The state's rabidly racist attorney general, John Ben Shepperd, argued before the Supreme Court in *Brown II* that Texans would resist desegregation. "Sixty-seven percent of the Negroes," Shepperd said, "70% of Latin-American whites, and 84% of other whites interviewed predicted trouble between white and Negro parents in the event of desegregation." He saw no reason to subject "our economy, our traditions, our state of social harmony or our children to the shock of forced

Juanita Craft (center) and a group of NAACP youth at the 1955 protest of the State Fair. This bold demonstration revealed the NAACP's willingness to protest in favor of black rights. (Collections, Texas/Dallas History and Archives Division, Dallas Public Library)

or too-rapid integration." "It is our problem," Shepperd stated bluntly, "let *us* solve it."[58] Integration, he emphasized, would lead to violence. Indeed, serious racial conflicts over school integration occurred in Mansfield and Texarkana.[59] White-on-black violence provided grounds for authorities to continue segregating African American students. While violent groups like the Ku Klux Klan and the White Citizens' Council were weak in Texas, government officials stridently opposed *Brown*.[60]

Other public officials also opposed integrated education for African Americans. Commissioner of Education J. W. Edgar stated that his office "had no proper responsibility either in legislating or interpreting the Court's decision"—even though he had promised to support integration for Mexican

American students. Further, Edgar enacted a policy to ensure that all schools, whether segregated or not, would continue to receive state funding. He vowed to punish districts that integrated by withholding state funding. The *Brown* decision and desegregation seem to have profoundly offended Edgar, much as they did John Ben Shepperd.[61] Both men, therefore, instigated policies and advocated personal judgments that directly resisted integration. African American leaders found no help from the state government.

The attitude of state officials reinforced massive resistance at the local level. School administrators and local courts frequently conspired to slow integration. In Dallas, where officials had promised that schools would integrate willingly, the school board refused to implement a desegregation plan. Along with the Dallas School Board, district court judge William Atwell formed a bulwark against integration. Atwell made his views regarding segregation clear: "My personal feeling about segregation is that it is neither immoral nor unconstitutional."[62] When the Dallas Independent School District (DISD) failed to implement an integration plan, the NAACP took the DISD to court in 1955. In *Bell v. Rippy*, Judge Atwell dismissed this case because he felt it was premature, which in legal parlance implied that the plaintiffs had suffered no injury and hence had no reason to sue. This assertion contradicted *Brown*, which had clearly shown that segregated education had pernicious effects on black children. Atwell declared: "When similar and convenient free schools are furnished to both white and colored . . . there then exists no reasonable ground for requiring desegregation." In other words, he completely ignored *Brown*.[63]

The Fifth Circuit Court of Appeals reversed Atwell's decision and remanded the case back to Dallas. Judge Atwell then took a hard line and ruled that the Supreme Court had overstepped its authority in *Brown*, saying: "I believe that it will be seen that the [Supreme] Court based its decision on no law but rather on what the Court regarded as mere authoritative, modern psychological knowledge." He posited that "we have Civil rights for all people under the national Constitution, and I might suggest that if there are Civil rights, there are also Civil wrongs." Atwell contended that white schools suffered from severe overcrowding and that desegregating these schools would displace white students in favor of blacks. If this happened, he asserted, the hardship would fall on the white students. Atwell misunderstood the very concept of integration and once again dismissed the *Bell* suit.[64]

The Fifth Circuit Court reversed Atwell a second time and remanded the case back to Dallas with instructions that the DISD draft a desegregation plan. When the district refused, the NAACP sued again in 1957. In *Borders v. Rippy*, an exasperated Atwell threw in the towel and ordered that all Dallas schools be desegregated by January 1958.[65] In what can best be described as a temper tantrum, Atwell ordered the DISD to integrate all schools and grades in less than six months. Because he literally demanded the impossible, in December 1957 the Fifth Circuit Court again reversed Atwell's decision, this time ruling that the district must design a reasonable plan for integrating the schools.[66] Frustrated by the desegregation cases, disdainful of the Supreme Court, and believing the *Brown* decision unconstitutional, Judge Atwell decided to retire in 1958.[67] Thanks to individuals like Atwell, the desegregation battles in Dallas and other cities would continue for years to come.

The influence of segregationists such as Judge Atwell at the local level and John Ben Shepperd, J. W. Edgar, and Governors Alan Shivers and Price Daniel at the state level pushed the Texas legislature to begin enacting measures to protect segregated education.[68] These efforts started in the house, which quickly adopted nearly a dozen prosegregation bills in 1957. The most important of these included House Bill (H.B.) 1, a bill responding to the Little Rock crisis that would prevent the use of soldiers to ensure desegregation. H.B. 32, an anti-NAACP bill, would bar NAACP members from holding local and state government jobs. H.B. 65 prohibited school districts from integrating until local residents voted in favor of integration. H.B. 231 engineered a pupil placement law—probably the most common mechanism used by southern states to circumvent *Brown* in the 1950s—that allowed local school officials to decide whom they would admit to their schools. H.B. 232 would exempt students from compulsory attendance at integrated schools. H.B. 235 authorized the payment of vouchers so white parents could send their children to private schools later known as "seg academies." H.B. 236 empowered the attorney general to prosecute groups or individuals who challenged segregation. And last, and perhaps the most distasteful to civil libertarians, H.B. 239 required persons advocating integration "in such manner as to cause racial tensions" to register with the secretary of state.[69]

While these bills made their way through the legislature, Attorney General Shepperd declared war on the NAACP. Alabama had banished the NAACP in 1956, and states throughout the South followed their example.[70] In *Texas v. NAACP*, held in the small Tyler courtroom of Judge Otis T. Dunagan, Shepperd sought to enjoin the NAACP from operating in Texas because it had violated barratry laws that prohibited attorneys and organizations from soliciting clients.[71] Prominent NAACP attorneys William J. Durham and Crawford B. Bunkley, along with Thurgood Marshall, defended the association.[72] Marshall dropped everything to defend the state NAACP. Indeed, his presence through-

A forlorn looking Thurgood Marshall (far left), with Dallas attorneys Crawford B. Bunkley (second from left) and William J. Durham (third from left), during the trial of the NAACP. Marshall, Bunkley, and Durham put up a spirited defense, but the state ultimately won the case. (Collections, Texas/Dallas History and Archives Division, Dallas Public Library)

out these proceedings indicates the national importance of affairs in Texas.[73] One of the most salacious pieces of evidence introduced at trial claimed that NAACP officials planned to appeal to Mexican Americans to send their children to black schools to force desegregation. While the NAACP ultimately rejected this idea, state officials openly detested this strategy, as did many Mexican Americans.[74] In October 1956 Judge Dunagan ruled in Shepperd's favor and issued a temporary restraining order against the NAACP.[75] In May 1957 Dunagan granted Shepperd a permanent injunction, which brought the trial to an end.[76] But Shepperd would not get all that he desired. Dunagan issued his injunction with a number of strings attached, which allowed the NAACP to continue functioning. Over time the organization learned to evade the restrictions.[77]

The trial hurt many NAACP branches in Texas. The Houston chapter, in particular, had great difficulty recovering from these blows. The state had forced branch president Christia Adair to turn over the chapter's membership records.[78] This exposure forced many blacks, afraid of losing their jobs, to flee the association. In other places in Southwest and West Texas, where the NAACP did not have a strong following to begin with, the organization crumbled. But other branches bounced back. The Dallas NAACP regrouped quickly. By June 1957 the Dallas branch had called an emergency mass meeting and by November the Texas State Conference of NAACP Branches chose Dallas as the host city for the association's annual meeting.[79] Equally important to the state was the San Antonio branch, which also recovered promptly. Reverend Emerson Marcee, its president, announced with only slight disdain that the San Antonio branch "is now open and ready for business with the same operations we were engaged in prior to the processing of the lawsuit in Tyler." Branches in Fort Worth, Corpus Christi, and Austin resumed operations as well.[80]

But much work remained. The state forced the NAACP from the offensive to the defensive. While local chapters recovered from the state's assault, it took several more years for the association to regain its initiative. Since local blacks centered their civil rights activities in the NAACP, the group's travails affected African American activism in many ways and on many levels. Black Texans held their breath while the state waged war on the NAACP. Once the attacks ceased, these activists began to push again for civil rights. Certainly the trial of the NAACP diverted energy and precious resources from more important endeavors. However, the fact that the NAACP in many parts of the state recovered so quickly demonstrates the hard work and dedication of black activists. Despite setbacks, the black community brought educational inequality into the mainstream and helped set the stage for the activism of the early 1960s.

■ ■ ■

While both the Mexican American and African American civil rights movements won significant victories in the 1950s, they continued to travel on parallel tracks. Unification seemed all the more difficult since the two groups fought so many different battles. NAACP leaders occasionally called for unity, but they did not often follow through on their requests. For example, in 1953 and 1957 the association proposed forming coalitions with organizations like LULAC and the G.I. Forum. In 1953 A. Maceo Smith, executive secretary of the Texas State Conference of NAACP Branches, after conferring with a few Mexican American leaders, urged "closer cooperation between Negroes and people of Mexican extraction" to eliminate "common problems."[81] The same year NAACP leaders noted that the two groups "had many problems in common . . . each suffers discrimination in employment, health, housing, and in other phases of public life."[82] In 1957 state president H. Boyd Hall argued that Mexican Americans would assist blacks. "Please don't make the mistake of presuming that all non-Negroes are your enemies," Hall said. Mexican Americans "and their leaders well know that the segregation laws if permitted to stand will be used against them. . . . When they have an opportunity, they help you to the very best of their abilities. Contact them and get their cooperation when desired."[83]

While black leaders like Hall and Smith hoped to unify with Mexican Americans, their calls for coalition building were infrequent. African Americans wanted Mexican Americans to help the NAACP — especially after the association's trial in 1957 — but they did not acknowledge how the NAACP might help Mexican Americans. The NAACP also did little beyond calling for cooperation with Mexican Americans: they offered no specific plans and did not follow through on their pronouncements, only broaching the concept of coalition building rhetorically. Hall and his colleagues appealed to Mexican Americans when it seemed advantageous for them to do so. Once the NAACP's crisis had passed, its calls for cooperation ended.[84] Further, some association leaders damaged chances for coalitions at the same time that others called for unity. Thurgood Marshall argued in 1955 that blacks "are now in the last stages of desegregation and more and more people are climbing on the desegregation bandwagon . . . we will welcome them aboard . . . but make no mistake about this, there is room for only one driver on that bandwagon and that is the NAACP." This statement so angered George Sánchez that he privately accused Marshall of wanting to lead desegregation efforts so he could accrue legal fees for himself.[85] While African American and Mexican American leaders would continue to sporadically pay lip service to the idea of unity, infrequent communication and inconsiderate rhetoric like Marshall's divided the two groups.

Mexican American leaders balked at the idea of joining with African Americans in the 1950s. In 1953 LULAC national president Albert Armendariz observed: "There is only one sure way to kill the insidious seed of racial discrimination . . . we must never allow ourselves to show offense." Armendariz hoped to turn the cheek as opposed to unifying with the NAACP. He desired unity with Anglos, not blacks. His solution to discrimination was to "include Anglos in our affairs [and to] invite them to our homes."[86] Armendariz continued LULAC's policy of appealing to whites as allies in the Mexican American quest for rights. "Perhaps the greatest advance that we have made in the last ten years," he suggested, "is in our relationship with the so-called

Anglo. We have made great friends among them."[87] Shortly after H. Boyd Hall's call for cooperation in 1957, LULAC national president Felix Tijerina firmly rebuffed the concept of African American/Mexican American unity. "Let the Negro fight his own battles," Tijerina stated, "his problems are not mine. I don't want to ally with him."[88] Armendariz and Tijerina were both certain that Governor Price Daniel, L. A. Woods, and J. W. Edgar would assist Mexican Americans, not African American leaders such as Maceo Smith and H. Boyd Hall.

Although many Mexican American civic groups opposed uniting with the NAACP, not all Mexican Americans were unfriendly toward blacks. George Sánchez (by now chairman of the University of Texas's Department of the History and Philosophy of Education) asked John Herrera pithily, "What is LULAC for? The LULAC mountain labors mightily and . . . gives birth to a mouse!" He wanted to put some teeth into LULAC, even if that meant organizing with blacks.[89] Gus Garcia agreed. He called leaders in LULAC and the G.I. Forum "eager-beavers" who did nothing.[90] Moreover, the G.I. Forum's efforts were "haphazard" and "penny-ante." Leaders of both groups "all make hellacious speeches at the LULAC and Forum meetings, but I'll be goddamed if they will stick their necks out." Garcia told Sánchez to "tell the A.C.L.U. to stop being so concerned about the NAACP, which in spite of all its tribulations is doing so damn well."[91] Much like H. Boyd Hall, Mexican American leaders such as George Sánchez and Gus Garcia rhetorically addressed the concept of unity. They wrote letters to each other promoting unification, but they seldom wrote to black leaders.[92]

George Sánchez and Gus Garcia's calls for greater militancy, and their rhetoric regarding interethnic solidarity, disturbed Mexican American leaders who did not want to associate with African Americans. Tensions between blacks and Mexican Americans reached a critical point when the Texas legislature began drafting the segregation bills in 1956 after the *Brown* decision.[93] Nevertheless, the tribulations of the NAACP and the state's massive resistance program led to one of the most important events relating to race relations between African Americans and Mexican Americans. Indeed, the NAACP found one of its greatest defenders in a group of state legislators who referred to themselves as the *filibusteros*, led by the charismatic and boisterous Texas senator (soon to be a U.S. representative) Henry Barbosa Gonzalez. Henry B., as his constituents called him, hoped to improve the civil liberties of all underrepresented groups. He refused to engage in antiblack racism and white racialization like LULAC and the G.I. Forum. He also openly supported black rights.[94]

Gonzalez had long championed racial equality. He won election to the San Antonio City Council in 1953 and almost immediately began pushing for equal rights when he opposed a city housing plan that discriminated against African Americans and Mexican Americans. Reelected in 1955, Gonzalez helped desegregate several city-owned buildings. In 1956 he became the first Mexican American elected to the Texas Senate in the twentieth century. His appreciation of civil rights caused Gonzalez to rail against the state's racist legislation. As a freshman senator in 1957, his actions went far beyond what anyone might have expected.

Henry B. and his legislative ally Abraham "Chick" Kazen Jr. opposed all of the state's prosegregation bills. Gonzalez contended that the measures were "highly questionable, inflammatory and wholly undesirable."[95] But initially he and Kazen aimed their fire at H.B. 231, the pupil placement act. While the act was intended for black children, they knew, as did numerous Mexican American leaders, that the bill also threatened Mexican Americans.[96] Mexican-descent children did receive some protection from the bill when Senator Oscar Laurel, a former LULAC president, attached an amendment that prevented the state from using "national origin" and the "pupil's ancestral language" to deny a student's entry to a school.[97] But Gonzalez and Kazen had a more ambitious goal: to convince their fellow senators to kill the bill before it got out of committee. When they failed, the two senators initiated a filibuster.

The filibuster lasted thirty-six hours, allegedly the longest in the state's history. Chick Kazen started the fight at 11:15 a.m. on Wednesday, May 1. He spoke for fifteen hours. The son of Lebanese immigrants, Kazen had become familiar with the Mexican American community in his hometown of Laredo. He had also personally experienced racial discrimination in Texas.[98] Kazen labeled H.B. 231 "dangerous." He correctly believed it was only the first in a series of bills designed "to circumvent the Constitution of the United States and the decisions of the United States Supreme Court."[99] One of Kazen's senatorial colleagues remarked that "he doesn't seem to understand filibustering; he's talking sense!"[100] During the delaying action, Gonzalez and Kazen questioned each other about the merits of the legislation. To further frustrate their segregationist opponents, Gonzalez and Kazen frequently spoke in Spanish.[101]

By the time Henry B. took over for Kazen, the senators had grown weary of the filibuster. But Gonzalez injected an eloquence and an air of statesmanship that many found compelling. To those who argued that the senate had to pass the bills out of necessity, Gonzalez responded: "Necessity is the creed of slaves and the argument of tyrants." He warned that his colleagues had "sown to the wind and reaped a whirlwind!" "The Irish have a saying," he stated. "'It's easy to sleep on another man's wounds.' Well, what's the difference? Mexican, Negro, what have you. The assault on the inner dignity of man, which our society protects, has been made. . . . We all know in our hearts and minds that it is wrong."[102] Gonzalez put the filibuster in patriotic terms and made frequent references to liberty, freedom, and democracy. He acknowledged that blacks had fought and died in every American war. "I don't care what anyone thinks," he said. "This bill is odious to any free society and I am going to continue opposing it just as long as I can."[103] Gonzalez's passionate nature seeped into his argument. "For whom does the bell toll? You, the white man, think it tolls for the Negro. I say, the bell tolls for you! It is ringing for us all," he shouted, "for us all."[104]

Despite their best efforts, the *filibusteros* could not stop H.B. 231. After nearly twenty-one hours, Gonzalez decided to end the speech to preserve his energy for the next piece of legislation. The pupil placement act passed with ease, and Governor Daniel signed it into law. In a press release, Daniel vowed that the state would use the law only against African American children, not Mexican Americans.[105] Another prosegregation bill, H.B. 65, which would require local elections to decide if schools would desegregate, passed in mid-May after a ten-hour filibuster by Gonzalez and Kazen. Although Gonzalez seemed to know the filibuster would fail, he lectured the senators about the danger of the bill and declared that he had "faith in the ultimate righteousness of our opposition" to segregation.[106]

The *filibusteros* had more success with the next bill, H.B. 32, which targeted the NAACP.[107] Due to the previous filibusters, Gonzalez and Kazen had presented arguments sufficient to prevent the anti-NAACP bill from coming to a floor vote. Indeed, Senator Floyd Bradshaw, who had run on a segregationist platform, changed his position and voted against H.B. 231 after the filibuster. He later refused to allow the senate to vote on the anti-NAACP bill, which killed the measure.[108] It could be argued that a Lebanese American and a Mexican American saved the Texas NAACP. After H.B. 32 failed, the senate tried again. They passed Senate Bill 15, which sought to limit the activities of unnamed groups, surreptitiously the NAACP, that interfered with state control of schools. While this act represented another setback, the state never implemented the law.[109]

In late 1957, Chick Kazen and Henry B. launched another filibuster—this time against H.B. 1, which would allow the governor to close schools where integration required the presence of federal troops.[110] The state had called this euphemistically the "anti-troop bill" because it would prevent another Little Rock or Mansfield crisis. But the bill, like so many others, had a much more basic purpose—to stop integration.[111] One individual who favored integration argued that the title "anti-troop" purposefully misled the public because the bill was actually a "pro-mob, anti-school" bill.[112] When the measure came up for a vote, the *filibusteros* sprang into action.[113] In another twenty-hour filibuster, Gonzalez blamed the proposed act on "a few militant people who haven't caught up with the twentieth century." He also said that the "bill stems from the same witch's brew—hate." His efforts could not stop the anti-troop bill from passing.[114]

Despite the fact that most of the prosegregation bills passed, Texas never vigorously enforced these laws. The state supreme court later pronounced several of them unconstitutional, and the rest lay dormant until they expired. In the end, it seems, segregationists hoped to make a principled stand. Once they made their stand, local officials bore the onus for actually implementing the laws, and many refrained from doing so. Henry B. Gonzalez and Chick Kazen had also taken a principled stand, and they reaped the rewards for their efforts. In particular, Gonzalez, unlike any other Mexican American politician to date, earned the respect of black Texans. After the filibusters, Senator Gonzalez continued to speak in favor of racial equality around the state. He told a Catholic assembly in San Antonio that "in 20 years or less, the strained interpretations of the law and even the Scriptures by the segregationists will sound as foolish and stupid as those same arguments used to support slavery 100 years ago." At a Negro fraternal organization's meeting in Houston, he responded to the notion that African Americans desired integration solely for the purpose of marrying white women. Gonzalez repeated an oft-noted truism when he stated, "Negroes are extremely interested in being brothers, not brothers-in-law." At an NAACP gathering in Dallas in November 1957, Gonzalez received the association's prestigious Citizenship Award. The NAACP also named him 1957's "Texas Man of the Year" for his filibustering.[115]

The words and actions of Henry Gonzalez remained important to black Texans. The NAACP still had to recover from the recent trial in Tyler, and the senator surely inspired association members. The NAACP did not simply thank Senator Gonzalez and then forget him. Indeed, African Americans continued to express their gratitude in the coming months and years. For Christmas 1957, for example, various branches of the NAACP raised over one thousand dollars for the senator as a token of appreciation.[116] His frequent speeches to African American audiences in Houston, Dallas, San Antonio, and elsewhere, and the black community's positive response, encouraged

Gonzalez to continue the struggle. African Americans adopted Henry B. as one of their own. His actions and their loyalty set the stage for a gubernatorial run in 1958.[117]

Evidently Senator Gonzalez had pondered the idea of challenging Governor Price Daniel since the fall of 1957.[118] Many Texans correctly regarded Daniel as a prosegregation governor, the Orval Faubus or George Wallace of the Lone Star State. When *Sweatt v. Painter* reached the Supreme Court in 1950, then Attorney General Daniel had defended the state.[119] As governor he wholeheartedly endorsed antiblack legislation. Gonzalez had, in part, aimed his senate filibusters at this racist governor. For instance, during his speech to delay a vote on the anti-troop bill, Gonzalez said Daniel was "guilty of subterfuge" for supporting the awkwardly worded anti-integration legislation.[120] Once he began his gubernatorial campaign in 1958, these attacks became unceasing. The senator ran a ragtag campaign on a shoestring budget. He traversed the state in his station wagon, often giving speeches standing on the tailgate.

The state's liberal white and Negro presses extensively reported on the senator's campaign.[121] The *Texas Observer*, a weekly liberal newspaper, noted that Gonzalez had many strengths but three essential handicaps: "He is a Mexican, he is a Catholic, and he is for integration." "There is something so brave and splendid about Henry Gonzalez running for governor," the paper observed, "[that] the formulae of the professionals may be unbalanced: the people may be moved."[122] In a speech televised statewide in June 1958, Gonzalez lambasted Price Daniel for "double-dealing, double-crossing, racialism, and bigotry."[123] He told a gathering in Austin that he was disturbed by men "who take a constitutional oath, on their honor, to defend the people, then defend only a certain percentage of the people." He noted that his opponent emphasized differences in skin color and religion. "But we've reached the point in Texas now," he emphasized, "that we must realize that we're all in the same boat . . . that we have the same drives, the same hopes. . . . Our state needs leadership."[124] These sentiments caused the *San Antonio Register, Houston Informer*, and *Dallas Express*, the state's premier black papers, to endorse Gonzalez. Carter Wesley, the owner of the *Informer* and *Express*, believed that African Americans should support the senator because he "exemplified all of the things that we believe are right and in accord with law and order and good citizenship."[125] But Gonzalez was a long shot, and Price Daniel easily won reelection.

While African Americans heartily endorsed Gonzalez, Mexican American leaders found many of his ideas problematic. Some civic leaders approved of the senator's filibusters and gubernatorial ambitions but later retracted their support. The leadership of the G.I. Forum is a case in point. As an advocate of the whiteness strategy, Hector García wanted to avoid any association with the concept of civil rights and, by extension, black people. "We are not a civil rights organization," he maintained. "Personally, I hate the word. . . . We are not to be considered at all as a counterpart (Latin) of the NAACP." García clearly did not want the terms "civil rights" and "the NAACP" tied to the Forum because in the 1950s many people viewed the concept of "civil rights" and "the NAACP" as black phenomena.[126] Many of his lieutenants felt the same way. The Forum initially backed Gonzalez but later withdrew its support. LULAC leaders more vociferously opposed Gonzalez and the idea of black/Mexican American unity. While some Mexican Americans had proposed that the league and the NAACP join forces to combat H.B. 231, this never occurred. LULAC president Felix Tijerina emerged as a vocal opponent of Gonzalez's gubernatorial campaign and the unification of blacks and Mexican Americans. "Let the Negro fight his own battles," he said.[127]

A prominent and respected restaurateur, Felix Tijerina practiced a form of white supremacy that was common in the 1950s. For one thing, he took the unusual step of posting a detailed policy statement, titled "Negroes," on the serving of blacks in his Felix Mexican Restaurants. Most eating establishments simply hung a "whites only" sign. But Tijerina charted out specific situations and gave his staff stock statements to use if African Americans attempted to be seated at one of his restaurants. "If a Negro enters," the policy read, "the proper thing to say is 'I'm sorry, we cannot serve you.' . . . If the Negro refuses to leave . . . and becomes demonstrative," then his employees should call the police. "Remember," Tijerina explained, "we are operating a *private business*, not a '*public place.*'" The level of detail of this policy reveals his determination to uphold the segregation order.[128] Other entrepreneurs shared his view. G.I. Forum official Manuel Avila told Forum leader Ed Idar that if Mexican American business owners refused service to blacks, white businesses that declined to serve Mexican American patrons might rethink their segregative practices and open their businesses to Mexican Americans. "The Negro knows he can't go in [to white businesses]," Avila argued, "but he will try and use the Mexican as an ally and as self defense [unless] the Chicano says '*I'm white* and you can't come into my restaurant.'" Like Tijerina and other Mexican American businesspeople, Avila wished to show no sign of unity with African Americans in order to promote cooperative relations with whites.[129]

Tijerina was even more vocally antiblack outside his restaurants. In private meetings with LULAC leaders, he emphatically rejected the idea of cooperating with the NAACP since its leadership had called for a unified stand against the racist legislation. Around May 1957, Tijerina penned a letter widely distributed within LULAC explaining his opposition to joining forces with the NAACP.[130] LULAC national legal adviser Phil Montalbo also summed up his and Tijerina's position regarding the segregationist legislation. They felt it unwise "to jeopardize the good standing of the League by appearing to join forces with the NAACP" in opposing H.B. 231. While Tijerina and Montalbo thought that the legislation was unconstitutional, they agreed to postpone action until Mexican-descent children were "unjustly transferred to colored schools." They made no mention of what action they might take if the state sent Mexican-origin children to Mexican schools. Montalbo opined to Tijerina, "A stand taken by you on such bills would tend to admit to our anglo-american friends that we considered ourselves separate and apart from the majority of American citizens." In other words, siding with the NAACP might discredit the whiteness strategy. Montalbo noted that these issues would "be worked out with the help of our anglo-american friends and not with the help of the NAACP."[131]

Many LULACers agreed with this position. A. G. Ramirez of Laredo, for instance, unflinchingly supported Tijerina. He wrote Texas regional governor Pete Tijerina that "every one of my council is proud of the stand taken by our National President. . . . My District does not want to be affiliated with the Negro group."[132] Ramirez unequivocally told Felix Tijerina: "We don't never want to be affiliated with the Negroes . . . we don't want you to commit our National Organization to such things."[133] In a letter to LULAC Council #2 in San Antonio, Ramirez reiterated his support of Tijerina. "My district does not want our people and our beloved LULAC to be affiliated with the Negroes. We are white and furthermore re[garding] the bills which were passed are unconstitutional." Ramirez concluded this letter by berating those in LULAC who disagreed with Tijerina's stand on NAACP/LULAC unity, calling any criticisms of Tijerina "cheap chyster [sic] tactics."[134]

While Ramirez openly supported Tijerina's resistance to uniting LULAC and the NAACP, others were equally vocal in their opposition to Felix Tijerina. Indeed, the controversy over the segregationist legislation exposed a bifurcation within the Mexican American leadership. A liberal wing of the organization led by Albert Peña, Pete Tijerina, and John Herrera came to oppose the conservative wing presided over by Felix Tijerina, Phil Montalbo, and others. Pete Tijerina showed his displeasure by running against Felix Tijerina for the national LULAC presidency in 1957. He also upbraided the LULAC president and Price Daniel in the pages of the LULAC News.[135] Pete Tijerina understood that discrimination still existed for Mexican Americans, as it did for blacks. After touring the Batesville school district in West Texas and finding a Mexican school in operation, he complained to education commissioner James W. Edgar, and one of Edgar's assistants informed the district that it had violated the law. It is unclear if the school integrated, but the exchange demonstrated that segregation persisted for Mexican Americans. Some unity, Pete Tijerina averred, was necessary to solve common problems.[136] National president Felix Tijerina and others disagreed. Their faction held sway, and Felix Tijerina defeated Pete Tijerina in the 1957 LULAC election.[137]

Houston attorney John Herrera disapproved of Felix Tijerina's stance on the pupil placement law. As a former LULAC national president and an attorney who had worked on the *Pete Hernandez* case, Herrera's words carried some weight. In June 1957, speaking at a LULAC banquet in San Antonio, he chastised the league president. His speech, which Henry B. Gonzalez and Chick Kazen autographed, praised the actions of the filibusters as a "classic 'Man Bites Dog'" story. "The 'free choice' option given to school superintendents in Texas under House Bill 231 strikes at the very heart of the Delgado Decision," Herrera exclaimed. "It, therefore, taxed my utmost credulity," he lamented, "when I learned first hand at Houston, Texas, that our present Lulac Administration did not take a positive stand against House Bill 231 . . . no essence of help or encouragement was forthcoming and it never came from our present Lulac leadership." The only leadership against H.B. 231 came from the senators and the NAACP, not from the state's most important Mexican American civic organization. To a past national president like Herrera, this was inexcusable. Unless LULAC took a stand, he argued, Texas politicians would continue to enact such legislation. Herrera believed that this stand had to begin with Felix Tijerina's replacement.[138]

Moreover, in an angry letter to Phil Montalbo, Herrera complained about the actions of LULAC's legal adviser and the national president. "Let's face the issue squarely, Phil," Herrera wrote. "Our National President 'missed the boat,' either through lack of foresight and/or intestinal fortitude or through sheer ineptitude. . . . You and Felix apparently can not see the forest for the trees or just refuse to recognize the fact that HB 231 strikes at the very root . . . of the Delgado decision." Herrera recognized that the pupil placement law, while ostensibly aimed at black children, could also affect Mexican American students. "HB 231 opens the way again for our children to be segregated unjustly," he argued. Herrera chided Montalbo and Tijerina for not giving the NAACP aid in the fight against the racist legislation. By fearing African American/Mexican American unity, Herrera contended, Tijerina had sacrificed Mexican American children to a white racist agenda that applied equally to blacks and Mexican Americans. And in case they had forgotten, Herrera quoted from the LULAC Constitution to remind them that Mexican Americans had founded the league to *"help to defend the rights of all the people."*[139]

Other LULACers agreed with Herrera. The liberal wing of the league did succeed in passing a resolution at the 1957 LULAC convention denouncing the legislation because it undermined LULAC's previous education victories. Pete Tijerina approved the resolution over Felix Tijerina's objections.[140] He helped pass a similar resolution in 1958, but this effort did little—LULAC made sure that the language of the resolution applied only to Mexican American students, not African Americans.[141] Pete Tijerina commented to John Herrera that he felt "there were times when our [1957] convention seemed more like a White Citizens' Council meeting than a LULAC convention."[142] For leaders like Pete Tijerina, Herrera, Henry Gonzalez, and Chick Kazen, this was a damning accusation.

Nevertheless, Mexican Americans greatly respected Felix Tijerina. He ultimately served four terms as league president, a record matched only by Belen Robles in the 1990s. Tijerina's longevity in the league suggests that many Mexican Americans agreed with his ideas. The organization's conservative wing had ruled LULAC for decades and would continue to hold the reins of power. The league shied away from its traditional approach only occasionally—primarily when LULACers elected Alfred J. Hernandez president for two nonconsecutive terms in the 1960s.

The leaders of the G.I. Forum had similar disagreements. For example, the Forum's executive secretary Ed Idar Jr. had vaguely argued for Mexican American solidarity with blacks in an article in the Forum's *News Bulletin*. "The Mexican-American population of Texas," the bulletin intoned, "in a larger proportion even than the Negroes themselves, is in favor of doing away with the segregation of Negro children in the public schools."[143] Like LULAC, the G.I. Forum rebuffed Idar's message. Forum leader Manuel Avila feared that any mention of sympathy toward blacks might hurt the Mexican American cause. "I can already hear the Anglos saying," he wrote, "'those nigger lovers, look it came out in their official organ with their blessing.'"[144] As legal scholar Randall Kennedy has shown, being called a "nigger lover" not only implied that someone sympathized with blacks, it could also impugn one's own whiteness. A white person labeled a "nigger lover" became less white, something Avila and other Mexican Americans hoped to avoid.[145] Avila told Idar that he had "pulled a boner" because his ideas might convince whites that Mexican Americans stood "ready to fight the Negroes battles." He was afraid that the bulletin might arrest the progress Mexican Americans had made. "Sooner or later we're going to have to say which side of the fence we're on, are we white or not [and] if we are white why do we ally with the Negro?" Avila wrote. "Let's face it, first we have to establish we are 'white' then be on the 'white side' and then we'll become '*Americans*'[—]otherwise never." Avila had rather simple logic; as whites, Anglos were Mexican Americans' natural ally, not blacks. He also contended that Mexican Americans in California and Arizona had progressed because they "will *never* make an issue of defending the Negro." "To go to bat for the Negro as a Mexican-American," Avila emphasized, "is suicide."[146]

LULAC and G.I. Forum leaders found widespread support for their racial ideas. One vocal supporter, who engaged in his own form of racism and white supremacy, was Pedro Ochoa of Dallas. Ochoa, an auto parts salesman who wrote under the pseudonym Pedro el Gringo, published the widely read *Dallas Americano*. Big D had no established LULAC or Forum chapters in the 1950s, and the city's Mexican-descent population was less than 5 percent. To unify these residents, he printed his weekly paper. His viewpoint provides insight into working-class Mexican American political and racial thought. Like some other Mexican American leaders, he vehemently opposed any form of unity with blacks and actively promoted whiteness.

Pedro Ochoa vocalized a racism that reflected the dominant views of southern society. He frequently peppered his columns with racial slurs: "niggerianos," "niggerifos," "niggerote," or simply "nígger."[147] He also called those wishing black/Mexican American unity "pro-negreras" (pro-niggers) and claimed that "integration is solely for the aggrandizement of the black race."[148] Similarly, Ochoa believed that integration would lead to the loss of Mexican American businesses. "The integrationist is our worst enemy," he wrote, "and they intend to implant integration by force." He referred to integrationists as "brota la plaga" or a plague and reminded his readers that "all people who speak spanish are classified as white people."[149]

Ochoa also engaged in Cold War conspiracy theories in ways that other Mexican American civic leaders did not. The Cold War both retarded and encouraged the broader civil rights movement.[150] In Texas, Anglos primarily feared communist plots and Soviet takeovers. While Cold War issues were a concern, minority communities generally had more important matters to worry about. Consequently, Mexican American and black leaders did not engage in the anticommunist rhetoric that other Texans embraced. But Ochoa did. He linked the forces of communism and civil rights in a vague conspiracy that aimed to undermine the United States and end free market capitalism.[151]

He claimed that subversives had co-opted civil rights groups and planned a communist revolt in Texas. "The groups 'Mexico de Afuera,' G.I. Forum, Lulac, Naacp and other social dissolution subversives," he maintained, "agitate integration and disorient, disfigure and distort public school matters[,] instilling racial hatred. And contraband Mexican congresses accumulate weapons for the coup."[152] For Ochoa, groups like LULAC and the G.I. Forum were not conservative enough.

Ochoa opposed anything that might assist African Americans. Finding the newly created United Negro College Fund abhorrent, he wrote:

> Actually you will be hearing costly radio announcements that they have been spreading to some populations in favor of the Negro's intelligence. In these paid notices, perhaps leaning toward sympathy, they ask the public to listen, help and support the United Negro College Fund. The American G.I. Forum, the Lulac, the Naacp, and other nigger groups repeatedly have professed faith in integration to uplift the equality, intelligence and superiority of the black race. Meanwhile the Spanish speaking Texans eat mesquite bark, chew corn cobs and burn animal dung to boil beans.

While questioning the intelligence of blacks, Ochoa at the same time accused Mexican Americans, African Americans, and related "nigger groups" of neglecting the impoverished Spanish-speaking population in Texas. He equally indicted black and Mexican American civic groups.[153]

It is possible, of course, to overemphasize the influence of someone like Pedro Ochoa, since his views were so extreme. But the widespread dissemination of his paper points to his importance. In 1958 he extended his newspaper's range by starting regional organs throughout the state, including a *San Antonio Americano*, a *Corpus Christi Americano*, an *Alice Americano*, and a *Kingsville Americano*. He also moved his publishing enterprise to Corpus Christi to increase the readership.[154] The geographic reach of the *Americano* papers gave Ochoa access to readers in practically every corner of the state. At the same time, he became much more political. Ochoa had long promoted the payment of the poll tax and encouraged Mexican Americans to vote.[155] But he began to openly express his opinions when Henry B. Gonzalez decided to run against segregationist Price Daniel. Ochoa vigorously supported Daniel. "A great many Texano qualified voters are lining up in favor of Mr. Price Daniel," Ochoa wrote. "These Americano voters," he insisted, "are the ones who do not accept the integrant [*sic*—integrationist] precept at public schools, and perhaps at churches and housing projects."[156] Ochoa also began running half-page ads that asked voters to force politicians to express their stand on integration. "Preserve your white race," he advised, "vote against integrationists, don't look to a black future."[157] He implored voters to send "segregationist delegates" to local conventions, to "help your own children preserve their kind of public schools," and to remember that "forced association is godless."[158] After Daniel won, Ochoa congratulated Mexican American voters for reelecting him. He also warned them that "integration means slavery."[159]

While serving as a voice of white racialization for Mexican Americans, Ochoa was decidedly political. He encouraged his readers to become more politically active to support segregation. His vitriolic coverage surely frustrated many Mexican Americans. But Ochoa just as surely convinced some Mexican Americans that African American/Mexican American unity equaled communism and slavery. His extreme reaction to cross-racial associations pointed to a distinct discomfort with matters relating to race. Indeed, his opinions proved so reactionary that other Mexican American leaders were subjected to Ochoa's harassment. Since LULAC and the G.I. Forum were not conservative enough, Ochoa formed the Organizacion Habla Spaniola de Gente Blanca (Spanish-Speaking Organization of White People), a group in name only.

Despite Pedro Ochoa's opinions, LULAC leaders like Felix Tijerina were politically conservative. Tijerina openly supported Price Daniel's reelection, and he disapproved of Henry Gonzalez's filibustering of "segregation laws directed at Negroes" because such activity "tended to throw the Latin American in the classification of a minority group militantly fighting for its rights."[160] It may seem surprising that LULAC, an organization similar to the NAACP in structure, membership numbers, and legal successes, did not suffer a fate similar to that of the association. After all, LULAC had essentially won its version of *Brown* in 1948 with the *Delgado* decision. The group had also pressured the state to comply with this decision since its passage. Why, then, was LULAC not put on trial? Surely part of the reason revolves around how the league chose to fight for rights. Rather than trying to destroy the social order as it existed, Mexican American civic groups sought to include Mexican Americans on the white side of Jim Crow. Many whites in state government, including J. W. Edgar, L. A. Woods, and Price Daniel, all counted themselves as friends of Mexican Americans and appeared willing to include them as members of the white race and ease segregation. The NAACP desired a different kind of inclusion, one that many whites could not tolerate.[161]

Anglos did not mount a massive resistance movement against Mexican Americans. The governor's actions, the segregative bills, and the efforts of local officials certainly had an impact on Mexican Americans, but these measures were not directly aimed at them. Instead, the government in particular, and whites in general, purposefully enacted a program of opposition to African American rights. Mexican Americans did not receive a similar reception, partly because of Mexican American racial positioning. Whites in the government proved at least moderately receptive to the demands of Mexican Americans. Why would Anglos enact a program of massive resistance against people they were willing to consider nominally white? Even though school officials continued to separate Mexican-origin children based on language handicaps (or the excuse of a language handicap), the vociferous opposition African Americans experienced seemed muted for Mexican Americans. Because blacks attempted to step out of their traditionally defined social, political, and racial place, they met with considerable opposition.

Felix Tijerina's discomfort with blacks, his unwillingness to work with or defend them, and his focus on preschool education exposed divisions within Mexican American leadership structure. Mexican American leaders certainly were not monolithic in their beliefs and tactical focuses. Tijerina's statement that they should "let the Negro fight his own battles" specifically scolded Henry Gonzalez, George Sánchez, John Herrera, and others who thought blacks and Mexican Americans could work together.[162] Tijerina, Hector García, Manuel Avila, Pedro Ochoa, and others diverged from a viewpoint long advocated by liberally minded activists such as Gonzalez, Sánchez, and Herrera. The liberal leaders had held that segregating Mexican American children from white children, which said nothing about blacks, was wrong and pedagogically unsound. While the liberal leaders fought for the inclusion of Mexican-origin children in white schools and, more generally, the inclusion of Mexican Americans in the white race, they were not antagonistic toward blacks like Pedro Ochoa or Felix Tijerina. These liberal leaders did not oppose unity.

African American victories could have potentially generated unity because they benefited all people in Texas, not just blacks. The *Smith* case provided the franchise to blacks, poor whites, and Mexican Americans. *Sweatt* opened the University of Texas to all groups. *Brown* was supposed to desegregate all schools nationwide. But many successful Mexican American cases worked to separate Mexican Americans from African Americans. *Delgado*, for instance, integrated only Mexican American children. The *Herminia Hernandez* decision applied only to people of Mexican descent. Mexican American attorneys fought the *Pete Hernandez* case for Mexican Americans. Since these lawsuits posited whiteness for the purpose of desegregation, they could not work for African Americans. Instead of uniting blacks and Mexican Americans, these victories divided them. Additionally, the state government supported the eradication of Mexican schools because Mexican Americans were classified as whites. The state opposed desegregation for blacks. These differing stances frustrated blacks and contributed to disunity.[163]

Some leaders felt that whiteness was all that Mexican Americans needed. But the persistence of segregation exposed the inaccuracy of this philosophy. Many felt that Felix Tijerina, as the foremost Mexican American leader in the state, should lead without discriminating. The debate over H.B. 231 proved that this would not happen. As Tijerina biographer Thomas Kreneck concluded, "By choosing to side with their 'anglo-american friends' rather than with the NAACP and its Mexican American legislative allies [Gonzalez and Kazen], Tijerina definitively communicated that blacks could not look to him, as LULAC national president, for support."[164] Black people understood that Tijerina and other leaders would not support them. They also knew that whiteness distanced Mexican Americans from African Americans. As Fort Worth NAACP leader L. Clifford Davis argued, Mexican Americans had for many years "carried on the notion that 'me white, me white,'" which worked to separate them from blacks.[165] Whiteness halted the limited attempts to unify Mexican Americans and blacks. The NAACP, then, fought against school segregation with a very limited supply of Mexican American allies.

Some LULACers continued to disagree with Felix Tijerina's views. At a 1959 meeting of the league, Arcenio Gonzales, a member from New Mexico, feared that the group had lost track of the struggle for rights. He felt LULAC "should grasp the reings [sic] [and] help the minority groups." Most boldly, Gonzales averred that LULAC should "discard our conservatism policy." "When NAACP invited LULAC to join with them in their fight, we did not accept," he reminded his colleagues; "this perhaps was a mistake."[166] Felix Tijerina rejected these ideas, but others still strongly disagreed with him. Perhaps the most damning indictment of LULAC's national president came from John Herrera. In a personal document, Herrera wrote: "Felix Tijerina. 'Used Lulac.' Perpetuated himself in Lulac. Was going to make Lulac 'Rich.' Left us broke."[167]

H.B. 231 and the other segregationist bills denoted for many Mexican Americans that Mexican schools, which the courts had outlawed in 1948, would continue to operate. Black leaders had similar fears—that *Brown* would not lead to integration, and indeed it did not. Blacks had learned that, to acquire civil rights, they needed to confront segregation head on. Some Mexican Americans had also discovered this truism, but leaders like Tijerina, Avila, and Ochoa disagreed. This caused others such as Henry B. and Albert Peña to strike a separate path from LULAC and the G.I. Forum. Peña contended: "You had to confront people sometimes to force them to do what was right." When the prominent civic groups failed to "force" the situation, Peña "decided that belonging to all these, LULAC, GI Forum" would no longer work. "What we were doing," he said, "was we would sit down and pass a lot of resolutions, but there was no follow through. I decided then that the answer lay in becoming involved in the community, in becoming involved in politics."[168] Peña's strategy fit in well with the likes of Henry Gonzalez. It also prefigured the activities of Chicano political activists like José Angel Gutiérrez, Gregory Salazar, Yolanda Birdwell, and many others. Such tactics followed patterns already established in the black community. Like African Americans, an increasing number of Mexican Americans would turn to political activism, direct action, and protest in the turbulent 1960s.

... 3 ...

Nothing but Victory Can Stop Us

Direct Action and Political Action in the Early 1960s

In March 1960 black Texans began sit-in protests at segregated lunch counters and other public facilities. Students, ministers, lawyers, young, old, men, and women participated in the demonstrations. They followed the example of four youths from Greensboro, North Carolina, whose sit-ins in February of that year sparked a national movement. The *Houston Forward Times*, a black weekly, reported that protesters arrived at segregated lunch counters in the Bayou City and "in less than 30 minutes, 1) The white customers departed 2) The waitresses walked away . . . and a 'closed counter' sign was posted 3) Negroes then occupied all 30 of the counter's seats and the sit-in strikes rampaging across the south for nearly 40 days had arrived in Houston."[1] Other cities followed suit.

African Americans hoped Mexican Americans would join their cause. After all, many Mexican Americans continued to experience discrimination in schools, in housing, at the ballot box, and, depending on their skin color and local conditions, in public facilities.[2] But Felix Tijerina, the national president of LULAC, once again made cooperation impossible. In a patronizing, paternalistic letter published in the *Houston Chronicle*, Tijerina disparaged the sit-ins and the activists. Though claiming to sympathize with blacks because Mexican Americans had experienced discrimination in the past, Tijerina urged African Americans to show patience, arguing that protests "cause much more harm than good. . . . The ladder must be climbed one step at a time." "I am convinced," he wrote, that integration would not "be achieved with pressure, threats, demonstrations or picketing. And I, for one, will not agree to give in to such tactics." Tijerina hinted that white businesses could respond to protests with economic reprisals. "The Negro has much more to lose than the white man. For instance, and I pray it never happens, the employers could decide they could get along without Negro help in their businesses and homes. Such a decision would be a catastrophe for every Negro in Houston and in the South."[3]

Once more unification eluded Mexican Americans and African Americans. The racial positioning and accommodationist orientation of Mexican American civic groups guaranteed very limited cooperation. Black activism disturbed many Mexican Americans, much as it did Anglos and, indeed, some African Americans. Although blacks had engaged in protests previously, from theater stand-ins to pickets at the Texas State Fair, the level of direct action demonstrations in the 1960s made previous protests seem tame. The sit-ins occurred spontaneously and local people led them. Mexican American groups almost universally decried these demonstrations as dangerous and unwarranted. But segregation persisted for Mexican Americans and their quest for rights continued with programs such as the Little School of the 400, political campaigns, and appeals to the state government for the redress of wrongs.

The philosophical and tactical differences of the two movements continued to generate disunity. Yet some Mexican Americans had begun to tire of LULAC and the G.I. Forum's gradualist approach. They decided to implement their own program of protest and political activism, particularly in the South Texas town of Crystal City. African Americans largely ignored these events. Both Mexican American political activism and black protest activism occurred simultaneously. But blacks rarely joined Mexican American political actions, and Mexican Americans avoided black protests. Due to the racial divide created in previous years, there was little cooperation or communication between these groups in the 1960s.

For African Americans, the NAACP had long planned the "knockout blow for Jim Crow" and anticipated the coming of the direct action phase of the civil rights movement.[4] When the sit-ins began, the association both encouraged the demonstrations and joined the protests. Contrary to studies that have ridiculed the NAACP as opposed to direct action, the NAACP in Texas had long supported protest activity.[5] In addition, women continued to have important leadership roles. Althea Simmons presided over the State Conference of NAACP Branches in the early 1960s, Juanita Craft continued to guide the Dallas Youth Council while Minnie Flanagan served as president of the local branch, Maude Jackson shared the leadership stage with George Flemmings in Fort Worth, and Lillian Leathers directed the Corpus Christi branch. All of these leaders encouraged direct action. Other organizations developed to steer protests. The NAACP, combined with new groups, showed the vibrancy of protest activism in the state. As one NAACP member predicted, "Nothing but victory can stop us."[6]

Sit-ins began in Houston on March 4, 1960, when Texas Southern University (TSU) students filled the seats at a Weingarten's supermarket near the campus.[7] The youths wholly organized the protest themselves. As activist Quentin Mease remembered, one day TSU law student Eldrewey Stearns, an employee of Mease's at the south central YMCA, simply stated: "Meet the new president of the Student Protest Movement." Mease humorously responded, "The new president . . . I didn't know there was an *old* president." Stearns repeated himself and with several friends standing behind him exclaimed, "We're the sit-in movement in Houston."[8]

Indeed, Stearns and his cohorts *were* the sit-in movement in Houston. They had hoped to find support from groups like the NAACP, but local leaders proved unable to help them. The state's efforts to ban the association had decimated the Houston NAACP, which was unwilling to assist the students.[9] The students next approached leaders at TSU, particularly Reverend William Lawson who directed the university's Baptist Student Center. But Lawson discouraged their activism.[10] Some Baptist ministers did not want to join the demonstrations, although they did preach civil rights from the pulpit.[11] Finding no real support for their ideas, the students chose to go it alone and created the Progressive Youth Association (PYA) to organize the sit-ins. The PYA resembled another institution that would develop out of the sit-ins, the Student Nonviolent Coordinating Committee (SNCC). The PYA first targeted the lunch counters near TSU; they later set their sites on downtown department stores, theaters, and restaurants.

The PYA led organized, professional, nonviolent sit-ins. Students dressed in their Sunday best and carried instruction cards that explained how they should behave while sitting-in: "Don't leave your seat . . . don't block entrances to the store and aisles . . . do remember the teachings of Jesus Christ, Gandhi, and Martin Luther King."[12] Within a week they had begun to use pickets along with the sit-ins. When Weingarten's staff closed its lunch counter, students sat in at the nearby Henke and Pillot supermarket, a local drugstore, and Woolworth's. The protests reached a fever pitch after barely three days.[13]

On the night of March 7, violence struck the black community. Four white

The first sit-in in Houston, March 4, 1960. The PYA students engaged in carefully managed and thoughtful protests against Jim Crow. Despite the large number of Mexican Americans in Houston, none joined the sit-ins. (Courtesy of Houston Metropolitan Research Center, Houston Public Library)

men kidnapped 27-year-old Felton Turner and took him to a wooded area of the city. There, they beat him, hung him by his feet from a tree, and gouged two rows of the letters KKK into his abdomen. The men told Turner that the sit-ins had received too much attention, even though he had not participated in them.[14] Turner later recovered from the attack. This incident reminded blacks that violence could strike in Texas as quickly as it could in Mississippi or Alabama. Instead of deterring the protests, the actions of these racists crystallized the resolve of the activists.[15] The violence meted out against Felton Turner forced Houston mayor Lewis Cutrer to react to the protests. Cutrer had run for mayor on a segregationist platform. In fact, one of his campaign posters warned in bold type "Will the Negroes Rule Our City?" and added "Here's hoping all the white people vote for Lewis Cutrer."[16] Yet after only a few months in office, Mayor Cutrer had desegregated city swimming pools and the lunch counter at city hall. He first responded to the sit-ins by contradictorily proclaiming that he would arrest the students for breaking the law while acknowledging that they had broken no laws. The mayor finally decided to meet with the leaders of the PYA, including Eldrewey Stearns and two TSU undergraduates, Curtis Graves and Earl Allen. Cutrer asked the students to end the protests in order to "assist in removing any cause that would result in violence." The students asked for desegregation. Neither side got what they wanted.[17]

It took Mayor Cutrer another week before he made any substantive response to the sit-in students; he began planning to form a biracial committee. Southern governments frequently used biracial committees during this period to successfully negotiate desegregation.[18] Houston did not follow this pattern. Instead, Cutrer used the *idea* of a biracial committee in an attempt to coerce the activists to comply with his desires. Civic groups like the Harris County Council of Organizations (HCCO) and the Houston Council on Human Relations (HCHR) submitted names to the mayor in hopes of swaying him to appoint the committee.[19] The mayor replied, "As long as these demonstrations are going on, I'm going to withhold coming up with any final plan."[20] Cutrer had a simple goal: to stall the sit-ins.

In late March, the students finally agreed to suspend their protests to give the mayor time to act. Cutrer then formed a 37-member Citizens Relations Committee (CRC).[21] The CRC immediately broke into two competing factions. Aloysius M. Wickliff, a prominent African American attorney and president of the HCCO, led one faction. Wickliff supported the sit-ins and advocated immediate integration. Houston businessmen made up the other faction; they supported segregation. The lone Mexican American appointed to the CRC, LULAC's Felix Tijerina, joined the segregation faction.[22]

Tijerina continued to serve as a popular LULAC president.[23] He also kept on making his opinions on blacks known to the general pubic. His widely circulated letter opposing the sit-in movement stated that the Mexican American quest for rights had never

> been of a nature to arouse further antagonisms. . . . Sit-downs may be melodramatic and may focus attention on their desires but when they irritate . . . yes, even antagonize a large segment of the other population, they automatically setup [*sic*] larger and more difficult obstacles in the path of their progress. . . . There is also no law, fiat, or dictate that can assure social equality for white and black because everyone has the right and the will to freely choose their friends and associates in business and social affairs.[24]

Tijerina's words carried great weight not only in the Mexican American community, but also on the mayor's CRC. His opposition to black protests appealed to many; one individual called his words "pearls of wisdom."[25] As a wealthy restaurant owner, Tijerina seemed to fear, as did other business-people, that admitting African Americans could potentially drive away white customers who did not want to patronize integrated facilities. Beyond that, however, Tijerina's response to black protests again demonstrated the preva-lence of Mexican American antiblack attitudes. His words set the tone for the CRC's response to the sit-ins. When A. M. Wickliff's liberal faction of the CRC voted to desegregate immediately, Tijerina and the other members of the prosegregation faction agreed that the time had come for the CRC to disband. The committee folded having achieved nothing.[26]

The failure of the biracial committee did not stop the student activists from protesting. Indeed, African Americans seemed presciently aware that the committee would not accomplish anything. The *Houston Informer*, the city's leading black weekly, never wrote a story about the CRC, which indi-cates the value blacks placed on the committee. Eldrewey Stearns called it a "chicanery, you know, to stop me in my tracks." After the CRC disbanded, students organized a Mother's Day boycott of downtown businesses to show how much black patronage meant to white merchants. The boycott was hugely successful.[27]

Besides the protests, the students had learned that media coverage from local newspapers drew attention to their cause. As long as they attracted pub-lic interest through the chronicling of the sit-ins and their arrests, the PYA would exert pressure on the city. But Houston papers were aware of this tactic and agreed not to publish accounts of the protests. After the biracial commit-tee failed, black business leaders John Coleman, Mack Hannah, and Judson Robinson, as well as religious leaders such as M. L. Price and L. H. Simpson, met with white leaders Bob Dundas (president of Foley's Department Store), Oveta Culp Hobby (*Houston Post*), and John Jones (*Houston Chronicle*) to negotiate a settlement that would end the sit-ins. These leaders approved a continued media blackout. They also consented to quietly desegregate the city.[28]

As Reverend William Lawson has cogently noted, "The fact is that the de-segregation of Houston was not white altruism, it was, quite frankly, estab-lishment selfishness wanting to protect its image." While the biracial com-mittee and the media blackout weakened the movement, Houston did begin desegregating downtown businesses.[29] This unpublicized integration fore-stalled a violent, racist white backlash that might have been produced if city leaders had announced their plans. As the restaurants desegregated, several African American customers chosen by the black business and religious leaders patronized the newly integrated businesses. For many Houstonians, the change came so gradually that hardly anyone noticed. As Quentin Mease recalled, "Everything was accepted because of the plan that was worked out in advance. So all that [integration] was done very orderly, as I say, without any . . . not only violence, with no semblance of violence, but no outward . . . demonstrations of any kind."[30]

The sit-ins in Houston quickly spread to other cities, starting in Galveston a few weeks later. A group of black high school students sat in at eleven lunch counters in the Island City. They succeeded in closing these businesses, some of which removed seat cushions to deter the protests. Almost all of them integrated within a few months.[31] Students in Austin sat in at restaurants near UT. Three restaurants quietly dropped racial barriers at their lunch counters. This protest inspired students at Huston-Tillotson College, a historically black school in Austin, to plan their own sit-ins. They created Students for Direct Action (SDA), a group similar to the PYA in Houston, to organize the protests.[32] But the Austin sit-ins occurred sporadically. Mayor Tom Miller formed a biracial committee to negotiate with merchants for integration. Much like in Houston, the committee moved slowly, so students continued their intermittent sit-ins throughout mid-1960. They received broad support from local ministers, the NAACP, and even Quakers, but the sit-ins ceased by May 1960.[33] New demonstrations began in December, when students picketed theaters throughout the month and into early 1961. One activist, Booker T. Bonner, engaged in a hunger strike to protest theater segregation, but it did no real good.[34] The protests ended when the theaters refused to integrate. Months later, Bonner remained engaged in a one-man picket. It took until September 1961 for theaters to desegregate. Nearly two years later, city restaurants finally began lowering racial barriers.[35]

San Antonio boldly stood out in the statewide sit-in movement. The local NAACP had announced plans to desegregate downtown facilities on January 1, 1960. Although this declaration proved premature, it again signaled the association's willingness to push for integration.[36] Harry V. Burns, the president of the Texas NAACP Youth Council, warned in March that African Americans would sit in if San Antonio refused to integrate. The association sponsored a massive rally attended by over 1,500 people. Burns and Reverend Claude Black, a longtime activist and minister, warned that sit-ins would begin at all stores that operated lunch counters on March 17. Officials quickly organized meetings to determine an appropriate response to the NAACP's demands. On March 17, they stated their intention to drop color barriers in over forty restaurants. These included lunch counters that had received vigorous protests throughout the South: Woolworth's, S. H. Kress, and H. L. Green, among others. Reverend C. Don Baugh, one of the prime movers behind the city's integration plan, exclaimed that San Antonio desegregated because "it was a community problem, and we have risen above it."[37] Baugh's self-congratulatory comments hid a deeper truth. Reverend Black and Harry Burns had more than one thousand sit-inners — what they called their "sitting force" — ready to begin the protests. They had more than enough demonstrators to fill every lunch counter seat in the city.[38]

The negotiated desegregation in San Antonio inspired new demonstrations. These occurred at Joske's Department Store, a Texas institution headquartered in the Alamo City. Joske's management had asked for a thirty-day grace period when activists first threatened to sit in. When the thirty days passed and Joske's had done nothing, the NAACP began to picket the store and sit in.[39] The association also promoted an "I have quit Joske's" boycott. As with other lunch counter protests, Joske's closed its restaurant facilities. Prohibited from sitting in, blacks nonetheless continued to picket and boycott the store. In July, Joske's finally succumbed to the pressure. After two months of protests, management opened all dining facilities to African Americans. Overall, then, San Antonio integrated with surprising speed, peacefulness, and goodwill.[40]

Dallas experienced the most intense and longest-lasting sit-ins. In March 1960, on the advice of Juanita Craft, the NAACP Youth Council began sit-ins at the downtown H. L. Green drugstore. In April, the sit-ins spread to the S. H. Kress Department Store's lunch counter. On April 25, H. L. Green served three African American undergraduates from Southern Methodist University (SMU). The following day two Baptist ministers, one black and one white, sat at the S. H. Kress lunch counter. To their surprise, lunch counter staff served them. They left Kress to join the sit-ins taking place at H. L. Green. The movement appeared to score victories at Kress, though management quickly returned to its practice of refusing service to African Americans.[41]

To assuage the protesters, the Dallas Citizens Council, a local political machine, formed a private biracial Committee of 14 to investigate the possibilities for desegregation. This committee, composed of seven blacks and seven whites, opened a line of communication between white and black leaders and met more openly than did the biracial committees in Houston and Austin. Local blacks elected the African American members, who submitted weekly reports to the black community regarding the progress of the negotiations.[42]

While the Committee of 14 negotiated, the sit-ins continued. In August 1960, African Americans created the Dallas Community Committee (DCC) to organize the sit-ins.[43] The DCC and the NAACP reenergized protests. Reverend H. Rhett James, an important member of the DCC and pastor of New Hope Baptist Church, began a picket at the H. L. Green and S. H. Kress lunch counters. James also attempted to begin an informal boycott, explaining that since "H. L. Greens [sic] and S. H. Kress integrate the Negro customer's money and segregate its facilities to Negro customers. . . . This policy of segregated lunch counters . . . is not compatible to the American Way of Life."[44] At the same time, a new picket of the Texas State Fair began. NAACP officials reported that they had completed plans "to throw a picket line around the State Fair on . . . 'Negro Achievement Day.'" Althea Simmons reminded Dallasites of the 1955 pickets when she borrowed a line from the earlier protest, saying "We urge parents of children throughout the state not to sell their pride for a segregated ride." This picket exceeded the NAACP's expectations. Hundreds of blacks participated in the protests and numerous others refused to attend the fair. Juanita Craft helped organize the protest with Simmons. These activist women were convinced that an order from Mayor Robert Thornton, who also served as president of the State Fair Board, would eliminate racial barriers, but he issued no order.[45]

The DCC, much like the NAACP in San Antonio, issued a deadline of January 14, 1961, for the elimination of restaurant segregation and warned that if the deadline passed the committee would initiate new sit-ins.[46] When the deadline arrived and no action had been taken, students began sit-ins near SMU. Earl Allen, a theology student at SMU, started these protests. Allen, who had first participated in sit-ins in 1960 with Eldrewey Stearns and other TSU students in Houston, arrived in Dallas in late 1960 and began using the tactics he had learned in Houston. He and classmate Carroll Brown sat in at the University Drug Store near the SMU campus. When the manager asked Allen to leave (Brown was white), both men left. They returned with sixty friends and picketed the store for several weeks.[47]

These protests finally drove the DCC to act. The group called an Easter boycott of downtown stores. NAACP attorney W. J. Durham attempted to unite the DCC with the NAACP Youth Council to support the boycott. Hundreds of NAACP youths attended a "prayer demonstration" downtown and, with the guidance of Juanita Craft, began stand-ins at local theaters. The DCC continued to publicize its upcoming boycott. While the Easter boycott never officially occurred, numerous blacks participated informally.[48]

The threat of a boycott ultimately forced the local government and the Committee of 14 to respond. The committee did so for one reason: boycotts threatened business. The solution proved more complex: the integration of

downtown lunch counters, stores, and other facilities. Through careful negotiations, the city planned to achieve racial change without violence or loss of
business. In late June government officials announced a comprehensive plan
to achieve partial desegregation of hotels, restaurants, the State Fair, Love
Field Airport, and local schools. The *Dallas Times Herald* described the plan
as "a vast public conditioning program, believed the first of its scope in the
nation . . . to pave the way for peaceful desegregation of the city's schools next
month."[49] City leaders prepared a propaganda film, *Dallas at the Crossroads*,
and a pamphlet variation of the film, also titled *Dallas at the Crossroads*, to
prime the city for school integration. Officials distributed 100,000 copies of
the pamphlet, debuted the film at a variety of locations and eventually on television, placed messages in the paychecks of public and private employees to
discourage violence, placarded the city with posters to promote nonviolence,
and distributed another pamphlet known simply as the "blue book" to urge
the media to promote peaceful integration. The city began desegregating in
an almost tranquil fashion.[50]

The great failure of the sit-in movement in the Lone Star State occurred in
East Texas, its Black Belt. In particular, the farming town of Marshall resisted
integration. Race relations in Marshall were distinctly southern, and blacks
had to confront a most oppressive racial caste system. But they had some
advantages. Blacks made up 50 percent of the population, and two colleges,
Wiley and Bishop, provided a convenient site for organizing protests. Reverend Harry Blake, a local Baptist minister, and Cuthbert O. Simpkins, who
had helped form the Southern Christian Leadership Conference (SCLC) in
January 1957, engineered sit-ins in Marshall.[51] Blake was a graduate of Bishop
College and Simpkins of Wiley College; both men had experience organizing protests. After several meetings with hundreds of potential sit-inners in
attendance, they decided on a cautious plan of action. They would begin sit-
ins at Woolworth's on March 26, 1960. They would sit for half an hour and
then other demonstrators would replace them.[52]

When the protests began, Woolworth's manager closed the restaurant.
Blake and Simpkins then attempted to sit in at the Union Station bus termi-
nal, but the facility's manager closed its counter as well. The next day, more
students arrived to sit in, and police began making arrests. There were more
arrests the next day. When crowds of black youths began meeting at the town
square to support the arrested protesters, the local fire department arrived
on the scene with a pumper truck. For a short time, Marshall of 1960 became Birmingham of 1963. African Americans felt the sting of the fire hose,
although few people were injured.[53] This violence, and the presence of police

Two unidentified black youths picket the Fry-Hodge Drugstore in Marshall,
April 2, 1960. Police arrested the two men shortly after this picture was taken.
Two other blacks picketed the local Woolworths store and were also arrested.
Marshall police and Texas Rangers responded viscerally to the demonstrations,
killing a vibrant local movement. (AP/Wide World Photos)

dogs, frightened many black Texans. After a few more days of sporadic protests and arrests, the demonstrations ended having achieved no goals. White
resistance and the fear of violence doomed the movement in Marshall to a
short, unsuccessful life. It would take until 1964 for desegregation to come to
this small town.[54]

While the movement in Marshall fizzled, direct action demonstrations
continued elsewhere. The movie theater stand-ins that occurred in early 1961
were coordinated by SNCC and took place simultaneously across the state.[55] In
Houston, protests resumed in 1961 after the initial negotiated desegregation.

The PYA began pickets that forced Mayor Cutrer to integrate the newly built Astrodome.[56] The group also joined with CORE to protest segregated bus stations.[57] In 1963 the PYA planned a major sit-down protest to block a parade route honoring astronaut Gordon Cooper. But it called off the protest when the mayor agreed to further integration. As a result, the group lost credibility in the city and folded shortly thereafter.[58] In Dallas, protests never ceased. Students continued to picket theaters, and in 1961 the city government integrated all movie houses. The local government integrated all city parks in 1963.[59] San Antonio saw some of its most intense demonstrations when Mayor Walter W. McAllister refused to endorse a proposed city ordinance outlawing segregation. Black activists picketed and sat in at City Hall. McAllister finally secured the integration of 205 businesses to halt the protests.[60] In cities such as Austin and Fort Worth, major protests and integration only began in 1963.[61]

The sit-in protests proved remarkably successful in many Texas cities, where negotiated desegregation occurred almost without incident.[62] Other communities integrated even more easily. Corpus Christi, for example, had integrated restaurant facilities years before the sit-ins began.[63] By the time the federal government passed the Civil Rights Act of 1964, most cities had already integrated. The sit-in movement proved both vibrant and successful. Throughout the state, sit-ins, pickets, and boycotts generated considerable attention and led to integration. In many cases, white leaders acquiesced to black demands because they feared that protests would damage the business community. Rather than prolong the inevitable, they chose to integrate. The decision to integrate staved off a violent and reactionary white response. Blacks and whites could pat themselves on the back for engineering integration before the passage of the Civil Rights Act of 1964. This was a major accomplishment.

■ ■ ■

Meanwhile, the Mexican American civil rights movement in the early 1960s primarily focused on school integration and political action. The Little School of the 400 continued to operate as an important preschool language project and as a political program. Since its inception in 1957, the project had graduated more than one thousand pupils. Felix Tijerina continued to promote the Little Schools with state government officials. Other LULACers tirelessly advertised them, distributing 150,000 brochures throughout Texas to Mexican American families. LULAC received a boost when *Time* magazine ran a widely disseminated article about the project. The *LULAC News* and the Mexican magazine *Impacto* reprinted this article, which extended the league's promotional reach.[64] In the political realm, state officials like J. W. Edgar maintained their involvement with the program. Edgar ardently supported the Little Schools, calling Felix Tijerina and others like him "Good Samaritans."[65]

The Little Schools melded well with LULAC's focus on education as the key route to advancement. Education activist Jake Rodríguez of San Antonio directed the project in the 1960s. He had previously criticized the program but became a Little School convert after its initial success. Rodríguez, like Felix Tijerina (who remained Little School chairman), indefatigably promoted the program. He called the Little Schools "a crusade" to teach English as "the official language of our country" and increased the vocabulary from four hundred to five hundred words.[66] Additionally, Rodríguez helped produce a glowing report entitled "What Price Education?" that detailed the program's successes. The report firmly labeled segregation as immoral, stating: "Lack of education brings not only physical and financial misery, but moral and intellectual deprivation as well."[67]

Little School officials hoped to achieve a great deal—no less than the moral, intellectual, and financial uplift of an entire group of people. These goals were perhaps too lofty, but the program did go far in educating Mexican American preschoolers. The criticisms voiced by George Sánchez, John Herrera, and others did not disappear, but these leaders were unable to create an alternative program. Despite criticism, Jake Rodríguez expanded the project. For example, when confronted by superintendents who claimed they had no Mexican American students to place in Little Schools, Rodríguez began to include non-English–speaking European immigrants in the project.[68] In 1964, 182 districts and more than 20,000 children received English instruction in Little Schools. Two-thirds of them continued to progress through school a grade per year, a phenomenal improvement.[69] By late 1964 nearly 100,000 children had received English language instruction through the program.[70]

In the mid-1960s, the federal government's Head Start program began to supplant the Little Schools. Head Start offered additional social services like medical care and nutrition information. Texas reduced the scope of the Little Schools due to the federal program.[71] When the Little School program ended in 1968, it was a shadow of its former self.[72] Unlike the Little Schools, which encouraged monolingualism, Head Start embraced bilingual education. Educators had begun to realize the pedagogical value of bilingual education, which teaches to a child's strengths while inculcating non-English speakers with knowledge of the English language. Leaders in the 1950s had viewed monolingual education in the "national" language as essential.[73]

The emergence of new political organizations proved to be the most important development in the Mexican American quest for rights in the late fifties and early sixties. In Houston, John Herrera and Alfonso Vázquez, a photographer and political cartoonist, created the Civic Action Committee (CAC) in 1958 to assist the gubernatorial candidacy of Henry B. Gonzalez. The CAC registered thousands of voters to support Gonzalez. After he lost, the CAC continued to mobilize Mexican Americans by funding poll tax and voter registration drives. The group supported Gonzalez again in 1960 when he ran for the U.S. Congress.[74]

The CAC also engaged in activities that would become more common in the late sixties and early seventies. For instance, it joined forces with LULAC and the G.I. Forum to advocate a free lunch program in Houston's schools. When one school board member rejected the idea of free school lunches because Mexican-origin students would rather eat pinto beans (which the schools did not serve), the CAC was incensed. "*SHE IS WRONG!*," they intoned. The group noted that students appreciated the free lunches because the school lunch often constituted the only balanced meal they ate on a daily basis. The district eventually agreed to keep the free lunch program.[75]

Like other civic groups, the CAC drew on the whiteness strategy. For example, when the Houston Police Department (HPD) redesigned traffic tickets, it listed three racial designations: "W" for white, "M" for Mexican, and "N" for Negro. The CAC, LULAC, and G.I. Forum demanded the city change the tickets. "There are only three races," the CAC stated, "the Mongoloid the Negroid and the Caucasian." Listing "M" for Mexican was discriminatory, it asserted, because "when race is designated we belong to the Caucasian Race." The civic groups continued to vie for whiteness to win rights and to show a remarkable amount of touchiness when they perceived their whiteness threatened. City officials changed the racial designations to reflect the wishes of the CAC, LULAC, and the Forum.[76]

The CAC helped spawn other groups, particularly the "Viva Kennedy" clubs. Viva Kennedy clubs emerged in 1960 to assist John F. Kennedy's presidential campaign. In Houston, John Herrera and the CAC organized the first Viva Kennedy club in Texas. Herrera, an ardent Kennedy admirer, felt that with JFK as president Mexican Americans could win further civil rights. Though many of Kennedy's campaign promises to both Mexican Americans and African Americans went unfulfilled, Viva Kennedy clubs sprouted throughout the state. These groups proved so successful in mobilizing support for political candidates that Mexican American leaders hoped to continue this activism after Kennedy's election. To this end, they met in late 1960 to form PASO, an umbrella organization designed to politically mobilize Mexican Americans and increase the number of registered voters and voter turnout. The group also focused on minimum wage laws, welfare measures for poor or aged Mexican Americans, and educational reform. They chose Albert Peña as PASO's first chairman, while Hector García served as president.[77]

PASO chapters quickly formed throughout the Southwest. Many Mexican American leaders viewed this political association as a new weapon in their quest for rights. The Mexican-origin community "throughout the years has not been afforded as easy a time to get ahead as most other groups," PASO claimed. The group's leaders hoped to elect "political friends" to win civil rights.[78] "Why PASO?" they asked. "The answer is that at last Spanish speaking citizens are becoming aware of politics and how it affects their daily lives."[79] The group began gearing up for national elections very early in 1963. In 1961 Albert Peña had announced that PASO would support the Kennedy-Johnson ticket.[80] PASO held a ball for Kennedy in Houston in November 1963. The president electrified the audience. But the community wept when Lee Harvey Oswald killed Kennedy only a few hours later. John Herrera lamented, "Han matado a mi presidente" (They have killed my president). Many Mexican Americans shared his sentiments.[81]

President Kennedy's death could not stop the momentum of Mexican American political activism. PASO grew even bolder after his assassination. The *Texas Observer* rightly noted that PASO was "considerably more aggressive than most of the older Latin clubs and societies."[82] Certainly the group's more outspoken stance generated media attention and thereby contributed to the increased visibility of Mexican Americans. Changing political fortunes, exemplified by Henry B. Gonzalez's 1961 election to the U.S. House of Representatives and the victories of six Mexican American candidates to the Texas House all but guaranteed a political realignment in Mexican-dominant areas of Texas.[83]

While PASO proved more forceful than LULAC or the G.I. Forum, its racial politics often mirrored these older organizations. The group's Democratic primary endorsement of segregationist Governor Price Daniel at their 1962 nominating convention confirms this point.[84] Hector García and Ed Idar, both leaders in PASO and the G.I. Forum, had pushed PASO to back Daniel. Their action infuriated George Sánchez, Albert Peña, and others. Indeed, Sánchez walked out of the nominating convention, calling the endorsement "a complete violation of the principles under which PASO was established."[85] The group's support of a segregationist governor offended Sánchez. "How can you say 'Viva Kennedy' and 'Viva Price Daniel' in the same breath?" he asked sarcastically. If Daniel won reelection, "put an accent mark on your spelling of *Pasó*.[86] Ed Idar accused Sánchez of being so "deep in the ivory tower" that he could not tell his friends from his enemies. "You pursue your theories," Idar said sardonically, "we'll continue on our own way."[87] In a private letter to Hector García, Idar called Sánchez "nuts."[88]

George Sánchez stood correct about Price Daniel. Although Daniel had recognized Mexican American whiteness and apparently counted himself a friend of people of Mexican descent, he had long supported the segregation of blacks. African Americans understood this, and their political organizations universally endorsed John Connally for governor. Sánchez and an anti-Daniel wing of PASO separately endorsed the liberal Don Yarborough. Daniel (and PASO) lost and the primary election went into a runoff between Yarborough and Connally. PASO then endorsed Yarborough. Once again PASO backed the loser—Connally won the primary and the election.[89]

Despite these setbacks, Mexican American leaders continued to press for civil rights. Indeed, PASO enjoyed its greatest successes after these disputes. Its most significant victory occurred in the small town of Crystal City in 1963.[90] Crystal City lies in the heart of Texas's Winter Garden region, so named because crops grow well in the winter months. Anglo political elites had dominated the government for decades. They kept Mexican Americans, who comprised more than 80 percent of the population, from the voting booths through the poll tax and intimidation. Discrimination was so rampant that Mexican Americans referred to the town as *Cristal*, as if two cities existed. The situation began to change in 1962 when businessmen Andrew Dickens and labor leader Juan Cornejo began planning a voting drive. According to political scientist Armando Navarro, Dickens had a disagreement with town leaders over a property lease. To express his dissatisfaction, he and Cornejo decided to replace the Crystal City government. To better organize their campaign, Dickens and Cornejo formed the Citizens Committee for Better Government (CCBG). The CCBG soon began a voter registration drive that mirrored the activities of groups like the Community Action Committee and PASO.[91]

After initiating their political offensive, Cornejo and Dickens gained two important allies First, they met with Ray Shafer, the president of the San Antonio's Teamsters Union, who agreed to provide financial and organizational assistance for the poll tax drive. Second, they appealed to PASO for support, and Cornejo established a chapter of the group in Crystal City. With the aid of PASO chairman Albert Peña and state secretary Alberto Fuentes, the inchoate political organizing in *Cristal* quickened. The poll tax drive was a huge success; over three hundred people paid their poll tax. Mexican Americans now comprised 68 percent of all registered voters in Crystal City. Instead of simply running a poll tax drive, the CCBG decided to nominate their own slate of candidates for the city council.[92]

The CCBG acted as a nascent political party. For the 1963 city elections, it chose five well-known locals to run for the city council. "Los Cinco Candidatos," as they came to be known, included Juan Cornejo; Manuel Maldonado, a grocery store clerk; Reynaldo Mendoza, a photography shop owner; Antonio Cárdenas, a truck driver; and Mario Hernández, a salesman for model homes. The CCBG engaged in canvassing and rallies to encourage Mexican Americans to vote. The night before the election, several thousand people attended a rally to cheer "Los Cinco." Alberto Fuentes told the crowd, "We're here tonight because deep in our hearts, we're all Mexicans, and tomorrow we're going to vote for our people." When he began speaking Spanish, college student and future activist José Angel Gutiérrez translated for reporters. "Do not be afraid," Fuentes said, "the victory we win tomorrow is here tonight." Gutiérrez, in one of his first speaking engagements, stated: "They say there is no discrimination, but we have only to look around us to know the truth . . . we look at the schools . . . the houses we live in . . . the few opportunities . . . the dirt in the streets . . . and we know."[93] He electrified the audience.

Many whites in Crystal City regarded Los Cinco Candidatos and Mexican American political power with trepidation. Anglos resisted the CCBG in a number of ways: local voting officials refused to give the CCBG forms so the candidates could file for the election, they reduced the number of polling places for the Mexican American community from three to one, and they refused to authorize observers to monitor the election. All of these actions violated state voting laws, but the CCBG effectively countered Anglo resistance by demonstrating the illegality of these procedures and forcing local leaders to apply the laws equally. Whites also derided Mexican American political organizing. "The Mexicans are trying to take over our town," a white gas station employee declared. Indeed, Anglos used the term "take over" with increasing frequency. *Time* magazine called these political developments the "revolt of the Mexicans." These terms had a negative connotation implying that the Mexican-origin community had done something wrong. Clearly Anglos and Mexican Americans disagreed about the point of the election. Mexican Americans saw it as not only a fight for civil rights, but also participatory democracy at work. Whites viewed the city as idyllic and denied charges of racism. "We may have had social discrimination before the Teamsters started

Crystal City mayor Juan Cornejo (left) and council member Reynaldo Mendoza shortly after the contentious 1963 elections. The election of "Los Cinco Candidatos" was a momentous event in the Mexican American struggle for rights. Cornejo proved to be a capable mayor and attempted, unsuccessfully, to moderate disputes between white and Mexican American townspeople. (Photograph by Douglass Jones; courtesy of the Library of Congress, Look Magazine Collection, and Ms. Janice Byrne)

their hate campaign," one farmer explained, "but we had no race discrimination." Most Mexican Americans probably would have disagreed. Juan Cornejo, like José Angel Gutiérrez, noted quite clearly that he could "feel and detect" racism in the town.[94] Another white resident claimed that the election had nothing to do with race because "nobody is now or ever has been race conscious in this town." One Anglo blamed the problems on "'*Democracy Salesmen*' from out of town," who "went among the poor preaching discontent."[95] Cornejo tried to moderate these sentiments: "Let's take it easy; let's go slow and let's think things out." Most Anglos rebuffed his suggestion.[96]

Mexican American political activists feared that the white establishment would attempt to steal the election. The arrival of Captain Alfred Y. Allee of the Texas Rangers confirmed their apprehensions. Governor John Connally had dispatched Allee to "keep the peace." But Allee had an infamous reputation for dealing Mexican Americans well-placed blows from his cowboy boots or the butt of his pearl-handled pistol.[97] José Angel Gutiérrez and others referred to Allee as *el pinche rinche* (the fucking Ranger).[98] According to Texas law, all local police came under Allee's control when he arrived. The town suddenly developed an informal curfew solely for Mexican Americans. Police also indiscriminately began closing Mexican American bars and nightspots. And Allee abused local citizens. He assaulted Gutiérrez one night after a rally. Gutiérrez had attempted to intervene when Allee arrested several friends. The Ranger slapped him to the ground and kicked him in the abdomen.[99]

Violence and curfews could not stop the election, and Los Cinco Candidatos easily swept to victory. Local whites pledged to cooperate with the new government, but solidarity eluded most townspeople.[100] When the new city council elected a reluctant Juan Cornejo as mayor, Anglos began to retaliate. The grocery store owners fired Manuel Maldonado, and Antonio Cárdenas had his wages cut from $77 to $35 a week.[101] Mario Hernández also suffered economic reprisals. When confronted by Anglo elites after allegedly writing several bad checks, he switched sides and began accusing Los Cinco of racism.[102] Moreover, in July 1963 Zavala County commissioner Tom Allee, the brother of A. Y. Allee, attempted to initiate a recall election but it ultimately failed.[103]

Sporadic violence in *Cristal* continued. Shortly after the election, A. Y. Allee attacked Mayor Juan Cornejo for allegedly making derogatory comments about the Rangers. *El pinche rinche* threw him up against a wall and banged his head into the Sheetrock six times.[104] This event probably would have faded from public view, but when Los Cinco complained to Governor Connally, he sided with the Texas Rangers. Connally told the mayor that the Rangers "were sent to Crystal City for the sole purpose of maintaining law and order and to prevent violence." As if to needle Mexican Americans, he added, "Apparently their efforts have been successful." Perhaps political payback for PASO's lack of support in the recent gubernatorial election motivated Connally to make this statement. Whatever the reason, his words frustrated Mexican Americans in South Texas, who had long suffered the abuses of Texas Rangers; even in their victory such ill-treatment continued.[105]

The election triggered another divide within PASO. The organization had risen in popularity thanks to the *Cristal* experiment, but the divisions between the Albert Peña/George Sánchez liberal wing of PASO and the Hector García/Ed Idar conservative wing intensified after the election.[106] The conservative group disapproved of PASO's involvement in Crystal City. To show its displeasure, García helped establish a second PASO chapter in San Antonio. This move served as a slap in the face for Peña and Albert Fuentes who not only controlled the state PASO but also ran San Antonio's local chapter. García

San Antonio county commissioner and PASO leader Albert Peña in Crystal City shortly after the 1963 elections. Peña was an influential leader, serving the Mexican-origin community from the 1950s to the 1970s. He helped generate a great deal of in-fighting among Mexican American leaders in the 1960s, most notably within PASO after the Crystal City experiment. (Photograph by Douglass Jones; courtesy of the Library of Congress, Look Magazine Collection, and Ms. Janice Byrne)

also censured Peña for his militancy and demanded his resignation. Peña refused to resign. Indeed, he was reelected chairman of PASO at a June 1963 convention, prompting García to angrily walk out of the meeting.[107]

These events damaged PASO. The political infighting and the walkouts by George Sánchez and Hector García made PASO appear weak and foolish. The reemergence of LULAC also damaged PASO. LULAC's primary strength had come from urban communities; it had grown notoriously weak in rural areas.[108] But in 1963, state chairman William Bonilla decided the time had come to reestablish Crystal City's dormant LULAC chapter. Albert Peña complained that the league simply hoped to capitalize on PASO's successes. He reminded Bonilla that LULAC was apolitical and that involvement in *Cristal* constituted a political action.[109] The always outspoken George Sánchez responded to these developments. He too reminded Bonilla that "PASSO is a political association. LULAC *is not*" and cautioned him against siding with the anti-CCBG Anglos. He warned the state chairman not to "bring LULAC into this kind of game [and] on the wrong side, at that."[110] His words evidently fell on deaf ears as LULAC reestablished its Crystal City council.

Meanwhile, Los Cinco had a town to run. Alas, they found winning the election far easier than governing. Political infighting and controversy plagued Mayor Cornejo's administration. Most significantly, the mayor had hired San Antonian George Ozuna as city manager. But Crystal City had a council-manager government, which meant that Ozuna, not Cornejo, controlled the city. The mayor continually tried to fire Ozuna throughout his term. Beyond this, Los Cinco had little experience running a government.[111] Their lack of knowledge contributed to a decline in the popularity of the CCBG. Local whites and Mexican Americans who disliked the CCBG established the Citizens Association Serving All Americans (CASAA). According to the *Dallas Morning News*, the group formed "for the expressed purpose of kicking Mayor Juan Cornejo and his councilmen out of office and keeping any more such political groups from taking over civic affairs."[112]

The CASAA operated as an upper-class CCBG.[113] The group began organizing in 1964 for the 1965 elections. The CCBG, on the other hand, got off to a slow start. CASAA ran a slate of three Mexican American and two Anglo candidates in 1965. The CCBG endorsed Cornejo and four new city council contenders. Although the CCBG slate received the greatest number of votes on election day, a well-organized absentee ballot campaign guaranteed CASAA an easy victory. The new leaders attempted to build an Anglo/Mexican American coalition government. They also began a series of reforms to improve conditions in poor Mexican American neighborhoods.[114]

Crystal City did not simply return to the status quo after the 1965 election. As historian David Montejano eloquently put it, *Cristal* "symbolized the overthrow of Jim Crow."[115] The political activism generated by PASO, the Teamsters, and the CCBG spread to other parts of the Winter Garden region. In 1964 PASO and the CCBG prepared for county elections, which resulted in the victory of a Mexican American justice of the peace. Moreover, Mexican Americans in Mathis created the Action Party and elected two Mexican Americans and one Anglo to the city government in 1965.[116]

Mexican Americans engaged in a great flurry of activity in the early 1960s. Their efforts met with a good deal of success. The Little School program continued to instruct Spanish-dominant students for most of the rest of the decade. But political activism clearly demonstrated the vibrancy of the Mexican American civil rights movement. Long the political pawns in the state, by the early 1960s activists had begun to tire of casting votes for candidates who did not respond to community needs. Instead, Mexican Americans sought out their own candidates and elected leaders to the U.S. Congress, to the Texas legislature, and to local positions in places like Crystal City. Their victories helped shape the contours of American political history for decades to come. Indeed, the future looked quite bright for Mexican American political action.

■ ■ ■

While Mexican Americans and African Americans both won numerous civil rights battles, unification continued to elude them. For the most part Mexican Americans reacted negatively to black protest activism, and they largely ignored the negotiated integration that occurred in most cities in Texas. As Robert Goldberg noted for San Antonio, "for Mexican Americans the struggle for black civil rights had no meaning, and prejudice and economic competition heightened the barrier between the two minorities."[117] Business owners like Felix Tijerina resisted the sit-in movement and did not follow the mandates of the negotiated desegregation, which in most Texas cities remained entirely voluntary. Indeed, Tijerina did not desegregate his restaurants until the passage of the Civil Rights Act of 1964, although he did so willingly once the federal government banned segregation.[118] Tijerina had ridiculed the sit-ins in 1960, and many other Mexican American leaders publicly opposed black protest activism. In July 1963, for instance, LULACers debated passing a resolution praising Martin Luther King Jr. The measure failed when one member wondered "what the negroes had done to help us?"[119]

In August 1963, LULAC national president Paul Andow reaffirmed the league's commitment to gradual progress. He publicly denounced direct action before a crowd of ten thousand at the LULAC National Convention. Andow criticized those who used protests and reminded LULACers that their struggle had been dignified. "We believe this dignity is now being threatened throughout the nation by some minority groups who are fomenting discord by demanding justice through mob violence [and] by undignified public demonstrations," he stated. Such protests "cast aspersions on our government in the eyes of the rest of the world." He discouraged LULACers, and Mexican Americans generally, from participating in protests with blacks. He also told them not to join "pseudo–civil rights organizations," referring to the NAACP, because their "aims are more often political than humanitarian." He called any such unity "unhealthy alliances." These "unhealthy alliances," he contended, "will only drag us down and hurt our cause." Andow concluded by saying: "Getting swallowed up in the craze of picket lines, marches, sit-ins and chain-ins will not solve the problem. Neither will joining forces with questionable civil rights groups."[120]

Paul Andow repeated these sentiments more stridently at a meeting of LULAC's Supreme Council in 1963. In a league policy statement, he called the black freedom struggle's protest tactics "the present craze." He reminded LULACers that they had long fought for rights without resorting to demonstrations. "We have not sought solutions to problems by marching to Washington, sit-in's or picketing," he stated, because "mass meetings and mass gatherings often times leads [sic] to mass hysteria." Andow told the assemblage that several unnamed groups had contacted him to form "a coalition." While he did not name the NAACP, the association had rhetorically called for forming alliances with LULAC in the 1950s. The league had rejected this idea, and Andow again rebuffed any attempts at coalition building. "I caution you," he warned, "not to be a part of or align yourself with any pseudo political organization that professes to be the shining knight in a silver armor displaying the role of protector of human rights." He closed by saying, "Do not be led astray by promises of a glorious future."[121]

One year later, William Bonilla, the new LULAC national president, made similar assertions. Bonilla argued that social change for Mexican Americans had come from "sound education coupled with the recognition and exercise of the privileges of American citizenship." Change would not come from protests, he said.[122] Bonilla repeated these statements a few months later, noting that "Latin American citizens have moved in large numbers from positions of scorn and discrimination . . . to take an equal and active part in the life of their community and their nation." He implied that Mexican Americans had already accomplished all of their goals. "These changes have come about through recourse to those citizenship privileges and those legal processes guaranteed every American citizen," he said, "without transgressions into violence, social discord, and civil disorder."[123] Leaders like Bonilla viewed protests as undignified, violent encounters that impugned the image of the United States. "I am not a crusader," he maintained, "and I hope that I am not classified as a radical individual." LULAC's leaders thus continued to promote a version of uplift that opposed the tactics of the African American struggle.[124]

Many Mexican Americans opposed black protests at both the state and the national level. They did not participate in demonstrations with African Americans, and they generally detested the fact that blacks throughout America engaged in these protests. As labor leader Pancho Medrano remembered, LULAC, the G.I. Forum, PASO, and other groups always rejected protesting. "Even at their state conventions," Medrano stated, "when you tried to say, 'Start demanding or picketing or marching,' they say, 'No. We are above that.' Especially the LULACs; they say, 'We have more pride or education than that. You leave this to the Negroes.'"[125] Medrano clearly acknowledged that not all Mexican Americans disliked protests. But some leaders rejected demonstrations, others denigrated protests, and some went so far as to criticize the most momentous protest of the 1960s: the March on Washington. LULAC, for example, drew up a resolution denouncing the march. According to one LULACer, the league was the only national group not represented in Washington, D.C., a fact that made some members quite proud.[126] Although many Mexican Americans supported the passage of the Civil Rights Act, LULAC and the G.I. Forum remained silent on the legislation.[127]

Once again the league's leaders firmly communicated to African Americans that they could not look to LULAC for aid or support. Like Felix Tijerina before them, Paul Andow and William Bonilla made sure that association with groups like the NAACP would not besmirch LULAC's image. According to Sherrill Smith, a prominent Catholic priest and activist in San Antonio, for some Mexican Americans protests were "a bit too much . . . to get out in public like that and walk and protest . . . it was in a sense beneath them."[128] Perhaps more problematically, political scientist Benjamin Márquez noted that groups like LULAC were "especially troubled by the possibility that such displays of defiance and impatience for social change could be adopted by Mexican Americans."[129] By rejecting the concept of direct action demonstrations, LULAC undermined the potential for working not only with blacks, but also with other Mexican Americans who disagreed with the league's accommodationist approach. If leaders like Albert Peña, Pancho Medrano, or George

Sánchez even cursorily read between the lines, what message could they take from LULAC's leadership? The league had an our-way-or-the-highway approach, one that ensured that only "dignified" action would be tolerated. Old copies of the *LULAC News* can give the impression that Mexican Americans were surprised, even jealous, that black protests won so much. Mexican Americans had engaged in a steady, cautious approach that had produced some results over the years. Now African Americans had, in a relatively short period, won rights through a program of direct action that Mexican Americans affiliated with LULAC abhorred. Black victories made groups like LULAC appear immobile. LULACers did not respond by changing tactics. Rather, they reaffirmed their loyalty to dignified progress. At a LULAC convention in New Mexico, past national president William Flores observed that the league had long fought discrimination "in the spirit of friendship, understanding, and dignity, and not by strikes, sit-ins, picketing, public demonstrations or emotional discontent, which could have disrupted the peace and tranquility of our country." Flores acknowledged that black protests had given Mexican Americans "food for thought," but he insisted that "our position has always been and still is that we take no active part in such demonstrations." Flores's message was clear: demonstrations were beneath Mexican Americans. The LULAC way remained the only way.[130]

Of course, not all Mexican Americans read the *LULAC News* or joined the league. And not all Mexican Americans opposed the black civil rights movement. Henry B. Gonzalez emerged as one of the few Mexican American leaders vocally supportive of the sit-in movement. At a meeting at Huston-Tillotson College in Austin, Gonzalez praised a large group of student activists. White leaders "should know that such ideas of the Sit-ins is an irresistible urge for human dignity and freedom," Gonzalez stated. He reminded the students of his earlier commitment to integration when he had served on the San Antonio City Council. Then as a state senator, he found that those leaders who resisted the quest for civil rights did so out of cowardice. They spoke of violence and loss of business, he implied, without considering what was right. "I say to you here today," Gonzalez said, "continue your course toward total freedom. . . . Freedom must come to all and there is nobody who can stop it." He uttered similar pronouncements at the NAACP's annual convention in 1961, telling attendees "the New Frontier has no room for racial bigotry." In all of his statements, Gonzalez diverged from Anglos and Mexican Americans who disapproved of direct action.[131]

Like Gonzalez, Juan Cornejo appealed to African Americans. In 1963 Cornejo sent a telegram to Martin Luther King Jr. while King was incarcerated in the Birmingham jail for his protests in that city. "Our hearts are with you in your effort to do away with the ugly practices of segregation and discrimination," he wrote. "We know how it feels to be abused under disguise of law and order." Oddly, the telegram ended with the thought, "Wish we could be with you to help."[132] If Cornejo hoped to win black friends, his effort failed. King made no reply, probably because he had already been released from jail before the telegram arrived. Interestingly, Mayor Cornejo made no appeals to Texas's black leaders. But he seemed to have understood that Mexican American political activism mirrored black protest activism.

Henry Gonzalez, George Sánchez, and Juan Cornejo, among others, continued to sympathize with the black freedom struggle. Despite this support, the racial positioning of many Mexican Americans and the disparagement of the sit-in movement damaged relations between African Americans and Mexican Americans. According to Earl Allen, William Lawson, Claude Black, and Ernest McMillan, no Mexican Americans participated in the sit-ins in Houston, Dallas, and San Antonio.[133] This suggests that Mexican Americans across the state had received the message communicated by LULAC and G.I. Forum officials. Membership in the league reached record numbers in the early 1960s, when the *LULAC News* had its greatest circulation to date.[134] Over ten thousand LULACers attended the 1963 annual convention, which points to the league's vitality. In short, LULAC influenced the general public through its organizational affiliation and through the *LULAC News*. It generated a discourse about race and rights, one that separated the black and Mexican American civil rights movements.

The African American response to Mexican American activism also proved somewhat bleak. Black leaders understood that Mexican Americans did not want to be their allies. As San Antonio activist Harry Burns recalled, Mexican Americans "didn't necessarily want to join forces with us."[135] The black press ignored both Mexican American activities, including those of the CAC and PASO, and political victories. Indeed, the Negro press rarely mentioned Mexican Americans at all. Problems in the black community most concerned African American leaders, so they disregarded the Mexican American community.

Geographic distance proved a crucial factor in the division between the two movements at this time. Few blacks lived in South Texas. In Crystal City, for instance, African Americans comprised only 2 percent of the population, or less than two hundred people. As one black resident observed, "This is one place where I'll never be in the minority. I just ain't." Obviously he was in the minority, but his sentiments implied that problems in Crystal City were specific to Mexican Americans, not blacks. His community's problems remained in large cities and in the Black Belt of the state. This individual, like other blacks in the area, did not consider himself part of the Mexican American struggle. Few blacks traveled to Crystal City to join the political protests. By the same token, few Mexican Americans from South and Southwest Texas went to cities like Dallas and Houston to take part in the sit-ins. Moreover, African Americans *in* Crystal City backed the Anglo political machine and refrained from voting for Los Cinco Candidatos.[136]

Mexican American and African American groups continued to have difficulty uniting. PASO, for example, had problems as an organizational entity and in its relations with black people. Its rejection of John Connally in favor of Price Daniel—later Don Yarborough—and events in Crystal City caused much controversy in Mexican American leadership circles.[137] Arthur W. Molina, a community leader in Fort Worth, derided the endorsement of Yarborough. In a letter to PASO, Molina expounded on a number of overtly racist subjects. He claimed that his neighborhood had been "inundated by the Negroes" and only Price Daniel could stop this, that social programs were "bedazzling the Negro people," and that Governor Connally's refusal to aid Mexican Americans was a step in the right direction. Moreover, he continued, labor unions had become part of the problem; hence Connally's resistance to unionism, which would come to a head during the Minimum Wage March of 1966, was the right course of action. Molina's basic concern with PASO appeared rather simple: "You sound too much like the NAACP. . . . For a dish of pottage your [*sic*] going to sell your birthright" to whiteness.[138] But PASO did not act like the NAACP. And the group's limited appeals to black Texans ensured almost no African American support for their efforts.

Another factor explains why blacks did not join forces with PASO. Some Mexican Americans in the group continued to rely on the whiteness strategy. Like the splinter San Antonio PASO, the Corpus Christi chapter opposed Albert Peña's leadership and withdrew from the national body; it also sustained its protest of the designation of Mexican Americans as nonwhite. Hearkening back to previous efforts by Hector García and Luciano Santoscoy to require health officials to classify Mexican Americans as white, PASO complained to Memorial Hospital in Nueces County in 1963 because hospital forms listed three races; Negro, white, and Latin American. PASO called this classification "Un-American . . . discriminatory, prejudiced, and illegal." It was "unacceptable, unwarranted . . . and is a thinly disguised method of continuing prejudice and discrimination so long enforced against Latin-Americans in Texas." The hospital finally removed the Latin American category from the form. This case confirms that white racial positioning still served as a tool in the Mexican American quest for rights. It further shows one reason why blacks and Mexican Americans did not unite.[139]

Like PASO, LULAC continued to promote the whiteness strategy. In a letter of May 1963 to the TGNC, Texas regional governor William Bonilla complained about segregation at a Texas resort. In a pamphlet, the resort made clear that "No Latin Americans or Colored People [Are] Accepted." Bonilla protested the "attitude" of people who would explicitly state that "no Latin Americans are allowed." As in the 1950s, he indicated that use of the words "colored" and "Latin American" in the same sentence constituted the real problem. If it could not repair this particular situation, Bonilla implied, then the TGNC had failed. The commission's Frank Kelley then wrote to remind the resort's owners that in Texas "the Latin race is a purely white race."[140] This example again demonstrates that Mexican Americans continued to appeal to the government for support. It also shows that LULACers still promoted whiteness in the fight for Mexican American rights.

The objectives of African Americans and Mexican Americans paradoxically contributed to disunity. The basic goals of each group appeared identical; to end discrimination, secure rights, eradicate poverty. For many blacks and Mexican Americans, pickets, sit-ins, and political activism resembled each other. In fact, the two groups used similar tactics, although the contexts differed. The CCBG did political canvassing and conducted poll tax drives. The NAACP and groups like the HCCO also directed voting drives and politically mobilized black Texans. The CCBG and PASO conducted rallies in Crystal City and beyond to secure Mexican American support. Rallies functioned as a major component of the black civil rights experience as well. Though Mexican Americans did not sit in, they did march and carry signs, much like their black counterparts. So each group had similar goals and tactics, but the overall emphasis of the two movements differed. This contributed to the lack of African American/Mexican American unity.

Politics also created divisions between Mexican Americans and African Americans. In previous decades, Mexican American leaders had worked diligently to nurture a close working relationship with state leaders, but their endorsement of Price Daniel over John Connally soured this relationship. In the 1960s African Americans saw a much more productive future with the segregationist Daniel out of office and a governor like Connally in the State House. Because of black support, and because JFK's assassination convinced many whites to look more favorably upon black civil rights, black Texans received more state support.[141] Thus, a transformation took place in the Texas government as African Americans became the beneficiaries of state support while Mexican Americans received more hostile treatment. The evolution of the government's role in minority communities served to once again divide the movements. Blacks and Mexican Americans ultimately found themselves in competition for state support, not in cooperation.[142]

As far as governors go, John Connally proved almost as bad as Price Daniel. Although a confidant and close friend of Lyndon B. Johnson, Connally was no liberal and remained lukewarm toward the Mexican American and African American quests for rights.[143] On the whole, however, he viewed the black struggle more positively than he did the Mexican American movement. But even African Americans had trouble dealing with Connally. Booker Bonner, the Austinite who had engaged in the one man theater stand-in, began another one-man protest against Connally. In addition, he organized a Freedom Now March to coincide with the March on Washington.[144] On August 28, 1963, three thousand blacks marched in Austin. A small number of Mexican Americans participated.[145] This limited support convinced some African Americans and Mexican Americans that the time for unity had come. In August 1963 blacks and Mexican Americans tried to form a four-group coalition composed of PASO and NAACP members, labor groups, and liberals. This Democratic Coalition turned out to be much smaller than anyone had hoped; it quickly devolved into the even smaller Bexar County Coalition, which remained limited to San Antonio. The group imploded in 1964, when each of its constituent elements endorsed a different candidate for a local election.[146] Coalition building once again met with limited success.

The rhetoric coming from Mexican American leaders also hurt coalition building. Beginning in 1960, these leaders began to magnify problems in the Mexican American community and minimize problems in the black community. Mexican Americans began to assert that they deserved more state support because people of Mexican origin suffered more than blacks. Leaders in PASO claimed that the Mexican American community "throughout the years has not been afforded as easy a time to get ahead as most other groups."[147] Similarly, LULAC president William Bonilla stated: "We citizens of Mexican ancestry have for years been faced with a struggle for an equal chance to participate in the activities around us. Ours has been in this area the ethnic group which has most often suffered the sting of bias and intolerance."[148] Hector García further argued that "the way some of our people have been discriminated against you would think that we didn't pay taxes; that we didn't help pioneer, settle and build this great state with our sweat, our brains and our sacrifices."[149] Even George Sánchez, someone unusually sympathetic to the plight of blacks, asserted: "The Indian, the Negro, the Filipino, the Puerto Rican, and all other peoples in a situation similar to that of the Mexican-American have been the object of our national solicitude, of our sense of social and moral responsibility. Not so the Mexican-American. He has been, and continues to be, the most neglected, the least sponsored, the most orphaned major minority group in the United States."[150]

The claim that Mexican Americans "suffered" more than African Americans frustrated unification with blacks. It signaled to black people that Mexican American leaders fundamentally misunderstood the African American experience in the United States. It indicated as well that Mexican American leaders viewed the poverty, discrimination, and racism that blacks endured as different from the poverty and discrimination that Mexican Americans experienced. While some of these sentiments certainly rang true, this rhetoric had rather predictable results. The competition for who had it worse insulted and offended blacks. It also ensured a poor working relationship between African Americans and Mexican Americans.[151]

The divide between Mexican Americans and blacks continued to exert itself in unusual ways. In early 1963 the Texas House of Representatives began committee hearings on a proposed minimum wage bill. A group of one hundred mainly blacks (represented by the NAACP) and Mexican Americans (supported by PASO) waited to testify. Both sides essentially said the same thing: low wages had damaged their community. Nevertheless, they approached the subject from separate paths.[152] "Only the mexicanos can speak for the mexicanos," George Sánchez maintained. Blacks were of the same opinion regarding their own community. These ethnocentric sentiments essentialized the experiences of blacks and Mexican Americans and made them unique to each group. But the experiences of both groups in the fifties and sixties pointed to the fallacy of such an opinion—Henry B. Gonzalez had clearly spoken for blacks when he challenged the segregation legislation in 1957 and supported the sit-ins in 1960, and NAACP leader H. Boyd Hall had at least attempted to speak to Mexican Americans in 1957. "Taken at its face value," Ronnie Dugger of the *Texas Observer* noted, such sentiments mean "not only that racial discrimination has to be experienced to be fully understood, but also in politics, mexicanos should elect only mexicanos. . . . Anglos can rationalize electing only Anglos. . . . Negroes can justify electing only Negroes." This was certainly how the movements in the early 1960s had played out.[153]

··· 4 ···

Venceremos

The Evolution of Civil Rights in the Mid-1960s

In August 1967 Father Antonio Gonzalez of the Galveston-Houston Archdio-cese described himself as the "Martin Luther King of the Mexicans." Speaking at a meeting of PASO, the priest detailed his own activism and commended "some of the nation's rioters" in Houston, Newark, and Detroit.[1] Although he urged Mexican Americans to "join hands politically with Negroes," Gon-zalez frequently waffled in his speech. After praising rioters, for instance, he vacillated and argued that riots were a last resort. Though he advocated Afri-can American/Mexican American unity, he later changed tracks, stating that "we intend to join many other organizations, even Negro perhaps." When asked why he wanted to ally with blacks, Gonzalez responded stereotypically that they made worthy allies because "they are intelligent, dignified and cul-tured."[2]

Father Gonzalez represented a new type of Mexican American civil rights leader in the mid-1960s. While he was unable to decisively articulate a vision of Mexican American and African American unity, his words clearly repre-sented a more open-minded approach to coalition building. Perhaps others could better fit the label of "Martin Luther King of the Mexicans," but Gon-zalez and his ilk represented a fundamental change in the attitude of many Mexican Americans toward the black civil rights movement. He also sym-bolized an important transformation in the Catholic Church, an entity that had not wholeheartedly embraced the notion of civil rights.[3] While LULAC, the G.I. Forum, and a number of other groups and individuals continued to promote civil rights by advancing Mexican American whiteness, others began to reevaluate the Mexican American movement and, more significantly, that movement's relationship with black people. For both groups, many problems remained. What strategies could blacks and Mexican Americans employ after passage of the Civil Rights Act and the Voting Rights Act? Desegregation of local businesses and the new laws gave blacks many of the victories they had fought for since their struggle began. How could Mexican Americans adopt the strategies of black activists, strategies that many leaders begrudgingly began to admit had worked very well, for their own purposes? Could unification produce good results? Leaders in both groups attempted to answer these questions during the mid-1960s.

Mexican Americans found new ways to become active in this period. Many discarded the LULAC model of gradual progress. Instead, direct action protests gave the Mexican American movement new life. Meanwhile, the black freedom struggle continued with full force. African Americans attacked the remnants of segregation and protested businesses that refused to desegregate. After 1964, they attempted to force recalcitrant businesses that would not integrate to comply with the Civil Rights Act. Blacks knew that they would have to demand that businesses obey the Civil Rights Act for the law to have any meaning. Both groups also worked at the grassroots level to make use of federal and local antipoverty programs. And while some leaders attempted to unify African Americans and Mexican Americans, significant unification continued to elude these groups. Many Mexican American leaders still employed the whiteness strategy, and divisions created in previous decades persisted in bifurcating each group.

As Jim Crow slowly died, Mexican Americans encountered a strategic problem. The previous method of achieving rights by racially positioning Mexican-origin people as white lost its effectiveness, and some of the protections granted by whiteness disappeared. Leaders were forced to initiate new tactics. One idea revolved around securing government aid through Great Society programs. Some also began to advocate the use of protests, something formerly derided and dismissed by many Mexican Americans. Finally, many leaders focused on labor activism to help secure better wages and working conditions for poor Mexicans and Mexican Americans.

In the mid-1960s, both Mexican Americans and African Americans began to make use of poverty programs established by the Johnson administration. Austin received a War on Poverty grant to implement a study of poverty. With federal aid Corpus Christi began a much-maligned, but nonetheless successful, birth control program. Most Texas cities used War on Poverty programs to fund tutorials and English language instruction similar to that provided by the Little Schools. Dallas made quick use of the Neighborhood Youth Corps program to add teachers, counselors, and tutors to local schools. Dallas, Houston, and many smaller towns opened Youth Opportunity Centers for job training.[4] In San Antonio, the NAACP had regular meetings with War on Poverty officials. The association also promoted use of the Volunteers in Service to America (VISTA) program.[5] The Community Action Program (CAP) also had the potential to assist poor people. Unfortunately, many Texas cities notoriously resisted the use of CAP. This resistance stemmed from fears about "welfare" and the federal government's encroachment into the South. Like many southern governors, John Connally controlled the purse strings and the types of programs that cities could use; this would create distinct problems for reformers as well as the governor in the coming years.[6]

Yet Mexican Americans achieved some of their greatest victories by taking advantage of these antipoverty programs. For example, leaders developed Operation SER in 1965 (also referred to as the Manpower Opportunities Project and as SER, Jobs for Progress, Inc.).[7] The original plans for SER originated when LULAC national president Alfred J. Hernández attended a meeting in one of Houston's barrios. After seeing conditions in this neighborhood, Hernández concluded that a job placement and training service could aid the working poor. LULAC formally opened the Houston Job Placement Center in April 1965.[8] The program's basic goal was to provide job training, counseling, and job placement and referral services for poor Mexican Americans. The league, with the G.I. Forum and California's Community Service Organization, formed a cooperative venture to fund SER throughout the Southwest. Houston, El Paso, San Antonio, and Corpus Christi initiated SER programs immediately. The project received an Office of Economic Opportunity (OEO) grant of nearly half a million dollars.[9]

SER's job training, education, and placement services had the potential of helping to eradicate poverty by giving poor people the tools to uplift themselves. The federal government's funding of the project and the state government's support of similar job corps and job training centers proved a boon to the efforts of LULAC and the G.I. Forum.[10] Beyond that, local government, business, and industry responded to the program. Many businesses found SER a worthy project. They not only gave financial support, but also hired individuals recommended or trained by SER. SER once again showed the willingness of the government to support Mexican American equality and uplift. The success of SER and the long-standing financial support provided by the government (the program exists today) shows that, like the Little Schools, Mexican Americans could still count on government aid.

In the mid-1960s Mexican Americans also began to engage in direct action demonstrations The most significant protests in Texas occurred in the Rio Grande Valley, the hub of the state's agricultural industry. Many of the issues in the Valley stemmed from the U.S. government's Bracero Program, which worsened the plight of Mexican American farm laborers. The program allowed guest workers, called braceros, to work in American agriculture and industry during, and long after, World War II. But the program had many problems. Lee G. Williams, a secretary in the Department of Labor, described the Bracero Program as little more than "legalized slavery."[11] San Antonio's Archbishop Robert E. Lucey referred to the braceros as "mobile serfs."[12] They experienced harassment, low wages, and job insecurity. As a result of the program, millions of legal and illegal Mexicans immigrated to the United States, which prompted the Immigration and Naturalization Services (INS) to begin "Operation Wetback" in 1954 to deport illegal immigrants. This punitive operation repatriated over one million Mexicans. Regrettably, the INS also deported a number of Mexican-origin children born in the United States and adult American citizens of Mexican descent.[13] Many Mexican American civic groups rejoiced when Congress declined to renew the program in 1963.[14]

The Bracero Program's demise did not end the farmworkers' problems. Farm laborers hoped for some financial aid when Congress proposed the establishment of a $1.25 minimum wage as part of the War on Poverty.[15] But Governor John Connally opposed the wage hike. The NFWA ultimately failed to convince the government to establish the new wage. When employers refused to voluntarily raise wages, the farmworkers resorted to the only tactic they had left—they went on strike.

In the summer of 1966, farmworkers organized one of the largest strikes in the history of the Rio Grande Valley. NFWA president Cesar Chavez dispatched union officers Dolores Huerta, Eugene Nelson, Hank Brown, and Antonio Orendain to organize the farmworkers. Huerta was Chavez's closest friend and second in command of the NFWA, while Nelson and Orendain were trusted officers.[16] These three individuals almost single-handedly organized the farmworkers' strike. On June 1, hundreds of Mexicans and Mexican Americans walked off the job.[17] The goal of *la huelga* (the strike) seemed simple enough: an official state minimum wage of $1.25. But as in Crystal City, the strikers found their efforts blocked by Texas Rangers. The Rangers, led by J. H. Preiss, joined with local growers to harass the Mexican-origin community. For instance, Preiss arrested Eugene Nelson on the first day of the strike.

El Malcriado, the union's newspaper, reported that "the big Texas landowners are supported by the guns and the boots of the fearsome Rangers in order to silence the Rio Grande Valley's melon strikers."[18] These events only emboldened the strikers.

After nearly a full month of striking, some of the farmworkers decided to transform into marchers. The strike's leadership planned a march from the Valley to Austin to garner media attention for the plight of the laborers.[19] They set out on Independence Day to highlight the symbolism of the protest. This nearly five-hundred-mile Minimum Wage March took over sixty-five days to complete. During the march, *la huelga* in the Valley continued. Many activists from across the state joined the march. On the first day, a group from Houston arrived in a bus chartered by PASO. LULAC president Alfred Hernández also participated, as well as many Christian ministers. Houstonians James Novarro, a Baptist of Mexican descent, and Father Antonio Gonzalez became the nominal heads of the protest. So too did Fathers Sherrill Smith and Robert Peña, two Catholic priests from San Antonio. The Catholic Church supported the march, and Texas's bishops signed a letter to Governor Connally asking him to meet with the marchers.[20] The church's avoidance of civil rights had begun to change when the San Antonio Archdiocese, led by the moderate archbishop, Robert Lucey, reexamined its relationship with poor people. The march proved an important, albeit controversial, step for the Catholic Church.[21]

Most of the strikers felt that government officials cared little for migrant workers.[22] This impression had some merit. But it would be inaccurate to assume that John Connally did nothing for poor Texans. He did support some antipoverty programs. For example, he authorized the Community Action Agency (CAA, a kind of mini-CAP) in many Texas counties. He also endorsed Head Start. And roughly one-third of federal funds from the OEO went to Texas for migrant workers. Connally was a strident advocate of the OEO's Camp Gary Job Corps Training Center, which offered vocational and technical training primarily to high school dropouts from across the United States. He called Camp Gary a "smashing success" that made up for "shortcomings in education." The facility, which trained thousands of minorities for technical jobs, is still in operation today.[23] But Connally ridiculed the minimum wage goal of the march. For this reason, the protest continued and the view that Connally did not care remained.[24]

As they traveled, the marchers sang songs, waved picket signs, and attracted more attention to their cause. Their numbers grew steadily. By the time they reached Austin, there were approximately ten thousand demon-

(From left to right) Dr. Clotilde García, Jane Valverde, Reverend James Navarro, and Dr. Hector P. García lead the Minimum Wage March out of Corpus Christi and on to San Antonio. The Valley strike and march represented a pivotal moment in the Mexican American quest for rights. (Dr. Hector P. García Papers, Special Collections and Archives, Texas A&M University, Corpus Christi, Bell Library)

strators. At rallies in places like Robstown and Corpus Christi, the marchers chanted *viva la huelga* (long live the strike) and *venceremos*, the Spanish version of the black movement's "we shall overcome."[25] Luz Orta, a forty-year veteran of farmwork, explained that "I'm marching to awaken the conscience of Texas. I'm old and I want to make a contribution before I die so that my grandchildren won't suffer as I did."[26] The Catholic priests also emboldened the strikers. Among them was Father Sherrill Smith, who spoke at many of the rallies. "We're giving notice to the whole world that we're going to march, march, march, until we've reached the hour of social justice," he yelled to the crowd at one gathering. The priests played an important role by blunting criticisms that the protest was anarchic or communistic.[27]

The marchers received broad support from Texas society. When they arrived in San Antonio, a number of politicians joined them. U.S. senator Ralph Yarborough, a Democrat, energized the marchers by addressing them in flawless Spanish.[28] Cries of "freedom," "justice," and "*venceremos*" echoed at a number of massive rallies.[29] Archbishop Lucey delivered a passionate sermon at San Fernando Cathedral, the seat of the San Antonio Archdiocese. Lucey turned the logic of the $1.25 minimum wage on its head when he said the church endorsed the wage "with a large measure of reluctance and regret." "No sane man," Lucey declared, "would consider *that* a fair wage." Lucey's kind words were a balm for the tired marchers. He brought many to tears when he closed his sermon by saying, "May God be with you as you march to Austin . . . may your reception there be in complete harmony with your dignity as human beings, American citizens and children of God."[30]

The marchers had hoped to meet with Governor Connally in Austin and persuade him to endorse the minimum wage proposal. But Connally refused to speak with them in Austin.[31] Instead, he opted to confer with their representatives at New Braunfels, a small town near the capital city. The governor arrived with Attorney General Waggoner Carr. Reverend James Novarro had personally invited Lieutenant Governor Preston Smith, but he declined to attend.[32] Novarro, Antonio Gonzalez, Eugene Nelson, Sherrill Smith, and several others represented the marchers. They met on the highway under the hot Texas sun. Gonzalez and Novarro greeted the governor warmly and again invited him to meet the marchers in Austin. Connally again refused. The discussion became tense when Father Smith warned the governor that Mexican Americans would refrain from voting in the next election. When Smith asked him what he would do to keep these voters, Connally fumbled for words. Smith then asked him if the march was a "bad way to come and see you." Connally replied, "Yes, I think basically it is, Father Smith, because of what is occurring elsewhere in this land with respect [to] marches that have resulted in riots, bloodshed, loss of life and loss of property." In other words, the governor came to New Braunfels to prevent violence. But so far, only Texas law enforcement had acted violently, which made the governor's words appear trite. The meeting ended abruptly.[33]

It took the Minimum Wage March another five days to reach the capitol. When the approximately ten thousand marchers arrived, an equal number of sympathetic demonstrators awaited them. Congressman Henry Gonzalez, Senator Ralph Yarborough, state senator Barbara Jordan, five other state senators, and fourteen other state representatives joined the protest. Yarborough told his massive audience that "one hundred years ago, we ended physical slavery, today we are here to end poverty and economic slavery."[34] Gonzalez praised the marchers, noting that "today is really a day of departure" for Mexican Americans. After the speeches, the demonstration moved away from the capitol to a nearby park. A huge rally and celebration ensued. The marchers rejoiced when Cesar Chavez addressed them. His remarks were short, concise, and incredibly moving. "We have suffered," he said, "We have struggled.

We will continue to struggle. We will continue to suffer. We will, we must, and we know in our hearts that we shall overcome."[35]

Though the crowds dissipated a few days later, the farmworkers continued the strike for another year. Support for the strike remained high, but most predicted it would fail.[36] In the end, the strikers did not secure the desired minimum wage. Yet their march succeeded beyond the wildest dreams of most. It showed many Mexican Americans that a nonviolent, protest action need not be discordant, disorderly, or undignified. Labor leader Hank Brown had "never seen as much unity among Mexican-Americans as I see at this hour in Texas." Father Smith reiterated these thoughts. "What Connally did," he asserted, "really stirred up Mexican-Americans. It was a slap on the hand, a Great White Father–type of thing." But, he acknowledged, it allowed them to become active: "they rallied themselves."[37] Six months later Smith spoke even more harshly, assailing Connally as a "gringo." "Governor Connally is the symbol of gringo paternalism," Smith contended. "I could see that out on the road that day. He was the tall Texan looking down and patting the Mexican on the head."[38] But this had inspired the struggle. This seemingly unsuccessful event radicalized the Mexican American protest movement.

Not all Mexican American civic groups approved of the strike, however. LULAC national president Alfred Hernández's decision to participate in the march generated a good deal of controversy within the league. A number of LULAC councils opposed the strike, still considering protests anathema to league activities. The Laredo council stated that it would "naturally oppose actual participation in the march" and invited Governor Connally to speak in Laredo.[39] There, he told LULACers that strike leaders were "itinerant paid purveyors of division, distrust and dissension."[40] Past national president William Flores again voiced his aversion to protests, saying LULAC was "opposed to marches, sit-ins and similar demonstrations."[41] San Antonio's LULAC withdrew its support for the march when rumors emerged that communists supported the strike.[42] Indeed, many councils gave hope and comfort to the enemies of the marchers by denouncing the strike or praising the governor.

During the strike and the march, other important developments played out on the national scene. Among these, several Mexican American leaders began to criticize the way the Johnson administration addressed poverty issues.[43] Alfred J. Hernández and many others believed the federal government was giving too much to African Americans while neglecting Mexican Americans. Carlos Truan, who coordinated LULAC's relationship with antipoverty programs, argued that "Latin Americans . . . constitute the ethnic group hardest hit by a chronic and unnecessary poverty in the Southwest."[44] Hernández also argued that *"we are being denied our fair share in government employment, housing and education."* He wanted LBJ to increase the number of Mexican American appointees. "Our government officials are hiding behind the pretext that appointments cannot be had because they cannot find qualified persons of Mexican-American extraction," he said. Signaling another strategic shift, Hernández asked: "What does it take? What must we do? While I do not condone violence, it may be that we too should resort to marches, sit-ins, and demonstrations."[45]

This was a bold declaration. Alfred Hernández openly endorsed what many LULACers considered abhorrent. He carried out his threat to protest when he resorted to demonstrations in March 1966. The LBJ administration called a meeting of the Equal Employment Opportunity Commission (EEOC) in Albuquerque, New Mexico, in March 1966 to hear the grievances of the Mexican American community. Mexican American leaders had criticized Franklin D. Roosevelt Jr., the EEOC chair, because the commission "was geared entirely to the situation of the Negro."[46] Roosevelt promised to rectify the EEOC's inattention, but he did nothing.[47] When the EEOC met in Albuquerque, Chairman Roosevelt failed to attend the gathering, which galled Mexican American leaders further. To them, his absence once again signaled the administration's neglect of Mexican Americans.

On March 28, when the EEOC meeting had barely started, the Mexican American leaders — Alfred Hernández, Albert Peña of PASO, Augustin Flores of the G.I. Forum, Bert Corona of the Mexican American Political Association (MAPA), and others — each rose to voice their grievances.[48] Peña noted that the EEOC had not filed complaints against companies that discriminated against Mexican Americans. He criticized White House meetings that involved hundreds of African American leaders but only a handful of Mexican Americans. As Hernández observed, "Our employment problems are severe and complex, yet we have no one on the commission with any insight into them." After each leader had spoken, they all stormed out of the conference. Later that afternoon they held their own meeting and resolved to work together — an important promise. They also drafted a letter to President Johnson explaining their actions.[49]

The letter sent to the White House called the EEOC meeting "valueless." The leaders who walked out stated that the federal government had shown no interest in the problems facing Mexican-origin people in the Southwest. "The commission has been insincere in its relations with the Mexican-American community," they asserted. The message included eight specific demands, the most important of which were that the president appoint a Mexican American to the EEOC, that Mexican Americans be represented at White House meetings, that the administration include Mexican Americans in the forthcoming White House Conference on Civil Rights (more generally known as the "To Fulfill These Rights" Conference), and that the "entire program of the EEOC be reoriented" to focus on Mexican Americans. George Sánchez, who agreed with these demands, told Franklin Roosevelt Jr. that nothing "had been done for some six million Americans of Mexican descent."[50] Sánchez also congratulated Hernández, Peña, and the others who had walked out, praising them for showing Mexican American "mettle."[51]

Criticisms of the president continued after this meeting. Albert Peña lambasted Johnson and declared that the Southwest needed a "Marshall Plan for Mexican Americans."[52] Alfred Hernández said the president made "beautiful speeches and wonderful promises that never materialize." He called the programs offered by the LBJ administration "token." Hernández acknowledged that Johnson had agreed that Mexican Americans had "a legitimate grievance. . . . But we've been so quiet, patient and passive that we're being left out of everything." He said, more brashly: "If it takes picketing and marching, we're ready to go to it."[53] Hernández made bold statements for a LULAC president. At no time before had a national president advocated similar strategies.

And yet the more things changed, the more they stayed the same. Only a few months before the blowup with the EEOC, LULAC had protested the designation of Mexican Americans as nonwhite. An unnamed LULAC leader told the San Antonio News that "being non-White makes us inferior." The paper agreed, noting that denying Mexican Americans "the designation of 'White'" was more aggravating than "being discriminated against."[54] As in previous decades, use of "L.A." or "Latin American" on hospital forms to designate the race of Mexican American newborns also infuriated LULACers. "We all know there is no such thing as a Latin American race," LULACer Alex Alcozar intoned. The league sent letters to the governor, state legislators, and health officials to complain. Officials apologized for the "misunderstanding" and agreed to classify Mexican American infants as white.[55] The whiteness strategy remained.

Like LULAC, the G.I. Forum continued to promote rights by appealing to the wages of whiteness. For example, Hector García protested when a census of college enrollments required Mexican American students to choose "other" instead of white. As in previous complaints, García disliked the phraseology because it took Mexican Americans out of the white category and placed them with "Eskimos, Indian Americans and Orientals." LULAC's William Bonilla complained to the White House. Vice President Hubert Humphrey informed

Bonilla that the administration deplored the mistake. George Sánchez also voiced his concerns, reminding officials that such classifications violated the law, "which classif[ies] Americans of Mexican descent as 'white.'" Sánchez explained that "we Americans of Mexican descent resent being placed in a category that (improperly) connotes inferiority to the lay mind." In other words, he disliked categorization as nonwhite because it connoted blackness. Federal authorities agreed to classify Mexican Americans as white on the college census.[56]

The White House attempted to improve relations with the Mexican American community by inviting prominent leaders to attend planning sessions for the "To Fulfill These Rights" Conference.[57] These efforts did not impress Mexican American leaders. Those involved in the Albuquerque walkout continued to goad the government to action and founded the Mexican-American Ad Hoc Committee on Equal Employment Opportunity (Ad Hoc Committee). Headquartered in Washington, D.C., the Ad Hoc Committee acted much like a political action committee, attempting to pressure the administration into making concessions favorable to Mexican Americans. Among its members were Alfred Hernández, Augustin Flores, Bert Corona, and Rodolfo "Corky" Gonzales of the Crusade for Justice.[58]

Like other groups, the Ad Hoc Committee continued to promote rights by comparing problems in the Mexican American community with those of blacks. Again, this tactic relied on a rhetoric that elevated Mexican American suffering over black suffering. LBJ had recognized "employment problems of Mexican Americans," the Ad Hoc Committee pointed out, and "publicly stated that this ethnic group suffers under similar or worse conditions of discrimination as does the American Negro." And yet, it argued, he did nothing.[59] The group incorrectly blamed blacks for the situation because "the 'big six' Negro leaders [Martin Luther King Jr., Ralph Abernathy, Roy Wilkins, James Farmer, Stokely Carmichael, and Whitney Young] and the administration are adamant on the exclusion of Mexican-Americans." The Ad Hoc Committee therefore made plans to boycott and picket the forthcoming civil rights meeting.[60]

Leaders on the Ad Hoc Committee became so infuriated over these issues that they started referring to the civil rights gathering as the "White House (all Negro) Civil Rights Conference."[61] They also kept their promise to picket the meeting.[62] But the civil rights conference proved unsuccessful. As James Farmer of CORE remembered, it operated as a smokescreen to hide increasing tensions between the administration and African American leaders who had begun to advocate for Black Power. In Farmer's words, "The White House Conference was an attempt to tell people to be quiet, and cut out this [Black Power] nonsense."[63] In fact, it failed to please anyone and degenerated into a cavalcade of criticism of the president. Little discussion about Mexican Americans occurred. Only Aaron Henry, a well-known NAACP leader in Mississippi, commented on the absence of Mexican Americans. "The Chicanos were largely upset because it did not seem that the White House Conference was meant for them," Henry recalled. "We wanted all people of whatever racial hue that had a difficulty finding its way into the mainstream of American life to be given a hand, to be given a lift. And this did include, in our thinking, the Chicanos, if they had told them to come to the convention."[64] He indicated that the lack of Mexican American involvement was the administration's fault. In fact, the meeting exemplified the division of the Mexican American and African American civil rights movements. By most accounts it was for blacks, not Mexican Americans.

The EEOC walkout and the criticisms and picket of the White House Conference on Civil Rights were somewhat unfair. President Johnson had frequently shown great sympathy toward the Mexican American community in Texas and for poor people generally. Certainly the state and federal government had offered Mexican Americans much assistance over the years, from the TGNC, which still operated, to educational reform, jobs programs, and Great Society programs. As Craig Kaplowitz has observed, "The accomplishments of the Johnson administration were not insignificant for Mexican Americans."[65] But leaders in groups like the Ad Hoc Committee continued to feel ignored and neglected.

Mexican American criticism of President Johnson did increase attention from the federal government. When LBJ learned of the displeasure over the White House meeting, he attempted to appease Mexican American leaders by inviting them to a separate gathering that preceded the White House Conference on Civil Rights. Johnson viewed this meeting as a precursor to what would hopefully become a more fruitful relationship with the Mexican American community.[66] This conference took place near the end of May 1966 and, based on postmeeting opinions, appeared to have been quite successful. Bert Corona, Alfred Hernández, Hector García, Augustin Flores, Roy Elizondo of PASO, and a number of other prominent leaders attended.[67] A short time later, the administration began planning for an exclusive Mexican American Conference on Civil Rights to be held in late 1966.[68] The White House also created the Interagency Committee on Mexican American Affairs

(From left to right) MAPA president Bert Corona, American G.I. Forum chairman
Dr. Hector P. García, LULAC national president Alfred J. Hernández, Roy Elizondo of
PASO, and LBJ special assistant Joseph Califano meet with President Johnson and adviser
Robert McPherson (with their backs to the camera) in May 1966. Although these
leaders were pleased with the president's attention, criticism of LBJ continued
after this meeting. (Lyndon Baines Johnson Presidential Library, Austin)

(ICMAA) to help alleviate tensions. The president appointed Vicente Ximenes,
a Texas native and prominent New Mexican leader, as chairman of the ICMAA
and also as a member of the EEOC.

In 1967 President Johnson began to promote poverty programs and civil
rights exclusively for Mexican Americans. His February message to Congress
focused almost entirely on poverty, and many Mexican American leaders
found it heartening.[69] Similarly, John Connally helped initiate a Texas Conference for the Mexican-American in San Antonio, where he made a rather
passionate speech on education and human rights. The governor vaguely
promised continued support from Austin.[70] At another civil rights conference called by the U.S. Civil Rights Commission, leaders exposed many of
the miserable conditions on Texas farms, in schools, and within the state government. The commission agreed with Mexican Americans that the "Texas
Rangers are a symbol of oppression."[71] At the same time, the LBJ administration continued to plan for another Mexican American conference, which
would finally take place in October 1967 in El Paso. Although the meeting was
not all that leaders had hoped for, it did allow Mexican Americans to press for

government aid and to articulate differences between African American and Mexican American approaches to antipoverty.[72]

Shortly after the El Paso conference, the Texas Rangers committed a series of atrocities that confirmed for Mexican Americans how little the government cared for them. Governor Connally had once again dispatched A. Y. Allee to the Rio Grande Valley in the name of maintaining law and order.[73] George Sánchez retorted that the Rangers were "the private strong arm of the Governor."[74] Allee immediately began arresting strikers on a variety of fictitious charges. He first targeted five Mexican American women, perhaps to intimidate male workers. The Rangers also harassed strikers, broke a newsman's camera, slapped a priest, and beat strikers with their shotguns.[75] Then, the Rangers arrested Magdaleno Dimas and another Mexican American man. In what became known as the Dimas Incident, Allee and his Rangers beat these men throughout the night and refused to give them appropriate medical treatment. Dimas later received hospital care for broken bones, internal bleeding, and a concussion. Allee insisted that Dimas was a notorious criminal and had fired a gun at a farm owner, but no proof existed to support these claims.[76]

These events provoked another response from Washington. This time the Senate Subcommittee on Migratory Labor met in Rio Grande City under the leadership of Harrison Williams (D-N.J.) and Edward Kennedy (D-Mass.). Kennedy, as a relative of JFK, electrified the audience of approximately two hundred Mexican Americans, many of whom were still on strike. The senator from Massachusetts openly criticized the Texas Rangers and A. Y. Allee. When growers maintained that they wanted peaceful relations with farmworkers, Kennedy retorted sternly, "Then why are the Rangers here?" The crowd applauded loudly. The subcommittee had requested that Allee attend the meeting, but he refused, leaving Senator Williams to joke: "Well, one thing I think we can all feel secure about, we are not going to be arrested by any Rangers today."[77]

The senators hoped to ultimately bring migrant laborers under the protection of the National Labor Relations Board. This would have important implications for individuals working in the farm industry and for those abused by law enforcement. But their visit came to naught. No new legislation emerged from Washington, and Magdaleno Dimas found no justice. After continued violence and a hurricane in September, *la huelga* finally ended.[78]

The Mexican American movement in the mid-1960s clearly had evolved. The use of antipoverty programs and projects like Operation SER greatly aided the Mexican-descent population in Texas and the Southwest. Additionally, leaders had begun to promote protest tactics. The EEOC walkout, the Minimum Wage March and Valley strike, and the Mexican-American Ad Hoc Committee all symbolized a new radicalism. Certainly some leaders in LULAC and the G.I. Forum, and many individuals in the state, continued to promote a "dignified" and gradualistic strategy of uplift. And they still promoted whiteness. But on the whole, the Mexican American struggle entered new territory in this period. The old generation composed of George Sánchez, Alfred Hernández, Albert Peña, and others helped open the door for a new generation of leaders.

■ ■ ■

Throughout this period African Americans continued to fight their own battles. For the most part they concentrated on eradicating the vestiges of Jim Crow that still remained in the public arena and on forcing reluctant businesses to comply with the provisions of the Civil Rights Act of 1964. Dallas remained a hotbed of black activism. In April 1963 the NAACP launched a boycott against Skillerns drugstores in Big D. This "ghetto gouger" sold expired and defective merchandise at high prices in all-black neighborhoods. African Americans also protested Skillerns's refusal to hire black clerks, managers, and pharmacists.[79] Ernest L. Haywood, president of the Dallas NAACP, personally led the pickets and carried a sign that stated simply "No Hire, No Buy!"[80] Haywood reported that by the end of April the picketing had cost the store hundreds of dollars and that in "one hour some 18 cars of would be patrons [were] turned away."[81] In the end, however, this protest proved unsuccessful.

In late 1963 the NAACP threatened to initiate protests to push the Dallas Transit Company, which ran the city's buses, to employ black drivers. The company reacted to the threat by hiring two African Americans.[82] The local NAACP chapter also warned that it would lead demonstrations if the city refused to integrate municipal parks and swimming pools. African Americans throughout the South had long found segregation at parks and pools particularly galling. Indeed, the denial of access to these recreation sites had led to the protests of the Texas State Fair in Dallas, to the vicious use of fire hoses at Kelly Ingram Park during demonstrations in Birmingham, and even to major riots in Chicago in 1919, Detroit in 1943, and Birmingham in 1963.[83] In response to the threat of demonstrations in Dallas, local government officials quickly agreed to desegregate all city-run parks and swimming pools.[84] Again, the city calmly integrated.

After President Kennedy's assassination in November 1963, black Dallasites cautiously renewed their call for civil rights when they formed the Dallas Coordinating Committee on Civil Rights (DCCCR). Uniting a variety of civic groups, including the NAACP, CORE, and SNCC, the DCCCR functioned as an umbrella organization. Initially the new committee distributed fliers that asked, "Are demonstrations needed in Dallas?" The answer was yes—unless the city integrated its schools.[85] When public officials made no response, the DCCCR began picketing the school administration building in downtown Dallas. Earl Allen, who had graduated from SMU and now ran the local chapter of CORE, led the protest with Clarence Laws, the recently appointed Southwest regional director of the NAACP. Although he managed the NAACP in Texas, Oklahoma, Arkansas, Louisiana, and New Mexico, Laws spent most of his time in Dallas because of the city's activist commitment. Seventy picketers marched around the administration building for several weeks.[86]

In 1964 the DCCCR censured the DISD for continuing to segregate black students ten years after the *Brown* decision. The group distributed a flier entitled "Little Known Facts about School Desegregation in Dallas." In it, the DCCCR chided the district for its tokenism and described what it called "The Other Half of the Truth." Among other things, the flier exposed the school board's complicated transfer procedures to permit African Americans to enroll in white schools. Sixteen criteria governed student transfers and ensured the slow pace of school desegregation. The DCCCR noted that only blacks had to transfer, not white students. In short, the DCCCR claimed, the DISD had created insurmountable obstacles to integration.[87]

Because of the city government's failure to implement further desegregation, new protests began. In May, Earl Allen led CORE and DCCCR activists in major demonstrations in Dallas (as well as in Austin and Waco) to protest the Piccadilly Cafeteria, which was not among the forty restaurants initially desegregated in Dallas. Protesters blocked the cafeteria's entrance and ignored police requests that they disperse. Although detained by police but not arrested, Allen told reporters that the protest "is just the beginning." He tied the demonstration to the DCCCR's school protests, explaining that it grew out "of our failure to reach some type of agreement with the Dallas Public School Board."[88] Pickets continued for several weeks.[89] The activists had problems integrating the restaurant because it was not locally owned. By late June, CORE and DCCCR convinced the cafeteria's proprietors to integrate. The agreement was but a partial victory; President Johnson signed the Civil Rights Act on July 2, 1964, just a few days after the agreement was reached. The cafeteria's owners acquiesced but only because they knew LBJ would sign the bill.[90]

The passage of the Civil Rights Act did not end activism in Texas cities. In

Dallas, shortly after LBJ signed the Civil Rights Act into law, a group of African American high school and college students engaged in a "bowl-in" at the Bowlero Lanes bowling alley. White activists paid for a lane, and then the black activists joined them for integrated bowling. A short time later the manager closed the alley, but the activists refused to leave; they continued bowling, playing pool, and feeding money into the jukebox. Police arrested the group for trespassing.[91] A few years later, black youths engaged in a "skate-in" at a Dallas roller rink. When the rink's owners told them that the rink "don't skate colored," the young people marched out onto the rink to block white skaters. The black community also boycotted the business. The federal government eventually charged the roller rink's owners with violating the Civil Rights Act.[92]

African Americans in Dallas and many other cities in Texas became more vocal in early 1965. They engaged in massive demonstrations to condemn the murder of Reverend James Reeb, a white Unitarian minister beaten to death by a racist mob during the Selma Campaign in Alabama. On March 14, 1965, in a coordinated statewide protest, crowds descended on downtown centers. In Dallas, between three thousand and five thousand people marched from a downtown church to a rally at Ferris Plaza. Led by H. Rhett James and Clarence Laws, the marchers dubbed the protest the Alabama Sympathy March. The *Dallas Express* reported that "it was a peaceful demonstration which tugged at the heart strings of bystanders and marchers alike."[93] Similar protests occurred in Houston, Fort Worth, San Antonio, El Paso, and Austin. Each of these involved more than one thousand people. In San Antonio, Father Sherrill Smith served as march leader. In El Paso, activists gave speeches in English and in Spanish. The marchers hoped to send President Johnson the message that he should remove barriers to voting in the United States. Clarence Laws asserted that "while we applaud their [the Johnson administration's] promises—we getting weary of promises."[94] Texans awaited word from Washington that the federal government intended to protect the voting rights of black people. A few days after the marches, LBJ signed the Voting Rights Act.[95]

After the act was passed, the NAACP began a massive voter registration and poll tax drive in Texas. Previously, local branch presidents had coordinated voting drives. In Houston, the association and the local Negro press encouraged black residents to vote and pay their poll taxes. Additionally, groups like the HCCO and the HCHR conducted voter education and registration drives.[96] Similarly, in 1964 Volma Overton, the longtime leader of Austin's NAACP, organized a voting drive in the capital city that he labeled the "Vote the Rascals Out" campaign.[97] The statewide association wanted to register 100,000

NAACP southwest regional director Clarence Laws (carrying flag) leads the
Dallas contingent of the Alabama Sympathy March. The marchers decried police
brutality and demanded federal protection for black voting rights. Similar protests
occurred in almost every Texas city. (Collections, Texas/Dallas History
and Archives Division, Dallas Public Library)

new voters, a goal that climbed to 600,000 by 1967. The State Conference of
NAACP Branches succeeded in registering thousands, although actual numbers never came close to the goals.[98] Beyond the voting and poll tax drives, the
NAACP also expanded its operations and opened new branches throughout
the state. Leaders wanted to cement the association's power by decentralizing
local branches. For example, the NAACP split the Houston branch into eight
smaller branches, each of which could appeal to different segments of the city.
The same thing happened in Dallas, where activists referred to the new organizational structure as the "Neighborhood NAACPs."[99]

These voter registration drives proved remarkably successful. The increased
number of voters, combined with the reapportionment of voting districts in
Texas, resulted in several major political victories for African Americans. In
many cases, these were the first black candidates elected to public office since
Reconstruction. In San Antonio, Reverend Samuel H. James Jr. won a seat on
the city council in 1965. The first black to hold such a position, James won re-

election in 1967.[100] In 1966 Houstonian Curtis Graves, one of the sit-in leaders and organizers of the PYA, was sent to the Texas House of Representatives and Barbara Jordan won a seat in the Texas Senate. Jordan was the first black to serve in the senate since 1883 and the first black woman ever elected to that body. Blacks returned Graves to the legislature in 1968 and sent Jordan to the U.S. Congress in 1972. As the first black southern woman to serve in the House, Barbara Jordan perhaps best represented the fulfillment of black political aspirations in Texas.[101] In Dallas, Joseph Lockridge was elected to the Texas House in 1966. After his untimely death, Lockridge was replaced by Reverend Zan Holmes.[102] Dr. Emmett Conrad won a seat on the board of the DISD, the first African American to hold such a position.[103] Dallasites also elected George Allen to the city council in 1969; he won reelection for four consecutive terms.[104] The election of these officeholders represented the culmination of efforts to effect change in the African American community. After promoting the payment of the poll tax and educating voters for decades, black political activism came of age in the mid-1960s. The voter registration work that began both before and after passage of the Voting Rights Act greatly facilitated the election of black candidates.

In the mid-1960s, the most vigorous demonstrations occurred in the state's Black Belt. Much like Marshall, Huntsville refused to integrate, even after passage of the Civil Rights Act. As a consequence, a variety of activists traveled to Huntsville for demonstrations in 1965. Booker T. Bonner, Reverend Wallace "Bud" Poteat and other Houston ministers, and the AFL-CIO's Hank Brown, who would organize the Rio Grande Valley strike a year later, all joined forces to ignite the protests. Beyond these leaders, Martin Luther King dispatched the SCLC's James Bevel to help organize the demonstrations and SCLC project director Alfred Sampson to help direct them. Bevel had become famous, or infamous, for using children as protesters in Birmingham. As elsewhere, a cadre of high school and college students provided the backbone of support for the protests.[105]

This broad collection of activists hoped to begin sit-ins, pickets, and boycotts of Huntsville's downtown businesses. Leaders believed that blacks, Mexican Americans, and sympathetic whites from around the state would converge on Huntsville to assist in protests. But the demonstrations actually began with the formation of Huntsville Action for You (HA-YOU), which was almost entirely composed of local black people. After a series of planning meetings, HA-YOU had gathered approximately forty volunteers and began a picket at the Life Theatre. The theater still segregated African Americans to the balcony even after the Civil Rights Act. The demonstrators included Gilbert Campos, of Houston, one of the only Mexican Americans involved in the protest. The activists picketed the theater and engaged in stand-ins. But the protest proved anticlimactic because the theater quickly desegregated. Activists then tried to sit in at the Texan Café; after the manager locked them out, HA-YOU picketed the restaurant.[106]

The protest at the Texan Café continued the following day. But when served by the eatery's staff, the activists again felt disappointed. These protesters needed white resistance to legitimize their protests. So, believing they had no recourse, the HA-YOU activists refused to pay their check and police arrested them for theft. Once more they found their plans foiled when someone paid the check and the police released them. The group then decided to picket the downtown courthouse. This protest incited white resistance. One white man attacked a photographer and broke his camera. A white farmer beat an activist. Locals told Gilbert Campos he had no reason to protest and to "get the hell out [of town]." When Campos refused, police arrested him, only to release him a short time later.[107]

The demonstrations, which included large rallies, marches, and pickets, lasted for several more days. Some businesses continued to integrate voluntarily. For instance, the Raven Café desegregated after the protests at the Texan Café. But HA-YOU learned that this "integration" allowed only two blacks to enter the business at a time. So sit-ins began at the Raven, where Houston minister Bud Poteat play a prominent role. When the wait staff asked Poteat why he chose to sit in, he replied that he and his wife were "with HA-YOU." "If they tell us they've been notified that you're integrated," he told the manager, "we'll leave." The manager refused to integrate, and police arrested Reverend and Mrs. Poteat with twenty-four other demonstrators. Local blacks gathered at the courthouse to serenade the jailed activists with freedom songs. All were hoarse by the time HA-YOU bailed them out the following day.[108]

The demonstrations in Huntsville continued for the next several months.[109] Just as he had in Austin, Booker Bonner appealed to Governor Connally for aid. Complaining of "the enormous [number] of arrests" in Huntsville, he made a criticism that most Mexican Americans would understand—"The truth is," Bonner told the governor, "the Texas Rangers have done a lot of intimidation." He blamed their brand of "gunpowder justice" for the arrests and violence. It seems that the Rangers frustrated black activists as much as they had Mexican Americans. Bonner hoped to meet with the governor, but Connally once again refused to see him.[110] Nevertheless, the HA-YOU protests finally succeeded in desegregating the reluctant businesses in Huntsville. The protests demonstrate that, even after passage of the Civil Rights Act, black activism was required to end segregation.

Yet African Americans discovered that local officials and businesses often refused to comply with the new legislation. Even in places like Houston, Dallas, San Antonio, and Corpus Christi, cities that had voluntarily begun to integrate before it was so mandated by the government, white officials and business owners did not welcome the new law. African Americans thus continued to protest. Some black leaders pushed their local governments to adopt their own versions of the Civil Rights Act as a way to force businesses to desegregate. In San Antonio, the NAACP hoped the city council would adopt a local civil rights act "in an effort to gain full community support of the recently enacted civil rights law. . . ."[111] These efforts made perfect sense. After pushing the federal government to pass the Civil Rights Act, African Americans at the local level wanted to see an appropriate response. Instead, San Antonio proposed to seek a state version of the civil rights law. This delaying tactic was doomed to fail since the Texas legislature did not favor the Civil Rights Act. The San Antonio City Council ultimately passed a rather weak resolution pledging to cooperate with various federal civil rights agencies.[112]

Besides protests, African Americans also attempted to utilize both public and private antipoverty programs in Texas. In Houston, Dallas, and Austin, for example, black leaders developed branches of Operation Breadbasket, initially begun by the SCLC. The program had two basic goals: to use federal grants to help poor African Americans buy food and to boycott white-owned businesses that refused to hire blacks. The national leader of the program, the SCLC's Reverend Jesse Jackson, pioneered what he called "selective buying campaigns," or boycotts, to force employers to use black contractors and buy from black-owned businesses. Operation Breadbasket thus had both antipoverty and pro-black capitalist elements. Although this program would realize its heyday in the 1970s, it did increase the number of African Americans hired by local businesses.[113] Dallas introduced a similar program. Run by the Dallas County Community Action Committee (DCCAC), this local antipoverty program helped black families obtain nutritious, low-cost foods. The DCCAC also taught a variety of classes on how to prepare healthy meals, child care, home safety, and home renovation.[114] In San Antonio, black activists began planning antipoverty programs in 1965. The government facilitated these efforts when the city council folded all local programs into the citywide Economic Opportunities Development Cooperation (EODC). The EODC administered a number of antipoverty programs and organizations in

San Antonio, including Head Start, a drug rehabilitation program, and a legal aid service. In 1967 blacks initiated Project FREE (Family, Rehabilitation, Education, Employment) under the EODC. Project FREE, a family services program, attempted to do exactly what the acronym implied: grant freedom from poverty.[115]

Black protests in the mid-1960s worked to remove the remainder of the Jim Crow system in the public sphere. White business owners continued to resist desegregation, but black protests combined with the backing of the Civil Rights Act made their opposition seem trivial, especially when compared to the massive resistance of the 1950s. African Americans secured numerous victories during this period. The demonstrations at the Piccadilly Cafeteria in Dallas, the various Alabama Sympathy Marches, the Huntsville protests, the voter registration drives and election of black candidates, and the initial use of antipoverty aid demonstrated the continued vitality of the black freedom struggle. Moreover, blacks began to move away from destroying the legal, de jure aspects of segregation and to concentrate more forcefully on addressing the customary or de facto aspects of Jim Crow. As a result, joblessness, poverty, and politics gained increased attention, a focus that would remain for the next decade.

■ ■ ■

One area of hope for African Americans and Mexican Americans lay in the unification of their two movements. Indeed, efforts to unite them increased in frequency in the mid-1960s. Albert Peña's attempt to develop a coalition with PASO, labor, the NAACP, and white liberals in 1963 resulted in the smaller Bexar County Coalition. In 1963 Graciela Olivárez, a well-known Arizona activist, and several Texas leaders established the Southwest Conference for Political Unity in Arizona to align several "Negro, Mexican-American and Jewish" organizations.[116] But the group quickly broke into two competing factions and dissolved. The presence of black, white, and Mexican American activists at the various Alabama Sympathy Marches also signaled a new level of cooperation. Moreover, the call for unity by Antonio Gonzalez, the self-proclaimed "Martin Luther King of the Mexicans," certainly represented an open-minded approach to collaboration.

Like their Mexican American counterparts, African Americans were interested in building coalitions. The NAACP began again to promote unification, and the San Antonio branch proposed a coalition to help implement the Civil Rights Act. Harry V. Burns trusted that groups like the G.I. Forum would join hands with the NAACP to ensure that local officials respected the law, but no coalition materialized. G.I. Forum leaders still were reluctant to join forces with the NAACP.[117]

Similarly, Booker Bonner participated in the Rio Grande Valley strike and Minimum Wage March in the hope of receiving support from Mexican Americans for the protests he initiated in Huntsville. Bonner praised the farmworkers. When they started the march, Bonner announced that blacks would travel from Huntsville to Austin "to show Mexicans that Negroes are behind them." Bonner's group passed out leaflets during their march from East Texas to the state capital. One pamphlet argued that "Negroes and Mexicans are the 'poor people of Texas' . . . nobody benefits from poverty."[118] Their 200-mile trek ended when Booker Bonner and his cohort of around forty marchers joined the Minimum Wage March in Austin.[119] Although blacks did join the march, their participation was limited. With perhaps as many as one hundred protesters, this meant that African Americans made up less than 0.5 percent of all the marchers. No broader coalition developed out of the march.

A few other black activists also took part in the Minimum Wage March. One of the most important was Moses LeRoy, who marched with the strikers almost the entire route. LeRoy represented an atypical figure in Texas politics. As a labor leader and a communist, he viewed Mexican American and black social and labor problems as similar and stressed unity to achieve change. LeRoy, like Cesar Chavez, tried to organize minority labor into a unified force. During the forties and fifties, he had pushed for increased labor activism for Mexican Americans and blacks on the Southern Pacific railroads.[120] In 1958 he served in the gubernatorial campaign of Henry B. Gonzalez. LeRoy felt that businesses and white politicians used race and labor to divide minority communities. To combat this, he argued, minorities had to join forces.[121]

During the Minimum Wage March, LeRoy spoke at many stops along the route to Austin. When the demonstrators reached Corpus Christi, he told a crowd: "This is the greatest thing that has ever happened in a generation. It is a tragedy that we live in a state with the resources we have, in a Great Society that our great leader Lyndon Johnson has advocated, and we make less than $1.25 an hour. It's pathetic."[122] Although the NAACP had dispatched LeRoy to join the march, he was also a member of PASO. Indeed, he was one of the only blacks involved with PASO, serving on the board of directors of the Harris County chapter. Hence, during the march he represented two of the major civil rights groups in the state. But LeRoy largely acted independently. Most blacks did not subscribe to his kind of politics, and they did not join forces with Mexican Americans.

Francisco "Pancho" Medrano denoted an interesting counterpart to Moses

Moses LeRoy addresses farmworkers at a rally during the Minimum Wage March. While an important ally of the strike and march, LeRoy was one of the only black Texans to participate in these protests. (Courtesy of Houston Metropolitan Research Center, Houston Public Library)

LeRoy. In fact, the two men were friends.[123] Like LeRoy, Medrano served with both black and Mexican American organizations. For instance, Medrano was a member of the NAACP and served on the executive board of the Dallas branch.[124] A prominent labor leader in the United Auto Workers, Medrano participated in labor organizing and protests across the Southwest. In the Valley, Ranger Captain Allee arrested Medrano and several colleagues during the Rio Grande Valley Strike (interestingly, Allee chose not to physically accost Medrano, perhaps because Medrano was a former pugilist).[125] LeRoy and Medrano both embraced an equalitarian politics that welcomed cooperation and coalition building among Mexican Americans and African Americans. Part of their more broad-minded approach surely came from their work with the unions, which typically find the root of social problems in economics and class, not in race. An African American leader like Moses LeRoy could therefore bridge the racial gap with Mexican Americans, while a Mexican American like Pancho Medrano could bridge the racial gulf with blacks, by focusing on class instead of race. This allowed these leaders and others like them to see past the racial animosities shared by blacks and Mexican Americans. Their example is not inconsequential.

While LeRoy and Medrano cooperated during the Minimum Wage March, others involved in this protest continued to view each movement as distinct. As Father Antonio Gonzalez noted, "Our problem is different from [that of] the Negro."[126] The theme of dissimilarity became common throughout the period. *El Malcriado* had argued that "the march of Negroes from East Texas and of Mexican-Americans from South Texas is showing Texas growers that from now on we will work together and nothing will divide us."[127] But instead of bringing blacks and Mexican Americans together, activists viewed the Minimum Wage March as something distinctly Mexican American, despite the presence of blacks.[128] Even Booker Bonner grew disillusioned after he supported the Valley strike; only Gilbert Campos reciprocated by joining the Huntsville protests.

Much of the rhetoric that continued to emanate from the Mexican American civil rights movement doomed cooperative efforts. In appealing to the state and federal governments, many leaders persisted in elevating Mexican American suffering over that of black people. Such arguments downplayed the racism that black people had experienced for generations. It ignored slavery, Jim Crow, and lynching in order to win benefits solely for the Mexican American community. This did not endear Mexican Americans to blacks. Rather, it separated them. At the EEOC walkout, for example, Alfred Hernández and other leaders argued that the Johnson administration had failed to appoint Mexican Americans to important government posts. "*We are being denied our fair share in government employment, housing and education,*" Hernández said. "Johnson has given [appointments] to members of the Negro race"; these appointments were conspicuous due to the "lack of people with Spanish surnames or Mexican-Americans" receiving them.[129] He maintained that other groups had received more than their fair share of representatives. According to the leaders of the walkout, the EEOC "was geared entirely to the situation of the Negro."[130] For them, this meant that the administration had appointed too many African Americans. Perhaps the walkout leaders had not intended to communicate such a message. But they did. And for blacks, a group historically underrepresented in the local, state, and national governments, these words cut deeply. This did not make African Americans sympathetic to Mexican-origin people because their leaders had not acted sympathetically toward blacks. Instead of cooperation, government aid created a sense of competition between blacks and Mexican Americans.[131]

The Mexican American protests of the White House "To Fulfill These

Rights" Conference produced similar results. Certainly by relabeling the meeting the "White House (All Negro) Civil Rights Conference," Mexican Americans affiliated with the Ad Hoc Committee on Equal Employment Opportunity implied that blacks had acted with greed and had monopolized access to the government. In fact, the Ad Hoc Committee blamed the "'big six' Negro leaders and the administration" for excluding Mexican Americans from the meeting. Black leaders seemed generally perplexed by this response. Heretofore, Mexican Americans had received aid from the government. Now, they chastised African Americans for excluding them from government meetings. This contradictory attitude confused black leaders who had neither denied nor advocated for a Mexican American presence at the meeting. And by decrying the lack of Mexican American involvement in the conference, Mexican American leaders suggested that African Americans did not need assistance from the government. Worse, the Ad Hoc Committee protested the conference, which had the potential to help the African American community. For African Americans this added insult to injury.[132] Blacks had never threatened to protest something that might have assisted Mexican Americans.

It would be a mistake to hold African Americans harmless in generating disunity. Black leaders did relatively little to appeal to Mexican Americans. While Moses LeRoy, Booker Bonner, and a few others made some effort to unify the two movements, most blacks simply did not approach Mexican Americans about forming coalitions. Geographic distance continued to separate both movements. The Valley protests took place far from the areas where most black people lived. The Valley was particularly distant from East Texas and major cities like Houston and Dallas, sites where most black demonstrations took place. Geographic distance also explains why few Mexican Americans traveled to places like Marshall to protest. In short, the vast geography of the state of Texas separated blacks and Mexican Americans.

Other factors also explain disunity. For example, some blacks remembered and disliked Mexican American racial positioning. As white people, Mexican Americans became part of the group that opposed the black movement. "They thought they were white," several black activists remembered, and this made some blacks unwilling to work with Mexican Americans.[133] While Mexican Americans did participate in black protests like the sympathy marches for James Reeb, African Americans had organized these protests primarily for the black community. The same could be said for Mexican Americans in the Valley strike and Minimum Wage March. Elsewhere, Mexican Americans did not join blacks in their protests. According to Earl Allen, no Mexican Americans participated in the protests in Dallas at this time.[134] In East Texas, only Gilbert

Campos joined the black demonstrations. The EEOC walkout and the protest of the White House Civil Rights Conference certainly frustrated some blacks and thus contributed to disunity. But many of these issues remained peripheral for African Americans. In other words, the Mexican American struggle involved issues salient only to Mexican Americans. Blacks regarded the Minimum Wage March and the strike in the Valley in similar terms. According to Sherrill Smith, aside from Moses LeRoy no blacks were involved in the march or protests in San Antonio. As for cooperation, noted Smith, "There wasn't much . . . there was a tension between blacks and mexicanos. They didn't mix very well."[135] Similarly, the NAACP's Reverend C. Anderson Davis saw cooperation as limited: there was "not as much as you might think."[136]

Mexican American activism came alive in the mid-1960s. The Minimum Wage March and the EEOC walkout galvanized many Mexican-origin people who had begun to see fighting for white rights as a failure. Clearly, the whiteness strategy did remain, but new, more aggressive tactics displaced white racialization. These tactics showed that Mexican Americans could engage in dignified and successful direct action demonstrations. Many had learned these lessons from black southerners. Alfred Hernández, George Sánchez, Albert Peña, and others saw what African Americans accomplished and hoped to emulate the black example.

The protests engineered by Mexican Americans had great significance for the movement as a whole. Some noticed a change in the rhetoric of the Mexican American freedom struggle at this time. The *San Antonio Express* noted that when the Rio Grande Valley strike began, the rhetoric of strikers had "a civil rights overtone and the . . . tactics of marches and mass rallies were developed by civil rights workers." Mexican-origin people, the paper stated, had borrowed much from the black movement.[137] Some blacks also acknowledged the growing similarities between the African American and Mexican American movements. NAACP member Bill Crane observed that the phrase "civil rights," while associated with blacks, had become more universal.[138] Many Mexican Americans sympathetic to the strikers and tired of the whiteness strategy adopted a similar language. And while some Mexican American civic groups and individuals continued to advocate a cautious activism and promote rights by advancing whiteness, a significant portion of the population in the Southwest grew weary of this approach. They absorbed the rhetoric of the black civil rights movement and became more militant. Leaders like Father Sherrill Smith enjoyed this change in outlook. Smith and other religious leaders such as Reverend Bud Poteat began to more fully explore how blacks and Mexican Americans might unify. Indeed, these religious leaders hoped to develop a new activism, one that combined nonviolent protests with antipoverty programs. In this new struggle, Mexican Americans and African Americans would work together. As Father Smith seemed to realize, "What's wrong with the Negro and the Mexican-American doing the same thing?"[139]

... 5 ...

Am I My Brother's Keeper?

Ecumenical Activism in the Lone Star State

In the summer of 1964, Houston minister Wallace B. "Bud" Poteat established the Ecumenical Fellowship (EF) to eradicate social problems and racism in the Bayou City. He hoped to accomplish this goal by taking advantage of local and national antipoverty programs, by encouraging minority communities to vote, and, when necessary, by urging these same communities to protest. The EF soon founded its most ambitious program, the Latin American Channel Project (LAC Project). The new project was all grassroots; Poteat and other EF members worked and lived in Houston's poorest neighborhoods, particularly in the mixed African American/Mexican American ghetto near the Houston Ship Channel (east end of Houston), an area known simply as the Latin American Channel. Reverend Poteat had simple objectives: to end poverty and secure civil rights for Mexican Americans and African Americans before these groups resorted to violence in response to these problems. "The blight of poverty in our area must be stopped," he asserted. "Our city, our [part] of town must avoid the violence and stigma of . . . slums!"[1]

Poteat's voice joined an unusual chorus that gained increasing salience after passage of the Civil Rights Act of 1964 and the Voting Rights Act of 1965. Indeed, individuals like Bud Poteat appeared at a crucial moment during the civil rights period. As nonviolent protest and political activism gave way to Black Power and Chicano Power, many civic leaders feared the struggle might spin out of control. Moreover, some leaders worried that the radicalism of the late 1960s would cause whites to abandon the African American and Mexican American civil rights movements. These leaders thus attempted to create an alternative struggle that focused on ecumenical principles to secure rights.[2]

Scholars have long neglected the history of ecumenism, which downplayed religious doctrinal differences and embraced a blending of spiritual beliefs with the more secular message of civil rights and social justice. They have also largely ignored the period between the days of nonviolence and the days of Black Power and Brown Power. For many Americans, the nonviolent black movement and the Mexican American struggle simply appeared to end and Black Power and Chicano Power began. The ongoing activism throughout the period confirms the fallacy of this interpretation. Rather than one move-ment ending and another beginning, an evolutionary process took place—the Mexican American and African American movements evolved into some-thing different, and Black or Brown Power were hardly forgone conclusions. Ecumenical activism took root at this important juncture, roughly between the passage of the Civil Rights Act of 1964 and the early 1970s. The ecumeni-cal struggle actually formed a bridge between the days of nonviolence and the days of Black Power and Chicano Power.

Ecumenical leaders hoped to develop a different kind of movement. They wanted to build coalitions for the benefit of African Americans and Mexican Americans. Anglo leaders like Reverend Bud Poteat of Houston and Father Sherrill Smith of San Antonio, as well as African American leaders such as Reverend Peter Johnson of Dallas, all represent good examples of ecumeni-cal leaders. Secularly oriented groups like Lubbock's Ecumenical Council on Social Concerns (ECSC) also show how ecumenism impacted Texas so-ciety. Poteat became involved in the civil rights movement in the early 1960s, when he joined protests in Houston and in Huntsville, where he was arrested. Father Smith played an important role in Alamo City demonstrations and participated in the Rio Grande Valley strike and the Minimum Wage March. Reverend Johnson helped organize black Dallasites to resist a slum clearance program. These ecumenical organizers had one basic formula: they wanted to apply religious ideals to the world in a secular fashion. They sought to join the religious concepts of brotherly love, charity, and positive works with grass-roots community organizing, federal and local antipoverty programs, and tra-ditional civil rights protest activism. For these clergymen, spirituality inspired their actions, but they did not proselytize.[3] As Poteat made clear on more than one occasion, ecumenical activism through groups like the LAC Project had to remain nonproselytistic. The project "will not attract people looking for a suburban church," he maintained, "but those looking for something different."[4] Peter Johnson stated quite succinctly that the ecumenical struggle could not be a religious movement: "If you're gonna have people campaigning for their particular faiths you're gonna drive people away."[5] Similarly, Reverend Earl Allen noted that ecumenical activists "were all about social justice."[6] Instead of proselytizing, ecumenical leaders attempted to aid poor people because they felt duty bound as ministers, as Christians, to do so.[7]

Bud Poteat began his activities in Houston shortly after passage of the Civil Rights Act. In mid-1964 he established the Ecumenical Fellowship as an auxiliary institution of the United Church of Christ.[8] The United Church of Christ had a long history of supporting multiethnic ministries and progressive reform movements. The ecumenical focus of the National Council of Churches also appealed to Poteat and other Protestant ministers. The civil rights struggles of the fifties and sixties had deeply influenced the National Council, which began a number of secular and civil rights–oriented projects across the United States, most notably the Delta Ministry in Mississippi. This increased activism—coalitions both from above, including the National Council and the United Church of Christ, and from below, such as grassroots organizations like the Delta Ministry—directly influenced ministers like Bud Poteat. Poteat knew that Houston had experienced a great deal of civil rights activism throughout the 1960s. He wanted to continue tactics established in the movement, namely nonviolent, direct action demonstrations. But he also hoped to combine these strategies with new tactics, primarily grassroots antipoverty and job training programs. Ending poverty proved the issue of the day in the mid-1960s. So Poteat chose the poorest, most dilapidated slum in Houston to start the EF's antipoverty activities. That area, the Latin American Channel, became the site of the EF's boldest program—the LAC Project.

The LAC Project was the official vehicle of EF antipoverty activities. Poteat, who served as director of the project, and the other members of the EF moved into the Latin American Channel area, rented a home to serve as a base of operations, and began to promote their ecumenical vision. At first, many of their neighbors assumed that the EF had started a new church, but Poteat assured them that if the LAC Project was a church, it was "a peculiar type of church."[9] Indeed, he frequently warned project members and other volunteers that "no proselytizing is allowed." Another EF member, Reverend James Noland, believed the LAC Project "must get Negroes, Latins, and whites talking together about common problems. The real problem of the 'church' has been that it has been a consumer rather than a servant." Both Poteat and Noland maintained that "the church" could best meet the needs of the community by operating through secular groups like the LAC Project.[10]

The LAC Project's first goal involved remedial education for African Americans and Mexican Americans living in the community. This included literacy instruction, English-Spanish lessons, and other basic skills like managing personal finances and writing résumés. Second, the LAC Project offered employment guidance and job placement. And third, it provided information on voter registration and education so individuals could cast votes for candidates who would respond to their needs. The EF's small rented house served as a community meeting place and as a headquarters for the administration of the project. Local people could visit the house to chat with EF volunteers, shoot a game of pool, or drink a cup of coffee.[11]

To keep the project afloat, Poteat appealed to Houston's charity organizations for monetary support. Fortunately for the LAC Project, Poteat maintained a long-standing friendship with James Noland, the director of Houston's Protestant Charities. Reverend Noland agreed to cosponsor the project, providing a source of funding the EF would have found hard to generate itself. Additionally, the largest charitable organization in the city—the Houston Association—donated approximately ten thousand dollars to the LAC Project.[12] Other groups agreed to pay the rent and utility bills of the LAC Project headquarters. Poteat also appealed to business and industry in Houston by making them aware that the project cost only one hundred dollars a month. He told businesspeople that they could help alleviate social problems by making charitable donations to the EF and the LAC Project. The cost, Poteat emphasized, was "a small price, indeed, to help stop the cancer of urban blight which eats without warning into every neighborhood." He referred to the LAC Project as "building a wall of concern against this most persistent enemy." Local businesses and civic groups donated most of the project's funding.[13] Moreover, small monetary donations rolled into LAC Project headquarters throughout 1965, 1966, and 1967.[14]

The LAC Project expanded rapidly after the local chapter of Students for a Democratic Society (SDS) agreed to volunteer their time to get their "hands dirty and remove our minds from ivory tower unreality." The SDS students made up a significant portion of the tutors and community outreach volunteers that the EF needed for the project.[15] Even more importantly, the Johnson administration sent approximately fifty VISTA volunteers to Houston.[16] The volunteers arrived at an opportune time in 1966. While Reverend Poteat, other EF members, and SDS activists had moved into the Latin American Channel area as part of the LAC Project, they had not succeeded in convincing other Houstonians to join them. The VISTA volunteers fit in perfectly because the federal government envisioned the VISTA program as a domestic Peace

Corps with volunteers living and working in the communities they served. This demonstrates one of the ways the EF bridged its efforts with national antipoverty programs.

The arrival of the SDS activists and the VISTAS allowed the LAC Project to expand, and Poteat began several new programs with their help. The Lawyer Project offered Latin American Channel residents free legal aid, using volunteers who had attended law school or had legal training. Poteat also established a new LAC Project house with a specific interest in aiding Mexican American and African American youths. Named the Pachuco House by local teens, the home gave them a place of their own "without rigorous programs and without a moralistic or patronizing atmosphere."[17] Pachuco House offered neighborhood youths a job referral service and parent-youth counseling in the morning and afternoon. It also provided a pool table and basketball court for evening entertainment. While Poteat and the other volunteers primarily centered the Pachuco House programs on teenage boys, the LAC Project did not exclude girls. Before the Pachuco House idea even got off the ground, project leaders had twenty youths eager to help restore a possible house, and young women comprised a majority of those volunteers.[18]

The University of Thought proved to be the LAC Project's most ambitious new program. This idea, according to the project's leaders, involved a return to the concept of "students seeking outstanding teachers to learn from." Initially, a pilot project attracted youths from two nearby high schools. But in late 1966, when the University of Thought officially commenced, students from fifty local high schools participated. The school drew on VISTAS along with professors and graduate students from the University of Houston, Rice University, St. Thomas University, and Texas Southern University to provide "college-type courses to Houston area high school students." Since many poor students found making the leap from high school to college very difficult, this program assisted in their transition. Classes included history, geography, science, math, and English. At its peak, the school offered one hundred courses to over 2,500 students. Courses expanded between 1966 and 1971 to include Spanish, photography, and karate, among others. Alas, when the EF dissolved in 1971, so too did the University of Thought.[19]

While the LAC Project continued until 1970, it suffered a series of setbacks beginning in 1967. That year, an unknown group of arsonists burned down the Pachuco House. To make matters worse, the fire engine rushing to the scene collided with a local machinist's pickup truck. His death inadvertently tarnished the image of the LAC Project.[20] Bud Poteat blamed the arson on "*irrational fear* [which] acted to put a stop to our common efforts to overcome discrimination, apathy, and despair." Unidentified segregationists had attacked Poteat on several prior occasions. They beat him once and fired guns at him several other times. Poteat placed the blame for the fire squarely on the shoulders of white racism, but police never charged anyone with the crime. And, in a classic blame-the-victim scenario, local newspapers implied that the LAC Project had actually generated the attacks and arson.[21]

The most serious blow to the LAC Project resulted from violence on the campus of Texas Southern University.[22] Some of the VISTA volunteers allegedly participated in this disturbance. Many conservatives in Houston disliked the rhetoric of Black Power and Chicano Power advocates. These individuals lumped forms of civil rights activism that they deemed subversive and discordant into categories like "Black Power." For many Anglos, the LAC Project, the EF, and the VISTAS fell into this classification. As historian William Clayson has shown, local officials and conservatively minded individuals feared antipoverty activism would lead to a race riot.[23] The negative reaction of many Houstonians ultimately doomed the LAC Project. The generalized and unfair perception of many Houstonians that all forms of charity work—such as programs to combat poverty and attempt community uplift—equaled radicalism and violence killed the LAC Project. Further, since the federal government funded VISTA, the participation of VISTA volunteers in protests and perhaps in the TSU disturbance indicated to some that Washington had subsidized civil rights protests and a riot. Many Houstonians, whether conservative or otherwise, found such a thought abhorrent. They demanded that President Johnson withdraw the VISTA volunteers from Houston. Johnson ultimately refused, but the presence of the VISTAS complicated the work of the LAC Project. They had come to form the backbone of its support, but the bad press the VISTAS received also reflected negatively on the project. Poteat and the EF, therefore, began to curtail their use of the volunteers. By default, they also curtailed the LAC Project.[24]

These events frustrated Bud Poteat. The number of VISTAS he had to work with began to decline. He also found that Houston's charitable organizations reduced donations as the LAC Project became associated with radicalism. It remains a historical irony that Poteat, in part, began the EF and LAC Project as alternatives to Brown Power or Black Power, only to be labeled an advocate of Black Power. Poteat could do nothing to change the situation. Still, he tried. He implored Houstonians to continue supporting ecumenical organizing and the LAC Project. In 1967 he asked the people of the Bayou City, "Am I my brother's keeper?" Poteat had responded affirmatively through his words and deeds, but he answered himself by saying, "Yes, I am my brother's keeper!"

But he failed to convince a large number of people of the truth behind that statement.[25] Reverend Poteat ultimately decided that his presence also hurt the LAC Project, and in 1968 he resigned as project director. Earl Allen, the Methodist minister who had sparked protests in Houston and Dallas, stepped in to help run the project. But it took two years to replace Poteat. By then the LAC Project was dead.[26] In 1972 the Nixon administration withdrew all VISTAS from Houston.[27]

The EF and its LAC Project were important ventures in Houston, but local resistance clearly damaged their efforts. While local charities and businesses supplied donations for the project, EF members had trouble convincing individuals to do the hard work necessary for the program to succeed. Most Houstonians simply did not want to move into the barrio or ghetto to help poor people. This meant that the LAC Project volunteers had to work doubly hard, and in many cases they were stretched too thin. Yet Poteat and the other individuals involved in the program spoke often of its success. The LAC Project did benefit the people in the Ship Channel area and had great meaning for them. Residents respected and appreciated the assistance it offered. In particular, the community aid provided via the Lawyer Project was of considerable benefit; today, free legal aid to poor people remains an important vehicle for redressing wrongs. For local youths, the Pachuco House offered a place of safety for teenagers to meet and converse. Even more importantly, the University of Thought opened a door for the education of thousands of young African Americans and Mexican Americans. For many of these youths, college remained beyond the realm of the possible. But with the University of Thought they could gain entrance to the academy. For young people, this project served as a reminder that they could have something more than poverty, joblessness, and despair. The LAC Project, as Poteat had planned, gave them hope.

Perhaps the EF and the LAC Project's greatest success came in bringing Mexican Americans and African Americans together for a common purpose. The leaders of both groups had proved incapable of generating substantive and long-lasting unity between the two civil rights movements. But as a leader of a different struggle, as an impartial observer, Poteat appealed to local blacks and Mexican Americans. The EF's leaders volunteered their time not because they wanted to become major players in civil rights struggles, not because they desired to win election to high office, and not for the kudos that came with organizing people. Rather, they volunteered because they felt it was the right thing to do. For that moment in the mid-1960s, the ideas of leaders like

Bud Poteat had united poor blacks and Mexican Americans in a concerted effort.

In San Antonio, Father Sherrill Smith was much more radical than Poteat. The Catholic Church is not well remembered for its civil rights stance. While black denominations became closely associated with the movement, the Catholic Church largely ignored the Mexican American struggle for rights in Texas until the 1960s.[28] Although the moderate Archbishop Robert Lucey had created organizations like the Bishop's Committee on the Spanish-Speaking to assist Mexican American Catholics, he generally saw civil rights as a secular matter.[29] Father Smith disagreed with these ideas. The Catholic Church's unwillingness to join the Mexican American civil rights movement in the same way that the Baptist church had joined forces with the black movement frustrated Sherrill Smith. "I don't see how the church can be silent and be witness to injustice," Smith argued. "Necessarily it must speak through persons [like] bishops and priests." As an ecumenical activist, Smith opposed the church's stance and he proposed to help all people — not just Catholics. Like Poteat, he saw civil rights as both a religious and a secular issue.[30]

The radicalization of Catholic priests like Father Smith occurred throughout the 1960s. Three distinct trends influenced this transformation. First, the activism occurring on the ground and the deeply felt beliefs of priests across the country influenced the church's relationship with the black and Mexican American struggles. Father Smith openly embraced civil rights and what he called "social action."[31] Like other priests, he took all of his sacred vows seriously, but he showed special regard for his vow of poverty. He felt the vow of poverty made Catholic priests similar and beholden to the world's poor people. Under these circumstances, the opinions and beliefs of local priests facilitated their activism. Second, the Vatican under Pope John XXIII began to reconsider the role of the church in modern society. In 1962 Pope John convened the Second Ecumenical Council of the Vatican, or Vatican II, in Rome to address this issue. The meeting accomplished a number of goals, but for socially minded priests like Sherrill Smith the most important achievement was the church's reassessment of its responsibility in combating poverty, inhumanity, and social injustice. Third, and even more important, was the 1968 Latin American Episcopal Conference in Medellín, Colombia, where church officials adopted the ideal of liberation theology. Liberation theology emphasizes the duty of Christians to embrace social justice as a spiritual tenet, specifically to combat poverty and support the poor. Liberation theology particularly appealed to activist priests. Vatican II and the Medellín meeting, of course, meant nothing unless priests were willing to take up the cause of social justice and civil rights. The activism of the period, Vatican II, and liberation theology encouraged Catholic priests to engage in civil rights activities. And ecumenical activism became the perfect vehicle by which to make the transformations within the Catholic Church a reality in Texas.[32]

In 1963 Sherrill Smith began to more clearly express his vision of activism and his role in the ecumenical struggle. He became one of the few outspoken priests to promote the passage of the Civil Rights Act of 1964. Smith urged Governor Connally to support the civil rights bill in 1963.[33] The same year he spoke at Booker T. Bonner's Freedom Now March.[34] In 1965 he led the San Antonio contingent of the Alabama Sympathy March, and in early 1966 he joined the Rio Grande Valley strike. Later that year he sounded what became a mantra for the Minimum Wage March, stating at a Texas House labor committee meeting: "Some of us feel rather ashamed that we have to stand before the state and talk about 75 cents an hour." Alluding to poor Mexican and Mexican American farm laborers, he said that "no man has a right to sweat others."[35] Father Smith's radicalism and his willingness to confront the power structure made him a well-respected ecumenical activist.

In 1965 he noted that one of the things that bothered many Americans was "the role of the clergy" in social issues and "what he has to say about the world, racial justice, economic justice, social justice." "Mexican Americans and Negroes . . . have suffered the burden of discrimination," he argued; "certainly the Anglo hasn't."[36] In discussing the poor, Smith did not proselytize or attempt to convince people that the Catholic Church could solve community problems. Instead, he spoke as an individual, as someone personally concerned about social issues. For his efforts, African Americans and Mexican Americans came to greatly admire Smith. In 1967, for instance, the San Antonio NAACP honored him for his civil rights work. This accolade so moved him that he could not speak at the reception.[37]

Father Smith became more militant in 1965 after he marched with Dr. Martin Luther King in Selma, Alabama. As one of the few Texans involved in that protest, Smith's participation earned him the esteem of black people.[38] The Selma demonstration seems to have sparked his radicalism, for he soon began making more confrontational public statements. Smith assailed Governor Connally and other racist whites as "gringos."[39] He also used the term "Tío Tomas" or Uncle Tom to refer to conservative Mexican Americans. "Tío Tomas," Smith demanded, "let's get rid of them. . . . The time is past for politeness and pussyfooting around." He urged a large gathering of Mexican Americans at a PASO meeting to protest like African Americans. We

Father Sherrill Smith speaks to reporters shortly before he was banished to New Mexico in 1967. Smith represented the growing militancy within the Catholic Church. Project Equality proved to be an important vehicle for making his ecumenical activism a reality. (Courtesy of UTSA's Institute of Texan Cultures)

must "be ready to stand on street corners, to form neighborhood councils, to knock on doors. I personally am ready to do this sort of thing," he shouted.[40] Six months later he followed up these statements with action. In 1965 Father Smith, with Archbishop Lucey's support, began his own ecumenical project modeled on a national program called Project Equality.

Smith designed San Antonio's version of Project Equality as an economic program to push companies that did business with the San Antonio Archdiocese to employ Mexican Americans and African Americans equally. The project drew on "the hiring and purchasing power of Catholic church institutions to end employment discrimination."[41] While Smith and Lucey both argued that they did not intend the program to operate as a boycott, the economic aspect of Project Equality worked exactly like a boycott writ large. Smith hired a group of "investigators" to monitor companies doing business with the archdiocese; if they found discrimination, the church "would go elsewhere for its purposes." Beyond that, Smith said, the project would "give recognition to those who are complying." In other words, Project Equality would honor those businesses that adopted the equal employment model mandated by the project. Additionally, program volunteers distributed pledge cards to local businesses. By signing these cards, businesspeople agreed not to discriminate in the hiring and promoting of blacks and Mexican Americans. This was a bold strategy. Project Equality used the church's multimillion-dollar purchasing power as a kind of bully pulpit to force businesses in the San Antonio area to end discrimination. The project worked with approximately 450 businesses to secure their compliance with these economic goals. Project Equality's leaders also communicated with the parish churches in San Antonio to ensure that they adhered to the economic program. "The money we have," Smith argued, "will promote fair employment."[42]

The Catholic Church also turned its attention inward. Archbishop Lucey and Father Smith used Project Equality to spur parishes to promote equality in their churches. Lucey called upon ministers "to examine their own hiring policies and practices to be sure that we are not discriminating against our employees or potential employees because of their national origin, their color, or, excepting those positions for which religion is a bona fide requirement, their faith." Lucey and Smith established a review board to investigate hiring practices from the archbishopric to the smallest parish church.[43] Thomas Gibbons, one of Father Smith's subordinates, maintained that "Church institutions have a responsibility to spend their money in a moral manner, since through this spending they either enforce or weaken current discriminatory employment practices."[44] In other words, Project Equality operated in a manner similar to a boycott even within the church itself. By regulating its spending patterns, the Catholic Church could produce a type of affirmative action and lead by example.[45]

Finally, Project Equality served as a clearinghouse for charitable donations. Smith acquired contributions from many San Antonio businesses, then personally delivered food, blankets, and clothes to needy families. He and project volunteers also offered after-school programs for primarily Mexican American youths. These included a tutoring service that gave the children the chance to improve their English language skills. Another part of the program offered adults voter education. Though viewing Project Equality as open to all, Smith acknowledged that "the emphasis would be on Mexican-Americans and Negroes."[46]

While Project Equality earned Father Smith a great deal of local praise, many of his other activities irritated Archbishop Lucey and some local people.

Much like Bud Poteat, Smith found himself labeled a militant or radical for having participated—among other activities—in the Rio Grande Valley strike and the Minimum Wage March. Smith's own language caused problems. When he began to assail *gringos*, *Tío Tomases*, and *vendidos* (sellouts), he was speaking well outside of the norm for Catholic priests. But his overall message was equalitarian and aimed at unity. He believed that programs such as Project Equality and tactics like direct action demonstrations could unite poor people in Texas. He viewed civil rights and antipoverty as part of his duty as a Christian. He hoped that ecumenical ideas could win rights and eventually eradicate poverty. Smith saw the Mexican American movement, and in many ways the black movement in San Antonio, as too passive and unresponsive to poor people's needs. "We've had too many losses, too many failures," he declared in 1965. "If I sound impatient about it, good, I am," he said, "I'm going to keep impatient and obsessed." Smith intended to push these struggles in new directions.[47]

While a version of Project Equality still operates today, Sherrill Smith's involvement in the program lasted only a few years. Archbishop Lucey seemed to tire of the priest's militancy. When Lucey ordered him to stop attending union meetings and participating in *la huelga* in the Rio Grande Valley, Smith refused. The archbishop proceeded to remove him as head of Project Equality and banish him and several other activist priests to New Mexico in 1967. When the Mexican American community demanded Smith's return, the archbishop relented.[48] But Smith further angered Lucey when he wrote and asked Pope Paul VI to retire the aging archbishop. Rome agreed. Shortly before Lucey withdrew in 1969, he punished Father Smith by assigning him to a small parish in El Campo.[49] In 1971 the new archbishop, Francis J. Furey, assigned Smith to a church in Crystal City, a move that delighted Smith.[50]

Perceptions of Sherrill Smith's radicalism ultimately impeded his ability to lead the ecumenical struggle in San Antonio. Although he ran Project Equality capably, Archbishop Lucey believed his association with the strike and unions reflected poorly on the church. The Catholic hierarchy and local government also came to view Smith and his activism negatively. Father Smith found many of his activities unwelcome in the late 1960s. Moreover, his banishment to New Mexico damaged his credibility in San Antonio and his prospects for advancement in the church. Smith could do nothing to change the situation, but for him, this was immaterial. He believed in helping the downtrodden and enabling underrepresented groups such as African Americans and Mexican Americans to enter the mainstream of American society. Father

Smith welcomed his duty to serve the community, and his goal of bringing blacks and Mexican Americans together proved an important one. If that irritated church or civic leaders, Smith argued, so be it.[51]

Much like Bud Poteat and Sherrill Smith, Reverend Peter Johnson worked within an ecumenical framework. Johnson did not establish his own ecumenical program. Instead, he was a member of the SCLC. Johnson stated quite clearly that the "SCLC was an ecumenical organization."[52] Many SCLC programs, especially their focus on antipoverty and community uplift, mirrored the programs established by other ecumenical leaders. Johnson traveled to Dallas in 1969 to preview the documentary *King: Montgomery to Memphis*. A longtime activist in Mississippi, Johnson had chosen to stay in Meridian on a hot summer night in 1963 while his friends James Chaney, Andy Goodman, and Michael Schwerner headed off to Neshoba County. Local racists later murdered the three men. Johnson never forgot this event. He knew the face of vicious racism, but he saw something different in Dallas and decided to stay.[53]

Peter Johnson was deeply concerned about poverty in Dallas. Once he settled in Big D, he became increasingly interested in housing conditions in the Fair Park neighborhood in South Dallas. In mid-1969 the Dallas City Council scheduled the demolition of this primarily black neighborhood as part of a slum clearance program. The city wanted to destroy the homes to make way for a new parking lot to serve the State Fair. Homeowners began protesting at City Hall to stop the evictions.[54] In July 1969, for instance, Fair Park homeowners descended on the city council to protest the city's offer of one dollar per square foot—a paltry sum. One homeowner told Dallas mayor Erik Jonsson and the city council that "the city has done (in attempting to displace the homeowners) an awful thing. They have destroyed [the neighborhood] as a livable community." Peter Johnson agreed. He viewed the city's actions as a dereliction of duty and organized the Fair Park neighbors to stop the destruction of their community.[55]

Johnson first called in reinforcements by appealing directly to leaders of the SCLC. The conference's national president, Reverend Ralph David Abernathy, told Dallasites that "the city council of Dallas has not made adequate effort to get fair market value for property and relocation expenses, nor has it shown the least amount of humaneness in this matter."[56] The owners desired market value for their homes, which was $3.75 per square foot. The city rejected the proposal.[57] By December, Johnson and a group of "concerned citizens" engaged in a "ghetto pilgrimage" to dramatize poor conditions in the city's black neighborhoods.[58] Johnson also announced a Christmas boycott

The SCLC's Reverends Peter Johnson (left) and Herbert Wright protest hunger
on the steps of Dallas City Hall in 1971. Johnson became a major movement figure
in Dallas. Like other ecumenical activists, he was not opposed to working with local
Mexican American leaders. (Collections, Texas/Dallas History and
Archives Division, Dallas Public Library)

of merchants. "Between December 15–22," he said, "we will not spend one red cent in downtown Dallas . . . we mean to sock it to Dallas."[59] At the same time, Peter Johnson threatened to block the Cotton Bowl Parade, a New Year's Day celebration in Dallas and a nationally televised event, if the city government and Mayor Jonsson failed to negotiate a settlement with the Fair Park homeowners. On New Year's Eve, five hundred activists, including Mexican American leader Pancho Medrano, met at a local church for the protest. Shortly before midnight, the mayor capitulated. He could not halt the destruction of the neighborhood, but he offered residents fair market value for their homes, which always had been their sole demand.[60]

Peter Johnson continued to direct SCLC activities in Dallas after the conclusion of the Fair Park controversy.[61] In mid-1970 he led three hundred marchers through downtown in a demonstration memorializing Martin Luther King.[62] A few months later he led another three hundred marchers to protest the "repression of poor and black people in general and specifically the recent murders in Mississippi, Georgia, Ohio, and Dallas."[63] This demonstration included a number of Mexican Americans who were concerned about poverty and police brutality. Also in 1970 Johnson and Pancho Medrano organized a major campaign focusing on hunger and malnutrition. Medrano had the idea to present Mayor Jonsson with a basket of loaves and fishes and ask him to feed the multitude. When Reverend Johnson acted out this scene, it inspired local church people to begin working to combat poverty. With the help of ecumenical leaders, churches, and the city government, Johnson, Medrano, and the SCLC were able to open food pantries across the city.[64] Further, the SCLC boycotted local Safeway stores for three weeks to force them to hire more blacks and Chicanos.[65] The management of Dallas's Safeway stores quickly acquiesced to the SCLC's demands.[66]

Although the national SCLC recalled Johnson in 1972, his efforts rallied local blacks to resist the city's slum clearance program and both African Americans and Mexican Americans to protest poverty and economic inequality. These demonstrations showed the continued viability of nonviolent protest, the persistence of antipoverty activism, and the power of ecumenical ideals. Like Bud Poteat and Sherrill Smith, Peter Johnson appealed to all segments of Dallas society for the betterment of poor people. Mexican Americans and African Americans responded to this call and joined his protests. Pancho Medrano's support of Johnson's Fair Park protests and the hunger campaign serve as cases in point. The way Johnson challenged poor people to unite for their own benefit followed the ecumenical example. So too did his use of the SCLC, a civil rights and ecumenical organization. Johnson struggled on behalf of poor blacks and Mexican Americans because he felt it was his duty as a minister to do so. But like the other ecumenical activists, he did not proselytize.

The ECSC in Lubbock stands as an example of ecumenism in a small town setting.[67] Its formation in 1966 was spearheaded by local Methodist minister O. A. McBrayer. He tasked Robert "Bob" Bartley, a local funeral home director, and Darrell Vines, an engineering professor at Texas Tech University, to organize the ECSC to combat poverty and end social problems in Lubbock's poor neighborhoods. A number of ministers, businesspeople, and community activists joined Bartley and Vines. For example, Mary Vines signed up with her husband. Tom and Pansy Burtis, two longtime Lubbock activists, also participated. Tom traced his activist roots back to his great-grandmother, who worked in the Underground Railroad during the Civil War. Pansy served as secretary-treasurer and often recorded ECSC minutes. The group claimed over one hundred members by 1968. Like other ecumenical organizations, the ECSC concentrated on a broad array of goals: they supported local politicians friendly to minority groups, provided college scholarships to Mexican American youths, promoted integrated schools, and attempted to establish community centers and playgrounds similar to the LAC Project's Pachuco House. But the ECSC's most significant project was the "All-American Community."[68]

Joe Phillips, a local realtor, originated the idea of a "model integrated community," a neighborhood with equal numbers of black, Anglo, and Mexican American homeowners.[69] While other ECSC members saw the plan as a "pull a blighted area up by its own bootstraps" project, the All-American Community concept was much more than that. Indeed, Phillips viewed the program in egalitarian terms: it was needed "if social unrest is to be overcome, racial conflict prevented, and serious economic trends reversed." Phillips and Vines had located a relatively new subdivision in northwestern Lubbock where construction had been abandoned after an economic downturn in 1962. The builders had cleared the land and built several dozen homes, most of which stood vacant in 1968. With the recent passage of the Fair Housing Act and seed money available from the OEO, the ECSC hoped to revitalize the area with the specific objective of encouraging the "integration of Negro-American, Mexican-American, and Anglo-American ethnic groups" in one neighborhood. It also wanted to establish traditional community institutions like parks and swimming pools, as well as less traditional facilities such as a job training office and a meeting place for various social welfare agencies to use as an outreach center.[70]

Joe Phillips hoped to receive broad-based community backing for his housing idea. Instead, his support came almost entirely from the ECSC. Acting quickly, Phillips, Darrel Vines, Tom Burtis, and other council members formed a steering committee to oversee the program and began meeting with local people who could potentially move into this new integrated neighborhood. Phillips consulted with OEO and HUD staff in Washington, D.C., on the funding of the project. He also met with Lubbock mayor William Rogers Jr., who promised to use his office to promote the program. Governor Preston Smith got wind of the plan and vocally supported it. Smith believed that other cities would be interested in establishing their own All-American Community.[71] Additionally, an informal interracial group promoted the concept among families already living near the proposed site. This group, assisted by the ECSC, helped configure the neighborhood's community center. Weekly meetings, usually attended by over three hundred people, greatly expanded the project's visibility. After issuing a call for volunteers with electrical, mechanical, and plumbing expertise, the ECSC ultimately developed an "engineer's unit" to make improvements to the existing homes in the neighborhood.[72]

Despite this flurry of activity, the All-American Community project fizzled in the ensuing years. By relegating the program to its "Housing Committee," the ECSC shifted the development of the proposed new community away from the main ECSC council to a less important committee. Moreover, Joe Phillips and others had trouble securing funds for home loans. They also had difficulty recruiting families to live in the new neighborhood. When Phillips began cutting corners in the repair of existing homes (apparently he ignored city housing codes), the ECSC in a split vote decided to separate itself from the All-American Community. The ECSC's departure helped doom the project.[73]

The All-American Community concept demonstrated an important aspect of ecumenical activism. It showed, once again, how local people concerned with problems in their town hoped to apply religious ideals to the world in a secular fashion. By helping their fellow citizens find decent homes, the ECSC added to the variety of ecumenical activism. By promoting an integrated model community, they attempted to bring blacks, whites, and browns together. In an age of white flight and protests of school busing, the All-American Community proved a worthwhile venture.

The ECSC pursued other projects in the late sixties and early seventies, which perhaps explains why their efforts on behalf of the All-American Community did not bear fruit. Of these projects, the most significant dealt with school desegregation. The Lubbock Independent School District (LISD) had made little progress integrating schools. Like Dallas, LISD had established a complicated set of guidelines governing student transfers. One of these guidelines required students to pay the cost of transportation to an integrated school.[74] In 1968 the ECSC began a two-part program to recruit transfer students and to generate a fund to pay for their transportation. The council started with Mexican American students but found no volunteers. It had no better results with black families. The ECSC argued that this failure was "probably [the result of] poor communication between the races."[75] Once again, ecumenical leaders had great difficulty bringing African Americans and Mexican Americans together.

In 1969 the Department of Health, Education, and Welfare (HEW) intervened in Lubbock school affairs, demanding that the LISD submit an adequate desegregation plan. When the school board began holding open meetings to discuss integration, the ECSC frequently made its voice heard. The board considered a variety of schemes to prolong segregation, but the ECSC balked at these ideas and insisted that all schools be integrated.[76] The ECSC published an angry "bill of inditement [sic]" in several local papers, quite literally "indicting" the school district for failing to comply with the Brown decision.[77] After a federal lawsuit, the district finally submitted a fair desegregation plan, although violence in the schools caused an almost instantaneous resegregation of the district.[78] Many ECSC members could claim responsibility for bringing about this short-lived integration. Indeed, their public indictment seemed to motivate school board members to begin the process.

The ECSC dealt with many other issues in the late 1960s. It promoted a free lunch program in local schools throughout its existence.[79] In addition to the All-American Community, the ECSC supported urban renewal projects in Lubbock's Guadalupe, Greenfair Manor, and Posey neighborhoods.[80] It protested the location of sewage treatment plants, city dumps, and animal rendering plants in minority neighborhoods and publicized the health problems these facilities caused—all aspects of environmental racism.[81] The ECSC also supported local politicians and registered blacks and Chicanos to vote.[82] But by 1970 its efforts had begun to flag. The ECSC eventually merged with a group called the Concerned Citizens, ending the council's activism.

The LAC Project, Project Equality, and the ECSC were not the only ecumenical organizations created at this time. For example, Project ENABLE began in Austin and operated much like the LAC Project. Another group—the Texas Catholic Conference—funded job training programs and elementary education, and assisted the Rio Grande Valley strikers in 1967. In 1966 Reverend Earl Allen, who had engineered protests in Houston and Dallas and worked with the LAC Project, established HOPE Development, Inc., which operated like other ecumenical groups to aid the poor in Houston.[83] All of these associations were important for a number of reasons. As a bridge between traditional, pre–Civil Rights Act activism and the more militant activism of the late 1960s, ecumenical organizations and their leaders provided a mechanism for alleviating poverty and joblessness—two issues that the black and Mexican American civil rights movements would continue to pursue. These groups also showed that it was possible for liberal whites, African Americans, and Mexican Americans to have open, cooperative working relationships. Although the Mexican American and black movements existed separately, ecumenical organizations gave them the opportunity to come together for a unified purpose. Further, while helping to keep endeavors for political and social change alive in Houston, they encouraged greater activism in cities like San Antonio and Dallas. By pushing a religious agenda in a secular manner, they offered unique solutions to problems in minority communities.

Ecumenical leaders also helped African Americans and Mexican Americans unite after the state government began to cancel the VISTA program in Texas. VISTA had proved incredibly beneficial to ecumenical leaders and activists, as well as to other black and Chicano civil rights groups. The EF, HOPE Development, Inc., Project ENABLE, MAYO, and many other local ecumenical and civil rights groups all enjoyed the support of VISTA. When the state government attempted to terminate the program, minority communities rose up in protest.

The state's efforts to banish VISTA generated widespread animosity. John Connally had tried but failed to curb the program. Governor Preston Smith was more successful. For example, in Del Rio in Southwest Texas, Smith angered Mexican Americans when he canceled VISTA and attempted to shut down another project—the Minority Mobilization (MM) program—after local activists had a series of violent encounters with the Texas Rangers. But beyond this, Governor Smith and other state officials feared that the MM, the VISTAS, and local MAYO leaders had begun to merge their antipoverty activities. In other words, they had grown too powerful. When the Val Verde County commissioners' court requested that the government terminate the program in early 1969, Governor Smith complied.[84] In response, activists and a variety of ecumenical and civil rights leaders organized a massive march. The protests continued for several more weeks. Leaders also issued the Del Rio Mexican-American Manifesto to the Nation, which summarized Mexican American grievances. While noting the general climate of poverty and conditions in local schools and neighborhoods, the Del Rio Manifesto more explicitly asked the governor to restore the VISTAS to Southwest Texas. Smith

More than one thousand Chicanos march in protest in Del Rio in May 1969. The state government's cancellation of the VISTA program greatly angered local people across the state. (Shel Hershorn Photographic Collection, Dolph Briscoe Center for American History, University of Texas, Austin)

ignored this request.[85] Soon other groups such as the G.I. Forum got involved. Hector García wrote an angry press release praising the VISTA program and castigating Governor Smith. Walter H. Richter, the Southwest regional director of OEO, which managed VISTA, appealed to the county commissioners to reconsider their actions. García's statement, Richter's appeal, and the protests in Del Rio did nothing to stop the cancellation of the VISTA program.[86]

Governor Smith's actions convinced other counties to oust their VISTA volunteers. Harrison and Panola came next. These East Texas counties, located in the heart of the Black Belt, went one step further and voted to disband the entire CAP, which controlled VISTA in the region. The governor's agreement to cancel the programs angered local leaders, but they could not stop the cancellations.[87] Back in South Texas, Cameron, Hidalgo, and Willacy County officials disbanded their VISTA program after volunteers allegedly participated in protests and political campaigns.[88] Roughly a year later, La Salle County, also in South Texas, became one of the last counties to expel VISTA volunteers.[89] In addition to these events, Governor Smith vetoed a government grant for the development of a CAP that would have allowed Val Verde County to reinvigorate its antipoverty programs. Smith used a state's rights, local control excuse to justify his actions. When the county commissioners' court officially requested he veto the grant, Smith did so.[90]

The cancellation of the VISTA program in these counties frustrated activists. As in Del Rio, protests flared up in the small towns of Brownsville, Cotulla, and Marshall over the dismissal of the volunteers. Many volunteers, other non-VISTA activists, ecumenical leaders, and civil rights movement participants felt that protests remained one of the few strategies available to them. For many of the VISTAs, such participation proved a normal part of serving as a volunteer. Indeed, the VISTAs had done nothing wrong. According to the mandates of the program and widely distributed VISTA literature, as long as a volunteer took part in demonstrations "as an individual without invoking the name of the public antipoverty program for which he works," his or her protests were permissible. Those who desired to eradicate the program, from John Connally to Preston Smith, ignored such mandates and pointed to the protests as a reason to oust the volunteers. Although the VISTAs proved enormously beneficial, their beneficence did not last long.[91] Governor Smith attempted to moderate the tension over the VISTAs by forming a statewide Committee on Human Relations. While the committee did assist minority communities, many local activists considered it merely a consolation prize.[92]

Ecumenical leaders in particular and activists more generally were distinctly disappointed when the governor(s) began canceling the VISTA programs in Texas. VISTA had great potential to unite poor people in a movement to combat their own poverty. Since the ecumenical activists attempted to do the same thing, the end of VISTA ultimately contributed to the demise of both types of activism. The state government's war on federal aid damaged antipoverty efforts throughout Texas. Activists found it difficult to combat the cancellation of the VISTA program. Without the program, of course, they also found it hard to combat poverty.

One other project with the potential to unite Mexican Americans and African Americans originated at this time. Martin Luther King's Poor People's Campaign (PPC) attempted to shift the focus of the civil rights movement to the issue of poverty. King and the SCLC hoped that the PPC would constitute the "second phase" of the civil rights movement. The widespread work of antipoverty activists in Texas, especially Peter Johnson but also Bud Poteat and Sherrill Smith, demonstrates the importance of the SCLC's ideas.[93] Dr. King had argued passionately that the PPC "must not be just black people, it must be all poor people. We must include American Indians, Puerto Ricans, Mexicans, and even poor whites." After King's assassination, Ralph Abernathy took over the leadership of the SCLC and the planning of the campaign. Abernathy organized a massive gathering in Washington, D.C., to protest the nation's treatment of poor people. This demonstration attracted a number of activists from Texas.[94]

The PPC intended to expose the problems of poverty and magnify the inattention given to poor people by the federal government. The nation's capital offered the perfect venue to showcase the deleterious effects of poverty. Activists constructed the campaign's most visible symbol—Resurrection City—to house the activists who traveled to Washington and to serve as a launching site for protests around the capital. From Resurrection City, volunteers could march through the capital, picket the Supreme Court, and demand that Congress pass legislation that addressed the needs of the nation's poor. Most importantly, the PPC would protest how the government attacked poverty and the ways in which Washington wasted resources on the Vietnam War.

The protest in the nation's capital quickly spun out of control, however. Resurrection City, a conglomeration of tents and shacks, was largely segregated by race. The news media misrepresented the city as crime-ridden and vice-filled, assertions that exaggerated and caricatured some minor problems. Local police constantly harassed, detained, and arrested activists involved in the PPC.[95] Additionally, the FBI actively undermined and possibly infiltrated the PPC.[96] Equally problematic, the groups involved in the campaign had trouble working together. For instance, SCLC leaders at Resurrection City did not treat Chicano and Native American protesters particularly well. The Mexican American leaders—among them, Reies López Tijerina, Rodolfo "Corky" Gonzales, and Bert Corona—who mainly came from New Mexico, Colorado, and California, found that the PPC primarily focused on black people. Tijerina complained that "the black militants seem to have taken over out here and nobody gets a chance to talk."[97] He threatened to form a coalition of Chicanos and Indians and leave the campaign. He seemed to believe, as Mexican Americans did in other areas of the antipoverty movement, that blacks received too much attention and that African Americans monopolized the protest.[98] Mexican American civil rights groups wanted to see Chicanos better represented during the campaign.[99] The SCLC failed to do this. In response, Mexican Americans abandoned Resurrection City. Unhappy with their treatment at the hands of black leaders and with the poor living conditions in the tent city, Chicano activists abandoned the site and chose to live instead at the Hawthorne School, a private experimental high school. This demonstration once again showed some of the pitfalls blacks and

Chicanos had to overcome in order to work with one another. Although the campaign established a new agenda that focused on antipoverty, it did not succeed in uniting Chicanos and blacks in a concerted movement.[100]

The PPC occurred both locally and nationally. Blacks, whites, and Chicanos in Texas participated in local marches to support the campaign. In Dallas in 1968, the NAACP organized a march to raise funds to send local people to the nation's capital. Leaders from around Texas came to Big D, including individuals from Houston, San Antonio, Laredo, and El Paso. Groups like the DCCCR and SNCC also took part.[101] A march and rally in Houston mirrored the demonstration in Dallas.[102] Beyond such local protests, a group of Texans traveled to Washington, D.C., for the gathering there. These PPC participants included eighteen blacks, three Mexican Americans, and one white.[103] The PPC taught some blacks and Chicanos important lessons about working together. As Peter Johnson observed, it took the campaign to show a number of black people that Mexican Americans were in the same boat as African Americans.[104]

Civil rights leaders throughout the state were very busy at this time—from ecumenical organizing to the pro-VISTA protests to the PPC. Although activists lost many of these battles, their failures should not diminish their importance nor tarnish their legacy. Indeed, many of them, especially the ecumenical leaders, had new, exciting ideas about how to assist poor people. The LAC Project's push for community uplift and local control, Project Equality's model of an economic boycott writ large, Peter Johnson and the SCLC's defiance of Dallas's slum clearance programs and its antihunger project, and the ECSC's All-American Community all combined new tactics with the more traditional strategies of the civil rights movement. Nonviolent protest and antipoverty joined in a unique struggle.

Ecumenical activists had some unusual ideas about how to make their goals a reality. Clearly one of their most important objectives involved bringing Mexican Americans and African Americans together in a concerted movement. The black civil rights movement and the Mexican American struggle, as has been shown, historically had great difficulty uniting. More simplistically, African American and Mexican American leaders had many problems working cooperatively. The ecumenical activists offered a third path. Bud Poteat, Sherrill Smith, Peter Johnson, ECSC members, and numerous others worked to form a broader coalition of poor blacks and Chicanos. Together, minorities could rally themselves and help end problems in their own communities. As a movement conceived in ecumenical terms, one specifically designed for Mexican Americans, African Americans, and Anglo Americans, ecumenical activists attempted to develop a movement for all Texans. And for a short time, they did.

But the extreme reaction of many Texans to Black Power and Chicano Power ensured that the ecumenical leaders achieved little. Ecumenical activists had their efforts tarnished by baseless fears that they encouraged anarchism, discord, and subversiveness. Those same labels were applied to their activities in order to discredit their movement. Obviously, their true message differed greatly from these perceptions. The efforts of ecumenical leaders demonstrate that the civil rights movements in Texas did not have to remain disunited. Blacks, whites, and browns could all come together to combat racism and secure social justice. Ecumenical activism also provided a bridge between the days of nonviolence and the days of Black and Brown Power. Ecumenism shows that the black and Mexican American freedom struggles did not transform overnight into the Black Power and Brown Power movements. On the contrary, the work of ecumenical activists offered an alternative to more radical forms of activism.

... 6 ...

The Day of Nonviolence Is Past

The Era of Brown Power and Black Power in Texas

In a 1969 speech in San Antonio, activist José Angel Gutiérrez told a group of Chicanos: "We have got to eliminate the gringo, and what I mean by that is if the worst comes to worst we have got to kill him." Gutiérrez's words caused considerable controversy in Mexican American leadership circles, although some Chicanos agreed with him. In a similar statement before the Houston City Council in 1970, Ovide Duncantell, of People's Party II (PP2), the precursor to Houston's Black Panther Party (BPP), warned that blacks would "exterminate 10 pigs for every black brother [that] is killed."[1] Like Gutiérrez's in San Antonio, Duncantell's threat produced much disquiet within the black leadership of Houston. Throughout the late 1960s and early 1970s, the popularity of Black Power and Brown or Chicano Power increased in Texas. The radicalism of the era set the stage for some of the most dramatic moments in the broader quest for Mexican American and African American rights.

The civil rights struggles of both groups became more militant at this time. Some blacks, following the example of the Oakland, California-based BPP, established groups committed to self-defense and Black Power.[2] Chicanos primarily focused on political campaigns, although these offensives displayed a radicalism that leaders of previous political actions hardly recognized. Chicanos created MAYO and RUP to advance Mexican American rights.[3] Not all blacks and Mexican Americans identified with the Black Power or Brown Power advocates, and many disagreed with these ideologies. But adherents to

154

both philosophies gained increased influence at this time and redefined concepts that had heretofore served as the core values of the civil rights movement—concepts like integration and nonviolence. For these activists, integration had to be demanded, and, if not forthcoming, forced. Nonviolence, while still advocated by numerous groups, was replaced by self-defense. And while some Mexican Americans continued to rely on the whiteness strategy, Chicanos dismissed whiteness as a civil rights tactic. In so doing, they opened up new avenues for cooperative ventures with African Americans.

For many African Americans, Black Power ruled the day in the 1960s and early 1970s. Current scholarship on Black Power has begun to reevaluate the basic characteristics of this movement. To many Americans in the sixties and seventies, Black Power seemed nothing more than an angry cry for redemptive violence that betrayed the earlier goals of the struggle. Today's scholars downplay this one-sided definition and emphasize the multifaceted nature of Black Power. It was a movement with multilayered ideologies and agendas that accomplished a great deal nationwide. As historian Jeffrey Ogbar notes, "Black Power employed—even co-opted—the activism typified in civil rights struggles and operated on basic assumptions of rights and privileges. In essence, it demanded inclusion while advocating autonomy and self-determination. . . . Black Power was many things to many people and an enigma to most."[4] Similarly, Robert Self observes that "as a political and cultural credo, black power was an extraordinarily plastic concept."[5] Such was the case in Texas, where Black Power merged with nonviolent protest, antipoverty, and armed protection to produce a struggle more nuanced than popular perceptions of the movement. Black Power leaders sought community control, an end to police violence, better jobs, and the basic reframing of what it meant to be black in Texas.

Alas, many Texans feared that Black Power would simply generate violent hostilities between whites and blacks. Their apprehensions ultimately hindered the success of this facet of the freedom struggle.[6] After passage of the Civil Rights and Voting Rights acts, some African Americans became disillusioned with nonviolent activism. The struggle had won desegregation and civil rights legislation, but it had failed to eliminate real structural inequalities like poverty, crime, inadequate housing, and joblessness. While the government and ecumenical leaders offered antipoverty programs, these seemed insufficient. When blacks demanded more, the state and federal governments responded by ending projects like VISTA and CAP. Black Power responded to these issues. Blacks began to reject government aid, which many felt represented a form of charity, paternalism, or both. Many also repudiated nonviolence in favor of self-defense. In addition, the failure of school desegregation fueled black anger. The cities with the highest concentration of blacks—Houston and Dallas—worried state leaders the most. Sociologist Wilhelmina Perry confirmed these fears when she declared that in Houston "the whole community is a bomb. Negroes are repressed, and there is this latent anxiety. It's just a matter of providing the situation that will ignite the bomb."[7]

Indeed, the bomb Perry described had a short fuse. It threatened to ignite only a few days after she made this prediction in May 1966, when the HPD killed an unarmed black man for allegedly stealing a loaf of bread. Local blacks nearly rioted then, but a contingent of police officers and NAACP officials cooled the situation. This type of police violence had given southern law enforcement a bad name, and Africans Americans had long regarded the police as the enemy. In the early 1960s Houston police had experienced decent relations with blacks, primarily because of the cautious, pragmatic leadership of Police Chief Carl Shuptrine. But in 1964, Mayor Louie Welch replaced Shuptrine with Herman Short, an individual widely regarded as the "Bull" Connor of Houston. Short's actions almost single-handedly ensured violent confrontations with black Houstonians.[8]

Black Power activism in Houston had steadily increased since 1966, the year that Reverend Frederick Douglass Kirkpatrick had come to town. The six-foot-six, 230-pound Kirkpatrick struck an imposing figure, but most regarded him as a gentle giant. He had a storied past. Kirkpatrick helped form the Deacons for Defense and Justice in Louisiana, a self-defense unit that protected civil rights activists in the Pelican State. He also brought SNCC to Houston. And unlike other local black leaders, he openly advocated Black Power.[9] Kirkpatrick began his work in the Bayou City by attempting to boost student activism on the TSU campus.[10] Civil rights activities at the university had dwindled since the negotiated integration in the early 1960s. Kirkpatrick wished to rekindle the movement. He organized interracial teach-ins at TSU, Rice University, and the University of Houston to inspire student activism. Kirkpatrick also hoped that Mayor Welch would push local employers to hire African Americans. But when the mayor proposed Project Partner, a lame attempt to economically develop one black neighborhood, Kirkpatrick dismissed the idea.[11] He warned against the presence of police in black neighborhoods. "Why should the police be coming around the Negro neighborhood instilling fear into the minds of our people?" Kirkpatrick asked. He seemed to perceive potential confrontations, but Welch lacked Kirkpatrick's foresight.

The mayor called race relations in Houston "utopian." His optimism was erroneous and ill-timed.[12]

Welch's lack of insight, combined with black anger, led directly to violence on the TSU campus.[13] Trouble began at three locations, each a distinct protest that converged with the other two as the TSU disturbance.[14] The first incident occurred in March 1967 after the university fired Professor Mack Jones for promoting SNCC and banned the SNCC chapter. This infringement on academic and campus freedom infuriated students, who responded by boycotting classes and sitting in at university buildings. Kirkpatrick, SNCC leader Lee Otis Johnson, and Booker T. Bonner demanded that TSU reinstate Jones and that the city close Wheeler Street, which bisected the campus. Students hated Wheeler Street. White motorists driving down this thoroughfare spit at black pedestrians, yelled obscenities, and pelted them with trash. The students believed that if TSU were a white school, the city would have closed Wheeler Street long ago.[15] These protests lasted for several weeks. The second incident leading to the TSU disturbance occurred at Northwood Junior High School, where a fight broke out between white and black students in May. Officials suspended the students involved, but the whites received only a three-day suspension while the African Americans were dismissed for several weeks. Kirkpatrick, Johnson, Bonner and students sat in at the school for one day. The next day protesters arrived to find the school cordoned off by police, who arrested the black students. The arrests outraged parents and leaders, but students paid a one-dollar fine and the school reinstated them, which ended the protests.[16]

The last event leading to the TSU disturbance stemmed from a local tragedy. On May 8, 1967, eleven-year-old Victor George fell into a garbage-filled pond at the Holmes Road Dump and drowned.[17] City governments traditionally placed landfills in minority neighborhoods, and most Houston dumps were located in black subdivisions.[18] The black community reacted angrily to young George's death, its leaders demanding that the city drain the pond and close the dump.[19] When Mayor Welch refused to do so immediately, protesters began to sit in at the landfill. Police arrested dozens of demonstrators, including William Lawson, a prominent black minister. Each night after the sit-ins, protesters gathered for rallies. Unbeknownst to the activists, another group joined them: undercover Houston police officers.[20] These officers heard some of the protesters call for violence and inferred that SNCC leaders made these statements. Since most SNCC members attended TSU, the HPD assumed by default that TSU students had threatened violence.[21]

(From left to right) Lee Otis Johnson, F. D. Kirkpatrick, and James Alexander in a Houston courtroom after their arrest at the Northwood protest. Although they had broken no laws, police arrested the three men, as well as a number of students, as a means of harassment and intimidation. (Courtesy of Houston Metropolitan Research Center, Houston Public Library)

When students returned to TSU on the night of May 16, they found that police had attempted to blockade the campus. The activists fought back by throwing rocks and bottles at the officers and by setting fire to several garbage cans. Reportedly, they strategically placed these cans on Wheeler Street to block police access. The students fired at least one gun in the direction of the police. It remains unclear who fired the shot, but it escalated tensions. The handful of police at the scene quickly multiplied. The students retreated to their dormitories.[22]

At around midnight, Police Chief Short arrived on the scene. He had Reverend Lawson released from jail and brought to the campus. Short then assembled Lawson, Earl Allen, F. D. Kirkpatrick, and several other black leaders to quell the violence. After convincing Short to pull his officers back, the African American leaders approached the dorms. They found the students disorganized and scared but could not persuade them to surrender. The students demanded that the police withdraw and that the city close Wheeler Street. Lawson, Allen, and Kirkpatrick relayed these two demands to Short, who quickly refused both. The black leaders could only watch in horror as students again attempted to blockade Wheeler Street. Chief Short had had enough. He ordered a contingent of six hundred police officers to storm the dormitories.[23]

Houston police arrested nearly five hundred TSU students the night of the disturbance. Here, students lay prone, guarded by heavily armed police officers. Many students were forced to remain in these positions for hours while paddy wagons slowly ferried them to the city jail. (Bettman/CORBIS)

The officers opened fire and shot between 3,000 and 5,000 rounds of ammunition at the dorms. Then they charged. Amazingly, only one student suffered an injury; a bullet struck Morris English in the back, but he later recovered. The police did not fare so well. Two officers, Robert Blaylock and Alan Dugger, received minor injuries from bullet wounds. More seriously, rookie officer Louis Kuba fell to the ground as the police charged the dorms. He later died from a bullet wound to the forehead. Kuba was the night's only fatality. When the police finally made it to the dorms, they ransacked students' rooms, beat the youths, and forced them outside. They arrested nearly five hundred students that night. By 3:00 a.m. the violence had ended.[24]

The aftermath of the disturbance at TSU reveals a great deal about the prevailing racial climate in Houston. Politicians, the city government, and most newspapers blamed the students for the violence and for the death of Officer Kuba. Five undergraduates, chosen at random, would eventually stand trial for Kuba's death. The white press reported that students had armed themselves with an array of guns and Molotov cocktails. These reports were later proved to be false. The *Houston Chronicle* declared that the "police handled [the] riot well"[25]; a glowing report about Officers Blaylock and Kuba asserted that they had been wounded trying to "clean out a nest of snipers." Besides praise for the HPD, the *Houston Post* commended Herman Short: the police chief warned his officers to be careful because "there are innocent people in there and we don't want them hurt."[26] Both papers blamed antipoverty groups like the EF and HOPE Development, Inc., for the violence. These and other inaccuracies in the stories about this event illustrated the racial bias in Houston.[27]

The Negro press gave a more factual account. The reports published in the *Houston Informer* and *Houston Forward Times* mirrored the official version that emerged after a local investigation and a congressional inquiry. The *Informer*, for instance, blamed everyone involved—students, police, and local government.[28] Both papers maintained that the students had few weapons; the students shared one .22 caliber pistol, and no Molotov cocktails existed. The black press argued that a ricocheting police bullet had killed Officer Kuba. The papers accused Mayor Welch and Chief Short of racism. Instead of calling for caution, they reported, Short evidently told his men "Goddamn it, let's clean the place up."[29] SNCC more succinctly denounced the mayor, calling him a "functional retard" and a "beast with no moral sense of conscience."[30] SNCC blamed the riot on one thing: "cop violence."[31] According to William Lawson, the "riot" only began when Short, "without warning to anybody, gave what must have been the most blundering order of the evening": that his officers storm the TSU dorms. As Lawson observed, "riot" did not accurately describe what happened at TSU.[32] Activist Quentin Mease concurred: "It was police instigated. That's why we called it . . . a 'police riot.'"[33] The *Houston Informer* recognized one final fact: "The day of non-violence is past."[34]

In the following days police quietly released most of the students. But the five accused of Officer Kuba's murder remained in jail. This "TSU Five" elicited considerable sympathy from black Houstonians who distrusted the police. The *Texas Observer* offered the most detailed analysis of Kuba's shooting. Based on Kuba's location, the paper observed, students in the dorms could not have shot him. They would have had to shoot around a building to do so. The *Observer* also learned that police had analyzed the bullet's fragments and discovered that it was larger than a .22 caliber. In short, the HPD had killed Officer Kuba. Nonetheless, the trial of the TSU Five went slowly and inexorably forward.[35]

While the trial proceeded, the U.S. Senate Subcommittee on Investigations began an inquiry into riots that occurred in Houston, Detroit, Newark, and elsewhere. The committee generally held black activists responsible for these riots. Many Houstonians called to testify about the TSU disturbance repeated reports from local papers. Several witnesses testified that students used Molotov cocktails.[36] Students blamed the HPD. Law student Cleve McDowell argued that the HPD "actually instigated the incident by harassing the student body."[37] Reverend Earl Allen interjected perhaps the most eloquent testimony at the hearings: the Senate must recognize "that there exists a black minority that has been, is being and, from all indications, will continue to be forced to submit to cruel, inhuman, and unjust treatment by a white ruling majority." All conflict was rooted in this fact. Allen disagreed with those who blamed the riot on the EF, HOPE Development, Inc., VISTA, and other anti-poverty groups. But his testimony made no real difference. The investigation operated as a show trial to allay white fears and to give a semblance of sympathy for blacks.[38]

The trial of the TSU Five was also a show trial. The state charged TSU student Douglas Waller with Kuba's murder, though police had arrested Waller earlier in the day and he sat in prison when Officer Kuba died. Earl Allen had taken Floyd Nichols, another of the TSU Five, to his home in northeastern Houston earlier that night. Thus Nichols was miles from the campus but was arrested anyway. Charles Freeman, another black youth arrested for Kuba's death, had conversed with the black ministers before police stormed the dormitories. While at the scene, he had not participated in the riot.[39] John Parker and Trazawell Franklin, the only members of the TSU Five in the dorms that night, claimed to have slept through the conflagration. Such an assertion strains credulity, but they never admitted any involvement in the riot.[40]

The trial of the TSU Five began with Charles Freemen in 1968. It ended quickly when an all-white jury failed to reach a verdict.[41] It took almost three years for the state to try him again (the court delayed the trial to allow tensions to calm). The district attorney again charged Freemen with assault and murder in 1970. But the state could not prove that he had killed Kuba or that he had assaulted anyone. After pressure from the defense and from the black community, the state dropped all charges against Freeman in November 1970. Prosecutors then recommended that Judge Wendell Odom drop the charges against the rest of the men. Judge Odom agreed. The state finally admitted that Officer Louis Kuba most likely died from a ricocheting police bullet. The TSU Five, the *Houston Informer* announced, were "free at last."[42]

The TSU disturbance had a marked impact on the civil rights movement in Houston and in some ways across the state. The incident emboldened Black Power advocates throughout Texas. They saw police violence as proof positive of state-sponsored racism. Blacks in Houston soon formed PP2, an offshoot of the BPP, to defend the black community. Dallas, San Antonio, and Austin witnessed the formation of militant chapters of SNCC, the Black Panthers, and

Friends of the Deacons for Defense and Justice.[43] At the same time, however, the disturbance confirmed white fears of radicalism emerging from the civil rights movement. These individuals viewed black militancy in mostly negative terms and came to consider any protests, whether radical or not, as un-American.[44]

The Houston police, white government officials, and locals generally — both white and black (and Mexican American, to be sure) — quickly tired of Black Power. The city government had learned that it could silence radicals by arresting them, holding them in jail, and even killing them. The experience of the TSU Five bears that out. But the travails of Lee Otis Johnson even more clearly demonstrated police repression. Johnson, a charismatic Texan with Denzel Washington good looks, helped bring Black Power to Houston. Police first collared him after the protests at Northwood Junior High. They arrested him on various charges five more times in 1967.[45] In 1968 the HPD apprehended Johnson for offering a marijuana joint to an undercover police officer. He stood trial for the "sale" of marijuana in August of that year. Black supporters initiated a "Free Lee Otis" campaign that included a *Free Lee Otis* newspaper and the Lee Otis Johnson Defense Committee. The jury deliberated for ten minutes before finding him guilty as charged. For his crime, the state sentenced Johnson to thirty years in prison. The excessive sentence flabbergasted blacks and other radicals in the Chicano and antiwar movements.[46]

For blacks in general and SNCC leaders in particular, the arrest of Lee Otis Johnson epitomized police repression. Much like the TSU Five, Johnson was railroaded by the white establishment for speaking out against the status quo. His incarceration effectively removed him from the struggle. At an appeals court hearing, Johnson's lawyers presented an impressive list of errors that had occurred during the trial. They showed, for instance, that many jurors held prejudicial views of Johnson due to press coverage. The judge finally agreed and freed Johnson in 1972.[47]

Police repression in Houston continued. In 1970, 23-year-old Army veteran Larry Taylor spent a week in the hospital after police brutalized him. His friend Bobby Joe Conner fared worse — Houston police beat him to death. Officers A. R. Hill and J. A. McMahon had arrested Taylor and Conner after a traffic violation. They drove the two black men to a police station in Galena Park, a small community near Houston, and took turns beating them. One of the Houston officers told Galena Park police, "We're going to show you how to take care of a bad nigger." After a kick in the stomach, Conner fell to the floor. The officers kicked him several more times. Taylor later reported that

Conner "didn't move anymore. He just lay there . . . he was dead then."[48] The two officers later stood trial for Conner's death, but the jury acquitted them.

Events like the incarceration of Lee Otis Johnson and the murder of Bobby Joe Conner outraged local blacks. In response, Black Power advocates formed PP2 in 1970 to combat police violence. A militant defense organization modeled on the Black Panthers,[49] PP2 was led by 21-year-old Carl Hampton, its ideological spirit and chairman. Charles "Boko" Freeman acted as PP2's minister of culture. Hampton and Freeman opened a headquarters on Dowling Street in South Houston, an area some regarded as the center of Houston's vice trade. The activists patrolled the area to curtail crime and protect black residents from police. "We believe we can end police brutality in our black community by organizing black self-defense groups that are dedicated to defending our black community from racist police oppression and brutality," read one plank of PP2's platform. The group also initiated a clothing drive, established a food pantry for the local poor, and attempted to open a health clinic.[50]

Expecting trouble from the Houston police, Carl Hampton and Boko Freeman armed themselves and their PP2 colleagues with shotguns and pistols. But a rather minor event sparked their first confrontation with the HPD. On the night of July 17, 1970, police attempted to arrest PP2 member James Aaron for selling the *Black Panther* newspaper. Aaron fled inside PP2 headquarters. There, Hampton and several other activists stopped the policemen. Hampton allegedly placed his hand on the butt of his pistol, which caused the lead officer to withdraw his sidearm. All three HPD officers and three PP2 members then drew their weapons and chambered rounds. After a tense standoff, the police retreated. The incident angered the officers and Police Chief Herman Short, who vowed to destroy PP2.[51]

A ten-day standoff between police and PP2 activists ensued. Party members, along with white activist Roy Bartee Haile from the John Brown Revolutionary League (JBRL) and several individuals from MAYO, kept police out of the Dowling Street area for well over a week. Throughout this time tensions remained palpable. The situation grew more stressful when Ovide Duncantell appeared before the Houston City Council and told Mayor Louie Welch that PP2 would defend the black community and "fight until we're all dead." That was when he also declared, "We will exterminate 10 pigs for every black brother [that] is killed."[52] Carl Hampton enjoyed "10-Pig" Duncantell's grandiloquence but predicted that it would lead to violence. At a rally in front of PP2's headquarters on the night of Sunday, July 26, 1970, Hampton told the crowd that he knew the police "are gonna attack this building." His words seemed prophetic. After most of the crowd had dispersed and many of the activists from MAYO and the JBRL had left, Duncantell informed Hampton that armed men had occupied the roof of a nearby church. Hampton, Bartee Haile, and several other PP2 members gathered their guns and marched into the street. The men on the roof, plainclothes, off-duty police officers, opened fire using expanding "dum-dum" bullets. During the fusillade, Hampton was shot three times in the abdomen; two other party members were wounded, and Haile was shot twice in the arm. A few hours later, Hampton died on an operating room table. The firefight at Dowling Street continued into the night.[53]

The shooting of Carl Hampton was little more than premeditated murder.[54] Reverend William Lawson said the shootout was a "well-arranged trap."[55] Another activist stated: "Carl Hampton died at 21 of natural causes — racism."[56] Boko Freeman was more concise, characterizing the event as the "police assassination of Carl Hampton."[57] For these activists, the actions of police seemed intended to "do away with black people." According to James Aaron, who took over the leadership of PP2 after Hampton's death, "The pigs assassinated Carl in an attempt to destroy the party."[58] Police and local officials responded in kind, calling Hampton and his followers "human mad dogs with their guns."[59] The Dowling Street Incident, the sobriquet given to the murder of Hampton, heightened tensions between blacks and whites in Texas. It proved to many blacks the racist attitudes of police. For whites, the incident confirmed their fears about Black Power.

The Dowling Street Incident had another effect in Houston: it united African Americans and Mexican Americans. Like blacks, police frequently abused Mexican-descent people. The members of PP2 and other black activists joined forces with MAYO and the JBRL to protest police violence. These organizations unified in a group they called the "Rainbow Coalition." They met and "remembered the police riot at Texas Southern University in 1967; they remembered the stomping death in a jailhouse of Bobby Joe Conner; now they recalled the actions leading up to Hampton's killing," and they promised to work together to stop police violence. The group represented an important attempt at coalition building, but it was short lived.[60]

PP2 was reborn in 1971 as the official Houston chapter of the BPP. The Panthers took up PP2's call to open a health clinic for minority clients. Part of what the Panthers called their "Survival Programs," the Carl B. Hampton Free Health Clinic offered sickle cell anemia screenings, immunizations, prenatal care, and dental care, among other services. This important clinic helped local blacks who struggled to find adequate health care. The Panthers began another Survival Program that provided free breakfasts for neighborhood children and initiated a food drive for local African Americans. The BPP, according to one newspaper, delivered so much food that it was "everywhere raining bags of groceries." The Panthers also began a free neighborhood pest control program, arguing that "decent housing is a human right." The People's Pest Control Service inspected and treated neighborhood homes and apartments with rat, roach, and flea infestations—all at no cost. The Carl B. Hampton Free Health Clinic, the free breakfast program, and the People's Pest Control Service demonstrate one of the important aspects of the BPP at the local level— the Panthers responded to community quality-of-life problems with novel solutions. The BPP in Oakland was so impressed by the pest control project that it advertised the program in the *Black Panther* newspaper. The BPP in Houston disbanded in 1974 after the national Panther office in California recalled local chapters to assist in the Oakland mayoral race of Bobby Seale.[61]

The movement in Houston quieted after the Dowling Street Incident and the demise of the BPP. Police Chief Short held onto his job despite community pressure. Reform of the HPD did not begin until 1973, when a unified black electorate helped to vote Mayor Welch out of office. Short decided to resign after Welch's defeat.[62] Short's departure helped smooth relations between the HPD and the black community. But the HPD still troubled minority leaders. Both African Americans and Mexican Americans feared the heavy-handedness that the HPD seemed to universally embrace. Their apprehensions, of course, had a great deal of merit. It would take another violent encounter, the murder of Jose "Joe" Campos Torres and the Moody Park Riot in 1977, to force the police department to change its ways.[63]

Dallas also saw its share of Black Power activism, particularly from SNCC, which was led by Marion Ernest "Ernie" McMillan, a longtime Dallas resident.[64] McMillan helped SNCC grow to more than two hundred members by 1968. However, he found SNCC's activities unwelcome in Dallas. Indeed, local police and FBI agents closely monitored McMillan and SNCC.[65] This surveillance began in March 1968 after SNCC picketed Dallas's Federal Building to protest the arrest of SNCC chairman H. Rap Brown.[66] A few days later, police arrested McMillan for the first time when he and four associates drove around the city shouting Black Power statements through a loudspeaker.[67] McMillan and SNCC suffered from constant police harassment because of their activities. As McMillan noted, the actions of police "were like killing a fly with a cannon."[68]

McMillan's most notable protest began in July 1968, when SNCC picketed the OK Supermarket. The store operated as a "ghetto gouger": located in a black neighborhood but owned by whites, the store charged inflated prices and sold expired food. SNCC hoped the picket would force the owners to sell the business to African Americans. Yet the owners refused to sell.[69] Tensions escalated at the supermarket in July. Ernie McMillan and his colleague Matthew Johnson put pressure on the store's owners by filling grocery carts with items, taking them to the cashier, and then leaving. They disrupted business by creating extra work for the supermarket, which had to restock the items in the abandoned carts. One evening, about fifty blacks entered the store and began smashing eggs, vegetables, and other foodstuffs. McMillan, who was directly accused of damaging property worth $1.09, later returned and mockingly told a cashier: "These white people sho' keep a nice clean store." Police promptly arrested McMillan and Johnson for destruction of property.[70]

While out of jail on bond, the two mem continued to picket the OK Supermarket. SNCC again approached the store owners and attempted to convince them to sell the business. By early August, the owners agreed to sell for $600,000 if an African American buyer came forward within sixty days.[71] But SNCC could not find a buyer. A short time later Ernie McMillan and Matthew Johnson, much like Lee Otis Johnson, each received excessive, ten-year prison sentences for vandalizing the supermarket—for McMillan a year in jail for every dime of damage he caused. The prosecution accused McMillan of "rushing America to hell." His travails damaged SNCC in Dallas.[72] Although store owners agreed in 1968 to allow black employees to own 60 percent of the business, thereby granting African Americans control of the supermarket, the protests had long since ended. SNCC received no credit for bringing the events at the supermarket to a conclusion.[73] By this time McMillan had fled Dallas. Police caught up with him in 1971, and a federal court sentenced him to three years in jail for draft evasion.[74]

For white leaders in Dallas, SNCC represented the worst of the Black Power movement. Local perceptions, however, were biased by popular misconceptions of the group. Ernie McMillan and Matthew Johnson, for example, eschewed violence. McMillan encouraged nonviolence and self-defense. He explained in 1968 that "Dallas' Snick has never advocated or wished to incite a riot."[75] But the national SNCC endorsed Black Power and dismissed nonviolence at this same time. Dallas's leaders ignored McMillan's statements, preferring instead to see SNCC as a violent group. Accordingly, police harassed, arrested, jailed, and eventually drove McMillan from the city. As the *Texas Observer* noted, city leaders "were determined to set an example by falling on McMillan with the full force of the law. And they did."[76] SNCC continued

A group of Black Power youths affiliated with the SCLC protest police brutality
in Dallas in 1972. Although Mexican Americans suffered from persistent police abuse,
most notably the shooting of Thomas Rodriguez and the killing of Santos Rodríguez,
no Mexican Americans joined this protest. (Collections, Texas/Dallas
History and Archives Division, Dallas Public Library)

to protest meekly into 1970, changing its name to the Black Revolutionary
Action Party and joining forces with the BPP. The Panthers in Dallas mirrored
the BPP in Houston, offering a free breakfast program and neighborhood pest
control. The group disbanded in 1973.[77]

Other Texas cities had their share of Black Power activists. But unlike in
Houston and Dallas, city leaders elsewhere attempted to head off conflicts between blacks and the local government. In San Antonio, black leaders pushed
the city to address the apprehensions of blacks regarding public officials and
vice versa. Claude Black and George Sutton argued that "a more positive approach is to try to correct conditions out of which riots grow." Black and
Sutton criticized Mayor W. W. McAllister for warning a white voting league
that blacks might riot in San Antonio in 1967 and that police stood ready to
"shoot to kill." They dismissed the mayor's comments as "tactless" and said
that McAllister could alleviate violence by forming a civilian review board to
monitor the police.[78]

The death of Bobby Jo Phillips facilitated the formation of the police review
board that Black and Sutton had suggested. Phillips died after San Antonio

police beat him during an arrest in 1968. The police claimed that Phillips assaulted them with two knives. According to eyewitnesses, however, the officers had quickly disarmed Phillips and then proceeded to violently beat him. Phillips later died from these injuries. In a subsequent trial, the jury found the officers not guilty. When the black community rose up in anger, the mayor and police chief moved quickly to form the review board to calm the situation. Although the board exonerated the officers, the oversight provided by the commission helped ease tensions in San Antonio.[79]

Phillips's murder also assisted in the development of SNCC in the Alamo City. According to activist Mario Salas, who self-identifies as an Afro-Mexican and became SNCC chairman, the San Antonio committee was the last SNCC chapter to form in the United States. The group focused primarily on police harassment and murder of blacks. A year after the murder of Phillips, the San Antonio SNCC planned a major protest to commemorate his death and to decry police violence. In April 1969 approximately one thousand activists descended on downtown San Antonio. After being attacked by police, the protesters retaliated by breaking into downtown stores. They robbed a pawnshop of its guns and took the weapons to SNCC headquarters. Over two hundred police officers then stormed the headquarters and arrested numerous activists.[80]

The SNCC chapter in San Antonio eventually combined its focus on police brutality with the Survival Programs of the BPP. This SNCC/BPP hybrid began a free breakfast program and a food pantry in 1969. The SNCC activists also initiated a free health clinic and free legal aid in 1970. The San Antonio SNCC/ BPP hybrid operated until 1975; it was the final SNCC chapter to fold in the United States. The group received "posthumous" status as an official chapter of the BPP in the 1990s. Thus this hybrid became the last SNCC and the final BPP chapter formed in the United States.[81]

Public officials in Fort Worth took a number of steps to stave off violent encounters. In 1955 they established a Human Relations Commission, which morphed into the Citizens Committee on Community Relations in 1960. This group initiated the integration that occurred in Cowtown in the following years. The city also improved housing conditions and promoted school desegregation.[82] Although these measures satisfied many black leaders, civil rights activists began to protest in 1969 when the local government refused to tear down the Ridgelea Wall. This solid concrete fence separated white Fort Worth from the all-black Lake Como neighborhood. Dr. Eck Prud'homme, a prominent physician, appealed to the city council to destroy barriers that isolated black and Chicano neighborhoods from the rest of the city. Prud'homme

San Antonio riot police arrest an unidentified man during the 1969 riot.
As in other Texas communities, officials in San Antonio attempted to guard
against radicalism and cracked down hard on disruptive protests.
(Courtesy of UTSA's Institute of Texan Cultures)

warned the officials that, at a "time when America itself is threatened with
being torn into two or more distinct and mutually distrusted, if not actively
hostile, societies," the city should remove the wall. The city council agreed,
and sections of the wall were destroyed to allow for pedestrian and vehicular
traffic.[83]

Texas thus witnessed a great deal of Black Power activism, much of it aimed
at police brutality. Throughout American history, African Americans had extreme difficulties with law enforcement. Activists desired community control, aid to those in poverty, and an end to police abuse. They also sought to
culturally rearticulate what it meant to be black and American, as well as to
redefine aspects of blackness that many Americans regarded as negatives.

This included a celebration of the African culture shared by black Americans, especially artistic expression, cuisine, dress, and hairstyle. Black Power advocates called for recognition of the accomplishments of black people in the United States through the development of African American history curricula and Black Studies programs. They demanded inclusion, sought greater control over black communities, hoped to empower African Americans by reaffirming positive aspects of blackness, and insisted that government institutions such as police departments treat black people with respect. But local white leaders feared Black Power activism. To these public officials, Black Power had no positive value and contributed nothing to their communities. Despite the fact that Black Power activists engaged in many positive and constructive enterprises, they found themselves the victims of reactionary city governments, recalcitrant law enforcement, and the overbearing hand of a federal government that resisted and opposed their activities.

■ ■ ■

Like Black Power, Chicano or Brown Power had major obstacles to overcome. One of those barriers proved to be white perceptions of Chicano militancy. Many Texans came to abhor any indication of radicalism as they perceived it—whether black or brown—and they reacted viscerally to Chicano radicalism. Current scholarship on Brown Power has rearticulated the basic characteristics of this movement. Most importantly, *chicanismo* (literally chicano-ism) responded to the previous generations' failure to end racism. As historian Juan Gómez-Quiñones observed: "Despite the organizational challenge by Mexican Americans to discrimination in the forties, fifties, and sixties and economic gains resulting from postwar economic booms, the unequal position between Mexican Americans and Anglo Americans probably expanded rather than contracted."[84] Gómez-Quiñones alluded to the failure of the whiteness strategy, which Chicanos discarded in the late 1960s and early 1970s. Scholars today highlight the multifaceted nature of Brown Power. Ignacio M. García argues that "the Chicano Movement was not so much a singular social process as a coalescing of numerous philosophical and historical currents within the community that came together at a particular time and place during this century."[85] The Chicano movement had multiple ideologies and agendas that accomplished a great deal. Chicanos focused on community control, participatory democracy, an end to police brutality, and the redefining of what it meant to be Mexican in America.

The concept of chicanismo predated the Chicano movement. Historians have found similar examples of resistance going back to the *bandido* legacy of the late nineteenth and early twentieth centuries and in the *pachuco* culture that developed in the 1930s and 1940s.[86] Development of the intellectual underpinnings of chicanismo mainly occurred in the 1960s, however. One of the most important examples of this intellectual development took place at the 1969 National Chicano Youth Liberation Conference, which Corky Gonzales hosted in Denver. There, activists drafted *El Plan de Aztlán* (the Plan of Aztlán, or *El Plan*). They designed *El Plan* to unify the Chicano movement by giving activists a collective organizational focus and to instill cultural pride by maintaining that the Southwest was Aztlán, the birthplace of the Aztecs, so that Chicanos lived in Aztlán and descended from the Aztecs. *El Plan* began with a spiritual credo: "In the spirit of a new people that is conscious not only of its proud Historical heritage, but also of the brutal 'Gringo' invasion of our territories, We, the Chicano inhabitants and civilizers of the northern land of Aztlán, from whence came our forefathers . . . Declare that the call of our blood is our power, our responsibility, and our inevitable destiny." The language of *El Plan* turned much of American history on its head. Chicanos argued that the United States had stolen Mexican territory, that Chicanos rightfully owned the land, and that Americans were the immigrants. By referring to whites as "gringos," *El Plan* firmly identified the enemy of the Mexican American community. It also helped establish Chicanos as a brown people. *El Plan* referred to Chicanos as "bronze" and as "La Raza" (the people). In other words, *El Plan* began the first steps toward racially repositioning Mexican Americans as brown—not white—people.[87]

While *El Plan de Aztlán* contained many statements about Chicano cultural and ethnic pride, it was also, as the name implies, a plan designed to collectively organize Chicano civil rights activities. Economic development, political liberation, community control, and educational issues dominated its agenda. Chicanos would achieve economic and community control "by driving the exploiter out of our communities." Political liberation demanded Chicano electoral action "since the two-party system is the same animal with two heads that feed from the same trough." The plan called for the development of a Chicano political party, and it proposed an educational model that highlighted Chicano history and culture. *El Plan* also emphasized the need for Chicano control of schools; Chicano teachers, administrators, and counselors; and new educational programs. Finally, *El Plan* advocated armed self-defense against police brutality.[88]

The rhetoric and semantics of chicanismo caused tensions between Chicano activists and their critics. Indeed, Mexican Americans passionately debated the term "Chicano." Chicano (derived from "mexicano") had pejoratively applied to lower-class Mexican Americans for generations. But radicals in the 1960s reformulated "Chicano" as a positive ethnic identifier imbued with racial and cultural pride. The term signified a militant political awareness, a distinct connection with Mexico, and a brown racial identity.[89] The embrace of "Chicano" as the new descriptor of Mexican American ethnicity mirrored African American rejection of the word "Negro" and the adoption of "black" as the new term for persons of African descent. "Chicano" also reflected black use of the word "nigger." The word "nigger" provoked considerable controversy in Texas and the United States generally. "Chicano," while not a term of racist derogation, did the same thing.

Young militants wholeheartedly embraced "Chicano," while more conservative Mexican Americans generally disliked the term. They preferred "Latin" or "Latin American." Phil Montalbo, still a prominent LULACer, argued that Mexican Americans like himself felt "humiliated, defiled, and held up to scorn and ridicule by these so called leaders with the 'pachuco' word 'chicano.'" Many others felt similarly.[90] But some elder statesmen like George Sánchez and Albert Peña had long considered any reference to "Latin" just as problematic. Sánchez noted that "the people in El Paso and California want to be called Mexican-Americans, the rest of the people in Texas want to be Latin-Americans, the people in New Mexico want to be Spanish-Americans. Except of course when they're speaking Spanish—then you ask them and they answer, 'Soy mexicano!' [I am Mexican]."[91]

While many activists openly used "Chicano" as an ethnic identifier, others responded negatively to the term. Albert Peña humorously called this reaction the "wetbacklash."[92] For example, in a series of short booklets, an individual calling him/herself "The Author" reacted angrily to "Chicano." "The term 'Chicano' was, and is, an insult," he/she wrote:[93]

> For the last 123 years the Spanish speaking American of the Great American Southwest, has been thoroughly brainwashed by the dominant society, and his own political, educational and, even, some religious leaders into believing ... that he is: 1) a Mexican; 2) of Mexican descent; 3) a Mexican-American; 4) a Chicano; and that due to the foregoing, he has acquired and developed 5) Mexican-American culture; and, last but not least, that he belongs to a mystical something or other called 6) La Raza.

The Author argued that those who used such terms embraced "that fallacy of a 'Mexican Race.'" He/she called "La Raza" a "*racial hoax* ... conceived in *ignorance* and dedicated to the *perpetuation* of an *ethnic falsehood*." As citizens, The Author stated, "we are: *not Mexicans—not Mexican-Americans—*

certainly not Chicanos. We are Americans!"[94] In these booklets, The Author focused on race and correctly noted that no Mexican race existed. But the flipside of this assertion implied that individuals of Mexican descent were white.[95] Indeed, it seems that some disliked "Chicano" because it detracted from the whiteness strategy.

Despite disagreements over the use of the word "Chicano," the Mexican American community had many problems to deal with in the late 1960s and early 1970s. Like African Americans, Mexican Americans had great difficulties with "la chota" (Spanish slang for "the law"). As noted, the Texas Rangers meted out notorious violence on Chicanos throughout much of American history. A. Y. Allee most visibly symbolized Ranger violence during the farmworkers' strike and protests in Crystal City. Similarly, law enforcers in many cities treated Mexican Americans much as they did blacks. Like blacks, Chicanos responded angrily to police brutality. "I don't see how we can accomplish any change by peaceable ways," Yolanda Garza Birdwell of the Houston MAYO said. "I don't see how we can avoid revolution with guns." To the issue of police harassment, Birdwell had a simple response: "Get a gun, get it soon."[96] José Angel Gutiérrez, Gregory Salazar, and others also predicted violence.

Many activists hoped local governments would acknowledge problems and repair them before violence occurred. After the TSU disturbance, for instance, African American and Mexican American leaders both worked with local investigators and the congressional inquiry to prevent further encounters.[97] As we have seen, events in Houston did prompt San Antonio, Fort Worth, and other cities to begin forming police review boards as a method of circumventing violence. But review boards did not stop police brutality.

By the late sixties and early seventies, Chicanos began to rise up in protest when police killed Mexican-origin people. In July 1970, San Patricio County deputy sheriff Eric Brauch shot and killed Dr. Fred E. Logan Jr. in Mathis. On the night of July 11, Logan apparently got into a scuffle with Sheriff Brauch, who then shot the doctor at point blank range in the chest. Though he was not of Mexican descent, Mexican Americans regarded Dr. Logan as a "friend of Chicanos" and as "the Anglo who cared." He ran a health clinic that provided low-cost or no-cost services and medication to the local community. Hundreds attended Logan's funeral and turned the proceedings into a protest of police brutality.[98] When Corpus Christi police killed Mario Benavides during a botched arrest, MAYO organized a massive demonstration against local officials. Benavides had only recently returned from duty in Vietnam, so activists carried signs that read "Fight in Vietnam, Get Killed in Corpus Christi."

Although the police refused to discipline the officer, community anger abated a few days after Benavides's funeral.[99]

Dallas had a similar experience when police shot Thomas Rodriguez and his wife Bertha. Officers had stormed the couple's apartment searching for two murder suspects. They shot Rodriguez several times and wounded his pregnant wife. This event outraged the Mexican American community. Chicanos held a number of rallies and marches to protest police violence. Pancho Medrano and his sons organized a Dallas chapter of the Brown Berets to protect local people. The Brown Berets, a Chicano self-defense unit, had developed shortly before the high school "blowouts" in Los Angeles in 1968 and quickly spread across the Southwest.[100] Police eventually dropped all charges against Rodriguez. But the city did not establish a civilian review board, and the police officers went unpunished. The results proved catastrophic.[101]

The inaction of local officials led to one of the most repugnant examples of white racism in the state's history. On the night of July 24, 1973, Dallas police officers Darrell Cain and Roy Arnold witnessed three thieves burglarizing a gas station. Although the suspects fled, the officers thought they recognized two of the robbers as brothers David and Santos Rodríguez. To apprehend these "suspects," the officers drove to the Rodríguez home, entered the small edifice, woke the brothers, handcuffed them, and shoved them into their squad car. They then drove back to the gas station. David sat in the back seat with Arnold, while Cain sat with Santos in the front seat. In an attempt to elicit a confession, Cain began a game of Russian roulette with the twelve-year-old Santos. With his .357 revolver pressed to Santos's temple, Cain demanded that he confess. Santos refused, so Cain pulled the trigger. Nothing happened. "Tell the truth, hombre," Arnold demanded from the back seat, "this time he's going to shoot you." Cain pulled the trigger again. This time the gun discharged, killing Santos Rodríguez instantly.[102]

After the murder of Santos Rodríguez, events in Dallas progressed rapidly. The police department suspended Cain and charged him with murder, but he posted bond and was released. On July 26, Dallasites learned that fingerprints taken from the gas station did not match the Rodríguez brothers. At about the same time, community leaders discovered that Officer Cain had also killed an unarmed black man named Michael Moorehead in 1970.[103] In response, black and Chicano leaders planned a march to denounce police violence. On July 28, nearly two thousand Mexican Americans and a handful of African Americans proceeded to march peacefully through downtown Dallas. But when one woman falsely claimed that the police had killed her son, the activists turned on the police officers observing the march. They beat the officers

Dallas council member Pedro Aguirre and Chicano leader Rene Martinez address
the massive crowd at a protest denouncing the police murder of Santos Rodríguez.
Only moments later, the protesters erupted in anger, triggering the Dallas riot of 1973.
(Collections, Texas/Dallas History and Archives Division, Dallas Public Library)

and dispersed them, burned two police motorcycles, and looted more than
forty stores along Main Street. After forty-five minutes of rioting, police reinforcements restored order.[104]

Despite the large number of rioters and the use of police to end the melee,
only a handful of people received injuries. In November, a jury found Darrell Cain guilty of murder and sentenced him to five years in jail. This verdict
failed to satisfy most Dallasites. The Rodríguez incident remained an ugly
blight on the city. So too was the riot, the only major racial conflagration in
Dallas's history. While the DPD attempted to assuage the community by hiring
more Mexican American and black officers, this effort only went so far. The
whole affair seemed to stun city leaders and residents, so much so that the
shock actually helped calm the situation in Dallas. As far as civil rights were
concerned, for the next few months the city remained quiet.

The level of violence Mexican Americans suffered at the hands of police
proved extreme and pervasive. Indeed, they had a long history of violent
interactions with law enforcement, especially the Texas Rangers. Much like
blacks, Chicanos found police in many locales abusive, violent, and unfair. As
a U.S. Civil Rights Commission report accurately noted, police misconduct

United in anger, black and Chicano rioters burn two police motorcycles and destroy sections of downtown Dallas after the protests decrying the police murder of Santos Rodríguez. (Photograph courtesy of Jay Dickman)

against Mexican Americans was widespread and "acts of police misconduct result in mounting suspicion and incite incidents of resistance to officers. These are followed by police retaliation, which results in escalating hostilities." In other words, abusive law enforcement resulted in an ever-increasing progression of violence that Chicanos proved powerless to overcome. So they protested on numerous occasions to show their displeasure with the police.[105]

Chicanos developed a number of new organizations to protest police brutality and fight for their rights. One of the most important groups to form was MAYO. José Angel Gutiérrez, a volunteer for the 1963 Crystal City campaign of "Los Cinco Candidatos," spearheaded MAYO's development in 1967. Gutiérrez, like many Chicanos, was deeply disappointed by the failure of the *Cristal* experiment. He founded the group and later RUP, in part, to recapture the political successes of 1963. Gutiérrez formed MAYO with his college friends Mario Compeán, William "Willie" Velásquez, Ignacio Pérez, and Juan Patlán. These five, who called themselves "Los Cinco" in reference to the 1963 campaign, hoped to create the Mexican American version of SNCC. In many ways, they did.[106]

MAYO addressed numerous issues salient to the Mexican American community in Texas. The organization made educational reform, political organizing, and voter participation major goals. MAYO also took up labor issues and police brutality. According to the group's constitution, "the purpose of the Mexican American Youth Organization is to establish a coordinated effort in the organization of groups interested in solving problems of the Chicano community and to develop leaders from within the communities."[107] Los Cinco hoped MAYO would command protests in the state and lead the Chicano movement. In selecting Gutiérrez as president, the activists chose a fastidious organizer with an acid tongue who helped make this broader goal a reality. He would come to symbolize Chicano radicalism and Brown Power.[108]

The group's first foray into the national spotlight occurred during the 1967 El Paso conference, which the LBJ White House had sponsored to mollify Mexican American criticism of the president. Instead, the meeting served as a platform for Johnson's detractors as MAYO and its leaders joined a large group of critics. For the new Los Cinco, the conference proved inspirational. Reies López Tijerina and Rodolfo "Corky" Gonzales addressed the crowd. These prominent leaders tinged their speeches with calls for revolution and redemptive violence. Their rhetoric helped radicalize many Chicanos, and MAYO easily adopted this language.[109]

MAYO quickly organized numerous local chapters. In Houston, Yolanda Garza Birdwell and Gregory Salazar formed a MAYO chapter in 1968.[110] They focused on problems affecting poor people in the city's predominately Mexican American neighborhoods. The group borrowed the proposals of *El Plan de Aztlán* in creating "The Barrio Program" in 1970. Referring to the "Gringo oppressor," Birdwell and Salazar hoped to prepare local people for the "liberation of our stolen land." They called for armed resistance to white oppression, the boycotting of white-owned businesses, and control of community institutions like schools.[111] They also railed against the Catholic Church. Many Chicanos derided the church as an oppressor of Mexican-descent people. While Catholic priests, such as Sherrill Smith and Antonio Gonzalez, attempted to push the church in more radical directions, many activists dismissed the Catholic Church as an agent of change. "MAYO believes the Church is the enemy of the people," they argued.[112]

Although MAYO indicted Catholicism, the Presbyterian Church in Houston received most of its anger. Yolanda Birdwell and Gregory Salazar hoped to take over the vacant Christ Church in the Northside barrio to make their community control agenda a reality. Its white congregation had abandoned the church as Mexican Americans began to relocate to the area. MAYO intended to use the facility to offer students free lunches, as a community outreach center, and for job training. Instead, the Brazos Presbytery, which controlled churches in the region, said the mostly Mexican American congregation at Juan Marcos Presbyterian Church could occupy the vacant building. Although Juan Marcos's leaders agreed to implement a community outreach program, Birdwell and Salazar felt their plans neglected the community's secular needs. They believed that the Presbytery "gave the building to a Mexican-American congregation to avoid a confrontation with us." Salazar and Birdwell, therefore, decided to stick with their plan to use the building whether the Presbytery allowed them to or not. In early 1970, they broke into the vacant church, seized the facility, and proceeded to implement their own community plan.[113]

MAYO moved quickly to develop a community outreach program at the church, which the activists renamed the Northside People's Center. They introduced a morning breakfast service for barrio children, offered bilingual education, and provided job counseling on a limited basis. Unsurprisingly, the Presbytery harassed MAYO throughout its three week-stay at the church. Church leaders had the gas and electricity disconnected. They also obtained a restraining order that eventually evicted the MAYO activists. Frustrated by the Presbytery's actions, Birdwell and Salazar decided to picket First Presbyterian Church, the largest and wealthiest congregation in Houston.[114] Salazar engineered this protest as something akin to Martin Luther's dissent in 1517. On March 8, 1970, during Sunday services, Salazar posted a "Manifesto of the People," a list of grievances similar to Luther's 95 Theses, on the front door of the church. MAYO then picketed the church for several hours, chanting slogans in English and Spanish and generally disrupting the services. Birdwell denounced what she saw as the church's greediness. "They're denying [the community] the right to develop their self-determination . . . we're considering humanistic values and they are considering property values," she explained. Bertha Hernández, a barrio resident and one of the marchers, stated: "If they [the presbytery] would let us help ourselves we could get somewhere." The picketers left after services ended, shouting "We'll be back, we'll be back, Presbyterians" as they marched off.[115]

The youth organization continued to picket the First Presbyterian Church for several more weeks. The following Sunday close to one hundred protesters returned. On Sunday, April 5, the picketers entered the church during worship services and silently marched down the aisles with fists raised. They marched out quietly, but their intrusion angered church officials. The Presbytery sued the group again and obtained another restraining order, one that ended protests at the downtown church.[116] While MAYO did not succeed in creating an effective community program at the Northside People's Center, the youth organization inspired locals to call for greater church participation in the secu-

MAYO activists Yolanda Birdwell (second from right) and Gregory Salazar (behind Birdwell) pose with a group of Chicanos in front of the seized Christ Church, which they converted into the Northside People's Center. The facility provided important services for barrio residents, but it was short-lived. (Gregory Salazar Papers, Courtesy of Houston Metropolitan Research Center, Houston Public Library)

lar lives of Chicanos. Juan Marcos Presbyterian Church did begin offering neighborhood programs for residents, Birdwell and Salazar continued their activities in the Chicano movement.

While many other community organizations experienced resistance similar to Houston's MAYO, Chicanos found greater success in La Raza Unida Party (the United People's Party, or RUP). The prime mover behind RUP was José Angel Gutiérrez, who stepped down as MAYO chairman in 1969 and moved back to Crystal City. There he began to plan for what he called the "Winter Garden Project" in *Cristal* to initiate the community control model that *El Plan de Aztlán* detailed.[117] Gutiérrez used the project to galvanize support for a Chicano third party. At the 1969 MAYO convention, Gutiérrez, his wife Luz, and other activists convinced MAYO to form a political party. They officially founded La Raza Unida Party in Crystal City on January 17, 1970.[118]

RUP grew out of MAYO, and many MAYO chapters made support of the party a requirement for membership in MAYO.[119] Alas, RUP's eventual successes doomed its parent organization. Most of MAYO's leaders became the top officers in RUP. As a result, chapters throughout the state began to close. In Houston, for instance, Yolanda Birdwell and Gregory Salazar disbanded MAYO in 1971 to "avoid open disunity" with RUP. Others followed suit. By 1972, RUP had largely absorbed most MAYO chapters.[120]

RUP intended to elect candidates who would respond to the minority community's needs. With this objective, they implicitly criticized the dominant parties' neglect of Mexican American voters.[121] RUP broadcast this message across the Southwest. But the party first concentrated on elections in Crystal City. While much had changed since the victory and defeat of Los Cinco Candidatos, much remained the same. A group of Mexican Americans and Anglos ran the city council, but according to RUP the white power structure controlled these leaders. In short, they did not represent the people. RUP activists began to mobilize the Mexican American community to elect a new city council and school board.[122]

The party ran a slate of candidates in elections for city council and school boards in Zavala, Dimitt, and La Salle, three of the main counties in the Winter Garden. But RUP experienced many difficulties. Officials used procedural technicalities on petition forms and filing applications to kick RUP candidates off the ballot. Many whites, who remembered the 1963 "takeover" by Los Cinco Candidatos, resisted the party's efforts as well. The Texas Rangers also discouraged participation in RUP. Despite these problems, Mexican American voters elected a total of fifteen candidates in Crystal City, Carrizo Springs, and Cotulla. Gutiérrez won election as school board president in Cristal. In a humorous mood, he promised that Chicanos would not exclude Anglos from Crystal City politics. "We're going to extend to them bicultural and bilingual education."[123]

RUP's first political outing was an overwhelming success and inspired the Chicano community across the Southwest. In late 1970 the party spread to Colorado, where campaigns resulted in the election of two RUP candidates to the state house of representatives. Party leaders then planned for state elections in Texas. But the party ran into difficulties once again when voting registrars disqualified candidates due to filing irregularities. This forced RUP to rely on a write-in campaign. The election resulted in a resounding defeat for the fledgling party, which captured only one of sixteen seats. This stinging loss caused party leaders to reevaluate RUP's organizational structure.[124]

At this point, RUP was a poorly coordinated confederation of civil rights groups and activists. In 1971 party leaders met in San Antonio and, despite bitter factional fighting between Gutiérrez and Mario Compeán, drafted an official constitution and platform. RUP's constitutional "Preambulo" spelled out Chicano grievances, from "the hypocritical application of the law" to "economic injustice and racial discrimination." The platform focused on education, economics, social justice, and political rights.[125] The education plank noted that the "Raza Unida Party will work for a broadening of the educational policy of the State of Texas to include multi-lingual and multi-cultural programs for all educational levels, preschool through college." RUP further advocated "that all levels of school personnel including administration should be representative of the people of that community." Politically, the party pushed for a national voting age of eighteen and voting rights for immigrants, as well as an end to the war in Vietnam.[126] Finally, it organized local party caucus groups in most Texas cities to encourage voting.[127]

RUP reemerged in 1971 as a well-organized and reenergized third party. Its leaders chose "Venceremos en '72" as their campaign slogan and set their sights on the governor's race.[128] But to succeed, RUP would require more than a well-oiled party machine. They needed a candidate. Waco attorney Ramsey Muñiz proved a surprisingly viable contender. A former football star, he was handsome, intelligent, and a consummate campaigner. Muñiz spent much of the campaign traveling from city to city and glad-handing with local people. The party selected Alma Canales, a prominent MAYO activist and education expert, for lieutenant governor. Canales appealed to female voters. Some Chicano groups had a patriarchal and chauvinistic bent, and she helped moderate criticism that RUP opposed Chicana feminism. As an authority on public education, Canales also attracted voters concerned about school issues.[129]

Ramsey Muñiz interjected a humor into the campaign that appealed to his Chicano base and to radicals more generally. Scandals that plagued the state government in 1971 forced Governor Preston Smith to give up his bid for re-election. Therefore, Muñiz told a crowd, "I'm as qualified as anybody else to run a corrupt government." He also ridiculed Democratic candidate Dolph Briscoe as a racist who employed "wetbacks" on his cattle ranch. In his most personal attack, Muñiz claimed that Briscoe received shock therapy during the campaign and that he did not have the psychological competence to serve as governor.[130] Despite these efforts, the RUP candidates garnered only 6 percent of the vote (219,127 ballots), enough to throw the Democrats and Republicans into a runoff. Dolph Briscoe became the new governor.[131]

In spite of the loss, the gubernatorial race inspired RUP leaders. In late 1972 they called a meeting in El Paso to discuss the development of a national party. Nearly two thousand Chicanos attended and formed El Con-

ESTE ES EL LICENCIADO

RAMSEY MUÑIZ

CANDIDATO PARA GOBERNADOR

Ramsey Muñiz, RUP gubernatorial candidate in 1972. This campaign poster reads,
"This is the attorney Ramsey Muñiz, candidate for governor." Though he ran an excellent
campaign, he lost the election. RUP produced similar posters in English. (Courtesy of
Nettie Lee Benson Latin American Collection, University of Texas, Austin)

greso de Aztlán to administer the national RUP.[132] Instead of aiding the party,
El Congreso illuminated problems within the Chicano movement. José Angel
Gutiérrez hoped El Congreso de Aztlán would unite RUP with Corky Gonzales's Crusade for Justice and other civil rights groups. But Gonzales saw himself as the natural leader of El Congreso and hence RUP. He believed that his
ideas should hold sway and that El Congreso, the Crusade for Justice, and RUP
should all fold into one group. Gutiérrez disagreed. He pragmatically viewed

Although RUP's primary strength remained in Texas, José Angel Gutiérrez promoted the party across the United States. Here, he speaks to a group of Chicanos in Illinois. (Courtesy of Nettie Lee Benson Latin American Collection, University of Texas, Austin)

each group as an entity unto itself. Gutiérrez also believed that he should control El Congreso. The Congress thus split into two competing factions that accomplished few goals.[133]

At about this time RUP began to concentrate on the 1974 Texas gubernatorial elections. The party ran Ramsey Muñiz again, but the political infighting within El Congreso had seeped into RUP and damaged his candidacy. According to political scientist Armando Navarro, Muñiz and RUP chairman Mario Compeán had a dispute over campaign strategy. Muñiz wanted to push RUP into the mainstream by promoting it as a true people's party, whereas Compeán continued to view RUP solely as a Chicano party. While the party kept the "venceremos" campaign slogan (now "Venceremos en '74"), Muñiz frequently used his own English campaign slogan: "People Together."[134] To Compeán, the change implied that Muñiz had abandoned the Mexican American community. The feud culminated at the RUP convention in Houston, where the two men almost came to blows. Muñiz had the upper hand, and Compeán ultimately left the party. But the dispute occurred publicly. It was also visible in campaign materials. For example, a Muñiz speech contained the words "be *cool*—you are the *candidate*" written in bold letters as if to remind Muñiz that he was, indeed, the candidate. One wonders if his opponents needed such reminders.[135] These issues doomed his candidacy. While RUP scored several victories, including José Angel Gutiérrez's election as Zavala County judge, Muñiz lost (he received 190,000 votes or 5.6 percent).[136]

RUP's statewide defeats fractured the party. Ramsey Muñiz's subsequent arrests for drug trafficking further damaged the party's credibility.[137] The controversial statements of some RUP leaders also contributed to the party's demise. Among them was the "kill the gringo" reference made by José Angel Gutiérrez at a MAYO rally in 1969, when he told the crowd: "We have got to eliminate the gringo, and what I mean by that is if the worst comes to worst we have got to kill him." While "gringo" applied only to racist whites, many Anglos took such statements to mean that Chicano radicals, like their Black Power counterparts, wanted to kill white people. Gutiérrez tried to clarify his comments a few weeks later when he explained, "Kill the gringo. What I mean is we must kill the gringo economically and politically but not necessarily physically unless, of course, the worst comes to worst."[138] Albert Peña was more explicit: "The number one enemy of La Raza Unida is the gringo. When we talk about gringo we are talking about the white racist. Nothing more and nothing less."[139] But others were less diplomatic. At a RUP conference in Fort Worth, Ramón Tijerina, the brother of Reies López Tijerina, stated quite plainly that "the only good gringo is a dead gringo."[140] Whites came to view the words of Gutiérrez, Ramón Tijerina, and others with fear. This did not help RUP.

The reactions of Democratic and Republican rivals helped seal RUP's fate. Henry B. Gonzalez found RUP's "gringo" rhetoric reprehensible, calling it "the new racism." MAYO responded by censuring Gonzalez at its 1969 convention.[141] Gutiérrez and other Chicanos branded him a "vendido" (sellout) and a "Tío Tomas" (Uncle Tom). Answering the charge, Gonzalez said: "I have been called a Communist, I have been castigated as a 'Nigger lover' and I am certainly denounced as a 'dirty Meskin' [but] I oppose this new racism because it threatens to destroy that good will, that sense of justice that alone can bring ultimate and lasting justice for all of us."[142] Gutiérrez suggested that political rivals like Henry Gonzalez used his "kill the gringo" rhetoric to hurt RUP: "They tried the 'outside agitator' bit on me but it didn't work because I was born in Crystal City. So they changed gears. Then they tried the 'communist' one for a while—until they found out I was in the U.S. Army Reserves. Then somewhere they dug up my 'kill a gringo' thing." Such tactics were "the old tricks and lies of the gringo," and for gringos, he said, "I have one final message to convey . . . up yours, baby."[143]

As historian Ignacio García accurately summarized, "The years 1975 through 1977 were disastrous for La Raza Unida Party." The political infighting and perceptions of radicalism doomed RUP. The party's successes attracted increased competition from Democrats and Republicans, who began to co-opt RUP's message. By 1978, RUP was defunct.[144]

The late sixties and early seventies saw the headiest days of Mexican American civil rights activism. The Chicano movement challenged the status quo in a way that the more conservative leaders in LULAC and the G.I. Forum hardly thought possible. Activists in MAYO, RUP, and a number of other groups dismissed many of the tactics of the previous generation. In particular, they began to eliminate the whiteness strategy. As brown people, as part of La Raza, many activists found the whiteness strategy distasteful and insulting. For them, whiteness connoted membership in the gringo community, a thought anathema to Chicanos. Brownness more completely identified the majority of Mexican-origin people. It encapsulated the African, Indian, and European aspects of the Mexican American past. It embraced aspects of Mexican American cultural pride and reaffirmed the place of Chicano ethnicity in the United States. This change in ethnic identity went hand in hand with tactical changes in the Mexican American movement. Instead of asking to become a part of the system, they forced their way into the system. They also appealed to African Americans.

■ ■ ■

Mexican Americans and African Americans attempted to join forces during the Black Power and Chicano Power era; more unity occurred at this time than in any previous period. For example, the Rainbow Coalition established after the death of Carl Hampton united blacks and Chicanos in Houston. PP2, MAYO, and white radicals who were affiliated with the JBRL came together to demand an end to police violence. But the group proved short-lived, largely because blacks led the Rainbow Coalition and focused its energies on black people. Chicanos and whites abandoned the organization a few weeks after its formation. The coalition's spotlight on blacks frustrated Chicano groups like MAYO. Consequently, the Rainbow Coalition devolved into the Black Coalition, which fell apart, according to "Boko" Freeman, because the group was "impotent" and their efforts were "unsustained."[145] While it was a significant attempt to collaborate, the Rainbow Coalition once again demonstrated the limits of interethnic cooperation. Similarly, Dallas Black Panther leader James "Skip" Shockley recalled working with Chicano groups like MAYO, though he acknowledged that "a lot of Hispanics wanted to do their own thing."[146] And San Antonio SNCC/BPP leader Mario Salas noted that blacks and browns worked together in groups such as SNCC/BPP, the Brown Berets, and RUP. Salas pointed out that while only a few Chicanos joined the San Antonio SNCC/BPP, the organization attempted to cooperate with Chicano groups. Salas also joined RUP and ran unsuccessfully for a seat on the San Antonio City Council.[147]

The anti–Vietnam War movement was another area where blacks and Chicanos united successfully. African Americans did not create a distinct black antiwar movement. Mexican Americans had much larger demonstrations, primarily because Chicanos organized the National Chicano Moratorium Committee, an anti–Vietnam War protest movement. Though most of its demonstrations occurred outside of Texas, there were protests in the Lone Star State. Groups like the ACLU and SNCC joined the Chicano Moratorium in its opposition to the war. These organizations began to regard the Vietnamese as similar to nonwhite Americans. The people of Vietnam formed another brown-skinned community that the U.S. government oppressed.[148] The fact that the war was fought disproportionately by poor blacks and Chicanos signaled—for activists—a continued racism in the United States.[149]

One of the first antiwar protests occurred in Houston. At the demonstration, a group of U.S. Marines accosted an unnamed peace group. Lee Otis Johnson, shortly before his arrest and thirty-year jail sentence, explained that the fighting started after one marine called him a communist. Johnson responded, "That's better than 'nigger.' I'm coming up in the world." When another marine called him "boy," Johnson said: "That's why I'm not going to Vietnam, I have to stay here and fight for freedom." When he added, "I'll fight any one of you," the marines pounced on the peace group and wounded several activists.[150]

Other demonstrations followed—among them, protest marches on an antiwar Moratorium Day in November 1969.[151] That month, small groups demonstrated in downtown Houston and Dallas. The most significant protest occurred in Austin, where an estimated ten thousand people gathered at the capitol to hear antiwar speakers.[152] In ensuing years, protests followed a similar pattern. For example, in May 1970, in Austin and Dallas several thousand Chicano, black, and white protesters marched against the war. Although the marchers in Austin acted peaceably, police halted them at several points along the route. This intensified the demonstrators' anger, and they began to throw rocks and bottles at the police. The officers then fired volleys of teargas. They ultimately broke up the protest, beat several of the activists, and made numerous arrests.[153] An antiwar protest a few days later was more peaceful. In July 1970 MAYO organized an antiwar demonstration in Houston, where Chicanos and a few black activists marched and attended a rally.[154] At an Austin demonstration in 1971, activists shouted "Brown Power" and "Raza Sí! Guerra No!" (People yes, War no).[155]

The antiwar movement was one struggle that served to unite black, brown, and white people. Most antiwar protests in Texas involved white radicals. Chicanos engineered separate demonstrations. African Americans did not create their own antiwar movement, as they felt quite comfortable joining the one organized by Chicanos. And with blacks participating in their marches and rallies, Chicanos could lay claim to an even more radical movement. They had both Brown Power and Black Power radicals in their protests. The anti-Vietnam War demonstrations indicate that blacks and Chicanos appreciated the development of a united front against oppression and discrimination. The fact that so many Chicanos and blacks died in the war angered activists. As Ernest McMillan noted, blacks and Chicanos like himself were torn "by what was happening in Vietnam and especially with what was happening in terms of the number of deaths of young black men and young Hispanic men." Black Power and Brown Power activists came to appreciate anyone willing to help stop the war.[156]

The protests against the Vietnam War and groups like the Rainbow Coalition show that blacks and Chicanos often held attitudes about each other that were different from those of individuals in previous generations. They recognized the racism and segregation that each group experienced. Both groups focused on destroying deeply problematic structural inequalities. This common focus and the recognition of the similarities shared by blacks and browns encouraged a closer working relationship. Chicanos and Black Power activists came to rely on each other on several occasions. As Ovide Duncantell said, "We saw each others' poverty and we realized that we were all in the same boat." Chicanos, he suggested, figured out that there "wasn't any virtue in being white if you couldn't be white." Similarly, José Angel Gutiérrez pointed out that some blacks openly supported RUP. Ernie McMillan and Skip Shockley both stated that they appreciated Chicanos who opened a second front against oppression.[157] Cooperation for blacks and Chicanos in the 1960s and 1970s seemed to come easier than for Mexican Americans and blacks in the 1950s.

Despite the numerous examples of unification, blacks and Chicanos continued to have problematic race relations. Yet some Brown Power leaders discussed how Chicanos might model their movement on the black struggle. John Colunga, a MAYO activist in Dallas, stated that the "biggest thing we have learned from the Negroes is that . . . they have stayed unified."[158] But blacks did not look to Chicanos for inspiration in the same way. The leaders in SNCC and PP2 infrequently mentioned Chicanos. For them, issues in the black community remained paramount.[159] In some cases, blacks discriminated against Chicanos. On one occasion, a group of blacks attacked an antipoverty center catering to Chicanos in Dallas. They evidently envied the government aid that Mexican Americans were receiving. These blacks also saw Chicanos as white and as competitors. This discrimination helped divide blacks and Chicanos in Dallas.[160]

The policies of black and Chicano organizations contributed to disunity. MAYO guidelines limited black participation because the group did "not permit people of a non Bronze or non Spanish culture to be recognized as official voting members . . . such people may never publicly represent the organization." Since the concept of "bronze people" applied only to Chicanos, and since blacks did not have a Spanish culture, MAYO excluded blacks as well as Anglos.[161] While MAYO leaders felt strongly about ending racism, especially the racism that blacks and Chicanos harbored toward each other, MAYO policies were discriminatory. SNCC's own racial outlook mirrored MAYO's. Beginning in 1964, committee leaders debated the value of having white people in the organization. A few years later, when SNCC became a leading Black Power organization, they kicked all whites out of the group. These "whites" included Elizabeth "Betita" Martínez and María Varela, the only two Mexican Americans working with SNCC. SNCC dismissed Martínez and Varela even though neither woman self-identified as white.[162] These actions were discriminatory and undermined black/brown cooperation. In the Dallas SNCC, Ernest McMillan, who sympathized with Chicanos, expelled Jesus Arredondo—the only Chicano in the group. "When the Black Power movement began to pick up people who came around were looking at him [Arredondo] like 'Why is he here?'" McMillan explained, he told Arredondo "Why don't you go organize among your people, and let's stay in contact, but you can't be around us now." While McMillan later regretted this decision, the end result contributed to disunity with Chicanos.[163]

Parallel institutions allowed blacks and Chicanos to continue working separately. The programs developed by MAYO, SNCC, PP2, and the BPP show this parallel working relationship. For example, while MAYO ran the Northside People's Center, the Houston SNCC operated the King Center, an outreach program that duplicated the activities Chicanos introduced at Christ Church. Separate organizations allowed for each group to work for its constituent communities. While Brown and Black Power groups occasionally joined forces, there was no long-standing unification. Separate institutions, then, kept blacks and Chicanos separated.[164]

Like MAYO, RUP experienced difficulty cooperating with African Americans. The party had neglected the black vote in 1972 by appealing almost exclusively to its Mexican American constituency. Although the SCLC's Ralph Abernathy and Corretta Scott King endorsed Ramsey Muñiz for governor in 1972, only a few other black leaders in Texas did.[165] But in 1974, Muñiz made attracting the black vote an important plank in his gubernatorial campaign. He concentrated on winning the African American, Mexican American, and liberal white vote with his "People Together" campaign slogan.[166] At the same time, however, Muñiz moved cautiously, explaining at the RUP state convention in Houston that a "true black-brown coalition is possible only after Chicanos and blacks have first formed coalitions among themselves." As in previous decades, Muñiz essentialized the experiences of both groups. "I can't organize the blacks," he stated, "and the blacks can't organize me." While he spoke abstractly about unity, Muñiz's actions on the ground prevented a close working relationship with African Americans.[167]

Mexican American whiteness remained another barrier to unity. Some leaders continued to pressure the state and federal government to categorize Mexican Americans as white in the late 1960s and early 1970s. In 1967 George Sánchez complained about census designations for schoolchildren on HEW forms. Calling the department "ridiculous" and "bumbling," he demanded that it "place 'mexicans' in the variegated Caucasoid group."[168] HEW agreed to change the designations on the forms so Mexican Americans could classify themselves as white.[169] In 1968 the G.I. Forum endorsed Richard Nixon for president largely because Democratic challenger Hubert Humphrey misspoke when discussing Mexican Americans. "I have heard some people say that jobs for Mexican Americans and Negros [sic] can only come by taking them away from whites," Humphrey stated. "Let me tell you . . . that couldn't be more wrong." Forum leaders censured Humphrey because he "placed our Mexican American citizens in a category other than white!" As in years past, Humphrey's use of "Negro" and "Mexican American" in the same sentence had offended.[170] Moreover, Dr. Hector P. García attacked the head of Texas's welfare department for attributing Chicano poverty to ethnicity. García retorted, "We are white Caucasians as much as he is."[171]

The concept of Mexican American brownness developed slowly. It would take a number of legal precedents, usually involving school desegregation cases championed by the Mexican American Legal Defense and Education Fund (MALDEF), to make Chicanos brown. Activists widely debated the concept of Mexican Americans as a brown race. *El Plan de Aztlán* referred to the Americas as a "Bronze Continent" and to Chicanos as "a Bronze People with a Bronze Culture." The Del Rio Mexican-American Manifesto used similar language when it observed: "Brown is the common denominator of the largest number of us—a glorious reminder of our Aztec and Mayan heritage."[172] Radical groups like MAYO and RUP also made frequent references to Chicanos as brown people.[173] The shift to brownness represented a fundamental change in the racial outlook of many Mexican Americans. As an ethnic minority, they could more freely utilize the Fourteenth Amendment. Similarly, Mexican Americans could claim some of the benefits that blacks enjoyed, including developing affirmative action programs. Finally, brownness did ease tensions between Chicanos and blacks. As brown people, Mexican Americans could become the allies of blacks.

The evolving Chicano consciousness helped radicalize older Mexican American civil rights groups.[174] LULAC, under the leadership of its president Alfred Hernández—who had joined the Minimum Wage March and walked out of the EEOC meeting in New Mexico—began to support direct action protests. He also began to work more closely with black activists. He spoke at the 1967 Rice University teach-ins organized by F. D. Kirkpatrick,[175] and he called for increased Chicano militancy at the 1968 LULAC National Convention.[176] In a speech before the Dallas chapter of LULAC, Hernández praised black militancy. "Some say we pattern [ourselves after] the black American," he said; "I say more power to them because we are learning from them." He indicated that he had modeled the EEOC walkout after black protests.[177]

But LULAC still contained a very conservative faction, one that disagreed with Hernández's activism. Participation in protests led to Hernández's ouster in 1967 after two terms as president. He was replaced by the more conservative Roberto Ornelas, who opposed Black Power. In a 1967 message, LULAC specifically targeted Stokely Carmichael, the militant chairman of SNCC. The league claimed that Carmichael, SNCC, and Black Power advocates everywhere participated in a communist conspiracy. "The Mexican-American will assil [*sic*] the 'burn american' preachings of the psychopathic lunatic [Carmichael]," the LULAC News intoned.[178] Alfred Hernández countered this viewpoint at the 1968 LULAC convention, where he said: the "black people of this country are now setting the example for us to follow . . . the Mexican-American community has to run now to catch up."[179]

Clearly, then, in the late sixties and early seventies many rearguard leaders retained a prominent role in the Mexican American struggle for rights, existing side by side with their Chicano counterparts. And while animosity frequently divided conservative Mexican Americans and radical Chicanos, they continued to fight for the same basic goals. They also continued to fight alone. While they spoke about uniting with blacks, most of these leaders—whether they self-identified as Chicanos or Mexican Americans—actually did little to join with blacks. African Americans similarly failed to unite with Mexican Americans. Some blacks regarded Mexican Americans as whites; others saw Chicano problems as dissimilar to black problems.[180] As MAYO's Gregory Salazar honestly noted, "It is difficult for chicanos and black people to understand and work with each other because of the enormous cultural differences and especially because of the racist attitudes which both groups have toward one another."[181] While Salazar and others hoped to overcome these differences, they had difficulty doing so.

In addition to race, fear and competition kept Black and Chicano Power radicals divided. Some Mexican American leaders continued to believe that blacks would monopolize government aid and political power. "Many fear that the militancy of the Negro will leave the Mexican without a fair share of programs stemming from the war on poverty," Mexican American Studies scholars Joan Moore and Ralph Guzman argued. Those who appreciated black radicalism seemed to nonetheless misunderstand the relationship between brown and black people. Moore and Guzman maintained that "the problem of competition is less among people on the community level and more among the professionals," although they offered no proof for this assertion. However, they correctly noted that "minority coalitions have never done well in the Southwest."[182] Others were equally pessimistic about the chances of coalitions. For instance, a "tri-ethnic" committee in San Antonio disbanded after only a few weeks of operation because, according to one Mexican American leader, "the council was completely Negro-oriented."[183] SNCC leaders in San Antonio discussed forming a coalition with RUP in 1972, but a local RUP leader acknowledged that "it's going to be hard to change the generally hostile attitude the two minorities have toward political cooperation." The *San Antonio Express* pointed out that African Americans were apprehensive about coalitions with Chicanos.[184] This stemmed from the fact that Chicanos constituted a larger, more politically powerful minority. Coalition building for blacks meant having to share limited power with a more powerful group. As San Antonio activist Harry Burns asserted, cooperation "would cause some of the benefits to be split . . . they would be competing with us . . . for political positions."[185] African Americans in San Antonio were reluctant to relinquish their tenuous hold on power.

Others incorrectly conceptualized the point of black/brown coalitions. As Ramsey Muñiz stated, "I can't organize the blacks and the blacks can't organize me."[186] He reiterated these sentiments when he argued that he "would be deceiving the Blacks by saying I can save them, Black people will save themselves, Mexicanos are going to save themselves."[187] While this statement was realistic, Muñiz once again disassociated the experiences of blacks and Chicanos, making Chicano and black problems unique to each group. But Muñiz probably could have led blacks, and black candidates could have led Chicanos, if they had tried. Henry B. Gonzalez had proved this more than a decade earlier. Reverend Claude Black analyzed the essentialism of blacks and Chicanos as "a sense of oneness" that can destroy the potential for unity. Boko Freeman commented similarly when he said that PP2 and the Black Panthers wanted Black Power "for black people, but we also looked at brown power for brown people, yellow power for yellow people, and even white power for white people." While Freeman did not negate unity with other groups, he indicated that each group had to develop its own sense of "power" before unification could occur. Ernest McMillan contended that, while not the root cause of disunity, racial essentialism did divide blacks and browns. Essentialism "was more about looking at 'me first,'" McMillan explained; "it's a product of individualism."[188] Instead of uniting different groups, as these activists certainly hoped, their words showed the bifurcation of both movements.

Some black and Chicano leaders blamed each other for the divided black and Chicano relationship. Robert Hilliard, the only African American on the San Antonio City Council, said that competition created by poverty programs meant that "each group is fighting over the crumbs being given out." Similarly, San Antonio civil rights leader George Sutton noted that "the blacks are not the creators of discrimination, so it is not incumbent upon us to solve it." By dismissing a black role in battling discrimination, Sutton simultaneously rejected working with Chicanos to end discrimination.[189] In Houston, when MAYO dissolved, reporters asked Yolanda Birdwell if she would organize with blacks. "I can't identify with the . . . Black Panthers," she stated, "because we, Chicanos, are different, subject to the same oppression but we see things from a different view point."[190] While she acknowledged a shared oppression, she could not visualize working with African Americans to eradicate racism. Birdwell, Hilliard, Sutton, Muñiz, and others seemed to feel that blacks and Chicanos were too different for unification.

Chicanos and blacks both worked for community control, but they used different tactics to achieve this goal. While each group employed a confrontational rhetoric, Black Power radicals like Ovide "10-pig" Duncantell and Carl Hampton were far more extreme in their oratory than most Chicanos. José Angel Gutiérrez and Yolanda Birdwell may have made statements about violence, but they did not back up their declarations with gunplay. When fighting for community control, both groups stressed cultural pride and nationalism, but they did so differently and often only for their own people. As Mario Salas observed, both "narrow nationalism" and "revolutionary nationalism" existed during this period. "Revolutionary nationalism was the belief that you can have pride in your culture, in your ethnicity . . . but not at the expense of hating anyone else or raising yourself above anyone else . . . whereas the narrow nationalists [said] 'It's my ethnicity first, it's my culture is number one.'" This concept was echoed by the Chicano movement anthem "Mi Raza Primero" (my people first). Ernest McMillan recognized that ideas of "me, my people" damaged interethnic relations: "When you see your family as only those who speak your language, or dress like you, look like you, then you're not going to be open to helping anybody else." Salas and McMillan acknowledged that activist blacks and Chicanos had to battle the forces of "narrow nationalism," in some cases unsuccessfully.[191] In short, Chicano Power and Black Power were dissimilar.

Americans have generally vilified Black and Chicano Power. People living in the late 1960s and early 1970s saw both as indistinguishable. They represented identically distasteful themes of violence, racism, and anti-Americanism. But these perceptions proved false in Texas. Most Black and Brown Power activists did not advocate violence. Rather, they promoted self-defense, an altogether different concept with a long history in the United States. Blacks worked to create defensive groups to guard the black community. Aside from a few cases where Chicano formed chapters of the Brown Berets, most Chicanos did not develop self-defense groups. While Black and Brown Power may have demonstrated shades of racism toward whites, activists applied that racism only to those who acted prejudicially toward blacks and Chicanos. In the words of Chicanos, only the "gringo" was the enemy. Rather than being anti-American, many Chicanos and blacks desired a reformed vision of the American body politic—an integrated and nondiscriminatory America. They wanted greater inclusion and they stood ready to fight for it.

Categorizing Black Power and Brown Power in similar terms has led to some rather superficial generalizations about both movements. If Brown Power and Black Power mirrored one another, if they were the same, then surely blacks and Chicanos worked amicably together. Contrary to popular discernment, Black Power and Brown Power did not equal each other. Chicanos and blacks clearly overcame their differences to join forces on several occasions; just as often, however, these differences divided the movements and cooperation was short-lived. While the Black Power and Brown Power movements occurred simultaneously, unity proved elusive.

Pawns, Puppets, and Scapegoats

School Desegregation in the Late 1960s and Early 1970s

In 1970 the Houston Independent School District (HISD) implemented a new integration plan to comply with the *Brown v. Board of Education* decision. This plan integrated only African American and Mexican American schools, which Chicanos and blacks viewed as discriminatory. Chicanos protested by boycotting the HISD and forming separate Huelga Schools (strike schools). They hoped that blacks would join their cause. Indeed, a number of black civil rights groups supported the boycott, especially the NAACP. But African American backing of the Huelga Schools proved largely rhetorical. Since Mexican Americans protested the HISD's decision to integrate blacks and Chicanos, some African Americans worried that Chicanos simply did not want to attend school with blacks. When a few Chicanos uttered racist opinions about black people, the African American community felt betrayed. Unification once again eluded these groups.[1]

The African American and Mexican American civil rights movements both focused sustained attention on school issues in the 1960s and 1970s. With the advent of new integration strategies and the creation of bilingual education programs, the debate over school desegregation became wide ranging. Texans loved to flaunt their successes in integrating schools, and many found much to praise in the desegregation efforts. According to a variety of sources, Texas had the highest percentage in the nation of black students attending integrated schools. But that number amounted to only 34 percent.[2] And while local officials generally applauded the progress of integrating blacks, they could not say the same for Mexican Americans. According to the U.S. Civil Rights Commission, in terms of educating Mexican Americans, Texas ranked worst among all the states.[3] Indeed, Texas schools remained segregated in the 1950s, 1960s, and 1970s. As late as 1978, one study found that 101 schools in Houston — just over half of the total number of schools in the city — remained one-race schools. Houston also still had a large number of predominately Mexican American schools.[4] In Dallas, federal judges committed to segregation delayed integration for decades.[5] Although San Antonio, Corpus Christi, and other cities began integrating schools in the 1950s, most districts still had some ground to cover.[6] In South Texas, students continued to have significant problems with administrators over curriculum, dress code, and the establishment of bilingual education programs.[7]

Both civil rights movements persisted in their battles for integrated schools. Blacks continued to protest segregated education and demand integrated schools for their children. They also reacted to the busing debate that was sweeping the country. Blacks attempted to form coalitions with Mexican American allies to challenge segregated schooling. And like blacks, Chicanos developed new strategies in their fight for integrated schools. Among them was their dismissal of the whiteness strategy in favor of a brownness strategy. New groups like MALDEF pushed for legal recognition of Chicanos as an identifiable minority to promote integration. They also protested segregated schooling in many Texas communities.

Education issues and school desegregation continued to deeply concern Mexican Americans. They challenged racist and recalcitrant school districts by funding lawsuits and by pursuing direct action demonstrations. Brown Power remained the order of the day; to force schools to comply with their demands, activists began to work to make Chicanos brown. This debate over Mexican American brownness reached a fever pitch in the late 1960s. The formation of MALDEF proved a major development in this regard. The group evolved from discussions between LULAC president Alfred Hernández and Jack Greenberg, the head of the NAACP's Legal Defense Fund (LDF).[8] Greenberg was "quite anxious to extend its [LDF] services to Mexican-Americans who are experiencing the same kind of discrimination problems which Negroes have experienced in the South."[9] But Mexican American leaders, committed to founding a group dedicated to Chicanos, created MALDEF.[10]

The organization officially began operations in 1968, when Pete Tijerina acquired a $2.2 million Ford Foundation grant for five years of funding. The grant helped secure MALDEF's future, and Tijerina became its first president.

The group soon began challenging the discrimination of Mexican Americans throughout Texas and the Southwest. MALDEF's greatest achievement was to acquire legal recognition of Mexican Americans as a brown people. By racially repositioning Mexican Americans as an identifiable minority group, Chicanos could more easily rely on the equal protection granted by the Fourteenth Amendment.[11]

The legal debate over brownness came to a head in Corpus Christi in 1968. As in other locales, the city's school district implemented a desegregation plan that integrated blacks and Chicanos, a process soon to be known as "pairing" or "lumping." For example, grades 1 and 3 from a majority black school would integrate with grades 2 and 4 from a white school. But in most pairing or lumping plans, districts combined predominately African American and Mexican American schools. Because the state classified Chicanos as white, the pairing plans legally desegregated the schools. Of course, these plans left Anglo children unaffected by integration, the district's desired result.[12]

A group of Chicano and African Americans parents, assisted by the local steelworkers union and MALDEF lawyers, brought suit to end this practice. In *Cisneros v. Corpus Christi Independent School District*, attorneys James de Anda and Chris Dixie argued that the district discriminated against nonwhite students. Instead of maintaining that Mexican Americans were white and that the school district should integrate them with the Anglo children, the attorneys asserted that the district should integrate all pupils—black, white, and brown. De Anda and Dixie further contended that the district had violated the Fourteenth Amendment rights of blacks and Mexican Americans. But in order to prove this, the court had to acknowledge that Chicanos constituted an identifiable ethnic minority. Judge Woodrow Seals found that on the basis of language, culture, religion, and physical characteristics, Mexican Americans formed a distinct minority. For Chicanos, Seals had acknowledged that they were brown, not white. He also determined that the district had segregated blacks and Chicanos, contrary to *Brown*.[13]

While the plaintiffs won the case, the decision only affected Corpus Christi schools. Chicanos would need much more to win acceptance as a new minority group. Nonetheless, the *Cisneros* case was a necessary step in racially repositioning Mexican Americans. A suit in Denver, Colorado, finally served as the straw that broke the camel's back. Denver had a tri-racial population that was 20 percent Chicano and about 15 percent black. The city had created a de facto segregated school system based on population concentrations of minority groups. In 1972, a group of primarily black families sued to desegregate and argued that blacks and Chicanos constituted minority communities that the district segregated unfairly. The district court found in the plaintiffs' favor, but only for a small corner of the district. So both the district and the plaintiffs appealed. That appeal eventually made it to the U.S. Supreme Court.[14]

The Denver case, *Keyes v. School District No. 1*, presented the Court with a dilemma. Although the justices had found in the *Pete Hernandez* case, and local courts had found in *Cisneros*, that the Fourteenth Amendment offered a method of redress for any group in the nation, they had yet to rule on the separate racial identity of Mexican Americans. As historian Guadalupe San Miguel has written, "The Court had to define Mexican Americans as part of the white population and pair them with black students, or define Mexican Americans as an identifiable minority and pair them with Anglo students."[15] The justices finally agreed with the prevailing sentiments of many Chicanos, noting: "There is also much evidence that in the Southwest Hispanos and Negroes have a great many things in common." The Court went on to conclude that only blacks and Chicanos suffered the burden of integration (or segregation, depending on how you look at it), because each formed a minority that the district prevented from entering white schools. In viewing Mexican Americans and African Americans in a similar light, the Court ruled that Chicanos constituted a separate and identifiable minority group.[16]

Many Mexican American leaders viewed these events positively. They believed that the Court's decision officially acknowledged Chicano brownness and eradicated the whiteness strategy. They also hoped that brownness would solve the problems that the Mexican American population in the Southwest had experienced for decades.[17] Yet local communities and some federal officials resisted recognizing Chicanos as brown. So MALDEF continued to push the brownness strategy. The group also engaged in a number of other civil rights cases pertaining to Mexican Americans and, by extension, to blacks, in Texas. For one thing, they pushed the state to equally fund minority schools. Texas financed schools through a property tax, and poor districts consequently received fewer funds. In 1971, in *Rodriguez et al. v. San Antonio ISD et al.*, a district court agreed that the funding scheme discriminated against the poor. But the Supreme Court rejected this decision.[18] It would take until 1989 for MALDEF to win a similar case.[19]

While MALDEF relied on legal tactics, groups like MAYO used direct action to protest segregated schools. MAYO's most significant school protests occurred in South Texas in the late 1960s. Students in the Edcouch-Elsa school district began boycotting classes in 1968 because teachers punished them for speaking Spanish. The teachers also ridiculed and insulted students who belonged to civil rights groups like MAYO. Further, the district had few Chicano teachers and counselors. Students responded to these issues by sending a list of demands to the school board. They asked the board to hire Chicano counselors and teachers, to teach Mexican American history, and to cease punishing students for belonging to political organizations and for speaking Spanish. To dramatize their demands, the students participated in class walkouts. The district retaliated by suspending the boycotting students.[20]

In Kingsville in early 1969, MAYO activists engaged in walkouts that duplicated the Edcouch-Elsa demonstrations. MAYO handed the Kingsville School Board a list of demands similar to the list created by the Edcouch-Elsa students. When the district refused to accept the list, students began a series of rallies and marches. Police arrested approximately one hundred demonstrators for disturbing the peace. After several weeks of protests, the school board finally accepted the students' demands.[21]

The most turbulent demonstrations occurred once again in Crystal City. As in the Edcouch-Elsa and Kingsville districts, teachers in Crystal City punished students for speaking Spanish. The students also disliked the fact that only one Mexican American served on the school board. In November 1969, led by local high school student Severita Lara, the students issued a list of demands calling for bilingual education and Chicano counselors and teachers, among other things.[22] When the district turned them down, nearly one thousand Chicanos boycotted classes. They did not return to class in the following weeks.[23] Instead, acting on the MAYO community control model, they established a tutoring program and held classes at separate "liberation schools" that emphasized Mexican American history and culture. Although officials predicted the boycott would collapse over the Christmas holiday, students returned to the liberation schools after the holiday break.[24]

The Crystal City students ultimately won. After a four-week boycott, the school district agreed to nineteen demands, including bilingual and bicultural education, improvement of school facilities, and the easing of punishments for dress code infractions and Spanish language use. With this agreement, the students returned to school. The situation continued to improve when Mexican American voters elected José Angel Gutiérrez as school board president in 1970. A year later, Crystal City schools offered courses in Mexican American Studies and bilingual education. They also established a grievance committee.[25]

Other cities chose a more confrontational approach and reaped the whirlwind for their recalcitrance. Houston serves as a case in point. As elsewhere, teachers punished students for speaking Spanish and for dress code infractions. In response, a group of high school students in 1968–69 formed Advocating Rights for Mexican-American Students (ARMAS).[26] In 1969 ARMAS began school walkouts. On September 16, in commemoration of Mexican independence from Spanish colonialism, an estimated five hundred ARMAS students walked out of four Houston high schools. They picketed the schools, then held a rally at a local park, but their actions had no effect on the HISD administration.[27]

The HISD resisted changing its policies. For instance, although activists pushed the district to recognize Chicano brownness, the school district continued to classify Mexican Americans as white. They also implemented a discriminatory pairing plan. In 1970 federal district court judge Ben C. Connally demanded an integration proposal from the HISD that would satisfy HEW. The son of popular New Deal senator Tom Connally, Judge Connally was more open-minded and liberal than many other district court judges.[28] HISD handed Connally a pairing scheme whereby buses were to be used to transfer students to one-race schools for integration purposes. Instead of busing black, white, and brown students to paired schools, the district paired only black and Chicano schools. Since the HISD still classified Mexican Americans as white, by pairing Chicano schools and black schools the district achieved "integration." Chicanos would serve as symbolic "whites" for desegregation purposes—"pawns, puppets, and scapegoats" as one activist put it—thereby ensuring that predominately Anglo schools remained white.[29] "By classifying us as Anglos, the HISD used the Chicano to show the federal courts that [schools] could be integrated," one Chicano paper editorialized.[30] Curtis Graves noted that the district played blacks and Chicanos off one another. He mocked the school board, saying: "Now that we have these new white folks that just happen to have brown skin, we'll have them be our integration, and we'll still be able to keep our schools lily white."[31] The whiteness strategy had come back to haunt Mexican Americans.

These events greatly frustrated Chicanos who had begun to promote brownness. But the school board vehemently defended the plan. Board member Eleanor Tinsley explained that the law recognized Mexican Americans as white and therefore integration with blacks meant "white and Negro integration."[32] HISD superintendent George Garver agreed: "The fact of the matter is, in this city and state, Mexican-Americans are white."[33] Chicanos were incensed. As the *Papel Chicano* observed, "All 'integration' in Houston means is changing from one bad school to another bad school."[34] Despite legal challenges in Corpus Christi that recognized Mexican American brownness, the HISD refused to consider Chicanos as an identifiable minority. In consequence, MALDEF leaders sued the HISD in 1970. MALDEF attorneys

Mario Obledo and Abraham Ramírez contended that the district illegally segregated Chicanos and blacks.[35] They further alleged that Chicanos constituted a distinct minority group that the district should recognize as separate from whites.[36]

In *Ross v. Eckels*, Judge Connally ruled against the plaintiffs. He disagreed with the findings in *Cisneros* and instead argued that Mexican Americans were white. Even more discouraging, Connally asserted that integrating Chicanos and blacks was an effective way to desegregate schools. The MALDEF lawyers appealed, but the Fifth Circuit Court of Appeals ultimately sided with Connally.[37] The pairing plan would stay.

These events triggered the most intense Chicano protests in Houston's history. Mexican Americans first engaged in a march to show their displeasure with the pairing plan.[38] More importantly, several civic groups formed the Mexican American Education Council (MAEC) to initiate community control of Chicano education, an idea laid out in *El Plan de Aztlán*. The MAEC was an umbrella organization intended to unite Chicano school integration protests. MAEC demanded that the HISD halt the pairing plan and implement a fair integration program. When the school board refused, the group led a boycott of the school system.[39] On the first day of classes in 1970, an estimated 3,500 Chicanos, or approximately half of all Mexican-origin students, boycotted HISD schools. Instead, they attended the Huelga Schools, or strike schools, that MAEC established in churches and community centers throughout Houston's barrios. Here, students received three weeks of instruction in Chicano history and bilingual education.[40]

The MAEC canceled the Huelga Schools after the so-called HISD mini-riot. At a meeting of the school board in October 1970, Chicanos requested permission to speak. They hoped to convince the district to discard the pairing plan. But the board refused to hear them and an angry verbal exchange commenced. Gregory Salazar pleaded for time to speak, but a police officer restrained him. This turned the verbal exchange into a physical fight. Police then attacked Walter Birdwell, the husband of activist Yolanda Garza Birdwell. She went to her spouse's aid and a free-for-all ensued. After the fighting had ended, police arrested fourteen Chicanos, including Salazar and the Birdwells. This mini-riot most clearly showed Chicano anger and an unwillingness to endure segregation.[41] A few weeks later, the HISD agreed to appeal Connally's busing plan and revise the pairing program.[42]

Despite the agreement, the HISD issued an unrevised pairing plan in early 1971, which Judge Connally quickly approved. In response, MAEC repeated the Huelga School protests.[43] However, the going proved more difficult this

Chicano students and teachers cheer the end of the day's classes at a Houston Huelga School. The Huelga Schools represented one of the most momentous Chicano protests in Houston. Although the HISD integration schemes affected African Americans, few blacks joined the Chicano school boycott. (Gregory Salazar Papers, Courtesy of Houston Metropolitan Research Center, Houston Public Library)

time. The strike schools had financial difficulties and limped along until April, when MAEC secured a $65,000 grant from HEW. This allowed the Huelga Schools to survive until the summer break.[44] As the summer began and a new school year loomed, MAEC planned to continue the Huelga Schools. By this time thousands of Chicano students had not set foot in an HISD school for nearly a year, and the situation did not appear likely to improve for the 1971–72 school year. Judge Connally again validated the HISD's racial policies, once more arguing that integrating Chicanos with blacks successfully desegregated the schools. MAEC and the MALDEF attorneys were dumbfounded. MAEC's director Leonel Castillo and MALDEF's Abraham Ramírez both insisted that Connally should step down. Lamenting his decision, Castillo was "sorry Judge Connally couldn't see the real world."[45]

Ben Connally had overseen the desegregation efforts in Houston for over a decade. Unlike many other southern judges such as William Atwell and T. Whitfield Davidson, Connally wanted the schools integrated. By continuing to classify Chicanos as white, he followed established legal precedents and the wishes of many Mexican Americans. He thus reacted angrily to Castillo and Ramírez's comments. "Never in the 15 years since the initiation of this action have they (Mexican-Americans) complained of this treatment (being claimed as white)," he asserted. "Content to be white for these many years," Connally chastised the lawyers, "now, when the shoe begins to pinch, the would-be-intervenors wish to be treated not as whites but as an 'identifiable ethnic group.' In short, they wish to be 'integrated' with whites, not blacks."[46] The judge seemed to have hit the nail on the head. He castigated the attorneys and Chicanos more generally for acting hypocritically. Connally asserted that Mexican Americans could not escape the burden of integration that all Texans now had to shoulder. But Ramírez and Castillo responded with egalitarian words. Besides restating that Chicanos were brown, Castillo argued that MAEC wanted a "triethnic desegregation plan"; moreover, Chicanos did not try to "escape integrating with any group."[47] Ramírez was more succinct. "We do not want to be disintegrated with the blacks," he said, "as much as we want the whole community to be integrated, not just the blacks and Mexican-Americans."[48] Despite these contentions, Connally refused to alter his decision. The Huelga Schools seemed destined to continue.

For the 1971–72 school year, the HISD once again implemented a pairing plan that duplicated the previous year's design. Indeed, the district added one all-white school to the 1971 pairing plan to appease civil rights groups but later removed that school from the new proposal.[49] The boycott began again when classes started in August 1971.[50] MAEC held a number of rallies and organized pickets to generate support for the Huelga Schools.[51] But this time the schools were a failure. According to Guadalupe San Miguel, group infighting and the lack of support from middle-class Mexican Americans doomed the boycott.[52] Legal successes also contributed to the strike schools' downfall. After Judge Connally had ruled against MALDEF in the Ross v. Eckels case, the group appealed. In 1972 the Fifth Circuit Court of Appeals decided in MALDEF's favor. The court noted that, based on the Cisneros case, the district needed to consider Chicanos as an identifiable minority when creating an integration plan.[53]

Chicano youths had found much to like about the Huelga Schools. Teachers exposed them to a positive vision of Mexican American history, society, and culture, a view that many had never seen in HISD schools. As one student said, "I learned so much about our traditions, our economical problems, our ways of improving our ideas for the better future we are heading forward to." The positive aspects of the Huelga Schools were amplified by several ugly incidents that occurred in Houston schools. At one paired school a teacher referred to Chicanos as "brown monkeys." Teachers also humiliated blacks and Chicanos by proclaiming that "half of you are on welfare." At another school, a teacher called black students "niggers" and Chicanos "ugly Mexicans." One Mexican American child was told to "shit in her pants" when she asked to go the bathroom. Indeed, such treatment highlighted the continuing need for the Huelga Schools.[54]

Unfortunately, the pairing plan devised by the HISD proved a useful tool for maintaining all-white schools, and other districts quickly adopted the Houston plan. In Dallas, the district initiated a pairing program that locals labeled a "lumping" plan.[55] This generated a series of angry protests. In the sixties Chicanos had begun pressuring the DISD to treat Mexican-origin students fairly. The DISD responded in 1968 by implementing a hiring program to attract more Mexican American teachers.[56] But in 1971 the district adopted a busing plan, followed by the lumping program. Chicanos universally opposed the idea. They had observed events in Houston and felt betrayed that the DISD would treat them the same way.[57]

As in Houston, officials in Dallas refused to recognize Mexican Americans as an identifiable minority. Instead, the authorities classified them as white and began to lump black and Chicano students together to integrate the schools. "Our kids are simply being used," Frances Arredondo stated. One of the few Chicanas on an advisory board to the DISD, Arredondo was a vocal critic of the lumping plan. "Chicanos are being classified as whites but the percentages aren't true," she argued. Some high schools had no whites enrolled, "but because of the percentage of Chicanos, it looks like it is integrated with a good proportion of whites."[58] Dallas also bused black students to white schools in North Dallas, which meant that the district incurred the wrath of Mexican American families and the Anglo community. Whites opposed busing and, more generally, the presence of blacks in white schools. Chicanos appealed to the Dallas City Council and in particular to Anita Martinez, the lone Mexican American on the council, to change district policies. As in Houston, the DISD refused.[59]

Mexican Americans presented a unified stance against the lumping program. But the district continued to classify Mexican Americans as white and send them to predominately black schools. Dr. Nolan Estes, the superintendent of schools, openly criticized Chicanos for attempting to change their racial classification. "I don't know what a Mexican-American is," he stated. Estes maintained that Mexican Americans' brownness amounted to a fantasy; the move to change their racial classification was an attempt to create a type of "positive discrimination." Nevertheless, Chicanos forced Estes to meet with them and demanded that he cancel the lumping program. When he refused, they began planning for a case that would reclassify Chicanos as a new minority. Chicanos succeeded in August 1971, when Judge William Taylor agreed in *Tasby v. Estes* that Mexican Americans constituted a distinct minority group.[60]

The reclassification of Mexican Americans did not end problems in the school district. Despite the *Tasby* ruling, the DISD continued busing black students to Chicano schools and Mexican American students to black schools as a way of complying with the Taylor's integration rulings. But the district did try to allay fears and open a line of communication by creating the Tri-Ethnic Committee. Indeed, Dallas, Fort Worth, Austin, and several other cities formed tri-ethnic committees to oversee integration matters. Committee meetings in Dallas proved acrimonious, with blacks, whites, and browns denouncing the busing and lumping plan. But the tension in Dallas ultimately dwindled.[61] Other issues like the shooting of the Thomas Rodriguez family and the murder of Santos Rodríguez provided a distraction from school problems. At the same time, Judge Taylor's decision to recognize Chicanos as brown had a calming effect on Chicano demands.[62]

Dallas and Houston were not alone in experiencing problems with lumping/pairing programs. School boards across the state attempted to pair Chicano and black students for the purpose of creating an "integrated" school system. This occurred in Houston, Dallas, Corpus Christi, Port Arthur, San Antonio, Austin, and many other locales.[63] Since pairing, and desegregation generally, involved busing, these cities also experienced significant resistance to busing. Thus, although numerous cities attempted to address problems relating to education and segregation in the late 1960s and early 1970s, most did so unsuccessfully.[64]

Many Mexican Americans came to view bilingual education as the panacea for problems in education. Bilingual programs began to flourish after passage of the Bilingual Education Act in 1967. Previous "bilingual" projects like the Little School of the 400 used an English-only pedagogical model. Bilingual classes offered a much more comprehensive and student-centered education because instruction occurred in two languages. In many southwestern communities, bilingual schooling also served to instill cultural and ethnic pride. Activists viewed such instruction as a way to satisfy student demands for cultural and historical courses that emphasized Mexican American contributions to the United States. Additionally, because bilingual schooling required instruction in both English and Spanish, these programs offered a new avenue of employment for dual-language teachers.[65]

Communities across Texas established bilingual education programs between 1967 and 1970.[66] The one launched in late 1967 by San Antonio city schools not only offered traditional bilingual classes, but also developed a new type of bilingual teaching and learning. Traditional bilingual education relies on an oral/aural philosophy that usually involves teaching classes, say history or science, in two languages. But in San Antonio, educators crafted a program that emphasized cultural studies to reinforce children psychologically, as well as a culturally sensitive focus on traditional subjects like math and science so children could better relate to the subject matter. In this way, San Antonians introduced a new pedagogical approach to bilingual education while simultaneously fulfilling some of the demands of the Chicano movement for cultural instruction.[67]

Not everyone appreciated the trend toward bilingual education. LULAC, for example, resisted it,[68] as did Henry B. Gonzalez. When Congress originally debated the Bilingual Education Bill in 1967, Gonzalez said that the legislation was of "dubious quality and unpredictable result" and that it would lead to a "competition in grantsmanship" among school districts. Instead, he favored a plan that would train teachers to better instruct Chicano students, although he failed to explain what that meant.[69]

Bilingual education, the protests over paired/lumped schools, the school walkouts and boycotts statewide—all of these events showed the vibrancy of Chicano activism on the local level. Combined with RUP victories, protests over the cancellation of the VISTA program, and numerous other demonstrations, the late 1960s and early 1970s witnessed the most intense and forceful protests in the history of the Mexican American movement. School issues dominated much of the struggle. The rejection of the whiteness strategy complicated Mexican American integration efforts, but the brownness strategy ultimately facilitated some measure of desegregation. Mexican Americans throughout the twentieth century had done a great deal to convince Anglos that they were white. In many cases, Anglos resisted. In the Chicano movement, Mexican Americans had to go to great lengths to convince whites of their brownness. Interestingly, Anglos resisted reclassifying Chicanos, preferring instead to categorize them as white so they could use them as integration's "pawns, puppets, and scapegoats." In the 1940s and 1950s, whiteness had offered Mexican Americans the best chance for ending racism. In the 1960s and 1970s, brownness became the best hope for doing so.

■ ■ ■

Like Mexican Americans, African Americans continued to push for school desegregation as part of the civil rights and Black Power movements. In Houston, the HISD largely refused to negotiate with activists. The HISD board repeatedly stalled on the integration issue. Black parents began trying to enroll their children in white schools shortly after 1954. The schools rejected them. Indeed, school board members proved so dilatory in their debates on integration that the best they could come up with was a "two per cent" plan, whereby blacks could enroll in white schools until a 2 percent quota had been reached. Tiring of these delays, the parents of two black students filed suit. In January 1957, one of these cases made it to the courtroom of Judge Ben Connally. He ordered the HISD to submit a desegregation plan and to integrate "with all deliberate speed."[70]

Connally's "deliberate speed" concept, one borrowed from the Supreme Court, allowed the district to delay integration. The school board repeatedly asked for additional time to create an appropriate plan for desegregation. Local blacks found they could not expedite the effort even after they elected an African American to the school board. In 1958 Hattie Mae White was the first person of color to be seated on the school board in the history of the HISD. But she found it extremely difficult to pressure the other board members to integrate.[71] In early 1960, however, Judge Connally ordered the school district to present a plan by June 1 of that year. The school board finally submitted a proposal to the judge in August. The HISD had created a stair-step integration plan, one that desegregated one grade per year. This would allow the district to stretch integration over a twelve-year period. Connally called the proposal "a palpable sham and subterfuge designed only to accomplish further evasion and delay."[72] The plan resulted in the admittance of eleven black children to three white schools for the 1960 school year. The district also engineered a complex system that governed how blacks could transfer to white schools. This system included a medical checkup, the requirement that parents obtain the signatures of three school officials to complete a transfer, and most oddly a "brother-sister" rule that prevented the admission of a child to a white school if his/her sibling attended a Negro school. Such procedures slowed integration to a crawl.[73]

Five years later blacks still harangued the HISD about delays. In March 1965, Hattie Mae White delivered a stinging indictment of the school board for doing "only what it is forced to do."[74] African Americans vigorously protested the failure of desegregation in Houston schools—but only sporadically.

In September 1964 a boycott of a Houston school had not materialized after three months of planning. A large group of black mothers intended to picket the school, but neither community leaders nor picketers arrived on the scheduled day. This flabbergasted Macel White, one of the main organizers of the protest. White later discovered that "someone claiming to be calling for me, contacted hundreds of mothers . . . and advised them that the boycott had been called off." Evidently a duplicitous segregationist foiled the demonstration. White said, "The phone calls threw a monkey wrench in our plans . . . but we are not going to let it sidetrack us." Contrary to her pronouncement, the fiasco successfully derailed the protest.[75]

In 1965 Reverend William Lawson began to speak out against the slow pace of integration in the HISD. Early that year he joined with the NAACP and helped create People for Upgraded Schools in Houston (PUSH) to work for accelerated desegregation.[76] PUSH soon organized a massive picket of an HISD school board meeting to demand the immediate desegregation of all grade levels.[77] On May 10, 1965, PUSH led a boycott of schools in which 90 percent of the city's black schoolchildren took part. Lawson also planned a major protest march. His Wheeler Avenue Baptist Church hosted a sign-painting party, and in May the march proceeded with over two thousand parents and high school students participating. Signs read, "Space Age Houston-Stone Age Schools" and "Jim Crow Must Go." The HISD resisted and agreed to make no changes to the speed of integration.[78]

Later that month, PUSH announced that it would sponsor a tour of Houston's slums and black high schools. The group invited HISD board members to attend so Lawson could demonstrate the problems in black schools. He also proposed a massive rally for the following Saturday to further spotlight the desegregation efforts. Lawson asked to meet with the school board's leaders in an effort to convince them to integrate the schools. Instead, the board proposed a meeting between PUSH and HISD's Community Relations Committee. Lawson balked at the idea, remarking "We will not talk to any small committee."[79] In June 1965 PUSH planned another massive march to protest a new HISD plan for desegregating several grades over the next few years. Declaring that blacks "can't be satisfied any longer with bones," Lawson demanded that all school grades be integrated immediately. "I personally feel the School Board has stuck a shiv in us," he declared, decrying the new integration plan.[80] He worked with PUSH through the summer of 1965, but the protests lasted only two months. Once again, however, PUSH brought school integration issues to the attention of Houstonians.

Despite the ultimate demise of PUSH, black Houstonians continued to fight for desegregation. They launched another school suit in 1966 after the HISD began a massive $50 million building program aimed at equalizing black and white schools. In other words, a dozen years after *Brown* the district tried to make separate equal.[81] The district's plan ultimately failed, but it slowed the integration debate. Also in 1966 the HISD introduced a "freedom of choice" integration scheme that allowed parents to enroll their children in any school of their choice, but this plan too failed to desegregate schools.[82] It took the school board four more years to move forward with a busing plan, which, when advanced, elicited considerable criticism from local whites.

Dallas also had significant problems integrating schools—mostly because of massive opposition on the local level and the fact that the judges overseeing integration supported segregated schools. In particular, Judge William Atwell acted as a local defender of segregation and firmly resisted the *Brown* decision. But after having his efforts blocked by the Fifth Circuit Court of Appeals on several occasions, Atwell retired. Alas, his departure did not end the desegregation fiascos. Instead, the more vociferously racist Judge T. Whitfield Davidson replaced Atwell. Davidson opposed *Brown* as much as Atwell, but he was much more vocal in his opinions than his predecessor. For example, in explaining the alleged shortcomings of *Brown*, Davidson declared: "When a child of one color is made to suffer an inferiority complex because of being segregated, then the child of the other color may likewise suffer an inferiority complex by not being allowed by law to be segregated." Thus he acknowledged (however facetiously) that blacks had suffered psychological harm because of segregation while simultaneously asserting that preventing whites from attending segregated schools would hurt them.[83]

Judge Davidson heard testimony on the next Dallas desegregation case in May 1960. In *Borders v. Rippy*, Davidson entered into the record one of the most bombastic defenses of segregation and the southern way of life in the history of the American legal profession. He began by explaining that "the City of Dallas has had exceptionally good relations between the two races and the question largely is how much haste can be exercised in applying integration by force." The judge reminded readers that the Supreme Court had left the speed of integration up to local officials. He then segued into a long-winded examination of ancient history, Negro slavery, and Reconstruction. But the heart of his argument appeared on page eight of his eighteen-page opinion. In a section entitled "Integration Rushes on to Amalgamation," Davidson wrote:

A law for integration of schools and consequent amalgamation of peoples was not made by the people of Texas nor its application invited by the schools of this city. . . . It is the belief of many thousands, no doubt the vast majority of the people in the Southern States, that racial integration will be followed by racial amalgamation. . . . Since most of the whites in the South desire to maintain their racial integrity, they would for that reason alone oppose integration in the schools.

In sum, integration would lead to the blending of the races, so Davidson threw the case out.[84]

In 1961, shortly after the *Borders* case, the school board submitted a new "salt and pepper" desegregation plan.[85] This proposal would keep the segregated school system, but "establish a third type of school for those who wished to attend an integrated school."[86] Known as a freedom-of-choice plan, the "salt and pepper" idea appealed to Judge Davidson because it continued segregated education while simultaneously allowing for some integration. But since the plan retained the segregated system, the Fifth Circuit Court rejected the proposal. The decision outraged Davidson; he called it "Un-American" and an "unhappy controversy." And while acknowledging the decree of the appeals court, Davidson declared that he felt "the effects upon the future [and he] must let the record show that at least one judge would dissent."[87]

By this time, much of the local populace, the school district, and the NAACP had grown weary of the court proceedings. The government, together with white business leaders and black civic leaders, decided to begin desegregating schools. The city engineered its "vast public conditioning program," and in September 1961 eighteen black first-graders desegregated schools in the DISD.[88] But for some blacks, these eighteen first-graders represented only token change. Such attitudes signaled that the desegregation cases would continue. Indeed, the DISD designed a complicated set of procedures for the transfer of blacks to white schools.[89] This kept the number of black students enrolled in previously all-white schools to a minimum.[90] In 1962, only sixteen new black students joined the sixteen (two of the original eighteen students having moved outside of Dallas) black first-graders who had integrated schools in 1961.[91] By 1964, a total of 72 black students, mainly in the first, second, and third grades, attended integrated schools. The NAACP therefore filed another case in 1964.[92] In 1965, the Fifth Circuit Court finally ordered the DISD to integrate the twelfth grade.[93]

Judge Davidson, angered that desegregation actually began, retired in late 1965. The far more liberal Judge William M. Taylor replaced him. President

Johnson appointed Taylor with the hope that he could implement an accelerated desegregation program. But Taylor found only stiff resistance from the
school board and local whites. The integration matters lingered for the next
few years with only token progress made. The first case Judge Taylor heard,
Tasby v. Estes, revealed many of the controversies that would come to haunt
school desegregation in the 1970s, especially in relation to busing. In October 1970 Sam Tasby filed suit against the Dallas school district. Tasby's two
sons had to ride a bus to attend a Negro school. Along the way, they passed
a more conveniently located white school. Tasby also had to pay to have his
sons bused to a segregated school. He and twenty-one others sued the district
to force a fair integration plan.[94]

Judge Taylor heard testimony on the *Tasby* case in November 1970. He first
needed to ascertain whether Dallas still operated a segregated school system.
A comprehensive investigation found "that in the Dallas Independent School
District 70 schools are 90% or more white (Anglo), 40 schools are 90% or
more black, and 49 schools [are] 90% or more minority [Mexican American
and African American] . . . 3% of the black students attend schools in which
the majority is white or Anglo." Judge Taylor argued: "It would be less than
honest for me to say or to hold that all vestiges of a dual system have been
eliminated, and I find and hold that elements of a dual system still remain."[95]
While he opposed "massive cross-town busing," Taylor implemented a busing
plan. Local opposition to busing materialized almost immediately. The judge
stayed his own order shortly after he issued it because Dallas did not own the
buses necessary to transport approximately seven thousand students. After
the Dallas Transit System agreed to supply the buses, the integration efforts
began again, although the furor over busing continued.[96]

Fort Worth also took a go-slow approach to integration. In the early 1960s
the city had the largest fully segregated school district in Texas. Local blacks
had started protesting segregated education in Cowtown in 1959. That October, an air force sergeant named Weirleis Flax attempted to enroll his daughter in a local elementary school. Herbert Teal followed Flax's example and
tried to enroll his six children in Fort Worth schools. In all seven cases, the
Fort Worth Independent School District (FWISD) rejected the applicants.[97]
The following month the two families brought suit. Fort Worth NAACP attorneys George Flemmings and L. Clifford Davis stridently fought for the
families involved. But the case landed in the courtroom of none other than
Judge T. Whitfield Davidson. The judge postponed hearing the case for a number of reasons, most childishly in 1961 because one of the district's superintendents was sick. As Flemmings pointed out, the superintendent was "a hired

Court-ordered bussing begins in Dallas. The district's bussing plan allowed for the local lumping program to commence. As this image demonstrates, bussing almost universally affected local black children. (Collections, Texas/Dallas History and Archives Division, Dallas Public Library)

employee and not a policy maker" who had "an abundance of assistants" who could appear in court. Judge Davidson, unsurprisingly, refused to continue the trial, calling it "not such an urgent matter."[98]

It took until 1962 for the suit against the FWISD, *Flax v. Potts*, to be heard. The case only went forward because it was transferred out of Davidson's courtroom and into the court of Judge Leo Brewster, a hardnosed Texas jurist appointed to the bench by President Kennedy. Brewster quickly ruled that the FWISD operated an illegally segregated school system in violation of *Brown* and ordered the district to integrate.[99] The FWISD appealed. The Fifth Circuit Court of Appeals heard *Potts v. Flax*, agreed with Brewster's ruling, and remanded the case back to Fort Worth with instructions that desegregation commence. The district, in essence, gave up and began integrating schools in September 1963.[100]

In some parts of the state, schools integrated only to resegregate a short time later. In Lubbock, a court order finally integrated schools in 1970.[101] The school district implemented a fair desegregation plan that sent blacks to white and Mexican American schools, and vice versa. After integration began, however, one frustrated white student shot and killed a black student in class. This horrific incident spawned a riot. Students fought in the schools, and a group of black parents beat up several whites and shot up the town. Police finally restored order, but the violence initiated an exodus of white and Chicano students from black schools. The city resegregated as quickly as it had integrated.[102]

Violence similarly afflicted other cities and other school districts. As noted in the previous chapter, fighting among students at Houston's Northwood Junior High School resulted, in part, in the TSU disturbance. Black and white students in many cases did come to blows once schools integrated. These students were part of the first generation to integrate schools and, as such, had some difficulty getting along. Black, white, and Chicano students bore the burden of integration, and sometimes tensions boiled over. But frequently the local media exacerbated the level of violence in the schools as a method of repudiating the concept of integration. Newspapers often made the situation appear quite bleak, an erroneous conclusion but one accepted by many Texans.[103]

As school integration issues proceeded into the 1970s, many school districts, like those of Houston and Dallas, implemented busing plans to achieve desegregation. Busing attempted to address one of the central problems with school desegregation: white flight. As urban locales began to integrate public facilities and schools, many whites moved to the suburbs.[104] With busing, schools could provide transportation to send black students to white schools for integration purposes. Districts usually did not bus white students to black schools. As historian Glenn Linden noted: "Busing was a one way street—for blacks only."[105] White flight removed a tax base that districts needed to support inner-city schools. Civil rights activists attempted to ease this problem by restructuring school financing, but the Supreme Court had nullified these attempts in the early 1970s. So districts and the courts used busing to "fix" school problems.

Busing created controversy throughout the United States, but it was an issue fraught with misunderstanding. After all, school districts had used the school bus for decades. Most Americans fundamentally misunderstood the purpose of busing. White people feared that districts would send their children to dirty, dangerous, and dilapidated ghetto schools to attend classes with black kids. Most white resistance to busing derived from this incorrect assessment. It also stemmed, more generally, from white racism. But busing never involved large numbers of whites. Instead, black children bore the brunt of busing. And when districts did bus white students to black schools, whites frequently boycotted classes. This happened in numerous cities but especially in Dallas and Houston.[106]

Anglos came up with a slew of arguments to counter busing. They said busing endangered their children, that the courts had overstepped their bounds, that busing was expensive, and that it did not improve the education of majority or minority students. The NAACP, in a report on busing, called these arguments "popularized myths." But perhaps the most often cited argument revolved around the fiction that students had to travel long distances by bus to integrate the schools. As the NAACP noted, this reasoning was suspect for several reasons. First, in most cases it was untrue. Second, if students had to travel long distances, those children had black skin. The NAACP stated quite simply that distance had little to do with opposition to busing. "It's not the distance," the NAACP contended, "it's the niggers." In short, busing had nothing to do with distance or safety. Rather, it had everything to do with white racism.[107]

In the early 1970s busing became a political issue. Politicians effectively used busing to mobilize a base of angry white voters.[108] In Texas, Governor Preston Smith encouraged foes of busing to complain to their elected officials. The public soon inundated Smith and other politicians with thousands of letters and telegrams.[109] Many citizens penned heartfelt messages expressing their personal displeasure over busing.[110] But others simply signed form letters created by local antibusing groups like Concerned Neighbors, Inc., the Concerned Parents Association of Corpus Christi, Concerned Citizens against Busing of Dallas, and Citizens for Neighborhood Schools of Fort Worth.[111] This campaign proved so effective that by early 1972 nearly 80 percent of Texans claimed to oppose busing, and over 70 percent favored a constitutional amendment that would forbid it.[112] Many state representatives opposed busing as well. Members of the Texas House attached an antibusing rider to legislation authorizing the TEA's budget for the coming fiscal year. The rider prohibited the use of state monies to fund busing programs.[113] Further, legislators approved a resolution demanding that the U.S. Congress call a convention to write an antibusing amendment into the Constitution. When this strategy failed, state lawmakers passed another antibusing resolution. But the vaguely worded motion did not specifically mention busing; rather, it more broadly called for a constitutional ban on integrated schools. This effort also did not succeed.[114]

African Americans experienced many obstacles in their quest for integrated schools. Of the battles they fought during the civil rights movement, school desegregation became their greatest failure. This situation was typical; throughout the nation school integration hardened white resistance to the goals of the movement. Much of this opposition came from white anxiety that desegregation might lead to "racial amalgamation," as Judge Davidson had stated. By the late 1960s, with Black Power on the rise, some African Americans began to distance themselves from the concept of integration and returned to the idea of equalization. If blacks had to attend separate classes, their schools should equal white schools in funding and facilities. This approach also met with limited acceptance.[115]

■ ■ ■

For both Mexican Americans and African Americans, unification remained elusive. A host of factors damaged race relations between the two groups. For example, brownness, much like the whiteness strategy, had the potential to complicate race relations with African Americans. The Huelga Schools exposed animosities between blacks and Mexican Americans. Some blacks openly supported the boycott,[116] but others found something disingenuous in the Chicano response to the pairing plan. If Chicanos protested pairing, which integrated blacks and Chicanos, what did that say about Mexican American attitudes toward black people? While the NAACP supported the boycott and the Huelga Schools, this support was primarily rhetorical. As Guadalupe San Miguel has noted, "Once the boycott began, neither the NAACP nor any other black group provided material or financial support."[117] Some blacks believed that Chicanos simply did not want to go to school with African Americans. Others viewed brownness as a tactic—Mexican Americans truly did not see themselves as people of color. Rather, they used brownness strategically in the same way whiteness had served as a tactic. As Fort Worth activist L. Clifford Davis argued, only "after the passage of the Civil Rights Act [and] we [blacks] begin to make some progress in the civil rights issue, you get the notion about 'do things for minorities,' they start hollering 'me minority too.'" Brownness was perceived as strategic, and blacks, therefore, did not boycott schools with Chicanos.[118]

The attitudes of some Mexican Americans confirmed African American opinions. For example, Chicano parents feared sending their children to black schools because they stereotypically viewed the schools as unsafe. They argued that blacks started fights with Chicano students. Individuals opposed to busing articulated similar themes.[119] "Black students are always bossing us around, picking fights," declared one Huelga School student.[120] "There's going to be trouble, fights," another intoned. And while many students maintained that they boycotted schools to protest the HISD's racism, others aired their own racist sentiments. One student said he would not attend his HISD paired school because he wanted to avoid being with blacks. Another claimed he would attend a Huelga School because there were "too many blacks" at his paired school.[121] Still another youth boycotted because "the niggers always get what they want—Chicanos never do!" One student attended a Huelga School because "there are no colored people" there.[122] A final student surmised that "the Blacks don't like to go to the Mexican-American [schools], and the Mexican-Americans don't like to go to the Black [schools], and the White people don't like to go to either one."[123] Such statements epitomized Chicano racism at the time and frustrated black and Chicano unity.

The HISD mini-riot also demonstrated animosities between African Americans and Mexican Americans. The NAACP's Reverend D. Leon Everett had attended the meeting that resulted in the mini-riot. Everett, the sole black member on the Houston school board, had sided with Chicanos and defended the school boycott. He had also pushed HISD to recognize Mexican Americans as an identifiable minority group. But Chicanos had insulted Everett on two separate occasions, once at an interracial meeting at the University of Houston and then at the school board meeting that devolved into the mini-riot. When a shouting match broke out at the HISD meeting, an unnamed Chicano yelled "We don't want to go to school with the Blacks because they are dirty!" This statement offended Reverend Everett. "Their position is quite clear to me," he said. "On the one hand they say they want recognition as a minority group. On the other hand, there is every reason to believe they are anti-Black." When asked if he would continue to support the Huelga Schools, he replied: "As a Black man, I have my hands full. I will join any group of oppressed people . . . but when that group employs the same form of discrimination that I have been up against all these years, I will cut them loose." Concluding his remarks, Everett stated: "Let them fight their own battles." Clearly Chicanos had alienated an important ally.[124]

The MAEC had great difficulty altering the sentiments of Chicanos involved in the Huelga Schools. More importantly, the group had trouble repairing the bruised feelings of African Americans. As a result, black support of the Huelga Schools remained largely symbolic.[125] Judge Ben Connally's statement that Chicanos boycotted the schools because the shoe had begun to pinch also demonstrated the fractured nature of African American–Mexican American race relations. Connally chastised Mexican Americans for what he viewed as hypocrisy.[126] By publicly reprimanding the Chicano lawyers and, by extension, the Mexican American community, Connally made light of the inconsistency in the legal strategies used to achieve Chicano school integration. Mexican Americans had, for decades, argued for integration based on the whiteness strategy. When that strategy backfired, they changed tracks and sought a separate racial identity. Why? Because, according to the statements of some students and parents, Mexican Americans did not want to go to school with blacks.[127]

Leonel Castillo and Abraham Ramírez certainly helped alleviate some of the tensions between blacks and Chicanos when they asserted that MAEC and MALDEF wanted a fair, tri-ethnic integration program. But the damage had been done. Most African American civic organizations only marginally supported the school boycott after 1971. In an attempt to calm this situation, MAEC organized a meeting of leaders in the Mexican American and black communities. The meeting failed because the two groups largely talked past one another. Chicanos attempted to get blacks to see the racism inherent in the pairing plan. African Americans tried to get Mexican Americans to appreciate their long fight against segregation. Chicanos censured black leaders for not bringing the Mexican American community into the integration process earlier. Blacks responded by accusing Chicanos of racism, both in the current debate and in years past, both when they were white and brown. Chicanos blamed black leaders for thinking that only African Americans fought for rights. Blacks then accused Chicanos of being "Johnny or Poncho come lately." The meeting devolved into a shouting match, with each side demanding that the other side recognize its sacrifices during the civil rights period.[128] These frustrations did not help blacks and Chicanos unite to integrate schools.

Events in Dallas also show the contentious nature of black/brown relations in Texas. As in Houston, many Chicanos in Dallas resisted lumping for racist reasons—they did not want to go to school with blacks. Similarly, African Americans did not want to attend school with Chicanos. In 1969 Mexican American leaders accused a group of black high school students of charging Chicano students "protection money." In exchange for their money, blacks agreed not to beat up the Chicanos. SNCC leaders met with Mexican American leaders about this situation. Matthew Johnson assured the Chicanos that the protection money schemes would stop and that SNCC had "never advocated warfare on blacks, browns or even white community children." But hostility was palpable. One African American leader supported the black students who had demanded the protection money and indicated that he disliked the Chicano leaders. The meeting accomplished nothing.[129]

The Tri-Ethnic Committee also achieved very little. Dallas leaders had created this committee to oversee school integration and help alleviate tensions between blacks and Chicanos. But the committee did not function as the leaders intended. Chicano and African American members fought primarily for their own racial/ethnic group, which led to frequent disagreements. The Dallas committee ultimately fell apart in 1973 after city leaders appointed an Anglo to head the organization.[130] Similarly, in 1970 Chicanos told local papers about an incident at a poverty center in which several African American youths had thrown rocks at Mexican American kids. The Chicanos wanted to meet with black leaders, but they refused. The press coverage angered African Americans, primarily because the reporting implied that the Mexican American leaders stereotypically believed blacks to be violent and aggressive.[131]

Black schoolchildren also were reluctant to integrate with Mexican Americans. When African American leaders aired their own racist sentiments about Chicanos, black students frequently followed suit. Three high school students described tensions in the paired schools in Houston. While asserting that they wished for "a big, open high school alliance . . . for whites, blacks, browns, everything," they implied that problems between blacks, whites, and browns resulted from intergroup jealousies. "We've got power," the students argued, "and the Mexicans don't have power and the whites don't have power. And they resent that." Power relationships within the schools obviously created interethnic conflict.[132]

Some of the solutions to school problems exacerbated these tensions. For instance, many Chicanos viewed integration as an auxiliary to assimilation. They coupled ethnic pride and resistance to integration/assimilation with cultural separatism. *Papel Chicano* columnist George Illueca accurately summarized how integration and acculturation affected the school desegregation discussion. He said that school districts hoped to inculcate American values in Chicanos students, but in so doing, they inoculated the students against their own cultural traditions. For him, schools served as a method of assimilation, something Chicanos should avoid. Thus, Illueca believed, "Chicano separatism can serve many positive purposes." MAYO also engaged in the politics of separation. Integration with whites, activists contended, implied the indoctrination of Chicanos with Anglo culture. Brown Power advocates wanted young Chicanos exposed to Mexican American culture, and separation granted that exposure. There is, of course, nothing inherently wrong with these goals, but in shunning "American" culture these leaders simultaneously distanced themselves from black people. Since school districts paired Chicanos with blacks, Chicanos did not refuse integration with whites, but with African Americans. Chicanos established strike schools for Chicanos. By their very existence, the Huelga Schools resisted integration. Instead of unity, Mexican Americans and African Americans came into open conflict over proposed desegregation plans. Integration included only blacks and Chicanos, which caused understandable friction between these groups.[133]

The assimilation/integration debate deeply affected black/brown relations. While African Americans could appreciate the cultural nationalism embraced by Chicanos, the "separatist" aspect of this nationalism applied to blacks as well as whites. The same thing could be said of black cultural nationalism. As Mario Salas noted, both movements struggled against the forces of this "narrow nationalism."[134] Blacks and Chicanos did appreciate each others' cultural nationalism. Indeed, they borrowed the intellectual underpinnings of cultural nationalism from each other. This borrowing, from music to food to tactics, and more directly the duplication of groups (Black Panthers and Brown Berets), in some ways reinforced each civil rights movement. Chicano and black cultural nationalism mirrored one another, and separatism and cultural nationalism often went hand in hand. By promoting separatism, however, blacks rejected integration with Chicanos, and vice versa. Separatism frustrated attempts at unity because, quite simply, separation *separated* blacks and Chicanos. By arguing for separate schools, Mexican Americans and African Americans both communicated that they did not want to attend school with each other. They dismissed the idea of working together and rejected unity.

By the late 1960s, some blacks and Chicanos had tired of the struggle over integration. White leaders and local governments had resisted school desegregation tooth and nail. Pairing, busing, and the hostilities they generated confirmed that schools would probably never totally integrate. Local districts used Chicanos and blacks as pawns and puppets in the integration battles, and both grew weary of this treatment. Given these issues, separatism is more understandable. A unified movement might have convinced local school districts to integrate all students. But this did not happen. Instead, each community looked out for its own interests. White resistance and black/brown separatism led to divided movements.

Throughout the school integration controversy, the rhetoric of Chicanos highlighted their suffering and downplayed problems in the black community. This further undercut a good working relationship with African Americans. Black educational gains in Dallas angered local Chicano leaders, who began promoting more radical tactics to obtain increased school funding from the government. "The Mexican traditionally has been nonviolent, obedient, even docile," attorney Frank Hernandez stated, "but now, with all the government's concessions to the Negro, the Mexican is beginning to say, 'Why should I put up with what my parents did?'" Although Hernandez's words certainly had merit, their tone helped separate blacks and browns. By asserting that the government had only made concessions to blacks, he implied that blacks hoarded government programs.[135] In Houston, Chicanos again argued that "of all the ethnic groups in the United States, Chicanos are the worst off." For blacks, this rhetoric was dishonest and hurtful. By downplaying black suffering, Chicanos elevated the moral imperative of their own cause while simultaneously discrediting the morality of the black struggle. Such ideas offended African Americans.[136]

Clearly school issues generated extreme tensions among all ethnic groups in Texas. The pairing/lumping plans exacerbated these tensions. Blacks and Chicanos tried to work together, although they often failed. But perhaps their willingness to discuss school issues points to a difference in the leadership of the 1950s and of the 1970s. At least in the Black and Brown Power era activists talked to each other. At least they tried to see what unity might mean. MAEC viewed racism as afflicting all groups. It tried to calm tensions by admitting that "some racism exists among Mexican-Americans toward blacks and anglos; just as some blacks are prejudiced against Chicanos and 'whiteys'; just as many whites are racist toward everyone else." The MAEC tried to persuade Chicanos of the benefits of integration, especially integration with blacks. This proved a necessary, albeit largely unsuccessful, attempt at smoothing race relations between the two groups. It is difficult to imagine a similar conversation occurring in 1955.[137]

Some blacks and Chicanos did attempt to form coalitions and merge their efforts to finalize school integration in the late 1960s and early 1970s. In Corpus Christi, Curtis Graves encouraged citizens to unite. "The thing you must do," he said, "is start building new coalitions, coalitions that obviously include all the racial minorities."[138] Certainly, some coalition building did occur. The development of tri-ethnic committees in Dallas, Fort Worth, Austin, and several other cities demonstrated attempts to assemble interracial coalitions. In Houston, blacks and Chicanos formed their own tri-ethnic organization in 1970. The Black and Brown Coalition (BBC) made an effort to involve all minority groups in the growing school crises. The BBC specifically disagreed with the pairing plan. In one flier, it stated;

The Black and Brown Coalition is a group of concerned blacks and Chicanos who are joining together to plan, coordinate and implement all efforts of the minority ethnic group communities in fighting the repressive and discriminatory practices inherent in the educational, the political, and the employment processes. We believe that the high ratio of our children's dropout rate is directly related to racist practices in our school system. We believe that the failure of our school system in educating our children academically and morally is the direct result of school officials' refusal to acknowledge and help minority group children. We feel that the present pairing plan insults the intelligence and dignity of blacks and browns and undermines the integrity of the U.S. Supreme Court. Following the successful methods of Christ, Gandhi, King, and Chavez, the Black and Brown Coalition pledges to fight our cause with every available means, and to promote the concept of human brotherhood.

Unfortunately, the BBC was short-lived. It did, however, serve as an example of one of the few groups that offered a unified stance against problems shared by both African American and Mexican American communities. But like other coalitions, the BBC ultimately failed to unite Chicanos and blacks.[139] At about the same time the BBC formed, Reverend William Lawson released a "Manifesto on Behalf of Black Children." This document, despite its title, recognized Chicano brownness and encouraged the school district to implement a fair pairing plan. But even Lawson only went so far. The fair pairing plan his manifesto foresaw joining "black and white schools or brown and white schools," but it made no mention of integrating black and brown schools or black, white, and brown schools.[140] Like most attempts to bring blacks and browns together, Lawson's manifesto saw unification in a limited capacity.

In 1972 the HCHR summarized race relations between African Americans and Mexican Americans in its aptly titled *The Black/Mexican-American Project Report*. Prepared by local educators, the report correctly noted that little information existed regarding relations between blacks and Chicanos because most Americans traditionally viewed "race" as a black/white issue. The report hoped to expand this view. It primarily concentrated on housing, newspaper coverage, antipoverty programs, politics, and schools. It found that both groups "retain negative stereotypes and misconceptions of each other." It also observed that social and economic inequalities contributed to interethnic tensions. The report generally blamed these tensions on Anglos because whites had prevented both groups from progressing economically and socially.

Some of the most provocative findings in *The Black/Mexican-American Project Report* dealt with race and the schools. For instance, the report argued that Mexican Americans suffered from a "double-minority" status. Because other groups perceived Chicanos as racially ambiguous—blacks and whites viewed them as neither white nor black—they suffered from neglect from both Anglos and African Americans. This conclusion did not consider how Mexican Americans had racially positioned themselves as white people throughout the twentieth century. But the study did accurately report other racial tensions—that Chicanos preferred the company of whites, while blacks preferred the company of Chicanos; that in schools blacks proved the least exclusionary of all three ethnic groups; that, contrary to popular opinion at the time, blacks were not more prone to fighting than other groups; and that all groups generally ignored race until racial tensions flared up. The study also found that 51 percent of blacks preferred attending black schools, 59 percent of Chicano students preferred attending predominately Mexican American schools, and 67 percent of whites preferred white schools. These numbers demonstrated that the majority of students favored attending their own schools, but also that blacks were the least preferential group of the three. As a corollary, 44 percent of Mexican Americans stated they did not want to attend classes with blacks, while only 11 percent of blacks said they did not want to go to predominately Chicano schools. The report noted quite clearly that "Blacks feel closer to Mexican-Americans than to Whites, but the Mexican-Americans do not reciprocate—they prefer to associate with Whites. As a result, Blacks are isolated from, and rejected by the other minority group in school."[141]

While these findings were thought-provoking, the report's suggestions for rectifying problems proved less than stellar. In fact, the study concluded rather blandly that whites should "seek to eliminate racism in the community." It also stated that blacks and Chicanos should work to reduce negative stereotypes, but made no real suggestion as to how they could accomplish this goal. While the study encouraged black, white, and brown students to meet in school for "reports, skits, and debates" so they could learn about each other, it did not suggest what the content of those modes of communication might be. The report did debunk the myth that black students were prone to fighting. It also noted that white and Chicano opinions that blacks caused fights reinforced negative stereotypes about black students. The study urged students to engage in verbal exchanges instead of physical fights but once again failed to explain how students could make that goal a reality.[142]

As a tool for uncovering the racism endemic to black, white, and brown students and their broader communities, *The Black/Mexican-American Project Report* did a relatively good job. But in developing a broader plan for combating racism, the report largely failed. In many ways, this study mirrored the larger debate that took place across Texas. Although Chicanos and blacks clearly understood the racism each held toward the other, no one seemed to know what to do about it. Instead of confronting racism, as the report suggested, both groups either accused the other of racism, talked past one another, or withdrew from the debate entirely by advocating separate schooling. This did not contribute to black/brown unity.

The school integration debates that occurred in the late 1960s and early 1970s duplicated the debates of the 1940s and 1950s. For the most part, African Americans and Mexican Americans in the 1950s did not unite for integration purposes, nor did they do so in the 1970s. While Chicanos racially repositioned themselves during the Brown Power era, the brownness strategy was only moderately more successful than the whiteness strategy. Some African Americans found the whiteness strategy offensive and the brownness strategy disingenuous. Blacks responded to both approaches by disregarding them. This, of course, did not endear them to Mexican Americans. Some Chicanos did not want to attend paired schools with blacks, which, of course, did not endear them to African Americans. Race had fractured the Mexican American and black movements in the 1950s. It did the same in the 1970s. Both groups continued to fight their battles separately.

Conclusion

The 2001 mayoral race in Houston pitted incumbent Democratic mayor Lee P. Brown against Republican challenger and Houston City Council member Orlando Sánchez. Mayor Brown, an African American political wunderkind, had served as police chief in Houston, police commissioner in New York City, and "drug czar" during the presidency of Bill Clinton before his election as mayor of Houston in 1997. Brown represented liberal, Democratic politics in the Bayou City. He made concerted appeals to Mexican American voters and had appointed a number of Hispanics to positions in his administration. Sánchez, a fair-complected, blue-eyed Cuban American, seemed politically out of step for the Mexican-origin community. He was a conservative Republican in a city where most Mexican Americans voted Democratic. And, of course, he was not of Mexican descent. Yet 72 percent of Hispanics voted for Sánchez, while 90 percent of African Americans voted for Brown.[1]

The Houston mayoral race demonstrated once again the Mexican American/African American divide in Texas. Mexican Americans voted for their candidate; African Americans voted for theirs. Despite Brown's appeals to Mexican American voters, he could not overcome Mexican American ethnic solidarity with Sánchez. By the same token, Orlando Sánchez failed to overcome black racial solidarity with Lee Brown. While this seemed to astonish many political observers, the broader history of African American and Mexican American relations shows that the political contours of this election were hardly surprising.

Throughout the twentieth century, and clearly into the twenty-first, unification eluded Mexican Americans and African Americans. While both groups fought a powerful and entrenched racial caste system, they ultimately did so alone. Blacks and Mexican Americans had many obstacles to overcome in their respective civil rights movements. Aside from combating segregation, poverty, disenfranchisement, and other forms of discrimination, they also had to overcome their animosities toward each other. In this effort, they largely failed.

African Americans and Mexican Americans began to challenge Jim Crow segregation in Texas in the early twentieth century. For blacks, the first task involved creating prosperous, stable communities. But segregation and racism hampered the feasibility of this approach. So blacks began to more forcefully challenge Jim Crow by pushing lawsuits such as the *Nixon* cases, *Smith v. Allwright*, and *Sweatt v. Painter*. Mexican Americans also hoped to establish prosperous communities, but they primarily focused on winning recognition as a group of white people. Successful legal challenges and appeals to state leaders demonstrated to Mexican Americans the efficacy of promoting white rights, although the whiteness strategy failed to eliminate racism. Between 1930 and 1950, the inchoate struggles of blacks and Mexican Americans gained momentum, but few leaders discussed uniting these separate movements.

In the 1950s, Mexican American and black civil rights groups began to engage in more confrontational tactics, especially when it came to the separate education of their children. For both communities, school segregation violated the principles of a fair and just society. Mexican Americans continued to argue that, as whites, their children should not suffer the burden of segregation. Leaders won a number of victories in securing white rights, but the whiteness strategy did not forge the promised integration that Mexican Americans desired. After *Brown v. Board of Education*, black civil rights groups urged state officials to fairly implement desegregation. In almost every case, elected leaders resisted these efforts. While both blacks and Mexican Americans engaged in similar attempts to eradicate segregated education, they did so separately.

The sit-in movement of the early 1960s exacerbated tensions between African Americans and Mexican Americans in Texas. Direct action demonstrations reenergized the black freedom struggle, which gave it many victories. Rather than face prolonged protests and possible racial violence, numerous communities began the process of integration. Mexican Americans seemed stunned. Many Mexican American leaders viewed direct action in a negative light. Protests lacked dignity and potentially tarnished the image of the United States. And while some Mexican-origin communities began their own, more aggressive demonstrations, particularly in Crystal City, on average Mexican Americans looked askance at black protests. Their negative perceptions damaged hopes for a unified movement.

Despite the opposition of some Mexican Americans to the sit-in movement, these protests ultimately helped radicalize the Mexican American struggle. When the Mexican-origin community engaged in the Minimum Wage March of 1966, it learned the value of direct action. More demonstrations followed. While the whiteness strategy remained, more aggressive tactics began to displace the fight for white rights. Meanwhile, the black freedom struggle continued with full force. Having fought and won numerous battles, African Americans focused on making the tenets of the Civil Rights Act a reality for black people. Some also hoped to unite with Mexican Americans. Booker Bonner, Moses LeRoy, and others looked to Mexican American leaders such as Albert Peña, Pancho Medrano, and Alfred Hernández for support and, perhaps, unity. This resulted in several short-lived alliances, but no long-standing unification.

The Black Power and Brown Power movements both held great potential for uniting blacks and Chicanos. Since Chicanos began to argue for a new racial status and to dismiss the whiteness strategy, they opened doors for cooperative ventures with blacks. For Chicanos, brownness most honestly encompassed the race of a majority of Mexican Americans. However, some African Americans seemed to oppose Mexican American racial repositioning as brown people, which blacks saw as disingenuous, opportunistic, or both. "Think about it," NAACP activist L. Clifford Davis said. "All prior to . . . 1964 and [196]5 in that timeframe, they were proclaiming themselves and trying to get the benefit of being white. But after, only after, the civil rights [act], when it became important—people were looking at color—that they started talking about 'me minority, me minority, me minority.'"[2] The black response to brownness frustrated Chicanos. Blacks also aired their own prejudicial sentiments about Mexican Americans, fought with them in the schools, and acted as competitors for antipoverty aid.

School integration in the late 1960s and early 1970s also bifurcated Chicanos and blacks. Both groups continued to press school districts to integrate fairly. But white resistance to school desegregation and the failure of integration offended African Americans and Mexican Americans. They demanded integration and were rewarded with pairing or lumping desegregation plans. Chicano opposition to the pairing plans, and the racist statements made by Chicanos in the Huelga Schools, damaged chances for cooperation between blacks and browns. Predictably, unity once again eluded African Americans and Mexican Americans.

A number of factors contributed to African American/Mexican American disunity. Certainly regional, cultural, and class differences generated friction between these groups. The regional breakdown of Mexican Americans and blacks frustrated a close working relationship between these two groups. Perceptions of cultural dissimilarities also played into the divisions between blacks and browns. The need for jobs and the desire for government aid and War on Poverty monies turned Mexican Americans and blacks into competitors, not allies. But race and racism provide the most consistent explanations for why these groups did not unite. Racial prejudice undercut chances for coalition building and cooperation.

The whiteness strategy proved particularly harmful to the development of a unified movement. The African American response to Mexican Americans and whiteness varied. Some blacks interpreted whiteness negatively. As activist Carol Sherman said, Mexican Americans "thought they were white. . . . There were Latinos and whites, and there were blacks."[3] Similarly, NAACP leader C. Anderson Davis recalled, "Mexican-Americans considered themselves white a long time. . . . They were not so proud to be allies with blacks."[4] Reverend Earl Allen also observed that "many Mexicans viewed themselves as part of the white community." For him and other blacks, whiteness "became an issue, it didn't make us feel very good. . . . We saw them as being as segregated as we were [but] they were somewhat split in terms of who they were and how they should proceed to establishing some degree of freedom."[5] The whiteness strategy offended these African Americans. White racial positioning reified the black/white binary and damaged black relations with Mexican Americans. As a result, some blacks came to view whiteness in a narrow light. "White" meant "anti-black," whether the white person was Anglo or Mexican American.

Whiteness was a complex phenomenon, and black people interpreted it in myriad ways. Some blacks simply chose to ignore white racial positioning and concentrate on problems in black communities. As L. Clifford Davis put it, blacks "were trying to fight our battles. . . . We just didn't get ourselves detoured from our mission because of what they [Mexican Americans] were doing."[6] Other blacks viewed whiteness as a contrivance foisted on Mexican Americans by deceitful Anglos. "The system had blacks and Hispanics split," argued Ovide Duncantell, because whites "had Hispanics under the impression that 'you can be white.'" But "they had no control, they could either accept what the system was offering to them or walk away." While Duncantell ignored the ways in which Mexican Americans positioned themselves as white, his analysis that the "system" split blacks and browns remains important. It shows that some blacks neither blamed Mexican Americans for the whiteness strategy nor held it against them.[7]

Of course, not all Mexican Americans embraced whiteness and not all Mexican Americans opposed the black civil rights movement. In the same way, white racialization did not mean that Mexican Americans automatically became prejudicial toward blacks. George Sánchez believed in whiteness but assisted the black movement when he could. It would be wrong to conclude that fighting for white rights meant fighting against black rights. It is equally incorrect to assume that Mexican Americans internalized white racism by claiming a white identity: whiteness and racism were not synonymous. Indeed, Mexican Americans had few alternatives and did the best they could with rather limited options and within a very harsh environment. They had great difficulties fighting for the Mexican-origin community and would have been hard pressed to fight for black people too. And, of course, black people did relatively little to fight for Mexican Americans. As historian Robert Goldberg observed for San Antonio, while "Mexican Americans were unsympathetic to the blacks, there is no evidence to suggest that blacks would have welcomed their involvement" in the civil rights movement.[8]

Beyond whiteness, racism in general contributed to disunity. Ovide Duncantell argued that "the black community may have been more of the villain" in this regard. Some blacks criticized the advantages that Mexican Americans received from Anglos, which "became a stigma between the two groups."[9] Reverend Peter Johnson said, "When I first came down here one of the fascinating things was how hostile black people were towards Mexicans."[10] According to Dallas politician Diana Orozco, Mexican Americans

> have to be very frank and very blunt about being truthful with ourselves and that is that we all grew up in the same society. So we all have prejudices. We all have racism, and racist notions and beliefs, that are part of our belief system. . . . And we have to fight them constantly . . . and so I think there is always going to be a problem because we were made, we were raised and learned in a system and a society that has many racist systemic problems.[11]

These leaders recognized that the prejudicial sentiments of Mexican Americans and blacks kept the two groups separated. Such racism in some cases prevented a close working relationship between blacks and browns.

While some African Americans and Mexican Americans reduced the causes of disunity to race, others tended to focus more on political and economic competition as the root of the black/brown divide. Former state representative Lauro Cruz recalled: "In Houston, you've had a developing divisiveness because the different ethnic groups have supported different local candidates. . . . I think that what's at the bottom of it is the fact that the overall community, the total community usually is only willing to give up so much of the pie."[12] In other words, political competition was a key factor in keeping African Americans and Mexican Americans apart. Chicano activist and University of Houston professor Tatcho Mindiola confirmed this viewpoint when he stated that one of the roots of black/brown conflict was "the political competition. . . . Blacks by far win whatever political competition we are involved in."[13] José Angel Gutiérrez concurred, stating that the cause of black/brown tension was "the competition for power."[14] San Antonio activist Harry V. Burns echoed these sentiments when he said that "the Mexican Americans were struggling themselves at that time, to acquire political power; and so as a result, in some areas there was some real opposition between the Mexican Americans and the blacks."[15] This political competition proved to be a major barrier to cooperation, one given the current political climate that seems likely to continue.

Economic competition, like political competition, also perpetuated disunity. Harry Burns stated that "sometimes we [blacks] feel that they [Mexican Americans] are our oppressors. . . . They try stepping on our heads to get ahead."[16] Similarly, Ernesto Calderón, a Chicano activist in Waco, argued:

> I think Blacks see the numbers [of Latino/as] increasing and that's going to threaten their position as those numbers increase. You know . . . we've tried before to work coalitions with Blacks. It's successful up to a point, but you can't get beyond that. If you start advocating for services to the Chicano that's where it stops. You know, the Black is not sharing that little piece of bone that they are getting, and I can't say that I blame them. But, the tension continues.

For Calderón, the increasing Latino/a population threatened blacks, especially since African Americans viewed those increases as taking away the "little piece of bone" that blacks had won.[17] In a like manner, Tatcho Mindiola noted that "economics, a perception on the part of many African-Americans that immigrants take jobs away from their community," bifurcated these communities.[18] The struggles of each group to eliminate poverty and joblessness were of paramount importance. The state and federal governments' restrictions on this funding, however, ensured that blacks and browns would conflict over scarce resources. Competition for limited funds pitted blacks against Mexican Americans, and vice versa.

The perception of cultural difference was an additional cause of conflict between these two groups. Mindiola stated that "some cultural issues like language and the speaking of language in the workplace, bilingual education, and speaking of languages generally" impeded coalition building. "I think many African-Americans, like many Anglo Americans in general, feel that they are threatened by that."[19] Mindiola believed that cultural differences led to black prejudice toward Chicanos. Such racism was distasteful to activists like Mindiola, and hence no unification occurred. Ernest McMillan made a similar observation when he said that "the whole question of color and language became barriers to building unity."[20] Some Mexican Americans and blacks regarded each other as culturally and socially dissimilar. The perception of difference did not encourage blacks and browns to work together. Instead, it contributed to disunity.

Geographic distance and unfamiliarity also prohibited a close working relationship. The majority of each group's population lived far away from the other—African Americans in East Texas and Mexicans Americans in South and West Texas. But even where blacks and Mexican Americans lived in close proximity, such as in major cities, leaders of both groups tended to ignore the other movement. NAACP field secretary Dr. David Williams remembered that "in West Texas I never saw a Mexican at all at any kind of meeting for civil rights—period."[21] Such a statement overlooks the constant and successful efforts of Mexican American civil rights activists in West and South Texas. Dallas NAACP leader Marion Butts criticized Mexican Americans because "they didn't really come in to fight and help." Butts ignored Mexican American activists in Dallas while blaming them for not assisting African Americans.[22] In a similar vein, José Angel Gutiérrez claimed not to have been influenced by the black civil rights movement. "I never knew of the black struggle," Gutiérrez said; "all I knew was my Chicano struggle that I was involved in and saw here, in SA [San Antonio], in Cristal, en el valle." Gutiérrez ignored the ways in which the black movement impacted other civil rights struggles. He also contradicted himself when he said that Chicanos "received vitamins from other movements."[23] The perception of distance and difference—of one group not helping or influencing the other—ultimately damaged relations between blacks and browns.

San Antonio activist Mario Salas offered the most sophisticated analysis of black/brown disunity. As a person of both African and Mexican heritage, Salas was perhaps uniquely positioned to comment on the subject. He held that, beyond racism, competition, culture, and geography, Mexican Americans and blacks had to overcome "the burden of history." From the 1850s to the present, Anglos had set these groups apart for the purpose of maintaining white supremacy. To acquire power from whites, blacks and Mexican Americans had to work against each other, producing what Salas called "a system of paternalism . . . that put these two communities at odds with one another. . . . The weight of history has really been convoluted along racial lines; call it colonialism on a local level . . . it's got very specific roots of how it separates people." Salas concluded that the long history of black/brown relations created a "superstructure of antagonisms" that divided these groups.[24] This burdensome history had erected obstacles to cooperation that appeared permanent and impenetrable.

■ ■ ■

The Texas example advances scholarship on civil rights in the United States. While Texas demonstrates once again that it is difficult to generalize about "the civil rights movement," there are similarities between the Lone Star State's struggles and those that occurred in the South and Southwest. As John Dittmer, William Chafe, Charles Payne, Adam Fairclough, and others have shown, blacks established organizing networks and initiated their own local civil rights movements in states like Mississippi, Louisiana, Georgia, and elsewhere.[25] Such was the case in Texas, where blacks built a movement from the ground up. Similarly, as Armando Navarro, Ernesto Chávez, Jorge Mariscal, Ernesto Vigil, and others have demonstrated, Mexican Americans began their own local civil rights struggles in states like New Mexico, California, and Colorado.[26] This was also the case in Texas, where Mexican Americans established grassroots organizations and local movements. When we compare Texas with Mississippi or California, many of the civil rights battles fought by blacks and Mexican Americans resemble the more well-known conflicts that occurred in the Deep South and the far Southwest.

Texas differs from its neighbors in the South and Southwest in that both the Mexican American and African American battles for rights occurred simultaneously within the state. No scholar has compared these two movements, and my hope is that the history offered in this book sheds new light on each freedom struggle. If nothing else, I hope I have exploded the concept of "the civil rights movement" and expanded the historiographical discussion regarding social justice, race relations, and the causes of the black/brown divide. While both movements garnered many successes, the inability of blacks and Mexican Americans to effectively unite ultimately hindered each struggle. When Mexican Americans opposed black protests, they strengthened the broader white opposition to black rights. This undercut the chances for black victories, although in most cases blacks won nonetheless. Similarly, when African Americans disregarded the Mexican American movement, they not only questioned the existence of the Mexican American civil rights struggle, they discredited it. In so doing, blacks aligned themselves with Anglos and damaged the prospects for Mexican American victories, even though Mexican-origin people were still victorious. The examples of cooperation—the filibusters of Henry B. Gonzalez, Moses LeRoy's support of the Minimum Wage March, Pancho Medrano's labor activism, the work of the ecumenical activists, the BBC—demonstrate that unity was possible and that it could advance both movements. Nevertheless, long-term unification eluded both groups.

The black/brown divide has continued into the post–civil rights period. In many ways, issues relating to black/brown relations that were pertinent to Texas and the Southwest have become national concerns in the late twentieth and early twenty-first centuries. African American prejudicial sentiments have caused many problems for black/brown relations during this period. Black people have felt threatened by the increasing number of Mexican Americans in the United States and have feared a loss of power as Latino/as became the nation's largest minority group in 2003. For example, in 1975 the Voting Rights Act of 1965 came up for renewal in the U.S. Congress. While the original voting protections of the act extended only to blacks, numerous Mexican American civil rights groups wanted persons of Latin American heritage included in the law's protections. The NAACP, fearing an erosion of black political gains, opposed including Mexican Americans in the Voting Rights Act's renewal legislation. This frustrated many Latinos because it showed, as they had argued in the 1960s, that blacks monopolized government programs. The Voting Rights Act of 1975 did ultimately include provisions for "language minority" groups. In 1982, when Congress debated an additional extension of the act, African Americans in the Leadership Conference on Civil Rights (LCCR) succeeded in diluting the "language minority provisions" of the legislation, which ultimately decreased the effectiveness of the act for Latinos. Mexican Americans, among other ethnic groups, once again felt rebuffed by the African American response to the Voting Rights Act.[27]

Reform of American immigration laws has also generated conflicts between blacks and browns. In 1965 the U.S. government tried to modernize immigration statutes with the Immigration and Nationality Services Act (INSA). This legislation put caps on the number of legal immigrants from Latin American nations for the first time in U.S. history. The act failed to curtail illegal immigration, however. So in 1976 the Gerald Ford administration tried again with the Western Hemisphere Act, which altered the caps established by the INSA. This law again failed to decrease illegal immigration. In 1986, Congress and the Ronald Reagan administration attempted to fix immigration statutes by passing the Immigration Reform and Control Act

(IRCA). The government designed IRCA specifically to reduce illegal immigration. This law criminalized illegal immigration and designated a series of punishments for companies that employed undocumented workers. The only positive aspect of this law was that it offered a road to citizenship for the two million illegal immigrants who resided in the United States.[28]

While many Latino civic organizations decried the IRCA, particularly the statutes that penalized companies that hired illegal immigrants, the NAACP supported the legislation. Black leaders felt that undocumented workers took jobs from African Americans. When a government study found significant discrimination against legal immigrant workers, Hispanic groups demanded that the NAACP and the LCCR support the repeal of IRCA. As immigrant rights activist Julie Quiroz-Martinez observed, the LCCR "ignored immigrant rights advocates and refused to take a position against the provisions."[29] This angered Latino/a activists, who protested at the annual LCCR meeting in 1990.[30] In 2006, when immigration reform returned as a hot-button political issue, thousands of immigrant rights protesters converged on major American cities to demand fair reforms. For the most part, blacks did not participate. Many blacks continued to feel that immigrants took jobs from the black community, and they viewed the increased number of Latino/as as a threat to African American political power.[31]

African American prejudicial opinions about Latino/as also surfaced in 2005 after Hurricane Katrina slammed into the Gulf Coast. While the aftermath of the storm unwittingly exposed problems of poverty in the United States, it likewise revealed simmering racial tensions between Mexican Americans and blacks. When New Orleans began rebuilding, numerous Mexicans, Mexican Americans, and other Latinos migrated to the city for work. African Americans greeted these migrants with much hostility, especially New Orleans mayor Ray Nagin. In an address to local businesspeople, Nagin wondered aloud: "How do I ensure that New Orleans is not overrun by Mexican workers?"[32] A few months later, he answered that racist question by stating unequivocally: "This city will be chocolate at the end of the day. This will be a majority African-American city. It's the way God wants it to be."[33]

Mayor Nagin vilified Latino/a workers, whom he portrayed as interlopers who displaced a black workforce. Many African Americans in New Orleans agreed. R. J. Rouzan, an African American who owned a construction business, made known his frustration at the presence of Hispanic workers: "They are allowing people to come in who are getting jobs while we as homeowners who built this city, they don't let us get access to our property." Another resident, Renee Langie, deeply resented that jobs were going to immigrants, arguing: "There could have been jobs right here for people to get. This is our city, we should be rebuilding it." Some blacks went further. Local contractor Mike Dunbar refused to hire immigrant workers from Latin America. "I'm not prejudiced," Dunbar stated, but he nonetheless vowed to hire only non-Latino workers. Other New Orleanians followed suit.[34]

Nagin's comments offended many people, but none more so than the Latino/as who arrived to help rebuild the city. Jairo Lopez thought the black response to immigrant workers was unfair. "Everyone needs to work," Lopez stated, "and it's not our fault if (local residents) don't have jobs here." Lopez hinted at one of the central ironies of this whole affair: "The people who lived here are in other states," which of course made it hard for them to work in New Orleans.[35] Arturo, an immigrant from Mexico City, said: "I don't know why they want to harass us. All we want is work. We came to lift the city up." Obed Irula, an immigrant from Honduras, argued further: "If Latinos come to work, they work hard."[36]

The situation in New Orleans is emblematic of the continuing racial divide between blacks and browns. The economic competition generated by the rebuilding of New Orleans unveiled some of the long-standing animosities between African Americans and Latino/as. While we must be wary of comments, like those of Arturo, that suggest immigrant workers went to New Orleans to "lift the city up," we must be equally wary of black comments that suggest Mexican Americans are taking over the Crescent City.

Relations between Latino/as and blacks have been even worse in other parts of the country. In California, Hispanics often cause friction between the two groups, especially in Los Angeles, where Latino gangs such as the Mexican Mafia have specifically targeted and killed African Americans in a campaign that political pundits and scholars have labeled "ethnic cleansing." Such murders result from the increased numbers of Latino/as who have moved into formerly all-black areas such as Compton. Gang members feel that these areas are now their territory. Aside from these territorial issues, long-standing economic and political competition in Los Angeles has exacerbated racial tensions. Some black gangs have responded in kind, killing Hispanics indiscriminately in retaliation for the death of African Americans.[37] In Georgia, New Jersey, Florida, and elsewhere, as the number of Hispanic immigrants has increased, African Americans have targeted random Latino/as for robbery, beating, and execution.[38] While this situation is extreme, it once again demonstrates the presence of a black/brown divide in the United States.

A recent poll by the *New American Media* has uncovered significant areas for concern in regard to black/brown relations. The poll "found that friction between ethnic and racial groups, which at times has erupted into highly-publicized incidents around the country, is clearly rooted in the mistrust that the groups harbor towards each other, as well as the sentiment that other groups are mistreating them or are detrimental to their own future." According to the poll, 44 percent of the Hispanics under study were "generally afraid of African Americans because they are responsible for most of the crime." On the other hand, 51 percent of African Americans felt that Latin American immigrants "are taking jobs, housing and political power away from the Black community."[39] Such sentiments do not auger well for the future of black/brown relations.

The 2008 primary and presidential contest in the United States also revealed some of the political divisions between African Americans and Latino/as. In particular, the primary campaigns of Senators Hillary Clinton (D-N.Y.) and Barack Obama (D-Ill.) demonstrated a continued black/brown political animus. Clinton was able to tap into long-standing community ties with Mexican American voters in California and Texas and ultimately won both states. Obama seemed less adept at courting Latino/a voters. But many political observers wondered if Latino/as simply did not want to vote for a black candidate. Clinton confidant Sergio Bendixen helped fuel this speculation when he noted that "the Hispanic voter—and I want to say this very carefully—has not shown a lot of willingness or affinity to support black candidates."[40] During the same period, Dallas activist Adelfa Callejo remarked: "Obama has a problem that he happens to be black." Callejo intimated that Obama would lose the Hispanic vote in Texas because blacks had not rallied to Mexican American causes. "When blacks had the numbers," Callejo stated, "they didn't do anything to support us. They always used our numbers to fulfill their goals and objectives, but they never really supported us, and there's a lot of hard feelings about that. I don't think we're going to get over it anytime soon." While Mexican American leaders roundly criticized Callejo and Bendixen, they nonetheless divulged a level of animosity among Latino/as toward Obama and, by extension, other black candidates.[41]

The presidential primary election caused numerous journalists to ask, "Will Latinos vote for Obama?" The question contained an underlying assumption that the black/brown divide would make Latino/as turn away from Obama solely because he was black. Certainly some cast votes based on race, or racist, assumptions about Senator Obama.[42] But such a question contained inherent contradictions. First, it ignored the significant campaigning that Senator Clinton carried out in the Southwest. She should receive credit for attracting Latino/a voters away from Obama. Second, it ignored the Latino/as who did vote for Obama. In Texas and California, Obama captured 32 percent of the Hispanic vote. In California, exit polling showed that 55 percent of Hispanic voters held a favorable opinion of Obama. And a national poll conducted by the Pew Research Center found that 74 percent of Hispanics had a favorable opinion of Obama. These numbers suggested that Latinos would vote for Obama and would do so in relatively significant numbers.[43]

The political competition in major cities like Houston, the economic competition in New Orleans, the racial issues exposed by the 2008 presidential primary, and the brown-on-black and black-on-brown gang violence has led many observers to wonder if a permanent division exists between blacks and Latino/as in the United States. For many Americans, unity among oppressed people would appear to be axiomatic: oppressed ethnic groups would naturally unite to battle racism. Hence, the violence witnessed in a city like Los Angeles, the tactless comments of New Orleans mayor Ray Nagin, and the ways in which race has played a role in political campaigns perplexes because these groups should join forces to solve problems. Author Nicolás C. Vaca calls this misconception the "presumed ideological alliance between Blacks and Latinos."[44]

While there remain significant areas for concern regarding black/brown relations, hope for cooperation still exists. The 2008 presidential election confirmed this point. Republican candidate John McCain (R-Ariz.) had trouble courting Latino/a voters. They ultimately turned out for Barack Obama in record numbers. Indeed, for the United States as a whole, 67 percent of the Hispanic vote went to the Obama/Biden ticket, while 31 percent went to the McCain/Palin ticket. States like Nevada, Colorado, and New Mexico, which often track Republican in presidential elections, all voted for Obama. According to several polls, 69 percent of Hispanics supported Obama in New Mexico while only 34 percent voted for McCain. A whopping 78 percent of the Latino/a population in California voted for Obama. In Nevada, 75 percent of Latino/as came out for him. Although Obama lost Texas, he garnered 63 percent of the Latino/a vote. Across the United States, Latino/as came out in force to vote for Obama.[45] These numbers indicate that Latino/as have no problem voting for black candidates. It also suggests that some of the dividing lines between black and brown may be starting to erode.

There are other areas where cooperation and goodwill between blacks and browns are evident. For example, while the New American Media poll found that 44 percent of Hispanics were "afraid" of blacks, 50 percent of Hispanics stated that they were not afraid of them. By the same token, while 51 percent of blacks felt immigrants took jobs, housing, and political power from African

Americans, 45 percent disagreed with that statement. Even more significantly, when the *New American Media* pollsters asked if African Americans and Latinos "should put aside their differences and work together on issues that affect their communities," 92 percent of Hispanics and 89 percent of blacks said yes. When asked if race relations between browns and blacks would improve in the future, 61 percent of Hispanics and 68 percent of African Americans thought relations would improve.[46] So, at first glance the black/brown divide appears very troubling, but on closer inspection black/brown relations seem less divisive than many Americans might think.

African Americans and Latino/as have come together for common purposes, have shared common interests, and have cooperated in other instances. In 1979, for instance, Congressman Robert Garcia (D-N.Y.) became one of the first national leaders to propose legislation for the creation of a holiday honoring Martin Luther King Jr. A few years later, President Reagan signed a version of Garcia's bill into law. Additionally, former MALDEF chairperson Mario Obledo served on the board of directors of the Martin Luther King Jr. Federal Holiday Commission, one of the few Mexican Americans chosen to do so. In 1987 Jesse Jackson handpicked Obledo to chair the board of directors of the National Rainbow Coalition. While largely a symbolic position, it nonetheless represented a model of ethnic inclusiveness within a prominent civil rights group. Jackson also reached out to Latino/as during his 1988 presidential bid. More recently, Jesse Jackson called for a "black-brown coalition" to address immigration reform and education issues. The Rainbow Coalition also began offering Spanish classes to familiarize blacks with spoken Spanish.[47]

While some parts of the country appear problematic for African American and Latino/a relations, other areas buck the trend. In San Antonio, blacks, Mexican Americans, and whites united in a broad coalition to elect Henry Cisneros mayor in 1981. In 1983 African Americans, Latino/as, and whites rallied behind the Denver mayoral candidacy of Federico Peña, who won a decisive victory.[48] Peña won reelection in 1987, and San Antonians reelected Cisneros three more times. In the 2005 Los Angeles mayoral race, Antonio Villaraigosa captured 50 percent of the black vote, won the election, and became the first Mexican American mayor of that city since the nineteenth century.[49] In Houston, while blacks and browns may have voted in blocs for Lee Brown and Orlando Sánchez, they have united behind other candidates, such as Congresswoman Sheila Jackson Lee (D-Tex.). Lee has long received a majority vote (usually 70–90 percent) from her district, which demographically breaks down along equitable lines between blacks (40 percent), Hispanics

(30 percent), and whites (30 percent). She has championed the cause of immigrant rights, which she calls "the civil rights issue of our time." Lee introduced a bill in the House that would have granted legal residency status for undocumented workers who have resided in the United States for five years and would have increased the number of family and work visas. Republican opponents voted against the bill. For Congresswoman Lee and other like-minded politicians, blacks and Hispanics have many common interests.[50]

Participants in the civil rights movement have commented on their hopes for better relations between blacks and browns. Ernest McMillan stated that, while color and language divided these groups, "I would love to find ways to overcome those things today because I see that happening, revisiting us even today."[51] He has attempted to overcome divisions by joining Mexican Americans to combat racism in Houston and Dallas. According to José Angel Gutiérrez, in the future "coalitions and alliances are going to be the name of the game."[52] Peter Johnson argued that "blacks and Mexicans could run the state of Texas if they stopped fighting among each other, they've got the political power to control this state."[53] These activists and others like them believe that while problems remain, blacks and Latinos can come together for common purposes. They also suggest that race relations will improve.

Yet racism continues to mar black/brown relations. Despite the racial transformations inaugurated by the black and Mexican American civil rights struggles, race offers the most consistent explanation for the black/brown divide. The United States remains a country with a decidedly black/white racial order. Many Hispanics continue to classify themselves as white. The 2000 census revealed that 48 percent of Latino/as self-identified as white.[54] Hispanics are the only ethnic group in the United States able to consider themselves white, a minority, and people of color. This is what historian Matthew Whitaker calls the Mexican American racial "escape hatch." Some blacks still view such racial positioning disapprovingly.[55] Both groups guard their own interests first, and these self-interests cause rifts that often seem irreparable. Blacks and Latino/as continue to view each other as competitors, not allies. This competition—over jobs, housing, political power—only exacerbates the racial dimension of the black/brown divide. And the growth of the Hispanic population has caused such sentiments to intensify among blacks. As the Latino/a community expands, these issues seem likely to persist.

As this book makes clear, Mexican Americans and African Americans have experienced a long history of disunification, especially during their respective civil rights movements. This disunity persists today, although there are moments when it dissipates and even disappears. Whether disunity will continue, intensify, or abate in the coming years remains a matter of conjecture. Certainly the examples of interracial cooperation during the civil rights era, and the instances of cooperation today, demonstrate that collaboration is an effective weapon against American racism. But intergroup racial acrimony reduces the chances for building effective coalitions and uniting the African American and Mexican American civil rights struggles. The rigidity of the American racial order and the persistence of racist sentiments suggest that the black/brown divide will remain. Race continues to be a divisive power in the United States. When combined with competition, distrust, and self-ishness, race is the most formidable obstacle to cooperation, coalition build-ing, and unification in the ongoing American civil rights struggles. As both movements proceed, it remains to be seen if Mexican Americans and African Americans will continue fighting their own battles.

Notes

Abbreviations

Archives

AHC	Austin History Center, Austin Public Library
BLAC	Nattie Lee Benson Latin American Collection, University of Texas, Austin
CAH	Dolph Briscoe Center for American History, University of Texas, Austin
DPL	Texas/Dallas History and Archives Division, Dallas Public Library
FWPL	Genealogy, History, and Archives, Fort Worth Public Library
HMRC	Houston Metropolitan Research Center, Houston Public Library
ITC	Institute of Texan Cultures
LBJ	Lyndon Baines Johnson Presidential Library
SAPL	Texana/Genealogy Collection, San Antonio Public Library
SHRL	Texas State Library and Archives Commission, Sam Houston Regional Library and Research Center
TAMUCC	Special Collections and Archives, Texas A&M University, Corpus Christi, Bell Library
TSLAC	Texas State Library and Archives Commission
TSU	Department of Special Collections, Robert J. Terry Library, Texas Southern University
TTU	Southwest Collection/Special Collections Library, Texas Tech University
UCD	Special Collections Department, Peter J. Shields Library, University of California, Davis
UH	Special Collections, University of Houston Libraries
UTA	University of Texas, Arlington, Special Collections
UTSA	Special Collections, University of Texas, San Antonio

Newspapers

AA	*Austin American*
AAS	*Austin American-Statesman*

AS	*Austin Statesman*
CCC	*Corpus Christi Caller*
CCCT	*Corpus Christi Caller-Times*
DE	*Dallas Express*
DMN	*Dallas Morning News*
DPT	*Dallas Post Tribune*
DTH	*Dallas Times Herald*
FWST	*Fort Worth Star-Telegram*
HC	*Houston Chronicle*
HFT	*Houston Forward Times*
HI	*Houston Informer*
HP	*Houston Post*
LN	*LULAC News*
PC	*Papel Chicano*
SAE	*San Antonio Express*
SAEN	*San Antonio Express and News*
SAL	*San Antonio Light*
SAN	*San Antonio News*
SAR	*San Antonio Register*
SSN	*Southern School News*
TO	*Texas Observer*

Introduction

1. "Houston's Latin American Leaders Back Varied Views," *HC*, December 8, 1958; "Everett Split with Mexican-Americans," *HFT*, September 19, 1970. On Tijerina, see Kreneck, *Mexican American Odyssey*; on the Huelga Schools, see San Miguel, *Brown, Not White*.

2. The literature on the black freedom struggle is extensive, but for some relevant sources see Branch, *Parting the Waters, Pillar of Fire*, and *At Canaan's Edge*; Dittmer, *Local People*; Carson, *In Struggle*; Charles M. Payne, *I've Got the Light of Freedom*; Eskew, *But for Birmingham*; Manis, *A Fire You Can't Put Out*; Fairclough, *To Redeem the Soul*; McWhorter, *Carry Me Home*; Thornton, *Dividing Lines*; Newman, *Civil Rights Movement*; Shabazz, *Advancing Democracy*; Morris, *Origins*; Kluger, *Simple Justice*; and Tuck, *Beyond Atlanta*.

3. The literature on Mexican American civil rights is broad, but for a good starting place see Carroll, *Felix Longoria's Wake*; Ernesto Chávez, *"¡Mi raza primero!"*; Ignacio M. García, *United We Win* and *Chicanismo*; Mario T. García, *Mexican Americans*; Gómez-Quiñones, *Chicano Politics*; Kaplowitz, *LULAC, Mexican Americans*; Mariscal, *Brown-eyed Children*; Muñoz, *Youth, Identity, Power*; Navarro, *Cristal Experiment* and *La Raza Unida Party*; Oropeza, *¡Raza Sí! ¡Guerra No!*; San Miguel, *"Let All of Them Take Heed"* and *Brown, Not White*; Vigil, *Crusade for Justice*; Olivas, *Colored Men*; and Vargas, *Labor Rights*.

4. There are relatively few comparative civil rights histories. See, e.g., Houston, "African Americans, Mexican Americans"; Behnken, "On Parallel Tracks" and "Fighting Their Own Battles"; Brilliant, "Color Lines"; Araiza, "For Freedom of Other Men"; and Mantler, "Black, Brown, and Poor." For a broader look at black/brown relations, see Piatt, *Black*

and Brown in America; Mindiola, Nieman, and Rodriguez, *Black-Brown*; Herzog, *Minority Group Politics*; and Romo, *Latinos and Blacks*.

5. On the field of comparative history, see Kocka, "Comparison and Beyond"; Marx, *Making Race and Nation*; Frederickson, *Comparative Imagination*; De Genova, *Racial Transformations*; and Woodward, *Comparative Approach to American History*.

6. See census data at ⟨http://www.census.gov/population/documentation/twps0056/tab58.pdf⟩ (January 20, 2007).

7. Woodward, *Strange Career*, 107–8. See also Packard, *American Nightmare*.

8. See Gilbert González, *Chicano Education*, and Donato, *Other Struggle for Equal Schools*.

9. Montejano, *Anglos and Mexicans*, 262.

10. Steven H. Wilson, "*Brown* over 'Other White,'" 17. For education more generally, see Ladino, *Desegregating Texas Schools*; Kellar, *Make Haste Slowly*; Linden, *Desegregating Schools*; Shabazz, *Advancing Democracy*; Barr, *Black Texans*; San Miguel, *"Let All of Them Take Heed," Brown, Not White*, and *Contested Policy*; and Blanton, *Strange Career*.

11. Montejano, *Anglos and Mexicans*, 39–40, 251–53; Barr, *Black Texans*, 79.

12. Wintz, "Blacks," 20. Novelist Jan De Hartog discusses the repugnant conditions in Houston's hospitals in the diary notes for his book *The Hospital* (New York: Atheneum, 1964). See "Notes and Diary," Jan De Hartog Collection, UH.

13. Darwin Payne, *Big D*, 5, 81–84; Mason, *African Americans*, 23–25, 36–38, 179–81; Goldberg, "Racial Change," 349–52; Schott, "Ethnic and Race Relations," 5–8.

14. Carrigan and Webb, "Lynching of Persons," 414. See also Carrigan and Webb, "Muerto por Unos Desconocidos," 35–74; Hall, *Revolt against Chivalry*; Brown, *Hood, Bonnet*; Bernstein, *First Waco Horror*; Carrigan, *Making of a Lynching Culture*; and Nevels, *Lynching to Belong*.

15. See Frederickson, *Racism*, 8–9, and Whitaker, *Race Work*, 6–8, 206–7, 272.

16. See Matthew Frye Jacobson, *Whiteness*; Ignatiev, *How the Irish Became White*; Brodkin, *How the Jews Became White Folks*; Lipsitz, *Possessive Investment*; and Roediger, *Wages of Whiteness*.

17. Du Bois, *Black Reconstruction*, 700; Roediger, *Wages of Whiteness*, title and p. 13.

18. Matthew Frye Jacobson, *Whiteness*, 43–44, 75, 95 (quotation—emphasis in original), title. For this process in California, see Almaguer, *Racial Fault Lines*, 1–10, 54–60, and chap. 1.

19. Carroll, *Felix Longoria's Wake*, 113.

20. Foley, "Becoming Hispanic," "Straddling the Color Line," "Partly Colored or Other White," and *White Scourge*; Guglielmo, "Fighting for Caucasian Rights"; Steven H. Wilson, "*Brown* over 'Other White'"; Sheridan, "'Another White Race'"; Phillips, *White Metropolis*.

21. On this subject, see Vasconselos, *La Raza Cósmica*; Schmidt, *Roots of Lo Mexicano*; Knight, "Racism, Revolution, and *Indigenismo*," 71–110; Graham, Introduction to *The Idea of Race*, 1–4; Miller, *Rise and Fall of the Cosmic Race*, 1–44, passim; Minna Stern, "From Mestizophilia to Biotypology," 187–210; and Foley, *Quest for Equality*, 43–44. See also Ruiz, "Morena/o, blanca/o."

22. San Miguel, *Brown, Not White*, 40. See also Avila et al., "Roundtable on the State of Chicana/o Studies," 144–45; Menchaca, *Recovering History, Constructing Race*, 1; and Laura E. Gómez, *Manifest Destinies*.

23. For a similar argument, see Gross, *What Blood Won't Tell*, 254–56.

24. Foley, "Becoming Hispanic," 65; Goldberg, "Racial Change," 362 (quotation); Phillips, *White Metropolis*, 163; Griffin interview; L. Clifford Davis interview; Duncantell interview.

25. Martínez, "African-Americans, Latinos," 213–22.

26. "Black Student Union," *Space City!*, n.d., Salazar Papers, HMRC; "Probes Mexican-American Unrest," *DPT*, July 5, 1969.

27. "Vatos' Views on School Zoning," *PC*, August 8, 1970; "Everett Split with Mexican-Americans," *HFT*, September 19, 1970; "La Raza vs. the School Board," *PC*, September 26–October 9, 1970.

28. See "Negro-Latin Talk Demand Renewed," *DTH*, October 28, 1970; "Black/Mexican-American Project Report"; L. Clifford Davis interview; "Black San Antonio V: Political Inroads," *SAE*, February 17, 1972; and "Chicanos," n.d., Salazar Papers, HMRC.

29. For black/brown competition, see Bauman, *Race and the War on Poverty*; Mantler, "Black, Brown, and Poor"; Clayson, "Texas Poverty"; and Jon Watson, "Crossing the Colour Lines."

Chapter 1

1. "Bombing Injures Man, Shatters Home Interior," *DE*, May 13, 1950; "Bombs Heard within Three Mile Radius," *DE*, June 10, 1950. See also "S. Dallas Blasted by Second Bomb in 24 Hours," *DE*, June 10, 1950; "Saturday Blast Wrecks House in South Dallas," *DTH*, June 4, 1950.

2. Eskew, *But for Birmingham*, chap. 2.

3. Schutze, *Accommodation*, 71–72; Phillips, *White Metropolis*, 126.

4. Phillips, *White Metropolis*, 124–26 (quotation, 124).

5. Hall, "Long Civil Rights Movement."

6. As quoted in SoRelle, "Emergence of Black Business," 105.

7. Dressman, "'Yes, We Have No Jitneys!,'" 116–25.

8. Govenar and Brakefield, *Deep Ellum and Central Track*, xix (quotation), 1–107; Darwin Payne, *Big D*, 144–45. On Deep Ellum's rebirth, see Phillips, *White Metropolis*, 172. For the blues scene in Houston, see Govenar, *Early Years of Rhythm and Blues*.

9. Barr, *Black Texans*, 158–60; Brown and Heintze, "Mary Branch"; Heintze, *Private Black Colleges*. For black education in general, the standard account remains James D. Anderson, *Education of Blacks in the South*. On Farmer, see Farmer, *Lay Bare the Heart*; Meier and Rudwick, *CORE*; and Arsenault, *Freedom Riders*.

10. Behnken, "'Count on Me,'" 67–69.

11. "The Christian Brotherhood Way of Practice in Social Life," n.d. (ca. 1940s), Simpson Papers, HMRC. See also Black interview by Wolfe and Griffin interview.

12. M. L. Price, "New Frontiers with Christ Leading in Social Life," 1965, pp. 1–2, Price Collection, HMRC (emphasis in original).

13. Chappell, *Stone of Hope*, 4–5. See also Dailey, "Sex, Segregation."

14. For the best treatment of these events, see Haynes, *Night of Violence*.

15. Gillette, "NAACP in Texas," 1. See also Berg, *Ticket to Freedom*; Jonas, *Freedom's Sword*; and Tushnet, *NAACP's Legal Strategy*.

16. Craft interview by Stricklin and Tomlinson, 25.

17. Pitre, *Struggle against Jim Crow*, 25–26. For the best account of the NAACP, see Gillette, "NAACP in Texas."

18. Gillette, "NAACP in Texas," 2; Durham, "Longview Race Riot."

19. See Bryson, *Dr. Lawrence A. Nixon*, and Hine, *Black Victory*. The Republican Party did exist in Texas, but it was so weak that Republicans rarely won state races.

20. *Nixon v. Herndon.*

21. *Nixon v. Condon.*

22. Hine, "Blacks and . . . the Democratic White Primary," 44–46, and *Black Victory*, 22.

23. Craft interview by Stricklin and Tomlinson, 45. For the activism of black women, see Harley and Terborg-Penn, *Afro-American Woman*; Hine, *Hine Sight*; Harley, *Sister Circle*; and Collier-Thomas, *Sisters in the Struggle.*

24. Pitre, *Struggle against Jim Crow*, 37.

25. Haynes, "Black Houstonians," 201; Hine, *Dark Victory*, 130, 168–75, chap. 8; Pitre, *Struggle against Jim Crow*, 22–23 (quotation).

26. *Grovey v. Townsend.*

27. On Marshall, see Rowan, *Dream Makers*; Tushnet, *Making Constitutional Law*; Juan Williams, *Thurgood Marshall*; and Ball, *Defiant Life.*

28. *Smith v. Allwright.*

29. Shabazz, *Advancing Democracy*, 66–68.

30. Ibid., 72, 79–86 (quotation, 84).

31. Pitre, *Struggle against Jim Crow*, 93–94.

32. As quoted in Shabazz, *Advancing Democracy*, 100.

33. Ibid., 102.

34. *Sweatt v. Painter.*

35. Shabazz, *Advancing Democracy*, 104. See also Rhoads, *Advancing the Cause*. I have borrowed my chapter title from Rhoads's book.

36. Barr, *Black Texans*, 80.

37. Enstam, "Dallas Equal Suffrage Association," 843–45; Darwin Payne, *Big D*, 209–10.

38. Barr and Calvert, *Black Leaders*; Dulaney, "Progressive Voters League."

39. These cases included *Sipuel v. Board of Regents of the University of Oklahoma* (1948), *McLaurin v. Oklahoma State Regents* (1950), *Lucy v. Adams* (1955) in Alabama, *Holmes v. Danner* (1961) in Georgia, and *Meredith v. Fair* (1962) in Mississippi.

40. On the development of the Mexican American community, see Achor, *Mexican Americans*; Mario T. García, *Desert Immigrants*; George J. Sánchez, *Becoming Mexican American*; De León, *Mexican Americans in Texas*; Buitron, *Search for Tejano Identity*; Anthony Quiroz, *Claiming Citizenship*; and Treviño, *Church in the Barrio.*

41. "Transcript of Treaty of Guadalupe Hidalgo," ⟨http://www.ourdocuments.gov/doc .php?doc=26&page=transcript⟩; del Castillo, *Treaty of Guadalupe Hidalgo*, 179–81.

42. See del Castillo, *Treaty of Guadalupe Hidalgo*; Rosenbaum, *Mexicano Resistance*; and Manuel G. Gonzales, *Mexicanos*. See also Abel G. Rubio's very interesting *Stolen Heritage.*

43. *Annals of Congress*, "Article 1, Section 8, Clause 4 (Citizenship) of U.S. Constitution," 561; for easily accessible text, see "Article 1, Section 8, Clause 4 (Citizenship)," The Founders' Constitution Webpage, ⟨http://press-pubs.uchicago.edu/founders/print_docu ments/a1_8_4_citizenships8.html⟩. The main clause of this act stated "that all free white

persons, who have, or shall migrate into the United States, and . . . intend to reside therein, and shall take an oath of allegiance, and shall have resided in the United States for one whole year, shall be entitled to all the rights of citizenship."

44. The racial prerequisite cases are discussed in Haney López, *White by Law*, chap. 3, 55 (quotation).

45. *In re Rodriguez*, reprinted in Bayor, *Columbia Documentary History*, 384. See also the short introductory essay by Mae M. Ngai, 307–36.

46. *In re Rodriguez*.

47. Ibid.

48. Foley, "Straddling the Color Line," 345.

49. Issues related to whiteness and civil rights were frequently debated throughout the early twentieth century. See, e.g., "La Cuestión de Razas en Texas" (The Question of Races in Texas), *La Crónica*, August 6, 1910, and "La Exclusión de los Niños Mexicanos de las Escuelas del Estado de Texas" (The Exclusion of Mexican Children from the Schools of the State of Texas), *La Crónica*, January 19, 1911.

50. Márquez, *LULAC*, 40–42.

51. Mario T. García, "Mexican Americans."

52. "Are Texas-Mexicans 'Americans?'" *LN*, April 1932. I located copies of the *LN* in BLAC, UT, and in the Carmen Cortes Collection, HMRC.

53. Juvencio Rodriguez to Congressman Joe H. Eagle, Rodriguez to Sen. Morris Shephard, Rodriguez to Sen. Tom Connely [*sic*], all November 25, 1936; Joe H. Eagle telegram and letter to SSB Director Frank Bane, November 25, 1936; SSB telegram to Joe H. Eagle, November 28, 1936—all in Eguia Collection, HMRC; De León, *Ethnicity*, 87–88.

54. "'Color' Rating Discussed," *El Paso Times*, October 12, 1936; Mario T. García, "Mexican Americans."

55. "Lest We Forget," *LN*, February 1937.

56. "Darkness Lifts to the Dawn," *LN*, April 1939; Fred Ponce Jr. to editor George Marquez, *LN*, April 1939. Both of these documents reference incidents similar to the Mc-Camant case.

57. "The 1940 Census . . . ," *LN*, November 1939. The letters from the second letter-writing campaign were reprinted in *LN*, November 1939. The announcement from the Department of the Census "that 'Mexicans' will be classified in the general White classification" appeared in *LN*, December 1939.

58. The exchanges between Salinas and the state government officials were recounted in "The School Questionnaire Incident," *LN*, November 1939, which reprinted the letters and responses verbatim.

59. "More Corrections on Racial Classification," *LN*, February 1940.

60. Steven H. Wilson, "*Brown* over 'Other White,'" 5–9, 19–21.

61. *Del Rio Independent School District v. Salvatierra*; San Miguel, "*Let All of Them Take Heed*," 78–80; Prewitt, "'We Didn't Ask to Come to This Party,'" passim.

62. See, e.g., Olguín, "Sangre Mexicana/Corazón Americano"; de la Luz Sáenz, *Los México-Americanos en la Gran Guerra*; and Rochin and Fernandez, "U.S. Latino Patriots."

63. Rivas-Rodriguez, *Mexican Americans and World War II*.

64. David G. Gutiérrez, *Walls and Mirrors*, 135, 154–55. See also Craig, *Bracero Program*;

Juan Ramon García, *Operation Wetback*; Anthony Quiroz, *Claiming Citizenship*; Blanton, "Citizenship Sacrifice"; *What Price Wetbacks?* Politicians began to make ludicrous claims that "open borders" allowed communists to enter the United States. In 1954 Benjamin Habberton, acting INS commissioner, warned that more than one hundred communists crossed the border daily. Critics later showed his assertion to be entirely fictitious. See "Commies Cross Border Daily, Officers Warn," *El Paso Herald-Post*, February 8, 1954, and "Border Patrol Tightens Check on Communists," *El Paso Herald-Post*, n.d., "Civil Rights, 1954," box 129, Texas Atty. Gen. Price Daniel Records, SHRL; "Identity of Border Commies Are Uncertain," *El Paso Herald-Post*, February 10, 1954; and "Brownell Denies Knowledge Reds Crossing Border," *El Paso Times*, February 19, 1954.

65. "A Resolution," n.d., Paul Andow Collection, BLAC; "Caucasian Race-Equal Privileges" Resolution, H.C.R. No. 105, April 15, 1943, in *General and Special Laws of the State of Texas*.

66. "Proclamation by the Governor of the State of Texas," June 25, 1943, Andow Collection, BLAC; "Commission Plans Lauded by De Pena," *Sentinel*, April 30, 1948; "Good Neighbor Group against Segregation, Secretary Declares," *Sentinel*, May 14, 1948. Special thanks to Grace Charles at the Corpus Christi Library for allowing me access to copies of the *Sentinel* she acquired while conducting her own research.

67. For a critical overview of the early years of the TGNC, see Perales, *Are We Good Neighbors?*

68. Efraín Domínguez Jr., to G. F. Dohrn, April 13, 1948, TGNC Papers, TSLAC.

69. An open letter to the Mission Chamber of Commerce from Hugo Dominguez, D.D.S., April 16, 1948, ibid.

70. Thomas S. Sutherland to R. E. Smith, April 20, 1948, ibid.

71. To the Members of the Good Neighbor Commission from Neville G. Penrose, October 12, 1949, ibid. See also unsigned draft of letter to Lions, Kiwanis, Rotary, and others, n.d., ibid.

72. See, e.g., Sub-Committee A meeting notes, November 21, 1949, ibid.

73. Albert Armendariz to State Health Officer [Henry A. Holle], August 26, 1954, ibid. Armendariz specifically cited Article 4477-A of Vernon's Texas Civil Statutes.

74. Henry A. Holle to Albert Armendariz, September 3, 1954, TGNC Papers, TSLAC.

75. Glenn E. Garrett to Morris A. Galatzan, September 7, 1954, ibid.

76. Henry A. Holle to Luciano Santoscoy, September 21, 1954, ibid.

77. W. D. Carroll [Texas Registrar of Vital Statistics] to Opal Talbot, January 10, 1955, ibid.

78. Henry A. Holle to Luciano Santoscoy, February 2, 1955, ibid.

79. Luciano Santoscoy to Henry B. Gonzalez, May 22, 1957, Gonzalez to Price Daniel, May 28, 1957, Henry A. Holle to Gonzalez, June 20, 1957, Holle interoffice memo to all concerned, June 21, 1957—all in box 350, folder "Gonzalez—Clippings—1958," Texas Gov. Daniel Papers, SHRL.

80. "Group Named on Human Relations," *FWST*, May 20, 1950.

81. On Dr. García and the G.I. Forum, see Carroll, *Felix Longoria's Wake*, and Ignacio M. García, *Hector P. García*. For a particularly interesting assessment of García, see Rivas-Rodriguez, "Framing Racism," 201–15.

82. Philip M. Hauser to Dr. Hector P. García, February 23, 1950, García Papers, TAMUCC.

83. John Vancronkhite telegram to Dr. Hector P. García, ibid. This communication followed a previous exchange between Congressman Richard Kleberg and Secretary of Commerce Daniel Roper regarding Census Bureau classification of Mexican Americans as "colored." Once again government officials were instructed to classify Mexican Americans as white. Roper to Kleberg, October 29, 1946, García Papers, TAMUCC.

84. Hector P. García to Ed Idar Jr., June 29, 1953, ibid.

85. Carlos I. Calderon to Hector P. García, September 3, 1953, ibid.

86. Hector P. García to Ed Idar Jr., December 23, 1953, ibid.

87. "Garcia Wages War on Birth Certificates," *News Bulletin*, February 1954.

88. San Miguel, *Brown, Not White*, 36.

89. De León, *Ethnicity*, 32–34 (quotation, 33).

90. Mario T. García, *Mexican Americans*, 146–74 (1st quotation, 147–48); David G. Gutiérrez, "Migration, Emergent Ethnicity," 498–500 (2nd quotation, 499), passim.

91. See Vargas, *Labor Rights*. See also Zamora, *Claiming Rights*.

92. Mario T. García, *Mexican Americans*, chap. 8; Urrutia, "Offspring of Discontent."

93. LULAC did occasionally protest and boycott schools; see San Miguel, *"Let All of Them Take Heed,"* 117–18.

94. Mario T. García, *Mexican Americans*, 62–83; San Miguel, *"Let All of Them Take Heed,"* 76, 85–86. See also "The Legacy of Eleuterio Escobar," ⟨http://www.lib.utexas.edu/benson/ escobar/escobar11.html⟩ (August 10, 2009). I could add the Good Government League to this list of groups, but it does not stand out as an activist organization. See Montejano, *Anglos and Mexicans*, 280–81, 293, and Rodolfo Rosales, *Illusion of Inclusion*, passim. For other examples of more confrontational leaders and groups, see Gabriela González, "Carolina Munguía," 200–229, and "Two Flags Entwined"; Orozco, "Origins of the League of United Latin American Citizens"; and Montes, "Working for American Rights."

95. See Houston, "African Americans, Mexican Americans."

96. As quoted in Green, *Establishment of Texas Politics*, 81.

97. See, e.g., the "plea" for desegregation of swimming pools, probably in Corpus Christi, undated [ca. 1940s], untitled, and unsigned court plea, Andow Collection, BLAC.

98. Foley, *White Scourge*, 209.

99. "Civil Rights Pledge Made by 'LULACs,'" *HC*, December 29, 1947.

100. Kaplowitz, "Distinct Minority," 196.

101. For some of this scholarship, see Mario Barrera, *Race and Class*; San Miguel, *"Let All of Them Take Heed"*; Montejano, *Anglos and Mexicans*; and Blanton, *Strange Career*.

102. Foley, *White Scourge*, 209–10.

103. Phillips, *White Metropolis*, 124.

104. "Bombing of Negro Home Here Spurs Move for Public Housing," *DE*, February 18, 1950; "Dallas Citizens Protest Housing Cut," *DE*, May 2, 1953; "Negro Area May Be First in Slum Clearance Project," *DE*, May 23, 1953; Schutze, *Accommodation*, 13–14; William H. Wilson, *Hamilton Park*, 10–44, passim.

105. George I. Sánchez to Robert K. Carr, May 6, 1947, Sánchez Collection, BLAC. See also Sánchez to Clifford Forster, May 24, 1947, ibid.

106. Goldberg, "Racial Change," 362.

Chapter 2

1. Peña interview by Roser, 1, 5; Peña interview by Gutiérrez, 4–15. This investigative work became a prime occupation of the G.I. Forum. See also Peña interview by Gutiérrez, 5–8; "Pecos School Segregation Aired before Edgar in Austin," May 15, 1953, "Aldrete Obtains Forum Win in Sanderson School Case," July 1953, and "Edgar Holds Conference on Mathis Schools Segregation," December 1954—all in *News Bulletin*; San Miguel, *"Let All of Them Take Heed,"* 126–34; Montejano, *Anglos and Mexicans*, 242–44; Ignacio M. García, *Hector P. García*, 140–43, 146–54; Carroll, *Felix Longoria's Wake*, 32–53; and Kells, *Héctor P. García*.

2. Ladino, *Desegregating Texas Schools*, 79–93, chap. 6; L. Clifford Davis interview; Griffin and Freedman, *What Happened in Mansfield?*, 1–17; "L. Clifford Davis Files Suit for Three Mansfield Youths in School Case," *Lake Como Weekly*, October 18, 1955; "A Special Text: Fifth Circuit Court Ruling in Mansfield School Case," *SSN*, August 1956; "Rangers Sent," *SSN*, September 1956. The response of the black residents represents an interesting aspect of African American culture: armed self-defense. On armed self-defense, see Tyson, *Radio Free Dixie*; Hill, *Deacons for Defense*; Strain, *Pure Fire*; and, most importantly, Wendt, *The Spirit and the Shotgun*.

3. Peña interview by Roser, 5–7.

4. On Edgar, see Stephen C. Anderson, *J. W. Edgar*.

5. Ruiz, "South By Southwest," ⟨http://www.oah.org/pubs/magazine/deseg/ruiz.html⟩ (June 19, 2010), and "We Always Tell Our Children"; Aguirre, *"Mendez v. Westminster School District"*; Salinas, "Mexican-Americans," 929–51; Arriola, "Knocking on the Schoolhouse Door"; Ramos, "Dismantling Segregation Together"; Strum, Mendez v. Westminster. Toni and Greg Robinson ("Limits of Interracial Coalitions," 93–119) have criticized scholarship on *Mendez* for too casually linking the NAACP and LULAC in a cooperative venture.

6. George I. Sánchez to Robert K. Carr, May 6, 1947, and Sánchez to A. L. Wirin, October 14, 1953, Sánchez Collection, BLAC.

7. See Steven H. Wilson, *"Brown over 'Other White,'"* 24–26; San Miguel, "Struggle against Separate and Unequal Schools"; Price Daniel, Opinion No. V-128, *Digest of Opinions*, 39; "Daniel Is Praised for School Ruling" and "Sanchez Lauds Daniel's Stand," *Daily Texan*, August 24, 1947; and "Daniel Praised for Racial Law Clarification," *AAS*, August 24, 1947.

8. Gus Garcia, Ed Idar Jr., and others first noted segregation in Bastrop in 1947. See Idar, Charles Kidder, and Cristobal P. Aldrete to Honorable Beauford Jester, October 1, 1947 and Beauford H. Jester to Idar, Kidder, and Aldrete, October 3, 1947, both in Idar Papers, BLAC; "Illegal Separation of Races in Schools Is Students' Charge," *SAEN*, October 3, 1947; "Governor Refers Discrimination Charges to 3 State Agencies," *AA*, October 4, 1947; and "Jester Recibe Mas Quejas Contra la Discriminacion" (Jester Receives More Complaints against Discrimination), *La Prensa*, October 4, 1947.

9. Barrientos interview.

10. George I. Sánchez to Clifford Forster [ACLU], May 24, 1947, Sánchez Collection, BLAC.

11. Clifford Forster to George I. Sánchez, May 19, 1947, Sánchez Collection, BLAC.

12. "Latin-Americans File Segregation Charges," *Daily Texan*, November 18, 1947.

13. Clippings, Correspondence, and Documents regarding *Delgado* case and segregation of Mexican Americans in Texas Schools, 1948–80, Herrera Papers, HMRC; *Delgado v. Bastrop ISD* (No. 388 Civil, final judgment), LULAC Council #60 Collection, HMRC; "Segregation Ban Decree by Federal Judge Climaxes 25-Year Fight by LULACs," *Sentinel*, June 18, 1948; San Miguel, *"Let All of Them Take Heed,"* 122–26; Mario T. García, *Mexican Americans*, 264.

14. In 1949 the Texas legislature abolished the Office of the Superintendent of Public Instruction and replaced it with the State Department of Education (later the TEA), headed by the commissioner of education.

15. L. A. Woods to All School Officers of County, City, Town, and School Districts of Texas, ca. 1948–50, Herrera Collection, HMRC. The same letter can be found in García Papers, TAMUCC.

16. J. W. Edgar to Superintendents of Schools, June 21, 1950, Edgar Correspondence, TEA Papers, TSLAC.

17. "Statement of Policy pertaining to Segregation of Latin-American Children," May 8, 1950, Edgar Correspondence, ibid.

18. "Texas' Forgotten People," *Look* magazine, March 27, 1951. .

19. Ed [Idar] to Hector [García], October 22, November 4, 17, 1950, Idar Papers, BLAC; Settlement agreement, signed by J. C. Hinsley, Gus Garcia, and J. W. Edgar, March 27, 1951, García Papers, TAMUCC.

20. To all National, Regional, and Local LULAC Officers from John J. Herrera, ca. May 1952, García Papers, TAMUCC; "Pecos School Segregation Aired before Edgar in Austin," May 15, 1953, "Edgar Says No Segregation at Pecos," December 1953, and "State Board Sustains Edgar in No Segregation Ruling," April 1954, all in *News Bulletin*; "State Board of Education Rejects Segregation Charges in the Pecos School Case," *LN*, April 1954.

21. Gus Garcia, Address Delivered before the United Nations, January 29, 1952, Obledo Papers, UCD.

22. George I. Sánchez to Hector García, July 23, 1970, García Papers, TAMUCC. This letter was obviously written after the *Hernandez* trial, but it does detail the planning of the case. Sánchez noted that they came up with the "class apart" theory because "the highest Texas courts had ruled that 'Mexicans' were 'White,' so it was useless to argue in those courts that 'Mexicans' were discriminated against because no 'Mexicans' were on the jury panel, jury, etc.," ibid. In legal terms, "class" is not associated with social status but rather is synonymous with "group."

23. *Pete Hernandez v. Texas*; "U.S. Supreme Court Bans Discrimination in Jury Service," *News Bulletin*, May 1954; "Hernandez Case Challenges Two Class Theory, 1954," *Forumeer*, 1978, Herrera Collection, HMRC; De León, *Mexican Americans in Texas*, 118–19.

24. *Pete Hernandez v. Texas*. For outstanding analysis of these events, see Haney López, "Retaining Race." See also Olivas, *Colored Men*, and Ignacio M. García, *White but Not Equal*. Hernandez was tried again in 1956, pled guilty, and was sentenced to a jail term of twenty years. See "Hernandez Tried Again: May Be Eligible for Parole Soon," *News Bulletin*, February, March 1956.

25. "Edgar Holds Conference on Mathis School Segregations," December 1954, "Edgar Hears Appeal on Kingsville School Segregation," January 1955, "Edgar Taken to Federal

Court on Segregation Cases," April 1955, and "Segregation Ending in September at Mathis and Carrizo," May, June 1955—all in *News Bulletin*.

26. *Hernandez v. Driscoll CISD*, in Andow Collection, BLAC; "Driscoll School Segregation Protest Laid before Edgar," *News Bulletin*, August 1955.

27. "Latin Segregation Is Curbed by Allred," *TO*, January 22, 1957. For a good discussion of Sánchez and his views, see Mario T. García, *Mexican Americans*, 252–72; Blanton, "George I. Sánchez"; Paredes, *Humanidad*. See also George I. Sánchez to Joe R. Greenhill, May 8, 1947, box 54, folder "Latin American Matters," Atty. Gen. Price Daniel Papers, SHRL; Sánchez to Ed Idar, November 5, 1956, Idar Papers, BLAC.

28. "In South Texas, Latins Protest Discrimination," *TO*, November 7, 1956; San Miguel, *"Let All of Them Take Heed,"* 133–34.

29. Mario T. García, *Mexican Americans*, 266.

30. *Hernandez v. Driscoll CISD*, in Andow Collection, BLAC.

31. Pete Tijerina to Felix Tijerina, February 11, 1957, Andow Collection, BLAC (quotation); LULAC Council #60 meeting notes, September 11, 1958, LULAC Council #60 Collection, HMRC. The same matter was discussed at the next Council #60 meeting; see LULAC Council #60 meeting notes, September 25, 1958, ibid.

32. Pete Tijerina to Felix Tijerina, February 11, 1957, Andow Collection, BLAC.

33. "Pupils Who Can't Speak English in Sad Plight," *HC*, December 2, 1958, 2.

34. "When Felix Tijerina Feels Like a Big Shot, He Thinks of Beer Truck," *HP*, August 8, 1955.

35. In 1956 Felix Tijerina initially promoted a program called the "escuelita del aire" (little school of the air), which would teach basic English to Mexican American children on the radio. The project did not proceed past the planning stages. Kreneck, *Mexican American Odyssey*, 210.

36. Quintanilla, "Little School of the 400"; San Miguel, *"Let All of Them Take Heed,"* 139–60; Kreneck, *Mexican American Odyssey*, 200–203, 218–21; De León, *Ethnicity*, 135–37.

37. "President's Message," *LN*, July 1958; Quintanilla, "Little School of the 400," 59; "Program to Aid 35,000 Latin Children Starts," *HC*, April 16, 1960.

38. "Statement about Tijerina," part of a letter from J. W. Edgar to Mr. Dean Pieper, November 25, 1959, and Felix Tijerina to Edgar, December 19, 1959, Edgar Correspondence, TEA Papers, TSLAC.

39. "Latin American Leaders Back Varied Views," *HC*, December 8, 1958. See also text of H.B.51/S.B.62, "Pre-school Instructional Program for Non-English Speaking Children," Quintanilla Papers, HMRC; De León, *Ethnicity*, 139.

40. "A Message to LULAC," ca. 1959, Sánchez Collection, BLAC. The Little Schools galled George Sánchez, and he contacted a variety of state leaders to complain. In 1959, for instance, he wrote Albert Armendariz: "Here comes Tijerina, the expert and savior, in the great tradition of the segregation of Mexicans, saying 'a little bit of segregation is good.'" Sánchez to Armendariz, June 23, 1959, Sánchez Collection, BLAC.

41. See Quintanilla, "Little School of the 400."

42. George I. Sánchez to A. L. Wirin, May 13, 1954, Idar Papers, BLAC.

43. For a good overview of these cases, see Kluger, *Simple Justice*.

44. *Brown v. Board of Education*.

45. "Segregation in the Schools: The Facts Are Not Altered," *DE*, September 19, 1953;

"NAACP, Dixie Argue School Issue before Supreme Court," *SAR*, December 11, 1953; "NAACP, Justice Dept. Say Jimcrow [*sic*] Illegal," *DE*, December 19, 1953.

46. "J. Crow Schools Outlawed," *SAR*, May 21, 1954.

47. "'Separate but Equal' Doctrine Outlawed by Supreme Court," *DE*, May 22, 1954.

48. "NAACP State Meet Opens Here, Today," *SAR*, October 23, 1953.

49. "NAACP to Kill Texas Jim Crow Fight Law," *SAR*, January 29, 1954; "Texas," *SSN*, February 3, 1955. The case, *Harvey v. Morgan*, was tried in 1954 and the decision handed down in 1955.

50. "Current Events," *DE*, January 7, 1950; "Boycott of 19th Urged," *DE*, June 20, 1953; "Mass Meeting Planned for Action on Bias," *DE*, August 15, 1953; "NAACP Sues, Attacks San Antonio Bias," *HI*, March 12, 1955; "Austin NAACP Challenges Jim Crow Bus Law," *HI*, November 19, 1955.

51. "'See Cinerama with Four Eyes,'" *DE*, March 19, 1955; "Pickets Melba Theatre, Hits Biased Entertainment," *DE*, March 19, 1955 (quotation). "Cinerama" was a projection process that involved three separate cameras simultaneously projecting the film. The Cinerama movie released in 1955 was *Cinerama Holiday*. The *Dallas Express* called the film *Cinerama*, and I have followed this convention.

52. "NAACP Pickets Movie in Jim Crow Protest," *SAR*, April 1, 1955.

53. Minutes of Dallas NAACP Youth Council, September 19, 1956, Craft Collection, DPL; "Large Crowds of Negroes Ignoring Fair," *DMN*, October 17, 1955.

54. "What Caused the Conflict between the Negro Chamber and the State Fair . . . ?," *DE*, October 22, 1955 (quotation). See also "State VP James Stewart, Segregation over at Texas State Fair Says" and "Youth Council to Picket, Gen Davis Refuses Award," *DE*, October 15, 1955; "Bunkley Resigns as Group Votes to Support Fair," *DE*, October 22, 1955. Aside from being contradictory, Thornton's statement was factually inaccurate. Two rides, "Laff in the Dark" and "Dodge 'em Scooter," were off limits to blacks because, according to the fair board, they allowed too much bodily contact between riders.

55. "Paraders Join Picket Line; Many Patrons Turn Away," *DE*, October 22, 1955 (quotation). See also "NAACP Youth Council on March in Protest of Fair Discrimination" and "NAACP Youth, C of C Differ on Fair Segregation Issue," *DE*, October 22, 1955.

56. Minutes of Dallas NAACP Youth Council, September 19, 1956, Craft Collection, DPL; Memo to All Local Branches from Edwin C. Washington, September 17, 1956, *State of Texas v. NAACP* Case Records, CAH; "State Fair Officials to Continue Segregation," *DE*, May 5, 1956.

57. "2 Railroad Depots Here Drop Segregation Rules," *FWST*, January 11, 1956; "Here's How Bus Desegregation Is Expected to Occur in Our City," April 29, 1956, "Van Zandt to Admit Negroes," July 6, 1956, and "First Grade Integration Is Talked," July 13, 1956—all in *Fort Worth Press*; "Integration in S.A. Schools Begins in Fall," *SAR*, July 15, 1955; "Segregation Ends at City Facilities," *SAR*, March 30, 1956. See also "Desegregation in S.A." *TO*, September 4, 1959; "Many Schools Integrate Peacefully, but Not All Try," *TO*, September 12, 1956; "S.A. School Integration Has Moved Smoothly," *SAR*, December 25, 1959; Goldberg, "Racial Change," 353–54; "Texas Advised 'No Hurry'; El Paso, San Antonio to Act," *SSN*, July 6, 1955; "A Special Report: School Desegregation in San Antonio," *SSN*, December 1955; and "Jim Crow Out on Dallas Buses, Bus Segregation to End at Once," *DE*, April 28, 1956.

58. Argument before U.S. Supreme Court, April 13, 1955, Shepperd Speeches, TSLAC. See also "Texas," *SSN*, December 1, 1954; "Report of the Legal and Legislative Subcommittee of the Texas Advisory Committee on Segregation in the Public Schools," September 1, 1956, 2.

59. Ladino, *Desegregating Texas Schools*, 41–42, 93–122, 124–25; "Many Schools Integrate Peacefully, but Not All Try," *TO*, September 12, 1956.

60. McMillen, *Citizens' Council*, 103–5.

61. "Districts Will Receive Funds Regardless of Action on Desegregation," *SAR*, July 8, 1955; J. W. Edgar to Mrs. Eugene Meyer, January 30, 1956, Edgar Correspondence, TEA Papers, TSLAC (quotation); "Legal Conflict," *SSN*, September 1957.

62. "Appeals Court Slows Dallas Desegregation Ordered for January," *SSN*, January 1958.

63. *Bell v. Rippy* (1955); "Federal Court Bars Early Desegregation of Schools in Dallas," *SSN*, October 1955.

64. *Bell v. Rippy* (1956); "Legal Action," *SSN*, June 1956; "Texas Judge's Rebuke; Legislative Plans Feature School Month," *SSN*, January 1957.

65. "Desegregation Ordered at Mid-Term in Dallas, No Other Choices, Atwell Declares," *DTH*, September 5, 1957. See also "US Circuit Court Orders Dallas Public Schools to Integrate," *DE*, July 27, 1957; "Dallas to Appeal Order for Mixing at Mid-Term," *SSN*, October 1957; "Dallas Schools Ordered to Integrate at Mid-Term" and "Dr E Rippy Speaks with No Authority," *DE*, September 14, 1957; and Linden, *Desegregating Schools*, 24. For unknown reasons, possibly because Albert Bell was no longer a minor, the *Bell* case went through several name changes, to *Brown*, back to *Bell*, and a new case was filed as *Borders*.

66. Skelton, "A Summary of School Desegregation Court Cases, 1896–1975," DPL, 1. See also "Dallas Desegregation Out; Atwell 'Goofed,'" *DE*, January 4, 1958; "Reversed and Remanded: 'Deliberate Speed' Time Element Reinstated," *SSN*, January 1958; "Order Entered in Dallas, Tex., Case; Protestant Ministers Sign Statement," *SSN*, May 1958.

67. Linden, *Desegregating Schools*, 26.

68. "Legislature Sidetracks Racial Row," *SAE*, January 9, 1957; "House Offered Plan to Bar Integration," *DMN*, January 23, 1957.

69. For a list of the prosegregation measures, see "Laws and Resolutions Enacted by the 55th Legislature," June 1957, Edgar Correspondence, TEA Papers, TSLAC. See also "9 Segregationist Bills Proposed," *SAE*, January 24, 1957; "11 School Segregation Bills Are Put in Hopper as Texas Legislators Meet," *SSN*, February 1957; "Five Racial Bills Set for Legislative Airing," *SAE*, March 13, 1957; "Bills to Promote Segregation Make Progress in Texas Legislature," *SSN*, April 1957; "Five Segregationist Bills Move Nearer to Final Action in House," *HC*, April 16, 1957 (quotation); and "Race Bills—Constitutional Analysis," *TO*, April 23, 1957.

70. On Alabama, see Eskew, *But for Birmingham*, and Gaillard, *Cradle of Freedom*.

71. See Shabazz, *Advancing Democracy*, 180–95, and Gillette, "NAACP in Texas," chap. VIII.

72. "NAACP Fights for Life against Odds," *DE*, October 6, 1956; "NAACP Ouster Effort, College's Integration Mark Texas Month," *SSN*, October 1956.

73. Ware, "NAACP-Inc. Fund Alliance," 327.

74. "Charges, Counter-Charges Fly at Tyler," *SAR*, October 12, 1956.

75. "NAACP Ban Order Filed," *DMN*, October 25, 1956.

76. "NAACP Is Halted in Texas," *DE*, October 27, 1956; "Texas Gets Anti-NAACP Injunction, 104 Districts Desegregated," *SSN*, November 1956; "State vs NAACP Suit Is Recessed for One Week," *DE*, April 27, 1957; "NAACP Trial Recessed," *DMN*, May 2, 1957. See also *State of Texas v. NAACP* Case Records, CAH; *State of Texas v. NAACP*, No. 56–469; Ware, "NAACP-Inc. Fund Alliance"; and "Background Information for Special Committee of National Board of Directors Appointed to Survey Texas Situation," 1957, NAACP Texas State Conference Papers (microfilm).

77. Members of the Texas NAACP had to comply with seven conditions: they could not practice law, solicit legal business, defend people in court, solicit lawsuits, hire lawyers, engage in political activity, and lobby against Texas laws. "The judgement," stated attorney C. B. Bunkley, "does not prevent the NAACP . . . from employing lawyers and filing lawsuits in which they have a direct interest." "Local NAACP Resumes Operations," *SAR*, May 17, 1957. The state legislature also attempted to ban the NAACP. See "House Adopts NAACP Bill," *DMN*, March 29, 1957.

78. "NAACP Fight Resumes Monday; Court Bares Records of Houston Branch," *DE*, October 13, 1956. In fact, an audit conducted in late 1962 found the Houston branch in shambles. See Richard B. McClain memo to Gloster B. Currant, December 12, 1962, NAACP Branch Department Files, Houston (microfilm).

79. "Dallas NAACP Meet Set Fri," *DE*, June 1, 1957; "NAACP Mass Meet Set for Sunday," *DE*, July 13, 1957; "NAACP Meeting Moved to Dallas," *DMN*, October 27, 1957; "NAACP Moves Regional Meeting from Longview to Dallas," *DE*, November 2, 1957; "NAACP Seeks to Revitalize Units in Texas," *DMN*, October 27, 1957; "The Resurrection of the NAACP," *HI*, May 25, 1957; Dulaney, "Whatever Happened . . . in Dallas?," 77.

80. "Local NAACP Resumes Operations," *SAR*, May 17, 1957 (quotation); Gillette, "NAACP in Texas," 341–43.

81. A. Maceo Smith to Chris Aldrete, October 29, 1953, Idar Papers, BLAC.

82. "Interracial Unity Urged," *DE*, November 7, 1953.

83. President's Address, 21st Annual Convention of the Texas State Conference of NAACP Branches, November 1, 1957, NAACP Texas State Conference Papers (microfilm). See also "Some Criteria for Effective Inter-Group Branch Action," January 30, 1956, ibid.

84. This was also true in Los Angeles after the Zoot Suit riots. See Jon Watson, "Crossing the Colour Lines," 1–10.

85. George I. Sánchez to Roger Baldwin, June 20, 1955, Idar Papers, BLAC.

86. "Hello from Our National President," *LN*, September 1953, 3, 14. Armendariz repeated these views in the October issue of the *LN*.

87. "Hello from Our National President," *LN*, November 1953.

88. "Latin American Leaders Back Varied Views," *HC*, December 8, 1958.

89. George I. Sánchez to John J. Herrera, June 16, 1953, Sánchez Collection, BLAC.

90. Gus Garcia to George I. Sánchez, May 16, 1955, ibid.

91. Gus Garcia to Dear Geo[rge Sánchez], October 24, 1956, ibid. The letter was labeled "personal (and damned confidential)."

92. Occasionally Sánchez did write to Thurgood Marshall, but rarely to black leaders in Texas. See Blanton, "George I. Sánchez," 590–97.

93. "The Case for Segregation," *TO*, March 19, 1957.

94. See Eugene Rodriguez Jr., *Henry B. Gonzalez*; Sloane, *Gonzalez of Texas*; Flynn, *Henry B. Gonzalez*.

95. "Gonzalez Raps Race Bill," *SAE*, March 22, 1957.

96. See G.I. Sánchez to Dear Doctor [Hector García], ca. 1957, Idar Papers, BLAC.

97. "Racial Bill Wins House Test," *SAE*, March 21, 1957; "Race Bills May Get House Action Tuesday," *SAE*, March 26, 1957; "House Votes Bill to Avoid Integration," *DMN*, April 9, 1957; "House Passes 6 Segregation Bills; 8 Wait Senate Action," *DMN*, April 18, 1957; "Segregation Measure Hits Snag in Senate," *DMN*, May 18, 1957.

98. Kazen discussed these issues in a lengthy interview; see "Chick Kazen: Segregation Bills' Foe," *DMN*, May 19, 1957.

99. "All-Night Filibuster Made in State Senate," *DMN*, May 2, 1957.

100. "Chick Kazen: Segregation Bills' Foe," *DMN*, May 19, 1957.

101. "The Segregation Filibuster of 1957," *TO*, May 7, 1957 (translation by *TO*). It was fortunate that newsman Ronnie Dugger was on the senate floor for the filibuster—his reporting was topnotch. As an example of the *filibusteros* questions in Spanish, Gonzalez asked Kazen: "A quien le dan tortillas que llora?" (Who cries if he gets tortillas to eat?). Kazen responded, "El lion juzga a todos su condicion" (All looks yellow to the jaundiced eye). These sayings were Spanish equivalents of "Don't look a gift horse in the mouth."

102. "The Segregation Filibuster of 1957," *TO*, May 7, 1957.

103. "Senators Kazen, Gonzalez Set Filibuster Record," *DE*, May 11, 1957.

104. "The Segregation Filibuster of 1957," *TO*, May 7, 1957.

105. "The Record Vote on H.B. 231," *TO*, May 7, 1957; Press release, May 23, 1957, box 494, folders "HB 231 and HB 65," Texas Gov. Daniel Papers, SHRL.

106. "Second Racial Bill Gets Senate Okay," *DTH*, May 15, 1957; "Gonzalez Starts New Filibuster," *DMN*, May 15, 1957 (quotation); "Texas Legislators Pass Pupil Assignment Law," *SSN*, June 1957.

107. "Senators Kazen, Gonzalez Set Filibuster Record," *DE*, May 11, 1957.

108. On Floyd Bradshaw, see "The Record Vote on H.B. 231," *TO*, May 7, 1957.

109. Gillette, "NAACP in Texas," 341–43.

110. "3 Segregation Bills Await Introduction," *DMN*, October 20, 1957.

111. "Daniel Says He Hopes to Hold New Session to Anti-Troop Bill," *DMN*, November 10, 1957; "Three Bills Offered for School Closing," *DMN*, November 14, 1957; "Second Bill Offered to Aid School Fight," *DMN*, November 15, 1957. See also "Message of Governor Price Daniel concerning Anti-Troops Bill," November 13, 1957, and "Press Memorandum," November 26, 1957, both in folder "Anti-Troops Bill," Texas Gov. Daniel Papers, SHRL.

112. Rev. Das Kelley Barnett, "A Speech Delivered at the Open Hearing of the Texas Senate on Senate Bills One and Two," November 18, 1957, folder "Anti-Troops Bill," Texas Gov. Daniel Papers, SHRL; "Foes of School-Closing Bill Attack Plan in Two Hearings," *DMN*, November 19, 1957.

113. "Anti-Troop Bill Constitutional, Will Wilson Tells Lawmakers," *DMN*, November 19, 1957; "Solon Raps Daniel on 'Troop Bill,'" *SAL*, November 5, 1957; "Gonzalez Talks All Day in 'Baby Filibuster,'" *SAE*, November 5, 1957; "Daniel Is Target of Gonzalez," *HP*, November 5, 1957; "School Legislation Being Filibustered," *HP*, November 22, 1957; "Kazen at Bat, Twin Talkathon," *SAL*, November 23, 1957.

114. "Senator Gonzalez' Filibuster Blocks Action on Troop Bill," *DMN*, November 22,

1957 (quotation); "Senate Passes 2 School Bills," *DMN*, November 23, 1957; "House Committee Quickly OK's Senate-Passed Anti-Troops Bill," *DMN*, November 26, 1957; "Texas Senate Passes Hate Bills Despite Filibuster," *SAR*, November 29, 1957.

115. "Senator Who Fought Race Hate Bill to Speak Here," *HI*, August 3, 1957; "Segregationist 'Minority' Assailed by Gonzalez," *HP*, August 6, 1957 (1st quotation); "Sen Gonzalez Lashes Bias," *DE*, August 10, 1957 (2nd quotation).

116. "Let's Give Sen Gonzalez a Present," *DE*, December 14, 1957; "Gonzalez Christmas Fund," *HI*, December 28, 1957.

117. "Senator Gonzales Speaks at TSU," *HI*, May 24, 1958. See also "Gonzales to Speak for Voters League," *DE*, December 28, 1957; "Sen Gonzalez Roosevelt Day Dinner Speaker," *DE*, February 15, 1958; "Senator to Highlight St John's Anniversary," *DE*, June 21, 1958; "Gonzalez Is UN Tea Speaker," *DE*, July 5, 1958; "Segregation Politics," *HI*, June 28, 1958; and "Latin Americans Ask Why Democrats Ashamed to Endorse Senator Gonzales," *HI*, July 21, 1958.

118. "Gonzalez Warns Hate Salons," *SAR*, October 18, 1957.

119. Press release, July 27, 1956[?]; Press release, n.d.; "Supreme Court Decisions on Separate Schools, Speech of Hon. Price Daniel of Texas," *Congressional Record*, 83rd Cong., 2nd sess. 1954—all in folder "Segregation," U.S. Sen. Price Daniel Papers, SHRL.

120. "Gonzalez Raps Daniel for 'Bias Law S[c]heme,'" *DE*, November 9, 1957.

121. "Senator Gonzalez Runs for Governor," *DE*, May 10, 1958.

122. "The Gonzalez Candidacy," *TO*, May 16, 1958.

123. "Double-Crossing, Bigotry Assailed by Sen Gonzalez," *HI*, June 14, 1958.

124. "Henry's Unorganized Organization," *TO*, July 11, 1958; "Gonzalez on Road, Rough, Tireless," *TO*, July 18, 1958; "Fair Play Caused His Filibuster—Gonzalez," *HI*, July 12, 1958.

125. "Candidates We Support," *DE*, July 26, 1958; "Durham Scolds Texas Dems for Failure to Endorse Gonzalez," *DE*, June 21, 1958.

126. Hector García to Gerald Saldeña, March 13, 1954, García Papers, TAMUCC.

127. "Latin American Leaders Back Varied Views," *HC*, December 8, 1958.

128. Felix Mexican Restaurant Personnel Policy, n.d., Tijerina Papers, HMRC (emphasis in original).

129. Manuel [Avila] to Ed [Idar], February 7, 1956, García Papers, TAMUCC (emphasis in original).

130. Despite a rigorous search, I have been unable to locate a copy of this letter. However, Phil Montalbo discussed this correspondence in a letter to Felix Tijerina on May 27, 1957, as did A. G. Ramirez in a letter to Tijerina dated May 30, 1957. See Montalbo to Felix Tijerina, May 27, 1957, and Ramirez to Felix Tijerina, May 30, 1957, LULAC Council #60 Collection, HMRC.

131. Phil Montalbo to Felix Tijerina, May 27, 1957, ibid. LULAC did not oppose H.B. 231 until early 1959. See "Proposed Segregation Bill Unconstitutional, LULACs Say," *LN*, March 1959.

132. A. G. Ramirez to Pete Tijerina, May 30, 1957, LULAC Council #60 Collection, HMRC.

133. A. G. Ramirez to Felix Tijerina, May 30, 1957, ibid.

134. A. G. Ramirez to LULAC Council #2, May 30, 1957, ibid.

135. "Memo from the Texas Regional Governor," *LN*, February 1957.

136. Pete Tijerina to J. W. Edgar, March 1, 1957, Edgar to Tijerina, March 6, 1957, and Bascom Hayes to J. R. Chapman, March 26, 1957—all in Edgar Correspondence, TEA Papers, TSLAC.

137. "The President's Message," *LN*, July 1957.

138. John J. Herrera, speech delivered at Installation LULAC Banquet, June 1, 1957, Herrera Collection, HMRC.

139. John J. Herrera to Phil Montalbo, June 14, 1957, Herrera Collection, HMRC (emphasis in original).

140. Text of "Resolution #3," June 29, 1957, signed by Pete Tijerina, Cortes Collection, HMRC. See also Carmen Cortes to Price Daniel, n.d. [ca. 1957], folders "HB 231 and HB 65," Texas Gov. Daniel Papers, SHRL.

141. "Resolution 21," *LN*, August 1958.

142. Pete Tijerina to John J. Herrera, July 17, 1957, Herrera Collection, HMRC.

143. "Mexican-Americans Favor Negro School Integration," *News Bulletin*, September, October 1955. Idar based his claims on a rather speculative and distorted reading of a survey conducted by the Texas Poll.

144. Manuel [Avila] to Ed [Idar], February 7, 1956, García Papers, TAMUCC.

145. Kennedy, *Nigger*, 20–22.

146. Manuel [Avila] to Ed [Idar], February 7, 1956, García Papers, TAMUCC (emphasis in original).

147. These terms were largely gibberish. There is no real Spanish-to-English translation for "niggerianos," "niggerifos," and "niggerote." These are simply Spanish-sounding terms that use as the root word "nigger." Special thanks to Lorena Oropeza and José Angel Hernández for help translating Ochoa's Spanish.

148. "Enterando a los Que Saben Leer" (Informing Those Who Know How to read), *Dallas Americano*, January 8, 1958; "¿Manda Usted en Su Propiedad?" (Do You Rule over Your Property?) *Dallas Americano*, January 8, 1958.

149. "Ochoa Periodista Loco" (Ochoa, Crazy Journalist), *Dallas Americano*, January 22, 1958 (1st quotation); "Organizacion de Gente Blanca" (Organization of White People), *Dallas Americano*, June 25, 1958 (2nd quotation).

150. For the Cold War and civil rights, see Carleton, *Red Scare!*; Dudziak, *Cold War Civil Rights*; and Borstelman, *Cold War and the Color Line*.

151. "Los Estorbos al Progreso Texano" (The Obstacles to Tejano Progress), February 5, 1958, "Communism Equals Hispanism," April 28, 1958, and "Integracion Gemelo Comunismo" (Integration's Twin Communism), May 7, 1958, *Dallas Americano*.

152. "Texanos Bajo Dominio Extranjero" (Tejanos under Foreign Domination), *Dallas Americano*, February 19, 1958. Ochoa repeated similar statements a few weeks later in "Texas Necesita a Sus Hijos" (Texas Needs Its Children), *Dallas Americano*, March 12, 1958.

153. "No Use Nopal Como Almohada" (Don't Use a Cactus for a Pillow), *Dallas Americano*, April 16, 1958. For similar sentiments, see "Damos Libertad Que No Tenemos" (We Give Freedom That We Don't Have), *Dallas Americano*, May 14, 1958.

154. The Corpus Christi, Alice, and Kingsville papers were produced, but it is unclear if the San Antonio paper actually appeared.

155. "Quire Mandar Sin Voz Ni Voto?" (Does He Want to Rule without Voice or Vote?), *Dallas Americano*, January 22, 1958.

156. "Pongase Listo a Todo lo que Sucede" (Get Ready for Anything That Can Happen), *Dallas Americano*, May 21, 1958. A few weeks later Ochoa encouraged Mexican Americans to "vote conservative" because other candidates, probably Henry B. Gonzalez, attempted to unite black and Mexican American workers. "Vote Conservativo; Use Pol Tax" (Vote Conservative; Use Poll Tax), *Dallas Americano*, July 16, 1958.

157. Advertisement, *Dallas Americano*, July 23, 1958. The exact phrase was "conserve su raza blanca." In this statement "raza" meant "race," but in later decades "raza" would come to mean "people." See also advertisement "American," *Dallas Americano*, July 2, 1958.

158. "Saturday Vote Conservative," *Dallas Americano*, July 23, 1958.

159. "El Texano Desamparado y Tonto" (The Tejano Defenseless and Foolish) and "News from Spaniol Heads," *Dallas Americano*, July 30, 1958.

160. "Latin American Leaders Back Varied Views," *HC*, December 8, 1958.

161. LULAC did protest H.B. 5, an anti-NAACP bill, because it required subversive "organizations" to register with the attorney general. LULACers feared the measure would allow the state to harm LULAC. See Felix Tijerina telegram to Gov. Daniels [*sic*], December 10, 1957, and Daniel telegram to Tijerina, December 10, 1957, box 481, folder "Second Special Session," Texas Gov. Daniel Papers, SHRL.

162. "Latin American Leaders Back Varied Views," *HC*, December 8, 1958.

163. C. Anderson Davis interview, 32–33; L. Clifford Davis interview.

164. Kreneck, *Mexican American Odyssey*, 207.

165. L. Clifford Davis interview; Sherman interview; Allen interview with author.

166. National Supreme Council meeting notes, Santa Fe, N.Mex., December 6, 1959, Cortes Collection, HMRC.

167. "LULAC National Presidents and Their Administrations," n.d., Herrera Collection, HMRC.

168. Peña interview with Roser, 7–8.

Chapter 3

1. "Local Portrait of a Sit-In," *HFT*, March 12, 1960. For the sit-ins generally, see Meier and Rudwick, *CORE*; Chafe, *Civilities and Civil Rights*; Oppenheimer, *Sit-In Movement*; Dittmer, *Local People*; Carson, *In Struggle*; and Charles M. Payne, *I've Got the Light of Freedom*.

2. Pete Tijerina comments on this segregation in his report to Felix Tijerina, discussed in Chapter 2; see Pete Tijerina to Felix Tijerina, February 11, 1957, Andow Collection, BLAC. Thomas Kreneck (*Mexican American Odyssey*, 269) notes that "discrimination because of skin color and their generalized 'fear of rebuff' prevented [Mexican Americans] from full participation in society." See also Ermelinda Holguin to Gov. Daniel, April 15, 1962, folder "Civil Rights," Gov. Price Daniel Papers, SHRL.

3. "Latin Leader Urges Negroes to Be Patient," *HC*, May 13, 1960. See also the original and edited version of this letter in Tijerina Papers, ca. May 1960, Tijerina Collection, HMRC.

4. "NAACP State Meet Opens Here, Today," *SAR*, October 23, 1953; "Some Criteria for

Effective Inter-Group Branch Action," January 30, 1956, NAACP Texas State Conference Papers (microfilm).

5. See Gillette, "NAACP in Texas"; Berg, *Ticket to Freedom*; Jonas, *Freedom's Sword*.

6. "Nothing but Victory," April 2, 1962 (author unknown), HCHR Papers, HMRC.

7. "TSU Students Fill Counter at Store," *HP*, March 5, 1960.

8. Mease, *On Equal Footing*, 93. Stearns recounts his version of this story in his transcript for *The Strange Demise of Jim Crow*, a videocassette directed by David Berman. "Transcripts Eldrewey Stearns," Cole Desegregation Papers, UH.

9. Richard B. McClain memo to Gloster B. Currant, December 12, 1962, NAACP Branch Dept. Files, Houston (microfilm). This 1962 audit found the Houston branch still in a shambles after the 1957 state trial against the NAACP (*State of Texas v. NAACP*).

10. Cole, *No Color Is My Kind*, 26–27; Lawson interview.

11. "Baptist Alliance Lauds Students," *HI*, March 19, 1960. See also Behnken, "'Count on Me,'" 61–78.

12. "TSU Students Fill Counter at Store," *HP*, March 5, 1960.

13. "Council of 60 Negro Groups Backs 'Strikes,'" *HC*, March 14, 1960; Earl Allen interview. See also "TSU Student Group Widens Its Sitdown," *HP*, March 6, 1960; "Newest Student Sitdown Move Ended Peacefully," *HP*, March 8, 1960; "Sitdown Students Move Campaign to 4th Store," *HP*, March 9, 1960; "Sitdown Demonstration Spreads to 5th Store," *HP*, March 10, 1960; "Usual Polite Manner Prevails," *HI*, March 19, 1960; and "T.S.U. Students' 'Sit-Ins,'" *TO*, March 11, 1960.

14. "T.S.U. Students' 'Sit-Ins,'" *TO*, March 11, 1960; "Felton Turner: 'They Said They Had a Job to Do,'" *HFT*, March 12, 1960; "Torture Linked to Sit-Down," *DE*, March 12, 1960; "French Press Raps Human Branding in Houston, Tex," *DE*, March 19, 1960.

15. Gloster B. Current to Francis L. Williams, March 9, 1960, NAACP Branch Dept. Files, Houston (microfilm).

16. Lewis Cutrer Campaign Poster, Miscellaneous Files, HMRC.

17. "Mayor Cautions Students on Sitdown," *HP*, March 16, 1960; Earl Allen interview; "Mayor Ponders Biracial Talks," *HC*, March 17, 1960; "Usual Polite Manner Prevails," *HI*, March 19, 1960.

18. Muse, *Special Report, Memphis*, 2, 7–8; Lawson, "From Sit-In to Race Riot," 262–67; Lofton, "Calm and Exemplary," 77–79.

19. On these groups, see Ann Dee Quiroz, "Black, White, and Brown"; HCHR Papers, HMRC; and Day, "Heart of Houston."

20. "Mayor Considering Sitdown Study Panel," *HP*, March 25, 1960; "Study to Await End of Sit-Down," *HC*, March 25, 1960.

21. "Mayor to Name Group to Study Biracial Problems," *HC*, March 29, 1960; "Six Accept Posts Here on Racial Group," *HC*, April 1, 1960; "Mayor Still Working on Biracial Panel," *HC*, April 4, 1960; "Houston Faces Integration," *TO*, April 1, 1960.

22. Jensen, "Houston Sit-In Movement," 217.

23. See "Mount Rushmore Image," *LN*, June 1959, which reproduced an image of Mount Rushmore with Tijerina's bust added to the monument. The caption under the illustration read "Among the Greatest."

24. Signed copy of Tijerina's letter opposing sit-ins, ca. May 1960, Tijerina Collection, HMRC. See also "Latin Leader Urges Negroes to Be Patient," *HC*, May 13, 1960.

25. As quoted in Kreneck, *Mexican American Odyssey*, 262.

26. "Café Issue Splits Race Committee," *HC*, May 10, 1960; "Mayor's Bi-Racial Group to Disband," *HP*, June 10, 1960.

27. "Transcripts Eldrewey Stearns," for *The Strange Demise of Jim Crow*, Cole Desegregation Papers, UH (quotation); Jensen, "Houston Sit-In Movement," 215.

28. What took place behind the scenes remains somewhat mysterious, although these events are discussed in greater detail in Cole, *No Color Is My Kind*, 54–55; Berman, *Strange Demise of Jim Crow* (videocassette); Jensen, "Houston Sit-In Movement," 211–20; Kuhlman, "Civil Rights Movement in Texas," 142–53; Mease, *On Equal Footing*, 92–103; and Behnken, "'Count on Me,'" 73–74.

29. Lawson interview; "'Sit-Ins Resume' at Downtown Lunch Counters in Houston," *HI*, July 30, 1960; "Stearnes Says Students Were Served at Joske's-Pay Refused," *HI*, August 6, 1960. See also "Houston, a Backwater of the Revolt," *TO*, November 15, 1963; "Houston in Forefront of Rights Move in Texas," *HC*, July 3, 1964; and Fisher, "Urban Sunbelt."

30. "Behind the Scenes," Quentin Mease transcript for *Strange Demise of Jim Crow*, Cole Desegregation Papers, UH.

31. "Galveston Race Trouble Closes 11 Lunch Counters," *HC*, March 13, 1960; "Galveston: A Contrast," *TO*, April 8, 1960; "Community Action," *SSN*, May 1960; "Galveston Gearing Calmly to Mix Races in Schools," *DMN*, August 15, 1961; "Integration in Texas," *TO*, March 6, 1964; Morland, "Lunch-Counter Desegregation," 12–18, and "Attachment B," 23–24.

32. "Protest at UT," *TO*, March 11, 1960; "Student Picketing Off to Start on Avenue," *AS*, April 27, 1960; "Lunch Counter Sit-In Shuts Bus Facility Here," *AS*, February 16, 1961; "In the Colleges," *SSN*, February 1961. See also "Report of Althea T. L. Simmons, Executive Secretary, Texas State Conference, NAACP," May 2–29, 1960, NAACP Texas State Conference Papers (microfilm).

33. "Jailings, Rope-Offs, Shovings in Sit-Ins," *TO*, May 6, 1960.

34. "Students Demonstrate against Texas Theater," *TO*, December 9, 1960; "Integration Group Mills at Theaters," *AAS*, December 11, 1960; "Stand-Ins Continue on Drag," *AA*, December 14, 1960; "UT Stand-Ins Will Continue," *TO*, December 30, 1960; "450 Protest at Theaters," *AA*, February 13, 1961; "Stand-Ins in Austin Reach Peak" and "Texas Cities Witness Protests," *TO*, February 18, 1961; "Segregation Protest Fast Continuing," *AS*, March 8, 1961; "Hungry Vigil—One Man's Protest," *TO*, March 18, 1961; "News from the States," *Student Voice*, March 1961.

35. "Ordinarily He'd Fight Back," *TO*, June 10, 1961; "2 Theaters Integrated for Students," *AS*, September 5, 1961; "Austin Theaters Give In," *TO*, September 9, 1961.

36. "Joseph V. Luter Elected President of Local NAACP," *SAR*, January 1, 1960; Goldberg, "Racial Change," 355–56.

37. "S.A. May Get Sit-Down Demonstrations," *SAR*, March 11, 1960; "S.A. Stores Integrate; White Held in Cutting," *TO*, March 18, 1960 (quotation).

38. "San Antonio Quietly Integrates Eating Facilities," *SAR*, March 18, 1960; "S.A. Firms Lauded by Youth Council for Integrating," *SAR*, April 8, 1960; Morland, "Lunch-Counter Desegregation," 6–11 and "Attachment A," 22; Philip Schug, "Crumbling Segregation Lines" (sermon), March 27, 1960, Peña Papers, UTSA.

39. "S.A. Firms Lauded by Youth Council for Integrating," *SAR*, April 8, 1960; "Joske's

Asks for 'Patience,'" *SAR*, April 15, 1960; "New Interracial Body to Take Over Dining Issue," *SAR*, April 22, 1960.

40. "Pickets, Sit-Ins at Joske's," *SAR*, April 29, 1960; "Joske's Closes All Dining Facilities," *SAR*, May 6, 1960; "Both Principals in Joske's Slapping 'Not Guilty,'" *SAR*, May 13, 1960; "Chuck Wagon Bars Lowered," *SAR*, July 1, 1960; Burns interview, 7–9; Goldberg, "Racial Change," 358; Morland, "Lunch-Counter Desegregation," 9.

41. "Negro Clergyman Served at Downtown Lunch Counters," *DE*, April 30, 1960; "'Sorry—Tea Room Not Integrated,'" *DE*, May 7, 1960; "Dallas: NAACP Negroes Militant," *TO*, March 11, 1960; "Dallas Blacks Recall Integrating Diners," *DMN*, April 27, 1985; Yvonne Johnson, "Desegregating Dallas," 27, 29; Dulaney, "Whatever Happened . . . in Dallas?," 80; Behnken, "'The Dallas Way.'"

42. Brophy, "Active Acceptance–Active Containment," 140–41; George Allen interview by Johnson, 4–5; Craft interview by Stricklin and Tomlinson, 79, 88–90.

43. "Dallas Group Organizes to End Racial Discrimination," *DE*, August 13, 1960. The DCC usually referenced the Dallas Citizens Council, but for my purposes DCC refers to the Dallas Community Committee.

44. "Interracial Group Pickets H L Green Store," *DE*, October 8, 1960; "Rev James Says Group Protests Integrating Dollar and Segregating Service," *DE*, October 8, 1960 (quotation); "Community Leaders Join in Picketing H L Green," *DE*, October 15, 1960; "NAACP Backs Picket Lines," *DE*, October 8, 1960; "Dallasites Picket Store," *TO*, October 14, 1960; "Dallas Leaders Throw Weight behind Picket Line at 'The H L Green Store,'" *DE*, October 29, 1960; "Green Store Issued Ultimatum in Integrating Facilities," *DE*, November 19, 1960; Dulaney, "Whatever Happened . . . in Dallas?," 80.

45. "Dallasites Picket Stores," *TO*, October 14, 1960; "Protest Bias at State Fair," *DE*, October 15, 1960 (quotations); "NAACP . . . Stage Picket Line Protesting Segregation at the State Fair," *DE*, October 22, 1960; Earl Allen interview.

46. "DCC Sets Deadline to End Jim Crow Counters; Actions Threatened," *DE*, January 7, 1961.

47. "New 'Sit-In' Demonstrations Strike in Dallas," *DE*, January 14, 1961; Earl Allen interview.

48. "DCC Plans Boycott of Bias Stores on the Eve of Big Easter Spending," "'Prayer Demonstration' to Be Held by NAACP Youths Sunday," and "Sit-Ins Note Abe Lincoln's Birthday," *DE*, February 18, 1961; "NAACP Youth Council Stages Downtown Prayer Demonstration for Freedom," *DE*, February 25, 1961; McMillan interview; "DCC Urges 'Old Clothes' for Easter," *DE*, March 4, 1961; Dulaney, "Whatever Happened . . . in Dallas?," 81.

49. "Forty Businesses Involved in Action," *DE*, August 5, 1961; "Dallas Starts Move toward Peaceful Desegregation," *DTH*, August 6, 1961 (quotations); "DCC Works for Peaceful Mixing," *DMN*, August 6, 1961; "Dallas Leaders Work to Prevent Violence," *SSN*, August 1961; George Allen interviews by Johnson, 6, and Saxon, 77–79; Conrad interview, 20–21.

50. "Blue Book," ca. August 1961, NAACP Campaign for Educational Equality, NAACP Papers (microfilm). See also Carmack and Freedmen, *Dallas*, 14; "Dallas Starts Move toward Peaceful Desegregation," *DTH*, August 6, 1961. The *Dallas Express* noted that "thousands of posters presenting the face of a happy Dallas and urging that its citizens avoid violence" were placed throughout the city ("City Girds to Accept Desegregation Honor-

ably," *DE* August 12, 1961). See also "Dallas Editors Urge Peaceful Desegregation," *SSN*, July 1961; "Dallas Leaders Work to Prevent Violence," *SSN*, August 1961; and "Index for Hopeful Change," *TO*, May 26, 1962.

51. On the SCLC, see Fairclough, *To Redeem the Soul*; Peake, *Keeping the Dream Alive*; Garrow, *Bearing the Cross*; and Branch, *Parting the Waters*, *Pillar of Fire*, and *At Canaan's Edge*.

52. "Bold Sit-Ins in Marshall," *TO*, April 1, 1960; Seals, "Wiley-Bishop Student Movement," 73–84.

53. "Intensive Report on Marshall Sit-Ins," "From Chapel to Dousings," "Dogs, Tear Gas," and "Marshall Becomes Tense, Suspicious City," *TO*, April 8, 1960; "Sit-In Demonstrators to Tell 'Marshall Story," *DE*, April 30, 1968; "Marshall Students Tell Dramatic Story of 'Sit-Ins," *DE*, May 7, 1968; Seals, "Wiley-Bishop Student Movement," 85–90.

54. Seals, "Wiley-Bishop Student Movement," 110–17.

55. "News from the States," *Student Voice*, March 1961.

56. Cole, *No Color Is My Kind*, 78–79; Mease, *On Equal Footing*, 84–87; Press release, ca. September 1961, and Clarence A. Laws to Francis L. Williams, September 11, 1961, NAACP Branch Dept. Files, Houston (microfilm).

57. "'Freedom Riders' Sought Cup of Coffee Here," *HFT*, August 19, 1961; "CORE Goes into Action Here," *HI*, August 18, 1962; "CORE Sets Public Workshop," *HI*, August 25, 1962; "Public CORE Workshop Saturday," *HFT*, August 25, 1962; Arsenault, *Freedom Riders*, 389.

58. Cole, *No Color Is My Kind*, 95.

59. "Integrated College Groups Stand-In at Tower Theatre," *DE*, December 9, 1961; "City Parks Integrated in Dallas," *DMN*, June 16, 1963; "Swimming Pools and Parks Desegregated," *DE*, June 22, 1963; "Dallas Theatres Are Now Open to All," *DE*, July 6, 1963; "Movies Here Wipe Out Color Lines," *DTH*, July 30, 1963.

60. "Sutton Wants City Law Amended," *SAE*, October 4, 1963; "City Seeks Voluntary Race Accord," *SAN*, June 5, 1963; "NAACP Puts Pickets at S.A. City Hall," *SAN*, June 12, 1963; "City Hall Picketing Criticized," *SAN*, June 13, 1963; "City Hall Pickets Set to Continue," *SAE*, June 17, 1963; "NAACP to Push Plan for Desegregating S.A.," *SAN*, June 18, 1963; "City Council Takes No Action on Desegregation Proposal," *SAE*, June 20, 1963; "205 Businesses Agree to City Integration Plan," *SAN*, June 27, 1963; "Desegregation Pledges Roll In," *SAE*, June 29, 1963.

61. Protest movements in cities like Austin and Fort Worth started much later than in the state's larger cities. See "City Restaurants Sign Integrate Pact," *AS*, June 6, 1963; "42 Restaurants Desegregated," *AA*, June 8, 1963; "Peaceful Integration—City Action Is Praised," *AS*, June 13, 1963; "City Schools to Integrate," *AS*, June 15, 1963; "Integration Advanced in Schools," *AAS*, June 16, 1963; "Hats Off to Austin," *Capital City Argus*, June 20, 1963; "The Transition of a Cowtown," *TO*, April 14, 1962; "Desegregation Steps Here Disclosed," *FWST*, June 23, 1963; "Texas Is Integrating," *TO*, June 28, 1963; "Quiet, Behind-Scene Efforts Bring Ft. Worth Integration" *SAR*, July 5, 1963; and "No Trouble Seen Here in Mixing," *FWST*, July 30, 1963.

62. "Racial Bars in Texas Are Quietly Disappearing," *HC*, June 30, 1963; "Few Changes Seen after Rights Bill OK'd," *DMN*, June 28, 1964.

63. Richard Morehead, news release "Corpus Christi," Morehead Papers, CAH (see box

3G429); "Report of Althea T. L. Simmons, Executive Secretary, Texas State Conference, NAACP," May 2–29, 1960, NAACP Texas State Conference Papers (microfilm); Morland, "Lunch-Counter Desegregation," 2–5.

64. "Program to Aid 35,000 Latin Children Starts," *HC*, April 16, 1960; Kreneck, *Mexican American Odyssey*, 255–56; "Texas Helps Her Little Latins," *Saturday Evening Post*, August 5, 1961.

65. J. W. Edgar to Felix Tijerina, July 5, 1961, Edgar Correspondence, TEA Papers, TSLAC.

66. Jake Rodríguez to Dear Sir or Madam, May 1962, Quintanilla Papers, HMRC.

67. Jake Rodríguez, "What Price Education?," 2, 7, ibid.

68. Jake Rodríguez to Dear Sir or Madam, May 1962, ibid.

69. Jack McIntosh to Jake Rodríguez, December 21, 1964, ibid.

70. "The Little School of the 400," *LN*, April 1965.

71. "Texas Communities Ask Federal Funds for 'Head Start,'" *SSN*, June 1965; Leon R. Graham to Jake Rodríguez, August 9, 1966, Quintanilla Papers, HMRC. See also Vinovskis, *Birth of Head Start*.

72. Jake Rodríguez to Alfred J. Hernández, June 10, September 29, 1966, and Hernández to Rodríguez, October 20, 1966, Quintanilla Papers, HMRC.

73. Historian Carlos Blanton has shown that in the nineteenth and early twentieth centuries many communities benefited from bilingual education. This knowledge was lost during the Progressive era. In the 1960s educators relearned the value of bilingual teaching. See Blanton, *Strange Career*, chaps. 4, 5, 8.

74. CAC, Bulletin No. 1, ca. December 1958 (quotation), Bulletin No. 2, ca. January 1959, Bulletin, March 9, 1960, Bulletin, September 1960, Bulletin, January 1961—all in PASO Collection, HMRC.

75. Civic Action Committee Bulletin, ca. January 1960, PASO Collection, HMRC.

76. Ibid.

77. In Spanish, "paso" as a noun means "pass" or "happen." PASO was also frequently called PASSO. On the "Viva Kennedy" clubs and PASO, see Ignacio M. García, *Viva Kennedy*, and Gómez-Quiñones, *Chicano Politics*.

78. "Political Association of Spanish Speaking Organizations, Harris County," ca. 1962, in LULAC Council #60 Collection and PASO Collection, HMRC.

79. Harris County PASO Bulletin, October 1962, PASO Collection, HMRC.

80. "'PASO'—Political Interests of Latins United," *TO*, September 15, 1961; "What Is PASO?," folder "PASO," ca. 1963, AHC. See similar document "What Is PASO?," Castillo Papers, HMRC.

81. John J. Herrera, "¡Han Matado a mi Presidente!" (They Have Killed My President), November 1963, Herrera to Carlos McCormick, November 29, 1963, and folder "Viva Kennedy" clubs—all in Herrera Collection, HMRC; De León, *Ethnicity*, 165–66; Ignacio M. García, *Viva Kennedy*.

82. "Latins and Votes," *TO*, January 19, 1962.

83. David G. Gutiérrez (*Walls and Mirrors*, 181) calls this political evolution "a significant shift in strategy and tactics." Certainly the development of PASO bears this out.

84. "PASO Solicita su Voto" (PASO Requests Your Vote), May 6, 1962, "Promises? Your Governor Price Daniel Does What He Says He Will Do," PASO advertisement, n.d. (ca.

May 1962), and Hector P. García to all PASO members, n.d. (ca. May 1962)—all in folder "PASO," Texas Gov. Daniel Papers, SHRL; "Unusual Racial Overtones Noted in Campaign for Governorship," *SSN*, March 1962.

85. Ed Idar to Salvador Guerrero, February 13, 1962, Garcia Papers, FWPL; "Latin Group Split on Endorsement," *TO*, February 16, 1962; Gómez Quiñones, *Chicano Politics*, 70.

86. George I. Sánchez to Hector García, April 24, 1962, García Papers, TAMUCC. See also George I. Sánchez to Ed Idar, May 16, 1962, Idar Papers, BLAC. With an accent on the "o," the word becomes the past tense conjugated verb "pasó" meaning "happened," signaling Sánchez's feelings that the organization was finished.

87. Ed [Idar] to George [Sánchez], May 17, 1962, García Papers, TAMUCC. Idar also closed an angry letter to Sánchez with the words, "Doc, you can go to hell!" See handwritten noted appended to George I. Sánchez letter to Ed Idar, May 16, 1962, Idar Papers, BLAC.

88. Ed [Idar] to H. P. García, May 17, 1962, García Papers, TAMUCC.

89. Gómez-Quiñones, *Chicano Politics*, 70; "Connally, Yarborough Lead in Primary for Governor," *SSN*, May 1962; "Conservatives Win Democratic Runoff by Slim Margin," *SSN*, June 1962. On Connally, see Reston, *Lone Star*.

90. See Shockley, *Chicano Revolt*, and Navarro, *Cristal Experiment*.

91. Navarro, *Cristal Experiment*, 20, 25–26. See also "Latin Americans in Texas Politics," *Texas Almanac*, May 13, 1963; Cornejo interview, 13–15.

92. "PASO Plans Drive from Crystal City," *SAE*, March 23, 1963; "Crystal City Vote to Get PASO Action," *SAE*, March 23, 1963; Navarro, *Cristal Experiment*, 27–29.

93. "Los Cinco Candidatos," *TO*, April 18, 1963 (quotations); Marc Simon Rodriguez, "Movement Made of 'Young Mexican Americans,'" 1–12. See also Marc Simon Rodriguez, "Cristaleño Consciousness," 146–69.

94. "A Town Divided: The Story of Crystal City," *SAEN*, April 13, 1963; "The Revolt of the Mexicans," *Time* magazine, April 12, 1963; "Mexicanos Take Over Crystal City Politics," *Daily Texan*, April 23, 1963.

95. Remarks by Capt. J. A. Loyall to Uvalde Rotary Club, ser. 40 40-21 PASO 1963–65, Connally Papers, LBJ.

96. "Crystal City View—Town 'Taken Over,'" *SAL*, April 17, 1963.

97. "Los Cinco Candidatos," *TO*, April 18, 1963; Samora, Bernal, and Peña, *Gunpowder Justice*, 91–94, 102, 104–7.

98. José Angel Gutiérrez, *Making of a Chicano Militant*, 43.

99. Navarro, *Cristal Experiment*, 32–33; Samora, Bernal, and Peña, *Gunpowder Justice*, 102.

100. "Crystal City Harmony Pledged," *SAL*, April 16, 1963; "Crystal City View—Town 'Taken Over,'" *SAL*, April 17, 1963; "Dealt a Poor Hand, Teamsters Take All," *DMN*, May 7, 1963; "Crystal City Gave PASO Pilot Project It Needed," *DMN*, May 7, 1963; "Latin-American Takeover of Town Watched by Nation," *SSN*, June 1963; "The Other Texans," *Look* magazine, October 8, 1963; Rivera, "Nosotros Venceremos," 56–64.

101. "Los Cinco Candidatos," *TO*, April 18, 1963; Medrano interview, 31–32.

102. Shockley, *Chicano Revolt*, 14–16.

103. "Crystal City Vote Probe Aid Offered," *SAEN*, April 13, 1963; "Crystal City: Con-

fusion, Sorrow, Hate," *SAEN*, April 14, 1963; "Cornejo Girds for Crystal City Showdown Fight," *SAN*, June 17, 1963; "While the Migrants Are Gone," *TO*, July 12, 1963.

104. "Shock Waves from Popeye Land," *TO*, May 16, 1963. Cornejo later pressed charges against Allee and sued him for $15,000 in damages. When no witnesses came forward, the suit was dismissed.

105. Samora, Bernal, and Peña, *Gunpowder Justice*, 113–24; "Cornejo Charges Attack by Ranger," *SAE*, April 30, 1963; "Crystal City Group Raps Governor," *SAN*, May 1, 1963; "Shock Waves from Popeye Land," *TO*, May 16, 1963; Bexar County PASO to The Reader, ca. May 1963, PASO File, SAPL.

106. I have borrowed the term "cristal experiment" from Armando Navarro (*Cristal Experiment*), whose work is the cornerstone of scholarship on Crystal City.

107. "Tactics by PASO Hit," *SAN*, April 15, 1963; "PASO Critics May Get Turn," *SAE*, April 17, 1963; "PASO Chief Seeks Peace in Crystal City," *SAEN*, May 4, 1963; "Shock Waves from Popeye Land," *TO*, May 16, 1963; "Deep Split Opens Up at PASO Convention" and "Dissension Erupts at PASO Meeting," *DMN*, June 9, 1963; "Pena [sic] Faction Keeps PASO Reins," *CCC*, June 10, 1963.

108. Kaplowitz, *LULAC, Mexican Americans*, chap. 2; Márquez, *LULAC*, 11–12, 58–59.

109. "Crystal City's LULAC Plans Election Meeting," *SAN*, June 17, 1963. Bonilla had challenged Peña for the chairmanship of PASO and lost. His efforts in Crystal City might have been motivated by a need for revenge against Peña. See also "LULAC Said Non-Political," *SAE*, June 26, 1963.

110. George I. Sánchez to William D. Bonilla, June 17, 1963, García Papers, TAMUCC.

111. Shockley (*Chicano Revolt*, 42, chap. 3) makes this point explicitly.

112. "CASAA Organized to Blockade PASO," *DMN*, August 26, 1963; Shockley, *Chicano Revolt*, 40–43; Navarro, *Cristal Experiment*, 42–43.

113. "CASAA Organized to Blockade PASO," *DMN*, August 26, 1963; "CASA, Not PASO," *Time* magazine, April 16, 1965; Navarro, *Cristal Experiment*, 38–42; Shockley, *Chicano Revolt*, 52–55.

114. Navarro, *Cristal Experiment*, 47–51.

115. Montejano, *Anglos and Mexicans*, 284.

116. Navarro, *Cristal Experiment*, 41–42; "Mathis Liberals Try Anew," *TO*, September 17, 1965.

117. Goldberg, "Racial Change," 372.

118. Notice to Employees from Felix Tijerina, July 3, 1964, Tijerina Collection, HMRC.

119. "El Torero" (The Bullfighter), *LN*, July 1963.

120. "President's Message," *LN*, August 1963; "LULAC Leader Assails Public Demonstrations," August 29, 1963, [probably *HC*] clippings files, LULAC Council #60 Collection, HMRC.

121. Paul Andow, "Civil Rights 'Quid Pro Quo,'" Statement of National Policy, speech delivered at National Supreme Council Meeting, August 25, 1963, Flores Collection, BLAC.

122. "United in Effort and Purpose," *LN*, July 1964.

123. "Minorities and Their Future," *LN*, November 1964.

124. William D. Bonilla to Frank Kelley, May 1, 1963, ser. 35 40-57-15 Race 1963, Connally Papers, LBJ.

125. Medrano interview, 39.

126. Pete Perez, speech delivered at the founding of a LULAC chapter in Fort Worth, January 31, 1967, TGNC Papers, TSLAC; "Latin American Unit Seeks Charter Here," clipping, [probably *FWST*], February 1, 1967, TGNC Papers, TSLAC.

127. "Rally Backed by Gonzalez," *DMN*, August 29, 1963; "Gonzalez Promises His Continued 'Rights' Support," *SAR*, February 28, 1964; "Gonzalez Pledges Rights Support," *HI*, March 14, 1964; "'If Elected, I Promise My Friends,'" *LN*, June 1964.

128. Smith interview by author.

129. Márquez, *LULAC*, 64.

130. "L.U.L.A.C.—Past, Present, Future," *LN*, June 1964.

131. "Senator Gonzalez Addresses H-T Student Body," *DE*, April 30, 1960 (1st and 2nd quotations); "Congressman-Elect Gonzalez Addresses NAACP Convention," *DE*, November 18, 1961; "State Attorneys Say NAACP Had No Part in Stirring Suits," *SSN*, December 1961 (3rd quotation).

132. "Cornejo Wire Goes to King," *SAN*, May 10, 1963.

133. Lawson interview; McMillan interview; Earl Allen interview; Goldberg, "Racial Change," 372. See also Griffin interview.

134. These things went hand in hand. The *LN* often had financial trouble, but these problems dissipated in the 1960s. More Mexican Americans joined the league, which stabilized the *LN* and helped attract new members. See Márquez, *LULAC*, 7, and Kaplowitz, *LULAC, Mexican Americans*, chap. 3.

135. Burns interview, 14.

136. "Crystal City: Confusion, Sorrow, Hate," *SAEN*, April 14, 1963; "Latin-American Takeover of Town Watched by Nation," *SSN*, June 1963; Gutiérrez interview; Smith interview by author.

137. "Texas' Latins Bid for Better Lot with Ballots," *FWST*, April 5, 1964.

138. Arthur W. Molina to PASO, August 16, 1965, ser. 40 40-21 PASO 1963–65, Connally Papers, LBJ.

139. Nueces County PASO to Memorial Hospital Officials and Board of Trustees, November 6, 1963, García Papers, TAMUCC.

140. William D. Bonilla to Frank Kelley, May 1, 1963, ser. 35 40-57-15 Race 1963, Connally Papers, LBJ; Frank H. Kelley to Ritchie's River Bend Camp, May 23, 1963, TGNC Papers, TSLAC.

141. Craft interview by Egerton, 12.

142. Cruz interview; Burns interview, 11–13.

143. Connally, for instance, had opposed President Kennedy's plans for a civil rights bill, arguing that "we have avoided the cold, arbitrary tool of governmental edict." See "A Special Message by Governor John Connally," ca. July 24, 1963, ser. 5(b), Civil Rights Speech Statewide Television Address, Connally Papers, LBJ.

144. "City Group Sets Protest to Connally," *AS*, July 29, 1963; "Negro Resumes Wait for Connally," *AS*, July 30, 1963; "40 Stage March around Mansion," *AA*, July 30, 1963; "Protestor Will See Governor," *AS*, July 31, 1963; "Negroes' Plan to March Okayed by City Council," *AS*, August 1, 1963; "Bonner Meeting Fails to Come Off," *AS*, August 6, 1963; "Bonner Skips Connally Meeting When Comrades Turned Away," *AA*, August 7, 1963; "Integrationist Admits Record, Plans March on State Capitol," *DMN*, August 8, 1963; "Texans March," *DE*,

September 7, 1963; "Who Is B. T. Bonner?," *DE*, August 24, 1963; Kuhlman, "Booker T. Bonner," 4–8. For an exchange that shows Connally's racial sensibilities, see A. W. Stinson to Gov. Connally, August 6, 1963, ser. 35 40-30-10 Civil Rights R-T, Connally Papers, LBJ.

145. "Five to Speak at Local March," *AAS*, August 25, 1963; "Pair of Racial Groups Slate Austin Marches," *AA*, August 27, 1963; "Parade by Negroes Called O.K." *FWST*, August 27, 1963; "Dallas Group to Join State Demonstrators," *DMN*, August 28, 1963; "Marches in Austin Go without Trouble," *AA*, August 29, 1963; "Freedom Now Parade," *Capital City Argus*, August 29, 1963; "San Antonians Join March on State Capital," *SAR*, August 30, 1963; "Teenagers Predominate in Rival Demonstration," *SSN*, September 1963; "Texans March," *DE*, September 7, 1963; Kuhlman, "Civil Rights March on Austin," 153–66.

146. "State's Liberals Join in Coalition," *DMN*, June 14, 1963; "A Four-Group Coalition," *TO*, August 9, 1963; "Bexar Coalition 'Weak Links' Out, Peña Says," *SAE*, September 19, 1964. The group was often referred to as Voters of Texas Enlist (VOTE).

147. "Political Association of Spanish Speaking Organizations, Harris County," ca. 1962, in LULAC Council #60 Collection and PASO Collection, HMRC.

148. "Minorities and Their Future," *LN*, November 1964.

149. CAC Bulletin, ca. January 1960, PASO Collection, HMRC.

150. "The Latin Citizen: His Hardship, His Promise," *TO*, March 9, 1962.

151. Burns interview, 15.

152. "A Dark-Skinned Throng before the Court," *TO*, March 7, 1963.

153. "A Comment," *TO*, April 18, 1963. On this type of racial essentialism, see Black interview by Wolfe. Dugger's "comment" referred to a 1961 letter from George Sánchez. For a discussion of that letter, see George Sánchez to Ed Idar, September 12, 1961, Idar Papers, BLAC.

Chapter 4

1. See Blair Justice, *Violence in the City*; Fine, *Violence in the Model City*; Belknap, *Urban Race Riots*; and Herman, *Fighting in the Streets*. The spelling of Gonzalez's is open to question. Historian Roberto Treviño spells it "Gonzales," whereas newspapers in the 1960s spelled it "Gonzalez." I follow the press's spelling.

2. "Priest Urges Latin-Negro Axis," *DMN*, August 13, 1967; "Sacerdote Catolico Elogio a los Amotinados en Conflictos Raciales" (Catholic Priest Praises the Rebels in Racial Conflicts), *El Sol de Texas*, August 18, 1967; Treviño, *Church in the Barrio*, 197–99.

3. On Mexican American ethno-Catholicism, see Matovina, *Guadalupe and Her Faithful*; Espinosa, Elizondo, and Miranda, *Latino Religions*; Treviño, *Church in the Barrio*; and Mario T. García, *Católicos*.

4. "The War on Poverty in Texas," "Corpus Program Teaches Birth Control," and "Other Cities Hesitating," *TO*, March 19, 1965.

5. "Job Corps, VISTA Applications Available in S.A.," *SAR*, February 5, 1965; "Poverty Panel to Be Feature of NAACP Meeting," *SAR*, February 19, 1965.

6. "Black Houston," *TO*, May 13, 1966.

7. "Message from the National President," *LN*, January 1966. SER stood for "service, employment, redevelopment." "Ser" is also the Spanish verb "to be."

8. Betty MacNabb to Bill Crook, August 8, 1966, Hernández Papers, HMRC; "History of

SER-Jobs for Progress," ⟨http://www.lulac.org/programs/economic/ser_jobs/index.html⟩; De León, *Ethnicity*, 171–72; Castillo interview, 38–41.

9. "Operation SER," condensed program version by Carl E. Craig, July 28, 1966, Hernández Papers, HMRC; "Current Experimental and Demonstration Projects Directed Primarily toward Spanish-Speaking Americans," OEO Office of Manpower, Policy, Evaluation, and Research, August 26, 1966, ibid.; "Operation SER, Bridge to the Barrio," excerpt reprinted from *Manpower Magazine* (a publication of the U.S. Department of Labor), December 1969, Eguia Collection, HMRC. For a local version of SER, see "The Dallas SER Project," ca. 1970; Press release, "13,000 Mexican Americans Win Jobs through Operation SER," Dallas SER, October 30, 1970; and "Dallas. . . . Manpower Plan 1971–72," Dallas SER, 1971—all in Martinez Collection, DPL.

10. "The Texas Front—1967. . . . In the Nation's War on Poverty," Annual Report of the Texas OEO, September 30, 1967, WHCF subject file box 126, EX FG 11-15 11/27/67–12/31/67, LBJ.

11. See "The Bracero Program," ⟨http://www.farmworkers.org/bracerop.html⟩.

12. "Four Boys in La Joya," *TO*, March 7, 1963. See also *What Price Wetbacks?*

13. See Craig, *Bracero Program*; Juan Ramon García, *Operation Wetback*; David G. Gutiérrez, *Walls and Mirrors*; and Blanton, "Citizenship Sacrifice."

14. "Bracero Bill Defeated," *LN*, May 1963. See also "Migrant Officials Ired by Migrants," *TO*, December 16, 1960, and "West Texans Aroused by U.S.," *Beaumont Enterprise*, December 7, 1961.

15. These debates went back a number of years. The $1.25 minimum wage was initially for youths involved in the Neighborhood Youth Corps. See "New State Agency Proposed to Assist Migratory Labor," *DMN*, December 16, 1956; "Council Asks State Migrant Labor Panel," *AAS*, December 16, 1956; "Moderate Program Explained," *SAL*, September 4, 1960; "Education of Migrant Workers Discussed," *Lubbock Avalanche-Journal*, March 9, 1962; "Migrants' Solutions Offered," *AA*, March 9, 1962; "The War on Poverty in Texas," *TO*, March 19, 1965; "Segregated and Self-Segregating" and "The Most Forgotten People," *TO*, June 10, 1966; and "A Struggling 'Minority': The Texas Mexicans," *TO*, December 9, 1966.

16. Alicia Chávez, "Dolores Huerta," 240–54. See also del Castillo and Garcia, *César Chávez*; La Botz, *César Chávez*; and Medrano interview, 40–67.

17. "'A Long Struggle with La Casita,'" *TO*, June 24, 1966; "On Being a Labor Organizer," *TO*, September 2, 1966; "Mexican-American Farm Workers in Texas March for Minimum Wage," *UAW News*, September 1966; "Easter Caravan for 'La Huelga,'" United Farm Workers Organizing Committee flier, ca. August 1966, VISTA Collection, HMRC; "La Huelga: Why Is There a Strike in Starr County?," United Farm Workers flier, ca. 1966, Migrant Farm Workers Organizing Movement Collection, UTA; Bailey, "Starr County Strike," 47–48.

18. *Un malcriado* is an ill-bred or back-talking child. The best English translation for this paper is probably *The Spoiler*. See "Gran Huelga en Texas" (Great Strike in Texas), June 16, 1966, "Editorial: Just a Wage," June 30, 1966, and "From the Day the Bridge Was Burned," ca. June 1966, *El Malcriado*; and "'A Long Struggle with La Casita,'" *TO*, June 24, 1966.

19. "Strikers in Valley to March," *SAE*, June 17, 1966; "Ripple along the Rio," *SAE*, July 5, 1966; "Unlikely Place for a Strike," *SAE*, July 6, 1966.

20. Robert E. Lucey et al. to Honorable John Connally, August 24, 1966, ser. 32 40-45-40

Migrant Workers March on Capitol, Connally Papers, LBJ. See also Treviño, *Church in the Barrio*, 187–94.

21. "Two Priests Join March of Striking Farm Workers," *DMN*, June 8, 1966; "Catholic Priests Join Protest March in Valley," *DMN*, June 18, 1966; "Continued March Planned in Valley," *SAN*, July 5, 1966; "Priests Active in Strike," *SAE*, July 7, 1966; "The Valley Strikers Are Walking to Austin," *TO*, July 22, 1966; "Marchers Say Purpose Is 'Justice,'" *SAE*, ca. August 1966, in Rio Grande Valley Strike File, SAPL; Bailey, "Starr County Strike," 50. On Archbishop Lucey, see Bronder, *Social Justice*. For the march's schedule of stops, see "Easter Caravan for 'La Huelga,'" United Farm Workers Organizing Committee flier, ca. August 1966, VISTA Collection, HMRC.

22. See, e.g., Carmen T. Rangel to Gov. John Connally, June 15, 1966, and Connally to Rangel, March 2, 1967, in ser. 32 40-45-40 Migrant Workers, Connally Papers, LBJ.

23. "A Different Kind of Job Corps Center," *Southern Education Reporter*, March–April 1966. For information on Camp Gary today, see ⟨http://gary.jobcorps.gov/about.aspx⟩ (accessed September 10, 2010).

24. Glenn E. Garrett to Honorable John Connally, July 15, 1966, Walter Richter statement to Connally, ca. July 1966, Richter memo to Connally, ca. July 1966, and Julian Weeks to Terrell Blodgett, July 12, 1966—all in ser. 32 40-45-40 Migrant Workers, Connally Papers, LBJ. See also Report, "The Texas Front—1967 . . . in the Nation's War on Poverty," Annual Report of the Texas OEO, September 30, 1967, WHCF subject file box 126, EX FG 11-15 11/27/67–12/31/67, LBJ.

25. "The March into Corpus Christi," *TO*, August 5, 1966. *Venceremos* can also be translated as "we will win." See also "150 Marchers Trek into Poth," *SAL*, August 21, 1966, and "Valley Marchers Nearing Austin," *AFL-CIO News*, August 20, 1966.

26. "Marchers Say Purpose Is 'Justice,'" *SAE*, ca. August 1966, Rio Grande Valley Strike File, SAPL.

27. "Priests Active in Strike," *SAE*, July 7, 1966. See also "An Army on the Move," press release for *SAE* and *SAN* by Henry J. Casso, August 1966, Gayton Collection, BLAC, and "Father Sherrill Smith Denies Strikers Tried to Halt Truck," *SAE*, August 10, 1966.

28. See Cox, *Ralph W. Yarborough*.

29. "From a Senator in Rain to a Church," *TO*, September 2, 1966; "Marchers Get New Backing," *SAE*, August 23, 1966; "Valley Marchers Told of Union Win," *SAE*, August 24, 1966; "Valley Marchers Plan Busy S.A. Schedule," *SAL*, August 26, 1966.

30. Sermon by His Excellency, Most Rev. Robert E. Lucey, August 27, 1966, Gayton Collection, BLAC.

31. "The March: A Triumph, a Task," *TO*, September 16, 1966.

32. Rev. James L. Novarro to Preston Smith, August 19, 1966, and Smith to Novarro, August 22, 1966, box 717, folder 9, Smith Papers, TTU. Speaker of the House Ben Barnes also attended the meeting.

33. "The Confrontation," *TO*, September 16, 1966. The *Texas Observer* reprinted the entire conversation between state officials and the marchers, which had been recorded by Ken Allen, a social worker from Dallas.

34. "Farm Workers End March at Capitol," *SAE*, September 6, 1966.

35. "Cesar Chavez' Plan" and "Labor Day in Austin," *TO*, September 16, 1966; "Farm Workers End March at Capitol," *SAE*, September 6, 1966; "Two Farm Workers Stay on

Capitol Steps after March," *SAL*, September 6, 1966; "Trabajadores Mexican Americans Marcharon Hasta Austin Para Reclamar Salarios Minimos" (Mexican American Workers Marched to Austin to Demand Minimum Wage), *El Sol de Texas*, September 1, 1967; "Marcharon los Trabajadores del Valle Sobre Austin" (The Workers Marched from the Valley to Austin) *El Sol de Texas*, September 8, 1967; Rhinehart and Kreneck, "Minimum Wage March."

36. "Two Farm Workers Stay on Capitol Steps after March," *SAL*, September 6, 1966; "Starr County: To Lose a Strike, but Nurture an Awakening" and "Movement Behind the Cactus Curtain," *TO*, December 9, 1966; "La Huelga's New Look," *TO*, February 17, 1967; Mario Obledo to All Officers and Councils, ca. January 1967, Flores Collection, BLAC. See also Rep. Lauro Cruz to Valley Farm Workers Assistance Committee, ca. January 1967, Flores Collection, BLAC, and "Valley Farm Workers Assistance Committee — State Board Meeting," January 13, 1968, Castillo Papers, HMRC.

37. "Labor Day in Austin," *TO*, September 16, 1966.

38. "Fr. Smith Assails 'Gringos,'" *SAE*, February 22, 1967.

39. "LULACs Approve Valley Strike Aid," *SAN*, July 18, 1966.

40. "AFL-CIO Plans Aid to Valley Workers," *SAE*, June 12, 1967.

41. "Press Release to *El Paso Times*," ca. June 1966, Flores Collection, BLAC.

42. "LULAC Group Vote Likely on March," *SAE*, August 11, 1966.

43. "LULAC and the War on Poverty," *LN*, January 1965.

44. "Latin Americans Hardest Hit by Poverty," *LN*, February 1965. See also "Plight of Latin in Texas Said to Exceed Negro's," *DMN*, September 1, 1966.

45. "Message from the National President," *LN*, March 1966 (emphasis in original); Kaplowitz, "Distinct Minority," 199–200.

46. "LULAC in the News," *LN*, April 1966.

47. "Information from the Equal Employment Opportunity Commission," *LN*, January 1966.

48. "Latin Leaders Walk Out on U.S.," *TO*, April 15, 1966; Jose Andres Chacon, "The Minority No One Knows," ca. 1968, Peña Papers, UTSA.

49. "LULAC in the News," *LN*, April 1966; "Latin Leaders Walk Out on U.S.," *TO*, April 15, 1966.

50. George I. Sánchez to Franklin D. Roosevelt Jr., April 5, 1966, Samora Papers, BLAC; "Equal Employment Opportunity Conference" press release, attached to Sánchez to Roosevelt, April 5, 1966, ibid.

51. George I. Sánchez to the Participants Who "Walked Out" of the EEOC Conference at Albuquerque on March 28, 1966, Samora Papers, BLAC.

52. "Needed: A Marshall Plan for Mexican-Americans," *TO*, April 15, 1966.

53. "Latins Ready to March, Leader Says," *HP*, April 21, 1966.

54. "Resent Denial of Designation," *SAN*, November 18, 1965.

55. "L.A. Label on Babies Draws LULAC Protest," *SAN*, December 3, 1964. See also "LULAC Wins against 'Other,'" *LN*, December 1967.

56. "Latin Americans Due 'White' Classification," *CCC*, October 13, 1967; "City Latins Satisfied with Ruling," *CCC*, October 14, 1967; George I. Sánchez to Sen. Ralph Yarborough, Flores Collection, BLAC. See also the letters relating to this matter in García Papers, TAMUCC: Ed Idar to Vicente Ximenez, September 23, 1967, Solomon Arbeiter

to Hector García, October 3, 1967, Peter Libassi telegram to J. W. Edgar, October 20, 1967, Libassi to Edgar, October 20, 1967, and Libassi to Yarborough, n.d.

57. Albert Piñon to Honorable Lyndon B. Johnson, November 1, 1965, and Lee C. White to Mr. Piñon, November 10, 1965, WHCF subject file box 23, EX-HU2/MC 10/27/65–3/11/66, LBJ.

58. Membership List, Ad Hoc Committee, April 22, 1966, García Papers, TAMUCC.

59. Rudy L. Ramos to John Macy (Civil Service Commission chairman), April 22, 1966, García Papers, TAMUCC.

60. "News Release," Washington, D.C. Office, G.I. Forum (Rudy Ramos was president of the Washington, D.C., Forum and Ad Hoc Committee), ca. May 1966, García Papers, TAMUCC. The "Big Six," a phrase attributed to Malcolm X, varied over time depending on who headed the major civil rights organizations.

61. "Washington Report," Ad Hoc Committee, ca. May 1966, and Rudy Ramos to Augustin Flores, ca. May 1966, García Papers, TAMUCC.

62. Pycior, *LBJ and Mexican Americans*, 170; "Washington Report," Ad Hoc Committee, ca. May 1966, García Papers, TAMUCC; "Washington, D.C., Report," Ad Hoc Committee, May 17, 1966, García Papers, TAMUCC.

63. Farmer Interview II, ⟨http://www.lbjlib.utexas.edu/johnson/archives.hom/oralhistory.hom/Farmer/farmer2.pdf⟩, 14–15.

64. Henry Interview I, ⟨http://www.lbjlib.utexas.edu/johnson/archives.hom/oralhistory.hom/Henry-A/Henry01.PDF⟩, 25–26. On Henry, see Henry, *Aaron Henry.*

65. Kaplowitz, *LULAC, Mexican Americans*, 121.

66. Announcement, "Dinner Tonight," May 26, 1966, and Press release, UPI-98 (Mexicans), May 26, 1966, WHCF subject file box 23, EX HU2/MC 5/25/66–5/31/66, LBJ.

67. Ralph C. Casarez to Pres. Lyndon B. Johnson, May 24, 1966, and Joseph A. Califano Jr. to Casarez, June 9, 1966, WHCF subject file box 24, HU2/MC 6/1/66–6/15/66, LBJ. See also Memorandum, Edward C. Sylvester Jr. to Honorable Clifford L. Alexander Jr., May 3, 1966, WHCF subject file box 22, Ex HU2/MC 4/14/66–5/24/66, LBJ; Abel Alvarez to President of the U.S.A., June 6, 1966, and Joseph A. Califano Jr. to Alvarez, June 14, 1966, WHCF subject file box 24, HU2/MC 6/1/66–6/15/66, LBJ.

68. See Armando C. Quintanilla to Pres. Lyndon B. Johnson, June 13, 1966, and Joseph A. Califano Jr. to Quintanilla, June 17, 1966, WHCF subject file box 24, HU2/MC 6/16/66–7/31/66, LBJ. The president's actions so impressed LULAC that the group passed several resolutions in support of him. See LULAC Resolutions, signed June 26, 1966, ibid; Belen B. Robles to The President, July 12, 1966, and Joseph A. Califano Jr. to Robles, July 24, 30, 1966, ibid.

69. Robert E. Lucey to Joseph A. Califano, March 31, 1967, and William D. Bonilla to Califano, April 4, 1967, WHCF subject file box 29, WE9 4/8/67–4/19/67, LBJ.

70. Remarks by Gov. Connally before Texas Conference for the Mexican-American, April 13, 1967, ser. (5a), San Antonio, Connally Papers, LBJ. See also "Message from the National President," *LN*, April 1967.

71. "Civil Rights Groups Takes Slap at Texas Conditions," *DMN*, June 18, 1967.

72. Memo, Lyndon Johnson to Secretaries Wirtz, Gardner, Freeman, Weaver, Shriver, and Ximenes, June 9, 1967, WHCF subject file box 386, EX-FG 687, ICMAA (1 of 2), LBJ; Weekly Compilation of Presidential Documents, 840–47, WHCF subject file box 386,

EX-FG 687 (2 of 2), LBJ; Report to the President, "The Mexican American—A New Focus on Opportunity," June 9, 1967, Aides Files—Barefoot Sanders, box 14, H. Barefoot Sanders Personal Papers, "Mexican Americans," LBJ; "L.B.J. Interviene Para Terminar Con La Discriminacion de los Mexico-Americanos" (LBJ Intervenes to End Discrimination of Mexican Americans) *El Sol de Texas*, September 15, 1967; Kaplowitz, *LULAC, Mexican Americans*, 117–20.

73. "The Rangers and La Huelga," *TO*, June 9, 1967.

74. George I. Sánchez to Honorable John Connally, June 1, 1967, Peña Papers, UTSA. See also Medrano interview, 66–74.

75. "Arrests Impede the Picketing," *TO*, June 9, 1967.

76. "Rally Protests Rangers in Valley," *Valley Evening Monitor*, June 4, 1967; "The Dimas Incident," "Conversation with the Captain," "'What Force We Deemed Necessary,'" "Medical and Press Matters," and "Arrests Impede the Picketing," *TO*, June 9, 1967; "From the Day the Bridge Was Burned," *El Malcriado*, ca. August 1967; "Testimony of Benito Rodriguez, ca. June 1967, Migrant Farm Workers Organizing Movement Collection, UTA.

77. "Little People's Day," *TO*, June 21, 1967 (quotations); "Bernal: Rangers Like an Appendix," *SAE*, June 12, 1967; "Allee and Garrison Deny the Allegations," *TO*, June 21, 1967; "Panel Told Rangers 'Brutal to Pickets,'" *DMN*, June 30, 1967; "Texas Farm Workers' Struggle Heard by Senate Committee," *UAW Washington Report*, July 10, 1967; "Senadores en el Valle" (Senators in the Valley), *El Malcriado*, July 21, 1967; "Senadores Investigan Acusaciones Contra los Soldados Rangers" (Senators Investigate Accusations against the Texas Rangers), *El Sol de Texas*, July 14, 1967; "Capt. Allee Told to Not Testify," *SAE*, July 13, 1967.

78. Bailey, "Starr County Strike," 58–60; "The Strike Is Beset by Woes," *TO*, June 9, 1967.

79. "NAACP Launches Selective Buying Drive against Skillerns Drug Stores," *DE*, April 13, 1963.

80. "Pickets," *DE*, April 20, 1963.

81. "Pickets to Continue at Skillerns," *DE*, April 27, 1963.

82. "Dallas Transit Hires 2 Negro Drivers as Result of Negro C of C Negotiations," *DE*, May 25, 1963.

83. For the protests in Birmingham, see Eskew, *But for Birmingham*, 265–69, 271, 281, and McWhorter, *Carry Me Home*, 330, 346, 366–78. On the Chicago riot, see Grossman, *Land of Hope*, 179–80, and Tuttle, *Race Riot*. On Detroit, see Shogan and Craig, *Detroit Race Riot*.

84. "City Parks Integrated in Dallas," *DMN*, June 16, 1963; "Swimming Pools and Parks Desegregated," *DE*, June 22, 1963.

85. DCCCR, "Are Demonstrations Needed in Dallas?" (flier), April 1964, DPL.

86. "Pickets March at Building of School Administration," *DMN*, April 28, 1964; "Dallas Negroes Picket Board," *SSN*, May 1964; Melosi, "Dallas-Fort Worth," 189; Craft interview by Egerton, 12.

87. "Little Known Facts about School Integration," DCCCR, May 31, 1964, DPL.

88. "Civil Rights Group Taken from Foyer," *DMN*, May 31, 1964.

89. "Negroes, Whites Stage 2d Protest at Piccadilly," *DMN*, June 1, 1964; "Groups Demonstrate Downtown," *DPT*, June 6, 1964; "15 Protestors Carry Flags at Cafeteria," *DMN*,

June 8, 1964; "Judge Sets Contempt Hearing," *DMN*, June 11, 1964; "Piccadilly Pickets Arrested," *DPT*, June 20, 1964; "Food Shared with Racial Protestors," *DMN*, June 21, 1964; "Negro Enters Cafeteria, Gets Food from Pair," *DTH*, June 21, 1964.

90. "Engineer Brings Harmony to Cafeteria Controversy" and "Few Dallas Changes Seen after Rights Bill OK'd," *DMN*, June 28, 1964; Yvonne Johnson, "Desegregating Dallas," 40.

91. "Nine Demonstrators Arrested in 'Bowl-In,'" *DMN*, June 22, 1964; "Integrationists Jailed Here," *DTH*, June 22, 1964; "Bowling Lane Suit Filed by Negroes," *DTH*, August 10, 1964; "Bowling Alley Suit Dismissed after Accord," *DTH*, September 1, 1964.

92. "Rink Owner Refuses Admittance," *DPT*, February 17, 1968; "Racial Refusal Claimed," *DTH*, July 7, 1968.

93. "Thousands of Dallasites March," *DE*, March 20, 1965.

94. "3000 March, Sing in Dallas Parade," *DMN*, March 14, 1965.

95. Ibid.; "'Untapped Reservoir of Goodwill'—Laws," *DPT*, March 20, 1965; "Dallas Marchers Awaiting Action from Washington," *DTH*, March 15, 1965; "You Were There!," *DE*, March 20, 1965; "NAACP March Lauded by Citizenry," *DE*, March 27, 1965; "Selma Victim Mourned at Alamo Rally," "1,000 Attend Service in Fort Worth," "1,000 Hear of Alabama in Houston," and "Reeb Memorial Held in Austin," *DMN*, March 15, 1965; "Selma Prompts S.A. March," "Big March in Dallas," and related stories on Houston, Fort Worth, Austin, and El Paso, *SAL*, March 15, 1965.

96. "Pay Your Poll Tax," *HI*, June 26, 1963; "The Price of Your Vote," *HI*, October 5, 1963; "NAACP Flash," *HI*, January 18, 1964.

97. "N.A.A.C.P. Poll Tax Call," *Capital City Argus*, January 16, 1964; "Local NAACP Steps Up Poll Tax Drive," *SAR*, January 24, 1964. See also Overton, *Volma . . . My Journey*.

98. "To Register 100,000 Goal of Dallas NAACP," *DPT*, December 11, 1965; "NAACP Opens Office for Voter Registration," *SAR*, January 19, 1967; "Texas Goal: 600,000 Registered Negroes," *SAR*, December 1, 1967; "NAACP Seeks to Register 600,000 Voters in Texas," *DE*, December 2, 1967; "NAACP Seeks to Register 600,000," *HFT*, December 2, 1967.

99. Gloster B. Current memo to Roy Wilkens, October 29, 1964, and "Houston to Set Up 8 NAACP Branches," NAACP press release, November 20, 1964, both in NAACP Branch Dept. Files, Houston (microfilm); "NAACP Plans More Branches," *DPT*, February 20, 1965.

100. "Rev. S. H. James Elected to City Council," *SAR*, April 9, 1965; "Rev. James Reelected," *SAR*, April 7, 1967.

101. "Three Negroes Elected in Texas," *HI*, November 12, 1966; Oliver, "Life and Time of Barbara Jordan." See also Jordan, *Barbara Jordan*, and Rogers, *Barbara Jordan*.

102. Barr, *Black Texans*, 179; Darwin Payne, *Quest for Justice*, 184–85.

103. "In Heated Runoff Conrad Elected to School Board," *DE*, May 6, 1967.

104. George Allen interview, 2.

105. "'Hey-You' in Huntsville," *TO*, August 9, 1965; Lewis, *King*, 192–95; Eskew, *But for Birmingham*, 254, 261–63, 265–66; Garrow, *Bearing the Cross*, 246–51; Branch, *Parting the Waters*, 754–76.

106. "Huntsville Businesses Told Negroes May Try Boycott," *HC*, July 26, 1965; "'Hey-You' in Huntsville," *TO*, August 9, 1965; Kuhlman, "Booker T. Bonner," 9–10.

107. "Café Serves Negroes, White Sit-Ins Are Jailed in Huntsville," *HP*, July 26, 1965; "'Hey-You' in Huntsville," *TO*, August 6, 1965 (quotation).

108. "King Aide Is New Leader of Huntsville Racial Protests," *HC*, July 27, 1965; "'Hey-You' in Huntsville," *TO*, August 6, 1965 (quotations).

109. "Klansmen Stage Huntsville March," *HC*, July 27, 1965.

110. Booker T. Bonner to Honorable John Connally, ca. January 1966, and Larry Temple telegram to Bonner, ca. January 1966, both in ser. 35 40-30-12 Texas Racial Problem 1963–68, Connally Papers, LBJ. The reference to "gunpowder justice" comes from Samora, Bernal, and Peña, *Gunpowder Justice*.

111. "Local NAACP Seeks Support of Rights Law," *SAR*, July 24, 1964.

112. "City Rights Law Urged on Council; No Action Taken," *SAE*, June 26, 1964; "Council May Consider Civil Rights Law for S.A.," *SAN*, July 9, 1964; "Civil Rights Act—City Pledges to Help," *SAL*, July 23, 1964; "S.A. Asks State Statute Authorizing Cities to Pass Rights Measures" and "NAACP Wants Reports of Civil Rights Compliance," *SAR*, July 31, 1964; "San Antonio Passes Rights Ordinance," *SAR*, November 12, 1965.

113. Harrison and Laine, "Operation Breadbasket," 223–35; Garrow, *Bearing the Cross*, 297, 438, 462, 469.

114. "War on Poverty Centers Selected," *DE*, January 13, 1968.

115. "Poverty Panel to Be Feature of NAACP Meeting," *SAR*, February 19, 1965; "Anti-Poverty Board Meeting Being Reorganized," *SAR*, April 15, 1966; Black interview by Sweeny; Clayson, "'The Barrios and the Ghettos Have Organized!,'" 158–83.

116. Meeting notes, Southwest Conference for Political Unity, November 14, 1963, Graciela Gil-Olivárez memo to Southwest Conference for Political Unity Organizers, December 2, 1963, and Gil-Olivárez memo to Southwest Conference on Inter-State, Inter-Group Affairs Organizers, ca. January 1964, Sánchez Collection, BLAC. See also Graciela Olivárez to George I. Sánchez, January 30, 1964, and Sánchez to Olivárez, February 7, 1964, ibid.

117. "NAACP Urges S.A. Rights Federation," *SAE*, July 20, 1964.

118. "Notes from Sympathy March," *TO*, September 2, 1966.

119. "Labor Day in Austin," *TO*, September 16, 1966.

120. Moses LeRoy to Greetings, November 12, 1948, LeRoy Collection, HMRC; Minutes of (Progressive Party) Founding Convention, April 25, 1948, LeRoy Collection, HMRC; LeRoy interview.

121. Henry B. Gonzalez, "Moses LeRoy: Touch of Greatness," *Congressional Record*, App., December 8, 1967, A6055; "Moses LeRoy Says He Believes Brotherhood to Come—Some Day," *HC*, August 29, 1971.

122. "The March into Corpus Christi," *TO*, August 5, 1966; Walter Katz to Dear Mose, December 2, 1967, LeRoy Collection, HMRC.

123. See "The LeRoy Dinner" program, December 2, 1967, Medrano Papers, UTA.

124. See Clarence A. Laws to Glover L. Pettes, Medrano Papers, UTA.

125. Press release from Richard Medrano, May 29, 1967, Medrano Papers, UTA; Medrano interview, 66–74.

126. "The Confrontation," *TO*, September 16, 1966.

127. "After 200 Miles: Marchers Shake," *El Malcriado*, August 12, 1966.

128. Smith interview by author.

129. "Message from the National President," *LN*, March 1966 (emphasis in original).

130. "LULAC in the News," *LN*, April 1966.

131. L. Clifford Davis interview; Gutiérrez interview; Lawson interview.

132. Henry Interview I, ⟨http://www.lbjlib.utexas.edu/johnson/archives.hom/oralhis tory.hom/Henry-A/Henry01.PDF⟩; L. Clifford Davis interview.

133. Sherman interview; Bryant interview; Smith interview with author; L. Clifford Davis interview.

134. Allen interview.

135. Smith interview by author.

136. C. Anderson Davis interview, 33.

137. "Ripple along the Rio," *SAE*, July 5, 1966 (quotations); "Leaders Eye Differences," *SAN*, November 19, 1965; "Speaking Out," *LN*, February 1967.

138. "Fr. Smith Honored by S.A. NAACP," *SAE*, April 17, 1967.

139. "Fr. Smith Assails 'Gringos,'" *SAE*, February 22, 1967.

Chapter 5

1. Wallace B. Poteat to Rev. Lawrence E. Noonan, September 30, 1966, VISTA Collection, HMRC. The first EF meetings occurred in November 1964. The group began under the name Ecumenical Council but switched to Ecumenical Fellowship after the first meeting. See minutes, November 1, 1964, ibid. Local residents and newspapers frequently referred to the LAC Project as the LACK Project. Additionally, in some cases the word "channel" was replaced by "council," making it the Latin American Council Project.

2. Freeman interview by author. For one of the few monographs that examines ecumenical organizing, see Newman, *Divine Agitators*.

3. For this reason, I categorize Sherrill Smith as an ecumenical leader. He was an ardent Catholic, but as a leader in civil rights protests he refused to proselytize. In other words, he did not join protests or attempt to help people with the idea of winning converts for his church. Rather, he felt a Christian duty to aid people in the secular world. And many of his statements reflected an ecumenical vision of civil rights activism. See Smith interview by Cohen, 38–39, Smith interview by author, and Mary Vines interview.

4. EF minutes, December 10, 1965, VISTA Collection, HMRC. Proselytizing was specifically banned by OEO, so when programs like the LAC Project began using VISTA volunteers they were federally mandated not to proselytize.

5. Peter Johnson interview.

6. Earl Allen interview.

7. See Newman, *Divine Agitators*, 21–22. Newman notes that Mississippi's Delta Ministry, a National Council of Churches organization similar to the ecumenical groups I describe, became so focused on its mission that "common religious observation did not become a part of its operations. . . . [instead] the Ministry became a significant civil rights group in Mississippi."

8. See EF minutes, November 1, 1964, VISTA Collection, HMRC.

9. EF minutes, December 10, 1965, and "Projected Program for LAC Project," 1965–66, ibid.

10. "Protestant Groups Open Community Organization Project in the East End," *HP*, November 13, 1965.

11. Ibid.; "Projected Program for LAC Project," 1965–66, VISTA Collection, HMRC.

12. EF minutes, December 10, 1965, ibid.

13. Wallace B. Poteat to Rev. Lawrence E. Noonan, September 30, 1966, ibid.

14. W. M. McKenzie to Terry McKenzie, November 15, 1967, and LAC Project meeting notes, December 7, 1967, ibid.

15. SDS Newsletter, November 12, 1965, ibid.

16. George F. Lord memo to Bruno Rantane, February 7, 1967, and LAC Project press release "VISTA Week," Rev. Wallace Poteat, March 9, 1967, VISTA Collection, HMRC. On the VISTA program, see "The Office of Economic Opportunity during the Administration of President Lyndon B. Johnson," November 1963–January 1969, Administrative History OEO, vol. 1. pt. 1, 412–55.

17. *Pachuco* is Spanish slang that generally referred to Mexican American hoodlums or gang members in the thirties and forties. Interestingly, the Pachuco House primarily attracted black teens. As a result, local papers often referred to the Pachuco House as the "Negro teen center."

18. HCHR-LACK VISTA Project proposal, ca. mid-1960s, VISTA Collection, HMRC.

19. Ibid.; "The University of Thought," *PC*, February 20, 1971.

20. "Arson Destroys Center; Fire Truck Crash Kills One," *HC*, January 3, 1967; "Four Alarm Harrisburg Fire Controlled," [probably *HP*], January 3, 1967.

21. The LAC Project *Voice*, by Rev. Bud Poteat, January 22, 1967 (emphasis in original); "Arson Destroys Center; Fire Truck Crash Kills One," *HC*, January 3, 1967.

22. The disturbance at TSU is discussed in more detail in Chapter 6.

23. Clayson, "War on Poverty."

24. "Nightmare in Houston," *TO*, June 9, 1967; "Student Firebrands Busy Last Fall," *HC*, June 18, 1967; "Allen Testimony," TSU Riot Papers, TSU; Clayson, "War on Poverty," 38–40.

25. The LAC Project *Voice*, by Rev. Bud Poteat, January 22, 1967.

26. LAC Project minutes, board meeting, February 21, October 23, 1968, ca. August 1969, VISTA Collection, HMRC. Earl Allen was debated as a possible replacement for Poteat.

27. "VISTA Program Closes," unidentified newspaper, February 2, 1972, VISTA Collection, HMRC.

28. For a good discussion of the radicalism of Catholic priests, see Martinez, *PADRES*. See also Treviño, *Church in the Barrio*; Espinosa, Elizondo, and Miranda, *Latino Religions*; and Matovina, *Guadalupe and Her Faithful*.

29. For information on Lucey, see Bronder, *Social Justice*.

30. "S.A. Priest Gets Involved for Justice," *SAEN*, October 3, 1965.

31. Smith interview by author.

32. Sherry, *A Brief History of Vatican II*; Lamb and Levering, *Vatican II*; Boff and Boff, *Introducing Liberation Theology*; Gustavo Gutiérrez, *Theology of Liberation*.

33. Fr. Sherrill Smith to Dear Governor, n.d., and John Connally to Smith, September 16, 1963, ser. 35 40–30–10 Civil Rights R-T, Connally Papers, LBJ.

34. "Freedom Now Parade," *Capital City Argus*, August 29, 1963.

35. "A Dark-Skinned Throng before the Court," *TO*, March 7, 1963.

36. "S.A. Priest Gets Involved for Justice," *SAEN*, October 3, 1965.

37. "Fr. Smith Honored by S.A. NAACP," *SAN*, April 17, 1967.

38. "Selma Prompts S.A. March," *SAL*, March 15, 1965.

39. "Fr. Smith Assails 'Gringos,'" *SAE*, February 22, 1967; Smith interview by Cohen, 3–9.

40. "Tio Tomas Must Go, Rev. Smith Tells PASO Rally," *SAE*, September 29, 1965.

41. "Catholics Launch Project Equality," *SAR*, August 20, 1965; "Information on Project Equality," ca. August 1965, Peña Papers, UTSA; "Project Equality Program Getting Excellent Response," *SAR*, October 1, 1965; Smith interview by author.

42. "S.A. Priest Gets Involved for Justice," *SAEN*, October 3, 1965; "Project Equality Pledge Card," The Archdiocese of San Antonio Social Action Department, August 1965, Peña Papers, UTSA.

43. Robert E. Lucey to All Pastors and Administrators of Institutions in the Archdiocese of San Antonio, August 11, 1965, Peña Papers, UTSA; Sherrill Smith to Dear Friend, August 12, 1965, Peña Papers, UTSA.

44. Press release regarding Project Equality, August 12, 1965, Peña Papers, UTSA; "Project Equality: A Program to Utilize the Purchasing Power of Catholic Institutions to Achieve Equality in Employment Opportunity," ca. August 1965, ibid.

45. "Information on Project Equality," ca. August 1965, Peña Papers, UTSA.

46. "S.A. Priest Gets Involved for Justice," *SAEN*, October 3, 1965.

47. "Tio Tomas Must Go, Rev. Smith Tells PASO Rally," *SAE*, September 29, 1965; Smith interview by author.

48. "Two Priests Backing Farm Union Are Ordered to Go to Monastery," *Valley Morning Star*, February 4, 1967; "Catholic Council Decides to Withhold Smith Statement," *SAE*, March 20, 1967.

49. "Fr. Smith Assails 'Gringos,'" *SAE*, February 22, 1967; "Roman Catholics: Revolt in Texas," *Time* magazine, November 8, 1968. In these articles and others, it is clear that Father Smith had angered Lucey and that his banishment was punishment for disobeying Lucey. Smith confirms this viewpoint in my oral history; see Smith interview by author and Smith interview by Cohen, 30–31.

50. "The Archbishop's Dilemma," *TO*, August 18, 1967; "Father Smith to Get Parish in Crystal City," *SAN*, December 3, 1971.

51. Smith interview by author.

52. Peter Johnson interview.

53. Ibid.; "The Jewish Role in Desegregating Dallas" (videocassette), January 6, 1998.

54. Schutze, *Accommodation*, 163; Barr, *Black Texans*, 224; "City: 'Take It or Turn It Loose,'" *DPT*, July 5, 1969.

55. Peter Johnson interview; "City: 'Take It or Turn It Loose,'" *DPT*, July 5, 1969.

56. "SCLC Calls Halt at Fair Park," *DPT*, November 22, 1969; "SCLC Supports Homeowners," *DPT*, December 6, 1969.

57. "City: 'Take It or Turn It Loose,'" *DPT*, July 5, 1969.

58. "Bishop Students and Citizens Support Ghetto Pilgrimage," *DPT*, December 13, 1969; "SCLC Tours Dallas Slums," *DE*, December 13, 1969.

59. "SCLC Proposes Xmas Boycott," *DPT*, December 13, 1969.

60. Peter Johnson interview; Schutze, *Accommodation*, 171–72; "Mayor to Meet with Fair Park Homeowners," *DE*, February 7, 1970; George Allen interview by Saxon, 56–60.

61. "Notes Interviews Peter Johnson," *Dallas Notes*, May 20–June 2, 1970; "March on City Hall Goes Off Peacefully," *DTH*, May 24, 1970; "SCLC March Opposes Oppression," *Dallas Notes*, June 3–16, 1970.

62. "State Representatives Help Lead March in Memory of Dr Martin L King," *DE*, April 11, 1970.

63. "March on City Hall Goes Off Peacefully," *DTH*, May 24, 1970; "SCLC March Opposes Oppression," *Dallas Notes*, June 3–16, 1970. In April 1970 an eighteen-year-old black youth had been shot thirteen times and killed by Dallas police.

64. Peter Johnson interview.

65. "SCLC Boycott Safeway," *DE*, August 1, 1970.

66. Peter Johnson interview; "SCLC and Safeway Reach an Agreement," *DE*, August 22, 1970; "SCLC Wins Agreement with Safeway," *Dallas Notes*, August 19–September 1, 1970.

67. On minority communities in Lubbock, see Andrés Tijerina, *History of Mexican Americans*, and Parks, *Remember When?*

68. Darrell Vines interview; Mary Vines interview; Burtis interview.

69. ECSC minutes, September 3, 1968, ECSC Papers, TTU.

70. "The All-American Community," n.d., ECSC Papers, TTU; ECSC to Joe B. Phillips, October 7, 1968, and attached sheet "The Plan for 'the all-american community' in Lubbock," ibid.

71. Governor Smith was particularly interested in urban renewal as it related to minority communities. In 1970 he formed the Texas Urban Development Commission to eradicate problems in urban communities statewide. See "Executive Order Creating the Urban Development Commission," n.d. [May 1970], box 528, folder 11, Smith Papers, TTU; "Toward Urban Progress: A Report to the Governor and the 62nd Texas Legislation," Texas Urban Development Commission, n.d. [ca. 1971], ibid.

72. ECSC minutes, November 1968, ECSC Papers, TTU; Darrell Vines to Dear Friends (calling for volunteers for the "engineer's unit"), November 19, 1968, ibid.

73. In fact, the minutes of ECSC meetings make no mention of the All-American City until February 1970. See ECSC minutes, February 9, 1970, attached draft letter to Joe Phillips, n.d., and Report of September 7 meeting of Housing Committee, ECSC Papers, TTU.

74. For most schools, the point was to force black students to transfer to white schools, and districts made this as difficult as they could.

75. ECSC minutes, September 3, 1968, ECSC Papers, TTU; Darrell Vines interview; Mary Vines interview; Burtis interview.

76. ECSC minutes, January, February 1969, ECSC Papers, TTU.

77. ECSC minutes, September, October 6, 1969, ibid.

78. These events are discussed in more detail in Chapter 7.

79. "Presented to the School Board," free lunch proposal by Rev. David H. Olson, November 4, 1969, ECSC Papers, TTU.

80. ECSC minutes, September 7, November 21, 1968, ibid.

81. ECSC minutes, January, February 1969, ibid.

82. ECSC minutes, February 9, 1970, ibid.

83. "Next Target Areas Chosen for Antipoverty Enable," *AS*, July 1966, in African American Miscellaneous Vertical File (AF-A4600), AHC; "Little People's Day," *TO*, June 21, 1967. See also *Voice of HOPE*, HMRC, and "Earl Allen—A Man of Strong Convictions," *HFT*, August 19, 1967.

84. Press release, March 13, 1969, box 89, folder 17, Smith Papers, 1930–75 and undated,

TTU; Preston Smith to Bertrand Harding, Acting Director of OEO, March 13, 1969, box 89, folder 17, ibid.; "Val Verde County Suddenly Awakened by VISTA Uproar," HC, March 23, 1969; "VISTA Given 'Kiss of Death' by Val Verde Commissioners," SAE, March 25, 1969.

85. "Pro-VISTA Fight Set at Del Rio," SAE, March 17, 1969; "Texas' Sleeping Giant—Really Awake This Time?," TO, April 11, 1969; "The Del Rio Mexican-American Manifesto to the Nation" and Memo from the Committee for the Issuance of the Del Rio Manifesto to All Mexican American Leaders in Texas and in the Country, both dated March 30, 1969, Peña Papers, UTSA; "The San Felipe Del Rio Mexican-American Manifesto to the Nation," March 30, 1969, García Papers, TAMUCC;

86. "OEO Man Made VISTA Appeal," SAE, March 30, 1969; "Statement of Dr. Hector P. García," press release, March 25, 1969, García Papers, TAMUCC.

87. Press release, October 10, 1969, box 263, folder 19, Smith Papers, TTU; "East Texas and the OEO," TO, September 26, 1969.

88. Ted Hall et al. to Honorable Preston Smith, October 27, 1969, box 527, folder 36, Smith Papers, TTU; "Panel Will Urge No New VISTAs," Brownsville Herald, October 17, 1969; "VISTA, Again Gov Smith's Problem," HP, November 14, 1969; "VISTAs Are Leaving Cameron, Willacy," HC, November 21, 1969.

89. "La Salle County Asks Smith to Remove VISTA Program," AA, October 30, 1970; Preston Smith to Joe J. Bernal, December 3, 1970, box 81, folder 156, Smith Papers, TTU.

90. Preston Smith to Walter Richter, August 27, 1969, box 527, folder 15, Smith Papers, TTU. Smith did not always decline government aid. Indeed, when local counties favored government grants he tended to side with the county. For example, when counties voted for CAP or VISTA funding, the governor approved the projects. This happened in Dallas County after the commissioners' court approved the establishment of a CAP. See Smith to Alvin Lawler, May 4, 1970, box 118, folder 3, Smith Papers, TTU. State support, or lack thereof, of antipoverty programs continued in the ensuing years. Gov. Dolph Briscoe, like John Connally and Preston Smith, resisted such programs. See, e.g., José Angel Gutiérrez to Abraham Kazen, August 26, 1976, and Gutiérrez to Mario Obledo, December 8, 1976, Obledo Papers, UCD; "Big Zavala Grant Gets Congressional Eyeballing," SAE, August 29, 1976; and "Briscoe: Grant Would Mean a Cuba-in-Texas," SAE, September 19, 1976.

91. "The Office of Economic Opportunity during the Administration of President Lyndon B. Johnson," November 1963–January 1969, Administrative History OEO, vol 1., part 1, p. 430, LBJ; "Panel Will Urge No New VISTAs," Brownsville Herald, October 17, 1969; "VISTA in Turmoil," Wall Street Journal, November 5, 1969.

92. "Remarks of Gov Preston Smith, Governor's Committee on Human Relations, 1st Meeting," October 21, 1969, box 225, folder 9, Smith Papers, TTU; "Human Relations Panel Begins Work," SAE, October 22, 1969; "Overcome Intolerance, Smith Urges," DMN, October 22, 1969.

93. "Statement of Goals and Objectives of Poor Peoples' Campaign by Rev. Abernathy and Delegation of Poor People," June 1968, Peña Papers, UTSA.

94. See Mantler, "Black, Brown, and Poor."

95. Ibid., 3–6, 191, 215–18.

96. See McKnight, Last Crusade.

97. "Latins Revolt In Face of Reality," El Sol, May 31, 1968.

98. "Attention Turns to Mexicans, Indians," DMN, May 28, 1968.

99. "Southwest Council of La Raza and the Poor Peoples' Campaign" Resolution, June 15, 1968, Peña Papers, UTSA; Luís Diaz de León interview, 114–22.

100. McKnight, *Last Crusade*, chap. 5; Branch, *At Canaan's Edge*, 715–17.

101. "Dallas Sparked by Poverty Rally" and "The Poor Are Marching," *DPT*, May 22, 1968.

102. "March to Draw Thousands," and "Special Mass Said for Poor People's March," *HI*, May 25, 1968.

103. "Dallas Section of Poor People's March Reports," *DPT*, June 1, 1968.

104. Peter Johnson interview.

Chapter 6

1. "Racism in Southwest Texas," *Congressional Record*, April 28, 1969 (1st quotation); "MAYO Members Most Active of Activist Chicanos," *SAE*, April 16, 1969; "Que Eliminar a Los Gringos: Gutiérrez" (Gutiérrez: To Eliminate the Gringos), *El Sol de Texas*, February 27, 1970; "Black Leader Dies at Second Run-in," *DMN*, July 28, 1970 (2nd quotation).

2. Scholarship on Black Power is extensive; for a good start, see Van Deburg, *New Day in Babylon*; Woodard, *Nation within a Nation*; Yohuru Williams, *Black Politics/White Power*; Glaude, *Is It Nation Time?*; Self, *American Babylon*; Singh, *Black Is a Country*; Ogbar, *Black Power*; Joseph, *Waiting 'Til the Midnight Hour* and *Black Power Movement*; and Countryman, *Up South*.

3. Scholarly work on Brown Power is considerable. See, e.g., Vigil, *Crusade for Justice*; Navarro, *Mexican American Youth Organization*; Hammerback, Jensen, and Gutiérrez, *War of Words*; Muñoz, *Youth, Identity, Power*; Gómez-Quiñones, *Chicano Politics*; F. Arturo Rosales, *Chicano!*; Ignacio M. García, *Chicanismo*; San Miguel, *Brown, Not White*; Ernesto Chávez, *"¡Mi raza primero!"*; Oropeza, *¡Raza Sí! ¡Guerra No!*; and Mariscal, *Brown-eyed Children*. In this chapter, I use "Chicano Power" and "Brown Power" interchangeably.

4. Ogbar, *Black Power*, 2,

5. Self, *American Babylon*, 218.

6. See "Many Texans Uneasy about Racial Troubles," *DMN*, September 26, 1966; "Emotions Boil in Rice University Racial Seminar," *Houston Tribune*, December 8, 1966.

7. "Black Houston," *TO*, May 13, 1966.

8. Blair Justice, *Violence in the City*, passim; Dwight Watson, *Race*, 70–72. See also Steven Harmon Wilson, *Rise of Judicial Management*.

9. On Kirkpatrick, see Hill, *Deacons for Defense*, 31–42, 45–48, 63–65, 103–7, 171–72, 254. Later in life Kirkpatrick had a recurring role as a singer on PBS's *Sesame Street*, where he played "Brother Kirk."

10. "Tell It Like It Is!!!!!" press release, Houston Chapter of SNCC, ca. 1967, Brode Family Collection, HMRC.

11. "Symposium Set on Civil Rights," *HC*, December 4, 1966; "Panelists Say City Drags Feet Assisting Minority Groups," *HC*, December 6, 1966; "Emotions Boil in Rice University Racial Seminar," *Houston Tribune*, December 8, 1966; "Students Demonstrate as Mayor Speaks at TSU," *HP*, December 14, 1966; "SNCC in the Space City" and "F. D. Kirkpatrick Is SNCC Leader in City," *HFT*, March 25, 1967; "Student Firebrands Busy Last Fall," *HC*, June 18, 1967.

12. "Welch Tells Mayors of Racial Peace," *HI*, January 27, 1967.

13. The violence at TSU has been referred to as the "TSU Riot" and the "TSU Police Riot." The latter description is the more accurate. However, since the violence was relatively minor, I refer to this incident as the "TSU disturbance."

14. "Four Incidents Led to the Most Terrifying Night," *HC*, June 18, 1967.

15. "Trouble at TSU, Court Stands on Rice Ruling," *HI*, March 25, 1967; "Words and Scenes at TSU on Protest Tuesday," *HFT*, April 1, 1967; "Trouble at TSU," *DE*, April 1, 1967; "You Cannot Train the Mind If the Heart Is Full of Poison," *HFT*, April 8, 1967; "Day with Friends of SNCC at TSU," *HFT*, April 1, 1967; "Rebellion without Discipline," *HFT*, April 8, 1967; "Nightmare in Houston," *TO*, June 9, 1967.

16. "20 Marchers Stage Protest at NE School," *HC*, May 15, 1967; "Northwood Demonstrations Stop," *HP*, May 17, 1967; "Trouble at Northwood," *HFT*, May 20, 1967; "Nightmare in Houston," *TO*, June 9, 1967.

17. "Boy Drowns in Pond at City Garbage Dump," *HP*, May 9, 1967; "Tragedy at City Dump," *HFT*, May 20, 1967.

18. See Melosi, *Garbage in the Cities*.

19. The city did drain the pond one week later but refused to close the dump. See "Pond Where Child Drowned Drained," *HP*, May 12, 1967.

20. "10 Protestors Arrested for Blocking Dump," *HC*, May 16, 1967; "Trucks Stopped, 36 Arrested at City Dump Protest," *HP*, May 17, 1967; "Dump Squabble in Sunnyside," *HFT*, May 20, 1967; Sherman interview; Griffin interview.

21. "Police Intelligence Units Step Up Their Watch on the Racial Situation," *Wall Street Journal*, September 10, 1968; "Postman Was Army Spy on Civilians in Houston," *HC*, January 28, 1971; "Army Spying on Texans Told," *HP*, January 28, 1971; "'Spying' Subjects Appalled," *HP*, January 29, 1971; "Houston Solons Said Spy Targets," [probably] *HC*, n.d., Graves Papers, TSU; "Military Snooping Made Graves Lose Faith in U.S." *HC*, February 25, 1971; "'Inches away' from Major Riot," *HC*, n.d. [ca. 1997], TSU Riot Papers, TSU; Sherman interview.

22. "Nightmare in Houston," *TO*, June 9, 1967; "Violence Erupts on Texas Southern Campus," *HFT*, May 20, 1967; "Eyewitness . . . of Sorts," *HFT*, May 27, 1967.

23. "A Second Look at the TSU Riot," *HFT*, May 27, 1967; "Students Shot in Riot at TSU," *HC*, May 17, 1967; "5 Charged in TSU Riot Fatal to Young Officer," *HP*, May 18, 1967; "Nightmare in Houston," *TO*, June 9, 1967; Griffin interview; Lawson interview; Earl Allen interview; Duncantell interview.

24. "Should Police Be Administrators?" and "Students in Jail," *HFT*, May 27, 1967; "Nightmare in Houston," *TO*, June 9, 1967; "Facts concerning the Crisis at T.S.U.," ca. 1967, VISTA Collection, HMRC; Earl Allen interview; Dwight Watson, *Race*, 77–85.

25. "Student Shot in Riot at TSU" and "Police Handled Riot Well," *HC*, May 17, 1967; "Students Say Pistol Shared during Riot," *HC*, May 18, 1967.

26. "Officer Blaylock Feels He's Lucky," *HP*, May 18, 1967.

27. "5 Charged in TSU Riot Fatal to Young Officer," *HP*, May 18, 1967; "Students in Jail," *HFT*, May 27, 1967; "Nightmare in Houston," *TO*, June 9, 1967.

28. "Was Everybody in Houston to Blame?," "Are the TSU Students at Fault?," "Was Mayor Welch at Fault?," "Was Governor Connally to Blame?," "Was Chief Herman Short at Fault?"—all in *HI*, May 20, 1967. The answer to each of these questions was yes.

29. "Facts concerning the Crisis at T.S.U.," n.d. [ca. 1967], VISTA Collection, HMRC.

30. Immediate Press Release, Houston SNCC Chapter, November 16, 1967, Brode Family Collection, HMRC.

31. "Will They Die?" and editorial, *SNCC Newsletter*, June-July 1967.

32. "Students Describe 'Nightmare' during All-Out Assault on TSU," "College Heads Shocked as Mayor, Gov. Blame Them"; "Informer Walks Beat with Students," and "After the Battle Comes the Calm"—all in *HI*, May 20, 1967; "A Second Look at the TSU Riot," photo editorial, "On the Yard . . . A Day Later," and "Eyewitness . . . of Sorts," *HFT*, May 27, 1967. See also "What Chance for Peace and Progress in Houston?," "If We Are—To the Students of TSU," "If We Are—To the White Leaders of Houston," and "NAACP Asks US Attorney General to Probe TSU Riot"—all in *DE*, May 27, 1967; "Will the True Story Ever be Told?," *DE*, June 10, 1967; "Riot—The Texas Southern University Incident," *Capital City Argus*, May 25, 1967; "Houston Police Accused of 'Vengeful' Rampage," *SAE*, May 26, 1967.

33. "Quentin Mease: On Equal Footing," interview transcript by Mease, Cole Desegregation Papers, UH.

34. "Was Everybody in Houston to Blame?" and "Are the TSU Students at Fault?," *HI*, May 20, 1967; "Local SNCC Looks to Revolution," *HC*, November 26, 1967.

35. "Nightmare in Houston," *TO*, June 9, 1967.

36. "Riots, Civil and Criminal Disorders," Hearings before the Permanent Subcommittee on Investigations of the Committee on Government Operations, U.S. Senate, 90th Cong., 1st sess., pts. I, III, TSU Riot Papers, TSU; "Chronology of Riot Traced for Probers," *DMN*, November 3, 1967; "Bush Lauds Police Action," *HC*, May 17, 1967; "Bush Backs Police on Riot Action," *HP*, May 18, 1967.

37. "TSU Student Says Police Started Riot," [probably *HP*, ca. 1967], Brode Family Collection, HMRC; "Four Incidents Led to the Most Terrifying Night," *HC*, June 18, 1967.

38. "Allen Testimony," TSU Riot Papers, TSU; Earl Allen interview; "Statement of Reverend Earl Allen," n.d., VISTA Collection, HMRC.

39. "Allen Testimony," TSU Riot Papers, TSU; Earl Allen interview.

40. "Arrest Stumps TSU Student," *HP*, May 20, 1967; "Charges Dropped against TSU 5," *Voice of Hope*, November 14, 1970.

41. "Five TSU Students Indicted in Uprising Fatal to Policeman," *HFT*, June 10, 1967; "First TSU Five in Court," *DE*, November 9, 1968; "Jury Fails to Reach Verdict in Trial of TSU Student," *DE*, November 16, 1968.

42. "NAACP to Defend Four Charged in TSU Disturbance," *HFT*, June 3, 1967; "Defense Calls TSU Students Scapegoats," *HC*, June 5, 1967; "Attorney for TSU Students Talks of Case," *HFT*, June 17, 1967; "The TSU Five Are 'Free at Last,'" *HI*, November 14, 1970; "Charges Dropped against TSU 5," *Voice of HOPE*, November 14, 1970; "Charges in TSU Riot Case Dropped," *HP*, November 5, 1970; "Texas Drops Charges against TSU Students," *SAR*, November 20, 1970; Dwight Watson, *Race*, 85–86.

43. On these groups, see Hill, *Deacons for Defense*; Strain, *Pure Fire*; and Wendt, *The Spirit and the Shotgun*. Scholarship on the BPP is extensive. See, e.g., Foner, *Black Panthers Speak*; Jones, *Black Panther Party Reconsidered*; Yohuru Williams, *Black Politics/White Power*; Cleaver and Katsiaficas, *Liberation, Imagination*; Jeffries, *Huey P. Newton*; and Austin, *Up against the Wall*.

44. On the evolution of the New Right, see Edsall and Edsall, *Chain Reaction*, and Hodgson, *World Turned Right Side Up*.

45. "Free Lee Otis Now!," *Free Lee Otis* (a newspaper published by Austin's Student National Coordinating Committee — SNCC had opted to remove "nonviolent" from its name in 1968), September 1969; "30-Year Pot Sentence: Justified or Political?," *HC*, May 18, 1969.

46. "Free Lee Otis Now!," *Free Lee Otis*, September 1969; "30-Year Pot Sentence: Justified or Political?," *HC*, May 18, 1969; "Lee Otis' Appeal," *TO*, November 7, 1969; "Lee Otis," *TO*, September 4, 1970; "Free Lee Otis Johnson" flier, ca. 1969, Afro-American Miscellaneous Collection, HMRC; "Black Panther Gets 30 Years for One Joint," ⟨http://www.hippy.com/php/article-156.html⟩ (May 15, 2008). Johnson became somewhat of a celebrity in the pro-marijuana community after his arrest.

47. "Lee Otis Backers Attend Hearing," *AA*, October 16, 1969; "Lee Otis' Appeal," *TO*, November 7, 1969; "Black Panther Gets 30 Years for One Joint." Johnson's life was never the same. His wife divorced him, and he was estranged from his children. He was in and out of jail before his death in 2002.

48. "Conner Begged and Pleaded for a Chance to Live," *HFT*, April 11, 1970; "Police Acts Terrifying and Unhuman, NAACP Head Says," *HFT*, April 18, 1970.

49. "Peoples Party Formed in Houston," *DE*, May 30, 1970; "What PPII Stands For," n.d., Salazar Papers, HMRC; Robinson Block, "History of People's Party II," ⟨http://houston.indymedia.org/news/2009/02/66654.php⟩; Freeman interview by author; Freeman interview by Indymedia, ⟨http://radio.indymedia.org/uploads/SavetillD10Boko_0.mp3⟩; "People's Party II Rally, [probably *Voice of Hope*, n.d.], ⟨http://www.itsabouttimebpp.com/Chapter_History/pdf/Houston/Houston_12.pdf⟩.

50. Freeman interview by author; "Black Leader Dies at Second Run-in," *DMN*, July 28, 1970; "In Case of Riot, Peoples Party II," *Space City!*, 6/20–7/3/1970; "Who 'Fingered' Carl Hampton?," *Sepia* magazine, November 1970.

51. "Diacritical View of Dowling Street Confrontation," and "Moments after Dowling Standoff," *HFT*, July 25, 1970; "Who 'Fingered' Carl Hampton?," *Sepia* magazine, November 1970; Duncantell interview; Freeman interview by author; "Space City Blues," recording of Pacifica news broadcast on Carl Hampton — special thanks to Boko Freeman for providing me a copy of this recording.

52. "Black Leader Dies at Second Run-in," *DMN*, July 28, 1970; "Diagnosis of 2828 Dowling," *HFT*, August 1, 1970.

53. "Black Militant Slain on Dowling," "Short Issues Statement Explaining Shootings," and "Black Amnesty among People's Party II Goals," *HC*, July 27, 1970; "Diagnosis of 2828 Dowling," "Was Carl Hampton Set Up?," and "Bad to Be Black on Dowling," *HFT*, August 1, 1970; "Who 'Fingered' Carl Hampton?," *Sepia* magazine, November 1970; Duncantell interview; Freeman interview by author; Dwight Watson, *Race*, 90–93; Freeman, "The Police Assassination of Carl Hampton," ⟨http://www.itsabouttimebpp.com/Chapter_History/Police_Assassination_of_Carl_Hampton.html⟩.

54. "Police, Militants Blame Each Other," *DMN*, July 28, 1970; "FBI Study Asked in Houston Killing," *DMN*, July 29, 1970; "Loudmouth 'General' Helped Kill Hampton," and "Eyewitness of Dowling Street Mini-War," *HFT*, August 1, 1970; "I Don't Mean to Frighten You," *Old Mole*, August 7–27, 1970; "Call Dowling Street Investigation a 'Cool Down' Play," *HFT*, October 3, 1970; Duncantell interview.

55. "Confrontation on Dowling," *DMN*, August 2, 1970.

56. "I Remember Carl," *HFT*, August 1, 1970.

57. Freeman, "Police Assassination of Carl Hampton."

58. "Who 'Fingered' Carl Hampton?," *Sepia* magazine, November 1970; "Peoples [*sic*] Party II Today," n.d., Salazar Papers, HMRC.

59. "Houston Slayings Inflame Tempers," *DMN*, July 30, 1970.

60. "Who 'Fingered' Carl Hampton?," *Sepia* magazine, November 1970; "Unifying Black Houston" and "Selective Buying Campaign Aimed at Downtown Houston," *HFT*, August 1, 1970; "The Police Allowed Her to Keep the Money," *TO*, August 21, 1970; "A Hung Jury in Houston," *TO*, July 30, 1971; Press release, The Coalition for the Defense of Peoples Party II, n.d., Salazar Papers, HMRC; "Police, and People's Party II in Warmup for 2nd Showdown," *Voice of HOPE*, February 20, 1971; "Constables Evict People's Party," *DMN*, May 17, 1971.

61. "Minority Contractors Rescue Health Clinic," *HFT*, August 14, 1971; "Everywhere It's Raining Bags of Groceries," [probably *Black Panther*, ca. July 1971], ⟨http://www.itsabouttimebpp.com/Chapter_History/Houston_Chapter_2.html⟩, (November 9, 2009); "Houston Branch Implements People's Pest Control Program," *Black Panther*, September 25, 1971; Freeman interview by author and e-mail responses to author's e-mailed questions.

62. "The Good, the Bad, the Imprisoned," *Houston Press*, December 30, 1999.

63. Dwight Watson, *Race*, chap. 5; Steven Harmon Wilson, *Rise of Judicial Management*, 247, 270; Behnken, "'We Want Justice!'"; Treviño interview.

64. Carson, *In Struggle*, 291–93; "The Black Revolution in Dallas and America," *DPT*, July 20, 1968.

65. Memorandum, Director, FBI, to the President et al., April 9, 1968, WHCF HU2, box 56, LBJ.

66. "Demonstrators Picket Court House," *DPT*, March 23, 1968.

67. "Five Arrested in Disturbance," *DMN*, March 28, 1968.

68. McMillan interview.

69. "SNCC Pickets OK Supermarket," *DE*, July 27, 1968; "Boycott of White Owned Business in South Dallas," *DPT*, July 31, 1968; "Black Power in Dallas," *TO*, August 9, 1968.

70. Gilliam, "Mama, Activist, and Friend," 48; *Johnson v. State of Texas*, 467 S.W. 2d 247 (quotation); "Property Destruction Charged," *DTH*, July 16, 1968; "SNCC Leader Jailed," *DE*, July 20, 1968.

71. "SNCC Heads Discuss Philosophy," *DPT*, August 3, 1968; "Black Boycott Successful," *Dallas Notes*, October 1–15, 1968; McMillan interview.

72. McMillan interview; "SNCC Attorney Studying Appeal," *DTH*, August 25, 1968; "SNCC Leaders Fouled in Court," *DPT*, September 4, 1968; "SNCC Leaders Convicted," *Dallas Notes*, September 4–17, 1968; "SNCC Members Shafted," *Dallas Notes*, September 18–October 1, 1968; "Black Militant Guilty though Innocent," *Dallas Notes*, October 1–15, 1968; "SNCC Fuse Sputtering Here," *DTH*, September 15, 1968.

73. "Control of O-K Supermarkets to Pass to O-K Employees," *DPT*, October 5, 1968.

74. See *Johnson v. State of Texas*, 467 S.W. 2d 247. They also appealed to the Supreme Court, but the Court declined to hear the case. *Johnson v. State of Texas*, 404 U.S. 951, 92 S.Ct. 273; "SNCC 'Bust of the Week,'" *Dallas Notes*, March 19–April 1, 1969; "Two SNCC Leaders Remaining in Jail," *DTH*, April 29, 1969.

75. "Declaration of Peace," *DMN*, August 15, 1968; McMillan interview.

76. "Lawyering the Left in Wimberly," *TO*, March 31, 2000.

77. "Ernie Gone . . . B.R.A.P Shapes Up," *DPT*, July 12, 1969; "'Snick', B.R.A.P., and Now Black Panthers," *DPT*, October 11, 1969; "Panthers Serve Breakfast Shot from Guns No More," *Dallas Notes*, November 20–December 4, 1970; "Dallas Chapter Details Success of Free Pest Control Program," *Black Panther*, November 9, 1974;

78. "'No Civil Disrespect or Disorder in San Antonio,'" *SAN*, July 26, 1976 (1st and 2nd quotations); "Negroes Criticize Mayor for 'Tactless' Riot Remarks," *SAE*, July 27, 1967 (3rd quotation); "Top of the News," *SAN*, August 1, 1976; "Civilian Review Board Is Outlined," *SAE*, September 2, 1967.

79. "Black San Antonio III: They Call It Police Brutality," *SAE*, February 15, 1972; "Black San Antonio V: Political Inroads," *SAE*, February 17, 1972; "Bobby Jo Phillips Investigative File 1968," box 10, folder 4, Salas Papers, UTSA; Salas interview.

80. Salas interview. See also "Student Nonviolent Coordinated Committee-S.A. (1 of 2), 1967–1975," box 8, folder 9, and "Student Nonviolent Coordinated Committee-S.A. (2 of 2), 1967–1975," box 9, folder 1, Salas Papers, UTSA.

81. Salas interview.

82. John Allan Long II to the Honorable J. Willard Barr, Mayor, March 30, 1967, and E. H. Denton to Long, April 13, 1967, City Managers Office Papers, folder "Ridgelea Wall," FWPL.

83. H. Grady Helm to H. D. McMahan, November 22, 1968, "Statement by Dr. Eck Prud'homme before the Fort Worth City Council," March 24, 1969, and "Informal Report to City Council Members," April 4, 1969—all in City Managers Office Papers, folder "Ridgelea Wall," FWPL; L. Clifford Davis interview.

84. Gómez-Quiñones, *Chicano Politics*, 99.

85. Ignacio M. García, *Chicanismo*, 4.

86. See, e.g., Paredes, *"With His Pistol in His Hand,"* passim; David G. Gutiérrez, *Walls and Mirrors*, 121–26; Meier and Ribera, *Mexican Americans/American Mexicans*, 82–84, 116, 162–65; and Manuel G. Gonzales, *Mexicanos*, 88–90, 108–9, 166–70.

87. "El Plan de Aztlán," March 1969, Gutiérrez Papers, UTSA. In some cases "la raza" meant "the race," but activists generally translated the term as "the people." Of course, in this instance "the people" were Chicanos, so "la raza" did have an ethnic significance.

88. "El Plan de Aztlán," March 1969, Gutiérrez Papers, UTSA.

89. Medrano interview, 39; "'Chicanos' Se Prepara para la Revolucion del Futuro" ("Chicanos" Prepare for the Future Revolution), *El Sol de Texas*, October 10, 1969; Hurtado and Arce, "Mexicans, Chicanos, . . . ¿Qué Somos?," 103–30.

90. "Backlash against 'Brown Power' Seen," *SAEN*, May 18, 1969; Hurtado and Arce, "Mexicans, Chicanos, . . . ¿Qué Somos?," 103–30; Martín Alcoff, "Latino vs. Hispanic."

91. "Semantics: Latin, Mexican, Spanish," *TO*, January 20, 1967; George I. Sánchez to Sen. Ralph Yarborough, September 26, 1967, Flores Collection, BLAC; "Mexican, Mexican-American, Chicano," *Compass*, December 1968; "Citizens for a Century Squabble over Image," *HC*, ca. 1970, in Salazar Papers, HMRC; "'Chicano' Call Pleases Some, Irks Others, Suit Yourself," *AAS*, July 10, 1971.

92. "Semantics: Latin, Mexican, Spanish," *TO*, January 20, 1967. "'Chicanos' Se Prepara para la Revolucion del Futuro" ("Chicanos" Prepare for the Future Revolution) (*El Sol de Texas*, October 10, 1969) puts "Chicano" in quotation marks as if it is not a real word.

93. The Author, "'Mexicans?" 'Mexican-Americans?' 'Chicanos?' All Wrong!" (San Antonio: Americanos Period of San Antonio, 1971), in Rodriguez Collection, BLAC.

94. The Author, "Exploring & Analyzing 'Mexican' Misnomers & Misconceptions" (San Antonio: Americanos Period of San Antonio, 1971), in Chicano File, SAPL.

95. The Author, "'Mexicans?" 'Mexican-Americans?' 'Chicanos?' All Wrong!," in Rodriguez Collection, BLAC.

96. "MAYOs Here Fold; New Group Foreseen," HP, March 2, 1971.

97. "Impractical, Unworkable, Intolerable," HI, August 3, 1968.

98. "FBI Will Probe Slaying in Mathis," HC, July 15, 1970; "Friend of Chicanos-Doctor's Death Stirs Town," DMN, July 19, 1970; "No Mathis Hearings, Says Dies," SAE, July 21, 1970; "MAYO to Protest Shooting of Doctor," HP, July 21, 1970; "Death Stirs Mathis Talks with MAYO," HP, July 22, 1970; Truan interview.

99. "Crowd Faces Police, Demands Resignation," CCC, October 9, 1970.

100. See Chávez, "¡Mi raza primero!," chap. 2.

101. "Chicanos, Anglos, y Negros Protestaron" (Chicanos, Anglos, and Blacks Protested), El Sol de Texas, March 5, 1971; "The Rodriguez Story," and "Chicanos Protest Shooting," Dallas News, March 10–24, 1971; "Guzman y Lopez por Tres Muertes" (Three Deaths by Guzman and Lopez), El Sol de Texas, March 12, 1971; "Chicanos y Negros Preparan Fuerte Boicot" (Chicanos and Blacks Prepare Tough Boycott), El Sol de Texas, March 19, 1971; "Chicanos March in Protest of Rodriguez Treatment," El Sol de Texas, March 26, 1971; "Chicanos Stage March to Protest 'Injustice,'" DMN, March 28, 1971; "Dallas Latins March in Protest," El Sol (Houston), April 2, 1972; "Raza Rallies against Repression," PC, [ca. April 1, 1971–June 12, 1971] [the paper was undated]; "Social Workers Take Stands on Rodriguez Case," PC, June 12, 1971; "Brown Berets Forman Comite para Recibir Quejas Sobrelos Abusos Policiales" (Brown Berest Form Committee to Receive Complaints about Police Abuse), PC, September 2, 1971; "Forman Comite Chicano Para Recibir Quejas Sobre los Abusos Policiales" (Chicano Committee Forms to Receive Complaints about Police Abuse), PC, September 16, 1971; "One Year Later—Rodriguez Family Still Survives," Iconoclast, February 25–March 3, 1972; "The Law Fails Rodriguezes," Iconoclast, March 31–April 7, 1972.

102. "Minorities Hope Child's Death Will Bring Change," Iconoclast, August 3–10, 1973; "Santos Rodriguez: Anniversary of a Murder," Tejano News Magazine, August 2–16, 1974; Achor, Mexican Americans, 148–53; Behnken, "'We Want Justice!'"

103. "N. Dallas Negroes Demand Further Probe of Slaying," DTH, June 9, 1970; "Policeman Involved in Previous Shooting," DMN, July 25, 1973.

104. "Questioning of Brothers Ends in Dallas Tragedy," DTH, July 24, 1973; "Policeman Involved in Previous Shooting," DMN, July 25, 1973; "Fingerprints Don't Match," DMN, July 26, 1973; "March Began in Peace, Ended in Violence," and "Angry Crowd Burns and Loots in Downtown Dallas Rampage," DTH, July 29, 1973; "City March Dissolves into Random Violence," DMN, July 29, 1973; "Police Security Guards against Disturbance Repeat," DTH, July 30, 1973; "Downtown Area Guarded," DMN, July 30, 1973.

105. "Mexican Americans and the Administration of Justice in the Southwest," Report of the U.S. Commission on Civil Rights (March 1970), 87. Austin also saw police brutality protests. These occurred after officers killed Oscar Balboa and Valentin Rodríguez. Austin implemented a new "gun discharge" policy to limit such shootings. See "Police to Sug-

gest Own Policy," [probably *AA*, July 13, 1968]; "Police under New Gun Rule," [probably *AA*, July 26, 1968]; "New Police Policy Is Changed," [probably *AA*, September 25, 1968]; Joseph P. Witherspoon, "The Austin Police, a Tragic Violation of the Law, and Recommendations," April 11, 1968—all in Obledo Papers, UCD.

106. "M.A.Y.O. Jefe Raps," *El Deguello*, June 1969; "New Wind from the Southwest," *Nation*, May 30, 1966; Gutiérrez interview by author; Navarro, *Mexican American Youth Organization*. Willie Velásquez is an interesting figure in Chicano history. His untimely death in 1988 is widely and correctly viewed as a tragedy. See Sepúlveda, *Life and Times of Willie Velásquez*; "Willie Velásquez, 1944–1988," *TO*, July 29, 1988.

107. As quoted in Ignacio M. García, *United We Win*, 21–22.

108. Ignacio M. García, *United We Win*, 17–22; Navarro, *La Raza Unida Party*, 24–26; "MAYO's Militant Cries Heard Again at Meeting," *SAN*, September 19, 1969; "MAYO Pressure Social Workers' Meet," *SAE*, September 19, 1969; "'MAYO' Grows in Lone Star State," *People's World*, April 19, 1970.

109. "Latin Revolution, U.S. Style, Next?," *DMN*, November 4, 1967; "Chicanos Staging Revolution," *DMN*, August 17, 1969.

110. Two MAYO groups operated in Houston: one at the University of Houston and a more militant group led by Salazar and Garza Birdwell. See MAYO to Dear Friend, n.d., MAYO, Houston, Tejas, Aztlán, policy statement, n.d., and "Requirements for All MAYO Members," n.d.—all in Salazar Papers, HMRC.

111. "The Barrio Program," MAYO, June 1970, Salazar Papers, HMRC.

112. "MAYO Positions," n.d., ibid.; "MAYO Demands Presented at Catholic Charities Parley," *HP*, October 1, 1969. For the radicalism of Chicano/a priests and nuns, see Martinez, *PADRES*, and Medina, *Las Hermanas*.

113. "MAYO Group Seizes Control of Church," *HP*, February 16, 1970; "The Church and the People," *Compass*, February 1970; Arnoldo De León, *Ethnicity*, 178–79.

114. "North Side People's Center," *Involvement Committee Newsletter*, November 1970; "Church Elders to Seek Agreement with MAYO," *HC*, February 18, 1970; "MAYO, Churchmen Debate Building Use," *HC*, February 20, 1970; "Church Sets Deadline at 3pm for MAYO to Vacate Building," *HP*, February 26, 1970; "Judge Tells MAYO to Evacuate Church," *HP*, March 7, 1970; "MAYOs March before Church," *HP*, March 9, 1970;"MAYO Out but Fighting," unknown paper, Salazar Papers, HMRC.

115. "MAYOs March before Church," *HP*, March 9, 1970; "Church Asks MAYO to Cease," unknown paper, March 10, 1970, and "MAYO Plans More Action at Churches," unknown paper, March 11, 1970, both in Salazar Papers, HMRC; Arnoldo De León, *Ethnicity*, 178–79.

116. "MAYO Pickets Church," unknown paper, March 16, 1970, "[Presbytery] Wants Ban on MAYO," unknown paper, April 6, 1970, "MAYOs Refused Entry to Services," *HP*, n.d., and "Presbyterian Church Sues MAYO," unknown paper, April 8, 1970—all in Salazar Papers, HMRC.

117. "Latin Youth Group Picks New Chief," *DTH*, May 14, 1969; "Crystal City Chicanos Claim Progress" and "MAYO Member Says He's Making Headway," *SAL*, November 30, 1969.

118. "700 Crystal City Dissidents March," *SAE*, December 11, 1969; "Crystal Teach-In Is Still Going On," *SAN*, December 26, 1969; "MAYO Meet Workshops Continue," *SAN*, December 29, 1969; Rivera, "Nosotros Venceremos" (We Will Win), 64–68; "Militance

among the Mexican Americans—Chicano Power," *New Republic*, June 20, 1970; Navarro, *La Raza Unida Party*, 29. The formation of RUP went hand in hand with school protests in Crystal City. School issues are discussed in more detail in the next chapter.

119. "The Barrio Program," MAYO Houston, June 1970, Salazar Papers, HMRC; "MAYO Projects," n.d., Gutiérrez Papers, BLAC; "'Viva La Raza!' [Long Live the People!] Has Democrats Worried," *SAN*, October 31, 1968.

120. Houston MAYO to Carlos Guerra, February 19, 1971, Salazar Papers, HMRC; "MAYOs Here Fold; New Group Foreseen," *HP*, March 2, 1971; "MAYO Muere" (MAYO Dies), *PC*, March 12, 1971; "MAYO Studies Shift toward La Raza Unida," *CCCT*, September 11, 1971; Navarro, *La Raza Unida Party*, 47.

121. Democrats had attempted to appeal to minority voters. See "Press Release–Preston Smith to Open Mexican-American State Headquarters in Austin" (ca. 1967), "Survey," Political Survey Result, November 10, 1967, and "Press Release" by Juan X. Ortiz and related material (ca. 1967)—all in box 615, folder 15, Smith Papers, TTU.

122. "Crystal City, Texas; La Raza Unida in Action," *International Socialist Review*, April 1971, 25; "School Bells for Crystal," *SAN*, January 6, 1970; "Student Victory Leaves Crystal City Divided," *SAL*, January 8, 1970; "Chicanos Forman Su Propio Partido Politico" (Chicanos Form Their Own Political Party), *El Sol de Texas*, January 30, 1970; "La Raza Unida, Tercer Partido Politico de Texas Puede Ser el Voto Decisivo en el Estado" (The People United, Texas Third Political Party Could Be the Decisive Vote in the State), *El Sol de Texas*, August 7, 1970. For background, see Shockley, *Chicano Revolt*; Navarro, *Cristal Experiment* and *La Raza Unida Party*; and Ignacio M. García, *United We Win*.

123. "Crystal City, Texas: La Raza Unida in Action," *International Socialist Review*, April 1971, 25; "La Raza Shows Political Muscle in South Texas," *SAN*, April 6, 1970 (quotation); "Chicano Huelga on School Board Vote," *People's World*, April 18, 1970; "Young Mexican-Americans Shedding Cloak of Silence," *AAS*, April 19, 1970; "La Raza May Hold Power Balance in Key Election," *SAEN*, August 2, 1970; "Latin Americans Gaining in Power," *DMN*, August 3, 1970; "US Journal: Crystal City, Texas," *New Yorker*, April 17, 1971; "Chicanos Troubled," *DMN*, September 20, 1970.

124. Navarro, *La Raza Unida Party*, 39–40.

125. The "Preambulo" read "la hipícrita aplicacion de la ley," "injusticias economicas y discriminación racial," and "terminar la probreza, la miseria y la injusticia." "Preambulo, Raza Unida Party, Crystal City, Tex." December 9, 1971, RUP Papers, BLAC. See also "Raza Unida Party," in folder "State Convention Material, 1971," RUP Papers, BLAC.

126. "A Chicano Youth Leader's Political Outlook," *Militant*, March 27, 1970; "Raza Unida Party, Platform Resolutions," October 30, 1971, RUP Papers, BLAC. See also "Juez Consigue Que el Partido La Raza Unida Intervenga en las Elecciones de Hidalgo" (Judge Decides That Raza Unida Party Intervened in the Hidalgo Elections), *El Sol De Texas*, October 17, 1970; "Una Mano No Se Lava Sola" (A Hand Can't Wash Itself), *Por Mientras* 1, vol. 3, December 1971, RUP Papers, BLAC.

127. "Estudiados los Problemas de los Mexico-Americanos en Dallas" (The Problems of Mexican Americans Studied in Dallas), *El Sol de Texas*, January 19, 1968; "La Raza Unida Meet Scheduled Saturday," *DMN*, January 4, 1971; Navarro, *Cristal Experiment*, chap. 3, and *La Raza Unida Party*, chap. 2.

128. "Venceremos en '72," RUP Papers, BLAC; "La Raza Seeks to Capture State's Chicano

Electorate," *HP*, February 13, 1972. See also Antonio Camejo, "A Report from Aztlán," 3–8, Mario Compean, "The Road to Chicano Power," 8–10, and José Angel Gutiérrez, "Mexicanos Need to Control Their Own Destinies"—all in *La Raza Unida Party in Texas* (pamphlet), 10–15.

129. Press release, "Ramsey Muñiz for Governor" and "Alma Canales for Lt. Governor," RUP Papers, BLAC; Canales interview, 60–67; "Muñiz Tops Raza Unida State Slate," *DTH*, January 11, 1972; "La Raza: Might It Tip the Scales?," *DMN*, March 12, 1972; "Ramsey Muñiz Comes to Houston for Raza Unida Party," *PC*, June 1, 1972; "La Raza Candidate Aims for Liberals," *DTH*, June 13, 1972; "La Raza Unida Effort Becomes Cutting Edge," *DMN*, August 13, 1972. On Muñiz, see Ignacio M. García, *United We Win*, 77–88. See also "Raza Unida Convention, Workshop: Women's Political Caucus," December 29, 1973, RUP Papers, BLAC; and *Chicanas Speak Out* (pamphlet).

130. "Muñiz Gains Confidence," *DMN*, October 26, 1972; "Briscoe Denies Treatment Charge of Opponent," *HP*, November 4, 1972; "Muñiz Charges Briscoe Using Alien Workers," *SAE*, November 5, 1972; "'Big Boys' Take Notice of Muñiz," *DMN*, November 5, 1972.

131. Navarro, *La Raza Unida Party*, 50; José Angel Gutiérrez to esteemed brothers, ca. 1973, Gutiérrez Papers, UTSA; "La Raza Still Seeking Major Political Clout," *DMN*, January 21, 1973; Castro, "La Raza Unida."

132. "Proposal for the Congreso de Aztlan," n.d., Gutiérrez Papers, UTSA.

133. "Gutiérrez Wins Heated Battle," *DMN*, September 5, 1972; "The Making of a Chicano Political Party," *Compass*, November 1972; "Crystal City Situation Anything but Clear," *SAE*, September 19, 1973; "'Getting It All Together," *Capital City Argus*, March 1, 1974; "La Raza Flexing Political Muscle, *SAL*, June 16, 1974; Navarro, *La Raza Unida Party*, 51–53, 244–47.

134. "Raza Unida—People Together" (pamphlet), ca. 1974, RUP Convention Papers, HMRC.

135. Campaign speech, ca. 1974, RUP Papers, BLAC.

136. "Ramsey Muñiz '74, Campaign Material," ca. 1974, RUP Papers, BLAC; "Ramsey Starts House to House Campaign," *El Informador*, May 24–June 7, 1974; "Ramsey Muñiz: Raza Unida," *SAL*, October 13, 1974; Carlos R. Guerra to Evey Chapa, May 31, 1974, RUP Papers, BLAC; Castro, "La Raza Unida; Ramsey Muñiz interview, *La Vida Latina en Houston*, October 1974; "Raza Unida Party Will Avoid Liberal Ties," *HC*, ca. 1974, and "Texas Raza Unida Party, 1974 State Convention" (pamphlet), 1974, RUP Convention Papers, HMRC; Navarro, *La Raza Unida Party*, 54–57.

137. "Muñiz Acusado de Traficar con Marihuana" (Muñiz Accused of Trafficking Marijuana) *El Sol de Texas*, August 6, 1976. For some strange reason, Muñiz and his brother Roberto had begun transporting large quantities of marijuana by car into Texas. Muñiz was tried for trafficking and received a five-year jail sentence. He was in and out of prison over the next decade. In 1994 the state charged him with drug possession and sentenced him to life in prison. See Ignacio M. García, *United We Win*, 197–200.

138. "Racism in Southwest Texas," *Congressional Record*, April 28, 1969; "MAYO Members Most Active of Activist Chicanos," *SAE*, April 16, 1969; "Que Eliminar a Los Gringos: Gutiérrez" (Gutiérrez: To Eliminate the Gringos), *El Sol de Texas*, February 27, 1970; "MAYO Leader Warns of Violence," *SAE*, ca. 1969, Peña Papers, UTSA.

139. Commissioner Albert A. Peña Jr., speech delivered at the University of Texas, September 23, 1971, Peña Papers, UTSA.

140. "Raza Unida Conference Huge Success," *El Sol de Texas*, January 15, 1971.

141. "Mexican-American Youth Vote to Censure Gonzalez," *HC*, April 20, 1969.

142. "Gonzalez to Report on 'Anti-Gringoism," *CCC*, April 8, 1969; "Gonzalez Hits Latin Racism," *HC*, April 16, 1969; "Gonzalez Says MAYO Quiz Waste of Time," *CCC*, April 29, 1969; "Liberal Gonzalez Details His Quarrel with Latin Radicals," *HC*, May 18, 1969 (quotations); "Militant Latins Preach Hate, Say 5 Texas Congressmen," *HP*, n.d., in Salazar Papers, HMRC; "Racism in Southwest Texas," *Congressional Record*, April 28, 1969; "Anglo 'System' Corrupt Says MAYO Speaker," *CCCT*, November 15, 1970; "Que Eliminar a Los Gringos: Gutiérrez" (Gutiérrez: To Eliminate the Gringos), *El Sol de Texas*, February 27, 1970.

143. José Angel Gutiérrez, "Mexicanos Need to Control Their Own Destinies," in *La Raza Unida Party in Texas* (pamphlet), 13, 15; "MAYO Leaders Urges La Raza Party," *La Raza* 1, no. 2 (1970); "Gutiérrez: Mexicanos Need to Be in Control of Their Own Destinies,'" *La Raza* 1, no. 2 (1970). See also "MAYOs Decry 'Gringo' Politics," *HP*, April 3, 1970, and "Three in Senate Race Ask Latin Support," *HC*, April 3, 1970.

144. "HBG May Request Grand Jury Proof" and "Ploch Asks Support for Gonzalez," *SAN*, April 9, 1969; "Bexar Official, MAYO Leader Nearly Have Fight," *CCCT*, April 12, 1969; "MAYO Members Most Active of Activist Chicanos," *SAE*, April 16, 1969; "Open Letter to Gonzalez" for La Raza Unida, n.d., Peña Papers, UTSA; Ignacio M. García, *United We Win*, 197.

145. Freeman, "Police Assassination of Carl Hampton"; Freeman interview by Indymedia.

146. Shockley interview, ⟨http://www.itsabouttimebpp.com/Media/Audio/Interview_with_James_Skip_Shockley-Black_Panther_Party-Dallas_Chapter.mp3⟩.

147. Salas interview.

148. Oropeza, *¡Raza Sí! ¡Guerra No!*, 91, 93–95, 99–101; "Chicano Moratorium August 29," *La Raza* 1, no. 2, 1970; "Chicanos and the War" and "Chicano Moratorium," *La Raza* 1, no. 3, 1970.

149. "Mexican Americans in the War," *HI*, October 21, 1967; "Austin Peace Group to Stage Anti War March," *Capital City Argus*, April 10, 1969; "Miles de Mexicanos Mueren en Viet Nam" (Thousands of Mexicans Die in Vietnam), *El Sol de Texas*, October 17, 1969.

150. "From the Halls of Montezuma to the Edge of Hermann Park," *TO*, August 4, 1967.

151. The first official Moratorium Day was in November 1969, followed by protests in May, August, and September 1970 and January 1971. See Oropeza, *¡Raza Sí! ¡Guerra No!*, 135–82.

152. "Moratorium Day in Texas," "Moratorium of News," and "We Can Prevail," *TO*, November 7, 1969; "Texas Moratorium Calmer Than Others across Nation," *HP*, November 16, 1969; "Space City Moves against the War," *Dallas Notes*, December 3–16, 1969; McMillan interview.

153. "None Dead; It's a Success," *DTH*, March 20, 1970; "Marcha de Chicanos en Austin Contra la Guerra en Vietnam" (March of Chicanos in Austin against the War in Vietnam), *El Sol de Texas*, April 24, 1970; "Antiwar Marchers Flee from Tear Gas Crown" and "Tensions in Austin Run High," *AA*, May 6, 1970; "Rioters Chased in Capitol," *DMN*, May 6,

1970; "Mob Damage at Capitol Texas' First," *SAE*, May 6, 1970; "No Riot for Police," "Shut-Down Refused, Teach-Ins Scheduled," and "Student Protestors Strike Campus," *Daily Texan*, May 7, 1970.

154. "Chicanos Told to Organize, Resist," *HP*, July 27, 1970; "CMC Organizes Chicano Moratorio," *PC*, August 8, 1970; "Chicanos Speak Out against War," *Dallas Notes*, August 19–September 1, 1970.

155. "Students to March Here Today," *AA*, May 8, 1970; "March in Austin Proves Peaceful," *DMN*, May 9, 1970; "GIs Count Dirty Cadence in Austin Antiwar March," *AA*, April 19, 1971.

156. McMillan interview.

157. Duncantell interview; Gutiérrez interview by author; McMillan interview; Shockley interview.

158. "Latins Demand Representation in City Council," *DMN*, September 10, 1968; "Latins Demanding 'Voice,'" *DTH*, September 11, 1968; "Democratic Way," *DTH*, September 17, 1968; "The Latins' Story," *DTH*, September 22, 1968; "Minority in Quest of Leader," *FWST*, July 26, 1970.

159. Duncantell interview; Freeman interview by author; McMillan interview.

160. "Arredondo Named to Head Citizens' Group," *DMN*, June 29, 1969; "Probes Mexican-American Unrest," *DPT*, July 5, 1969; "Negro-Latin Talk Demand Renewed," *DTH*, October 28, 1970; McMillan interview.

161. MAYO, Houston, Tejas, Aztlán, policy statement, n.d., Salazar Papers, HMRC.

162. Araiza, "For Freedom of Other Men," chap. 2; McMillan interview.

163. McMillan interview and e-mail responses to author's e-mailed questions.

164. "Progress Report—King Center," *Involvement Committee Newsletter*, November 1970.

165. See campaign document, entitled "The Poll List," which specifically calls for seeking the white liberal vote but makes no mention of the black vote. "The Poll List," ca. 1972, RUP Papers, BLAC; "Muñiz Hits 'Racism' in Texas," *AA*, August 18, 1972; "La Raza Unita? [sic]: An Appeal to Blacks," *DPT*, September 2, 1972; Gutiérrez interview by author.

166. "Raza Unida—People Together" (pamphlet), ca. 1974, RUP Convention Papers, HMRC; Carlos R. Guerra to Evey Chapa, May 31, 1974, RUP Papers, BLAC; "La Raza Unida Seeks Alliances with Blacks," *La Vida Latina en Houston*, September 1974.

167. "Raza Unida Party Will Avoid Liberal Ties," *HC*, ca. 1974, RUP Convention Papers, HMRC; "Ramsey Muñiz '74, Campaign Material," ca. 1974, RUP Papers, BLAC; interview with Ramsey Muñiz, *La Vida Latina in Houston*, October 1974.

168. George I. Sánchez to Ralph Yarborough, September 26, 1967, Idar Papers, BLAC.

169. Peter Libassi to Ralph Yarborough, ca. September 1967, and Libassi to J. W. Edgar, October 20, 1967, García Papers, TAMUCC.

170. "Attention Voters," ca. 1968, ibid.

171. "Texas Charges Prejudice against Mexican Americans," *DMN*, May 29, 1968. See also Dr. Hector P. García to Col. Morris Schwartz, October 14, 1969, García Papers, TAMUCC.

172. "El Plan de Aztlán," March 1969, Gutiérrez Papers, UTSA; "The Del Rio Mexican-American Manifesto to the Nation," March 30, 1969, Peña Papers, UTSA.

173. "Chicanos," n.d., Salazar Papers, HMRC.

174. "LULAC Chief Calls for Action," *HP*, June 14, 1971.

175. "Symposium Set on Civil Rights," *HC*, December 4, 1966; "Panelists Say City Drags Feet in Assisting Minority Groups," *HC*, December 6, 1966; "Emotions Boil in Rice University Racial Seminar," *Houston Tribune*, December 8, 1966; "Students Demonstrate as Mayor Speaks at TSU," *HP*, December 14, 1966.

176. "LULACs Advised for Their Rights to Be More Militant," *El Sol* (Houston), July 5, 1968. See also "LULAC Insiste en la Necesidad de Union Entre Mexican Americans" (LULAC Insists on the Need for Union between Mexican Americans) *El Sol de Texas*, December 24, 1969.

177. "Mexican Americans Wanting Equal Opportunity," *DMN*, August 21, 1969; "Equality for Latins Stressed," *DTH*, December 23, 1969.

178. "The Mexican-Americans Reply to Stokley [*sic*] Carmichael," *LN*, October 1967. A presidential message from Ornelas appeared next to the statement about Carmichael. Since LULAC presidents often wrote statements for the *LILAC News*, it is probable that Ornelas penned the attack on Carmichael.

179. "LULACs Advised for Their Rights to Be More Militant," *El Sol* (Houston), July 5, 1968.

180. L. Clifford Davis interview; Duncantell interview; Lawson interview.

181. "Chicanos," n.d., Salazar Papers, HMRC.

182. "New Wind from the Southwest," *Nation*, May 30, 1966.

183. "Only Ghost of Racial Forum Here," *CCC*, May 8, 1969.

184. "Black San Antonio V: Political Inroads," *SAE*, February 17, 1972.

185. Burns interview, 14.

186. "Raza Unida Party Will Avoid Liberal Ties," *HC*, ca. 1974, RUP Convention Papers, HMRC.

187. Interview with Ramsey Muñiz, *La Vida Latina in Houston*, October 1974.

188. Black interview by Wolfe; Freeman interview by author; McMillan interview.

189. "Angry Old Man We Got," *SAL*, November 29, 1972.

190. "MAYO Muere," *PC*, March 12, 1971.

191. Salas interview; McMillan interview.

Chapter 7

1. See San Miguel, *Brown, Not White*; "Chicanos, NAACP Will Seek Meeting on School Boycott," *HC*, August 22, 1971; "Moody Hosts Raza," *PC*, September 5–25, 1970.

2. "Texas Schools Desegregating Faster Than Most of South," *DMN*, June 13, 1965; "Texas Rates High on School Mixing," *DMN*, August 8, 1967; "Texas Called Leader in School Desegregation," *DMN*, May 29, 1968. See also "Texas School Desegregation . . . after Ten Years," *HFT*, June 6, 1964, and "Texas," Report to the Commission on Civil Rights.

3. "Texas Rated Worst," *DMN*, November 11, 1971; "Texas Schooling of Latins Lags," *DTH*, December 10, 1965; "Schools Fail Latin Students," *DMN*, April 15, 1967; "Que la Discriminacion Se Acabe para el Mexican American" (Discrimination Is Ending for the Mexican American) and "Discriminacion Contra Niños Mexico-Americanos" (Discrimination against Mexican American Kids), *El Sol de Texas*, April 21, 1967; Montoya, "Brief History of Chicana/o School Segregation."

4. "HISD Finds 90 Percent of Students in 101 Schools Are of One Race," *HC*, November 5, 1978; Kellar, *Make Haste Slowly*, epilogue; San Miguel, *Brown, Not White*, chap. 5; Luís Cano, "Illegal Discrimination and Segregation of Chicano Students in the Houston Independent School District," draft manuscript, n.d. [ca. 1975], Cano Papers, HMRC.

5. Linden, *Desegregating Schools*, 20–27, 29–32, 35–39; Beck, Linden, and Siegel, "Identifying School Desegregation Leadership Styles," 115–33.

6. See, e.g., "San Antonio Integrating 250 a Year," *DMN*, September 7, 1962.

7. See "Ethnic Isolation of Mexican Americans in the Public Schools of the Southwest," Report I of the U.S. Commission on Civil Rights (April 1971), 11–59; "The Unfinished Education: Mexican American Educational Series," Report II of the U.S. Commission on Civil Rights (October 1971), 7–41; "The Excluded Student: Educational Practices Affecting Mexican Americans in the Southwest," Report III of the U.S. Commission on Civil Rights (May 1972), 1–49; and "Toward Quality Education for Mexican Americans: Mexican American Education Survey," Report IV of the U.S. Commission on Civil Rights (February 1974), 1–70. In the 1950s, because leaders had pushed for "bilingual education," which taught English, it was really monolingual education. See Blanton, *Strange Career*, and San Miguel, *Contested Policy*.

8. This idea went back to 1966. See Betty Elder to Peter Tijerina, December 12, 1966, Herrera Collection, HMRC.

9. Jack Greenberg to Peter Tijerina, January 23, 1967, ibid. See also Alfred Hernández to Tijerina, February 4, 1967, ibid.

10. "Legal Services Should Be Equal to All Citizens," *LN*, ca. 1966, in Carmen Cortes Collection, HMRC; Leroy D. Clark to Pete Tijerina, January 24, 1967, Herrera Collection, HMRC; Richard J. Alatorre to Dr. Julian Zamora [*sic*], May 13, 1968, Samora Papers, BLAC; "Mexican-American Legal Defense," *SAE*, May 2, 1968; "La Raza Turns to the Courts," *TO*, April 11, 1969. On MALDEF, see San Miguel, *"Let All of Them Take Heed,"* 164–72; Ferg-Cadina, "Black, White, and Brown"; and Badillo, *MALDEF and the Evolution of Latino Civil Rights*.

11. Some Mexican Americans continued to promote the whiteness strategy. The G.I. Forum reminded those who wished to reclassify Mexican Americans that "the Mexican American is white"; Ricardo L. Garza memo to Ed Idar Jr., July 5, 1973, García Papers, TAMUCC. In 1973 attorney Ricardo Garza argued that while "being considered as a member of the white race was not always as advantageous as one would like to believe," Chicanos could take advantage of civil rights laws "without the necessity of proving that they are of a race that is other than 'white'"; Garza to Ed Idar Jr., June 27, 1973, García Papers, TAMUCC. See also "_____ Which Allegedly Discriminates against Mexican Americans" [the first part of the title of this document has been lost], prepared by the G.I. Forum, November 20, 1970, García Papers, TAMUCC; Idar memo to Sanford Rosen, July 10, 1973, Idar Papers, BLAC; Idar memo to Dr. Hector P. García, July 20, 1973, Sharon Province, and Garza memo to Idar, May 25, 1973, and "Education Mexican-American Children in the Southwest," ca. 1972—all in García Papers, TAMUCC; "MALDEF Litigation Program," 1974 MALDEF report, Leonel J. Castillo Collection, HMRC. And see Mario G. Obledo memo to Staff Attorneys, "Whether Mexican-Americans Are 'Non-White'" (May 7, 1973, García Papers, TAMUCC), which stated: "The conclusion that Mexicans are not of the

same race as 'whites' is supported by four separate reasons: (1) Mexican-Americans are primarily (often wholly) descended from the Indian population . . . ; (2) . . . Mexican-Americans are classified as a separate race in birth, death and arrest records . . . ; (3) Mexican-Americans are recognized and treated as a separate racial group by the generality of American opinion; (4) Mexican-Americans recognize themselves as a separate racial group." Yet Obledo and others still considered whiteness the best tactic. Finally, attorney Abraham Ramírez remarked on problems he encountered convincing Mexican Americans to fight for brown rights. He noted widespread hostility to brownness along the Gulf Coast: "I was faced with hostility from the Mexican American people because they felt that I was trying to sell them the idea that they were other than of the white race." He blamed this hostility on "the poor, uneducated sector of the Mexican American community" and the "professional (legal) Mexican American sector as well." His experience reminds us that the whiteness strategy cut across class lines. He also warned: "To sell Mexican-Americans that they are a 'race' separate and apart from the whites will result in chaos, in-fighting and hostility among ourselves the likes of which we have never seen . . . we should remain identified as whites." Abraham Ramírez to Ed Idar Jr., July 25, 1973, Idar Papers, BLAC.

12. "18 Stage School Board Sit-In," *CCC*, August 15, 1972; "Local School Case Highlights," *CCC*, June 27, 1973; "Historia Cronologica de la Discriminacion Contra el Estudiante Mejico-Americano y el Negrito por el Cuerpo Escolar Corpus Christi Texas, 1968–1975," (Chronological History of the Discrimination against the Mexican American and Negro by the Corpus Christi, Texas, School Body, 1968–1975), April 17, 1975, García Papers, TAMUCC; San Miguel, *"Let All of Them Take Heed,"* 177–81, and *Brown, Not White*, 84–87.

13. *Cisneros v. Corpus Christi Independent School District*; "Judge Seals Extends Integration to Latins," *El Sol* (Houston), June 12, 1970; "They Call the Issue Busing," *TO*, November 5, 1971; San Miguel, *"Let All of Them Take Heed,"* 177–78. On Mexican American legal history, see Soltero, *Latinos and American Law*.

14. *Keyes v. School District No. 1*.

15. San Miguel, *"Let All of Them Take Heed,"* 181.

16. *Keyes v. School District No. 1*.

17. San Miguel, *Brown, Not White*, 76–79.

18. *Demetrio P. Rodriguez et al. v. San Antonio ISD et al.*; "Court Finally Ends Edgewood Tax Fight," *SAN*, March 21, 1973. See also Sracic, San Antonio v. Rodriguez *and the Pursuit of Equal Education*.

19. *Rodriguez et al. v. San Antonio ISD et al.* For the 1989 case, see *Edgewood ISD v. Kirby*.

20. "Discriminan a Estudiantes Mexico Americanos" (They Discriminate against Mexican American Students), *El Sol de Texas*, November 22, 1968; "Growing Student Dissent in Valley Mirrored by Boycott," *HP*, November 24, 1968; "Mexican-Americans Boycott Elsa High School," *Compass*, December 1968; "Down in the Valley," *Petal Paper*, September 1969. See also "Chicanos Walk Out in Abilene," *TO*, December 5, 1969; Guajardo and Guajardo, "Impact of *Brown*"; Baldemar James Barrera, "The 1968 Edcouch-Elsa High School Walkout" and "'We Want Better Education!'"; and Arias, "Impact of *Brown* on Latinos," 1974–78. The protests mirrored the more famous Los Angeles blowouts.

21. "110 Mexican-Americans Arrested at Kingsville," *DMN*, April 17, 1969; "MAYO Sets Rally Today in Kingsville," *HC*, April 20, 1969; "MAYO Flag Raised in School Row," *DMN*,

April 22, 1969; "MAYO Protest March at Kingsville Is Peaceful," unknown newspaper, n.d., and "Kingsville Rights Workers Rapped," unknown newspaper, n.d., both in Salazar Papers, HMRC; "Board Bows to Demand for Student Hearings," *DMN*, April 23, 1969.

22. Lara interview, 13–18; "Crystal City Chicanos Claim Progress," *SAL*, November 30, 1969. See also José Angel Gutiérrez, *We Won't Back Down*.

23. "700 Crystal City Dissidents March," *SAE*, December 11, 1969; "Estudiantes Mexico-Americanos en Huelga" (Mexican American Students on Strike), *El Sol de Texas*, December 24, 1969; Marc Simon Rodriguez, "Movement Made of 'Young Mexican Americans Seeking Change,'" 26–36.

24. "Crystal City Students Vacation," *SAL*, December 24, 1969; "Crystal Teach-In Is Still Going On," *SAN*, December 29, 1969; "Rebelio Estudiantes Contra Discriminacion en Escuelas" (Student Rebellion against Discrimination in Schools), *El Sol de Texas*, December 31, 1969; "Aztlan: Chicano Revolt in the Winter Garden," *La Raza* 1, no. 4 (January 1971): 36–38.

25. "School Bells for Crystal," *SAN*, January 6, 1970; "Student Victory Leaves Crystal City Divided," *SAL*, January 8, 1970; "Crystal City Boycott—Many Changes a Year Later," *SAE*, December 6, 1970; "Crystal City, Texas; La Raza Unida in Action," *International Socialist Review*, April 1971, 25.

26. San Miguel, *"Let All of Them Take Heed,"* 189. The organization's acronym—ARMAS—suggests student militancy.

27. "Latins Demonstrate at School to Mark Mexican Holiday," *HP*, September 17, 1969; "Chicano Students' Walkout," *Space City!*, September 27–October 11, 1969. See also "ARMAS—Advocating Rights for Mexican-American Students" (protest flier), ca. March 1969, Salazar Papers, HMRC, and San Miguel, "'Community Is Beginning to Rumble,'" 136, 140–41.

28. "Geographic Plan Integration Goal Is Not Yet Met," *HC*, September 2, 1970.

29. "But We're Brown!," *PC*, August 22–September 11, 1970.

30. "Editorial: La Raza Fights Unfair Integration," *PC*, August 22–September 11, 1970.

31. Curtis Graves, "Together, a New Society," speech delivered to Corpus Christi NAACP, April 3, 1971, Graves Papers, TSU.

32. "But We're Brown!," *PC*, August 22–September 11, 1970.

33. "Massive Boycott of HISD Schools Brewing," *LN*, August 1971.

34. "Mixing Blacks and Raza, HISD 'Integration' Lies," *PC*, August 8, 1970.

35. Ramírez's involvement caused problems, as some Chicanos considered him an opportunist. Yolanda Birdwell and Gregory Salazar "refused to attend a banquet that is honoring a vendido [sellout] like Abe Ramírez." See "Mexican-American Youth Organization, Houston Chapter" (statement), December 15, 1970, and "Mexican-American Youth Organization, Houston Chapter" (telegram), December 15, 1970, Salazar Papers, HMRC.

36. "Chicanos Pose Special Problem, Board Says," *HC*, August 16, 1970; "League Files Suit," *PC*, August 22–September 11, 1970. See also "The Reality of Being Brown, Corpus and Houston," *PC*, September 26–October 9, 1970.

37. See *Ross v. Eckels*, 317 F.Supp. 512; *Ross v. Eckels*, 434 F.2d 1140.

38. "Concerning the Issue of Integration," Statement of MAYO, December 1970, Salazar Papers, HMRC; "MAYO on the Issue of Integration," *PC*, January 16–19, 1971. MAYO's ideas began with its Barrio Program; see "The Barrio Program," MAYO, June

1970, Salazar Papers, HMRC, and, more generally, "MAYO Projects," n.d., Gutiérrez Papers, BLAC.

39. "Huelga schools," MAEC flier, n.d., Salazar Papers, HMRC; Castillo interview, 41–42.

40. "Freedom Schools Will Open during Boycott," *HC*, August 30, 1970; "Schools Open Calmly; 3,500 Latins Absent," *HP*, September 1, 1970; "'Huelga' School Pupils Taught Word 'Boycott,'" *El Sol* (Houston), September 11, 1970; "Mexican-Americans Drop Part of Boycott," *HP*, September 13, 1970; "Another First in Houston," "La Raza vs. the School Board," and "MAEC Demands," *PC*, September 26–October 9, 1970; "The Truth about the Boycott," MAEC flier, n.d., Salazar Papers, HMRC. The boycott received widespread support. See "Reverendos Arturo M. Fernandez et al. to the Houston City Council and the Houston Independent School District Board," Huelga Schools Collection, HMRC.

41. "Brown Power!," "Confusion at HISD," "Struggle Never Ends," and "14 Arrested at HISD," *PC*, September 26–October 9, 1970; "Los Nueve" (The Nine), *PC*, October 10–23, 1970; "Chicanos Tell Houston School Board Not to Call Them 'White,'" *Muhammad Speaks*, n.d., in Salazar Papers, HMRC; "Brown Power," *Dallas News*, December 23, 1970–January 12, 1971. Nine of those arrested were later indicted for damaging school property. See San Miguel, *Brown, Not White*, chap. 7.

42. "Boycott Ends—MAEC Wins" and "¿Por Que La Huelga Escolar?" (Why the School Strike?), *PC*, September 26–October 9, 1970; "Community Gains from School Boycott," *PC*, October 10–23, 1970.

43. "Hell No, No Vamos" (Hell No, We Won't Go), *PC*, February 3, 1971; "Pairing Brings Picketers," "Adelante MAEC" (Forward MAEC), and "Huelga Schools Open," *PC*, February 20, 1971.

44. "Conservatives, Liberals, All the Same," and "MAEC Funded for $65,000," *PC*, February 20, 1971.

45. "Judge Raps Chicanos over Pairing Protest," and "Pairing Plan Ruled Unacceptable," *HC*, May 26, 1971.

46. "Pairing Plan Ruled Unacceptable," *HC*, May 26, 1971; "Houston Attorney Urges Appeal of Connally's School Ruling," *HP*, May 26, 1971. Both papers used almost identical quotations.

47. "Pairing Plan Ruled Unacceptable," *HC*, May 26, 1971.

48. "Houston Attorney Urges Appeal of Connally's School Ruling," *HP*, May 26, 1971; "Judges Differ in Integration," *El Sol* (Houston), June 4, 1971; "Judge Rules against La Raza," *PC*, June 12, 1971. Chicanos were generally incensed by Judge Connally's statements. For two examples, see untitled editorial and "The Supreme Duty," *PC*, June 12, 1971.

49. "HISD Announces Racist Pairing Plan Again," *PC*, July 15, 1971.

50. "MAEC—What It's All About," *PC*, July 15, 1971; "Justice—A Struggle but How Long La Raza?," *PC*, July 29, 1971; "Raza Marches from Hidalgo to Eastwood Park for Justice in Education" and "Huelga Schools Are Hope for La Raza Children," *PC*, October 14, 1971.

51. "MAEC Declares Boycott against HISD," "'Boycott the Hell Out of Them!,'" "MAEC Rally" advertisement, and "MAEC Calls for Boycott Support," *PC*, August 12, 1971; "2,000 Attend MAEC School Boycott Rally," *El Sol* (Houston), August 20, 1971.

52. San Miguel, *Brown, Not White*, 175.

53. In 1972, the Huelga Schools were transferred to the newly created Centro-Escolar

México-Americano (CEMA, Mexican-American Central Schools). CEMA broadened the program and attempted to create, in essence, a Chicano school district. However, CEMA faltered a short time later and the Huelga Schools ended. MAEC continued to operate until the late 1970s. See unsigned letter, May 25, 1972, Huelga Schools Collection, HMRC; "MAEC advertisement," *La Vida Latina en Houston*, July 1975.

54. "I Am" and "¡Chale! We Are Not Brown Monkeys," *PC*, October 10–23, 1970; "Franklin Parents Confront School," *PC*, ca. April 1, June 12, 1971.

55. "US Policy on Schools Predicted," *DTH*, April 22, 1970; "School Confusion," *DTH*, August 11, 1971; "Judge Taylors' School Busing Brews a Storm in Dallas," *DPT*, August 14, 1971.

56. "Latin Educators Will Be Recruited," *DMN*, September 10, 1969; "More Latin Educators Called Chicano Aim," *DTH*, December 11, 1969; "Desegregation Progress Continues," *DE*, April 11, 1970; "Mexican-American and Negro American Studies Offered in the DISD," *DE*, September 5, 1970.

57. "Lumping Requested," *DMN*, June 26, 1971; "Judge Taylors' School Busing Brews a Storm in Dallas," *DPT*, August 14, 1971; Linden, *Desegregating Schools*, 66–69.

58. "Latin-American Protest," *DMN*, June 28, 1971; "Desegregation and Chicanos," *Iconoclast*, July 16–23, 1971.

59. "Chicanos to Oppose Lumping," *DMN*, June 30, 1971.

60. "Inconsistent It Is" (quotations) and "Latins Due Talk with Estes," *DMN*, July 1, 1971; "Courts May Decide Chicano Point," *DMN*, July 15, 1971; "Texas Schools Mired in Confusion," *DTH*, August 15, 1971; "Desegregation in Dallas Derailed," *TO*, September 10, 1971; "Juez Excluye Chicanos de Plan de Integracion Educacional" (Judge Excludes Chicanos from Educational Integration Plan), *PC*, September 16, 1971; Linden, *Desegregating Schools*, 74–75; Contreras and Valverde, "Impact of *Brown*," 475; *Tasby v. Estes*, 342 F.Supp. 945, 947.

61. "Tri-Ethnic Panel May Probe 'Missing' Pupils," *DTH*, December 21, 1971; "Criticism Sparks Walkout," *DMN*, February 13, 1972; "Dallasites Asked to Obey Court," *DTH*, July 17, 1973.

62. Dallasites were also appeased when the *Keyes* decision was handed down. See "Dallasites Asked to Obey Court," *DTH*, July 17, 1973.

63. "How Long Ago Was 1954?," *TO*, August 13, 1971; "Back to the Back of the Bus," *TO*, September 10, 1971; "They Call the Issue Busing," *TO*, November 5, 1971. A number of cities created triracial committees to help diffuse tensions. See "Tri-Ethnic Group Discusses Schools" and "Race Panel Members Announced," *AA*, December 2, 1970; "East Austin Chicanos Fight School Board," *Echo*, April 14, 1970; "East Austin School Board Fight Continues," *Echo*, April 28, 1970; "East Austin Wins First Round in School Board Fight," *Echo*, May 19, 1970; "Bylaws," Human Relations Committee, Fort Worth Independent School District, ca. 1971, Collins Collection, FWPL.

64. "S.A. Student Busing Seen," *SAE*, October 4, 1968; "School District Must End Rights Violations," *SAR*, March 7, 1969; "SAISD Board Postpones Wheatley Zoning Action," *SAE*, June 6, 1969; "School Race Tensions Discussed," *SAE*, October 22, 1969; "San Antonio School Boycott," *PC*, January 16–19, 1971. For the situation in Austin, see "Storm Clouds Gather in Austin," *PC*, February 3, 1971; "How Long Ago Was 1954?," *TO*,

August 13, 1971; "Court Won't Clarify Austin School Order," *DMN*, January 4, 1973; and "NAACP Continues Fight for Integration of Schools," *Capital City Argus*, June 1, 1973.

65. "Why Not Bilingual Classes?," *TO*, June 9, 1967; "Language Barrier for Latins," *DTH*, October 19, 1969; Blanton, *Strange Career*, chaps. 8, 9.

66. "Bilingual Program Underway in Four County Districts," *SAE*, December 1, 1968; "Bilingual Plan Gains Support," *SAL*, December 1, 1968; "SAISD Bilingual Program Involves 4,000 Pupils," *Sun*, December 5, 1968; "U.S. Funds Okd for Bilingual Study," *HP*, February 28, 1969; Yolanda Navarro and Luis R. Cano, "Programs and Services of the Association for the Advancement of Mexican Americans," ca. 1970, Cano Papers, HMRC; "Language Role High in Dropout Problems," *FWST*, July 26, 1970.

67. "San Antonio Classes Use Two Languages," *Southern Education Reporter*, October 1967. See also Matthew D. Davis, *Exposing a Culture of Neglect*.

68. Minutes, LULAC Supreme Council meeting, 1968, pp. 1–3, LULAC Council #60 Collection, HMRC; "Lulac Seeks Education Course Funds," *SAN*, June 26, 1972.

69. "Gonzalez Opposes," *TO*, June 9, 1967.

70. "Texas Governor Is Showing 'Great Interest' in Interposition," *SSN*, February 1956; "Shivers Suggests Texas Vote, New District to Desegregate," *SSN*, March 1956 (1st quotation); "Houston's Integration Suit," *HI*, January 12, 1957; "Negro School Suit Scored as Unwarranted," *HC*, January 16, 1957; "Deliberate Speed Order Raises Questions of Progress," *HI*, October 19, 1957 (2nd quotation); "Houston Told: Proceed 'With All Deliberate Speed," *SSN*, November 1957. See also "Houston Plan—Selective Desegregation Proposed," *SSN*, April 1959. For a full account of school desegregation in Houston, see William Henry Kellar's excellent study, *Make Haste Slowly*.

71. "Whites, Negroes Unite to Elect Mrs C E White," *HI*, November 8, 1958; Kellar, *Make Haste Slowly*, 106–12.

72. "Segregation Itself Is a 'Sham and Subterfuge,'" *HI*, August 13, 1960; "'Sham and Subterfuge': Text of Judge's Order in Houston Case," *SSN*, September 1960; "Segregation Majority of Houston School Board Is Still Discriminating against the Negro Children," *HI*, September 10, 1960.

73. "Houston Desegregates; 11 Negroes Admitted," *SSN*, October 1960; "Court Rejects Liberalization of Houston Transfer Policies," *SSN*, April 1962; "Texas School Desegregation . . . after Ten Years," *HFT*, June 6, 1964.

74. "Integration Row Splits School Bd.," *HI*, March 13, 1965.

75. "Pickets Late . . . So Boycott of School Is Foiled" and "Who Called Off School Protest?," *HI*, September 5, 1964.

76. Davidson, *Biracial Politics*, 31. PUSH was also often called People for the Upgrading of Schools in Houston.

77. "2000 to Picket Houston School Board Meeting," *HI*, May 8, 1965; Lawson interview.

78. "The Response Was Gratifying," *HI*, May 10, 1965; Kellar, *Make Haste Slowly*, 154–55.

79. "'PUSH' Plans Tour of Ghetto," *HI*, May 15, 1965; Lawson interview.

80. "PUSH Plans Another Big Protest March," *HI*, June 19, 1965.

81. "Houston Bond Election Has Racial Overtones," *SSN*, June 1965; "School Suit Hearing Set," *HI*, May 28, 1966; "2nd Suit Filed in School Case," *HI*, August 6, 1966; "Itemizes New Integration Order of Houston Schools," *HI*, September 9, 1967.

82. Kellar, *Make Haste Slowly*, 155.

83. "Man on the Bench: Judge Maintains That Court Should Protect Both Races," *SSN*, August 1960.

84. *Borders v. Rippy*, 184 F.Supp. 402; "A Summary of School Desegregation Court Cases, 1896–1975," DPL, p. 2. The avowed racist had advised Price Daniel regarding the 1957 anti-integration legislation. See T. Whitfield Davidson to Price Daniel, September 12, 1957, and Daniel to Davidson, September 20, 1957, box 481, folder "Segregation Legislation," Texas Gov. Daniel Papers, SMRL.

85. Linden, *Desegregating Schools*, 36–37. See also "Implementing School Desegregation," 5–6, League of Women Voters of Dallas, April 1971.

86. "A Summary of School Desegregation Court Cases, 1896–1975," 2, DPL.

87. See *Borders v. Rippy*, 195 F.Supp. 732; "Excerpts from Court Decisions on Dallas Grade-a-Year Plan," *SSN*, March 1961.

88. "Dallas Starts Move toward Peaceful Desegregation," *DTH*, August 6, 1961.

89. "Little Known Facts about School Integration," DCCCR, May 1, 1964, DPL.

90. "Dateline Dallas," *DE*, August 5, 1961; "Dateline Dallas," *DE*, August 26, 1961. There were sixteen criteria governing transfers. See Carmack and Freedmen, *Dallas*, 17–18.

91. "16 More Negroes Enroll with Whites in Dallas School," *SSN*, October 1962.

92. "Suit Filed for Total Integration Immediately," *DPT*, August 15, 1964.

93. "Court Orders Dallas Integrate 12th in Fall," *DE*, July 10, 1965.

94. Linden, *Desegregating Schools*, 66.

95. *Tasby v. Estes*, CA-3-4211-C. See also *Tasby v. Estes*, 342 F.Supp. 945, 947.

96. Linden, *Desegregating Schools*, 79–84. Taylor implemented another busing plan for the 1971–72 school year that also caused a great deal of controversy. See "Judge Taylor's School Busing Brews a Storm in Dallas," *DPT*, August 14, 1971.

97. "Fort Worth Rejects Enrollment Try," *SSN*, October 1959.

98. "Fort Worth Suit Filed in Court," *SSN*, November 1959; "Fort Worth Lawsuit Set for Hearing on April 10," *SSN*, April 1961; "Illness of School Official Delays Fort Worth Case," *SSN*, May 1961 (quotations); L. Clifford Davis interview.

99. *Flax v. Potts*; "Fort Worth Ordered to Desegregate Next September," *SSN*, December 1961; L. Clifford Davis interview.

100. *Potts v. Flax*, 313 F.2d 284; "Integration Here Might Not Be for All," *FWST*, November 14, 1962; "Three New Desegregation Suits Filed," *SSN*, December 1962; "US Court Says Schools Here Must Integrate," *FWST*, February 7, 1963; "Fort Worth Makes Plans to Begin Desegregation," *SSN*, March 1963; "Judge Rules 1st Grade Integration for Fall," *FWST*, May 3, 1963; "Court Approves Fort Worth Plan," *SSN*, May 1963; "Desegregation Steps Here Disclosed," *FWST*, June 23, 1963; "No Trouble Seen Here in Mixing," *FWST*, July 30, 1960; "11 Negro Pupils to Mix Today," *FWST*, September 4, 1963; L. Clifford Davis interview.

101. "Local School System Faced with Federal Suit," *West Texas Times*, July 30, 1970; "Segregation Suit Filed against School District," *West Texas Times*, August 13, 1970.

102. Parks, *Remember When?*, 101–3.

103. "Trouble at Northwood," *HFT*, May 20, 1967; "Panel to Protest Protection Racket," *DMN*, June 27, 1969; "Black/Mexican-American Project Report," 35, 41–46.

104. Many local communities were aware of the problem of white flight, and local papers commented on the phenomenon with great frequency. See "Trio Tries to Stem White Exodus," *DMN*, February 7, 1965; "Scare Tactics Seen in Integrating Homes," *DMN*, Feb-

ruary 24, 1965; "'White Flight' Fought," *DTH*, March 19, 1972; and "White Flight," *DMN*, September 28, 1973.

105. Linden, *Desegregating Schools*, 83.

106. "Racist Expectation," *Iconoclast*, September 14–October 1, 1971.

107. "It's Not the Distance, 'It's the Niggers,'" 1–44, in Cano Papers, HMRC.

108. See, e.g., "S.A. Student Busing Seen," *SAE*, October 4, 1968; "A Case against Bussing," *TO*, June 4, 1971; "A Case for Bussing," *TO*, July 16, 1971; "R.I.P. Freedom of Choice, 1776–1971," *Life Lines* (a Dallas newsletter that billed itself as the "patriotic voice of freedom"), July 9, 1971, Huelga Schools Collection, HMRC; "Judge Taylor's School Busing Brews a Storm in Dallas," *DPT*, August 14, 1971; "How Long Ago Was 1954?," *TO*, August 13, 1971; "Texas Schools Mired in Confusion," *DTH*, August 15, 1971; "Statewide Antibusing Meet Planned for Dallas Sept. 11," *DTH*, August 23, 1971; "More Busing Due?," *DMN*, October 22, 1971; "Racist Expectation," *Iconoclast*, September 14–October 1, 1971; "They Call the Issue Busing," *TO*, November 5, 1971. See also Douglas, *School Busing*, and Boxill, *Blacks and Social Justice*.

109. "Press Release," August 2, 1971, box 257, folder 38, Smith Papers, TTU. See also Maurice Beckham to J. M. Ray (memo on Texas School Busing Survey), August 20, 1971, box 552, folder 24, Smith Papers, TTU.

110. Dolores Benavides to Preston Smith, July 14, 1971, and Jane Kerby to Smith, August 5, 1971, box 150, busing correspondence folders, Smith Papers, TTU.

111. These letters used stock phrases ("I oppose forced busing" or "I am for neighborhood schools") to exemplify their points. See Mrs. Irving Smith to Richard Nixon, August 23, 1971, Suzanne Stewart to Nixon, November 30, 1971, Mrs. Fred H. White to Preston Smith, June 30, 1971, and Citizens for Neighborhood Schools to Preston Smith, August 16, 1971—all in box 150, busing correspondence folders, Smith Papers, TTU.

112. *The Texas Poll*, Report #827, March 5, 1972, box 246, folder 20, Smith Papers, TTU.

113. "House Votes Anti-busing," *AAS*, July 2, 1972; "Rider Puts TEA Ban on Busing," *FWST*, July 3, 1972; "Texas House Prohibits Busing Expenditures," *AA*, July 3, 1972.

114. "House Antibusing Resolution Passes, Sent to Senate," *SAE*, July 6, 1972; "Texas House OKs Antibusing Plan," *FWST*, July 6, 1972; "No-busing Measure Past House," *AA*, July 6, 1972; "Busing Stand Urged," *HP*, July 6, 1972; "Texas House Members OK School Segregation Proposal," *HP*, October 10, 1972.

115. For a discussion of this viewpoint, see Kluger, *Simple Justice*; Irons, *Jim Crow's Children*; Kozol, *Shame of the Nation*; and Bell, *Silent Covenants*. Equalization represented a return to a late-nineteenth-/early-twentieth-century tactic. See also Lamothe interview.

116. See, e.g., Your Black Brothers to Gregory Salazar, September 1, 1970, Salazar Papers, HMRC.

117. San Miguel, *Brown, Not White*, 173.

118. *Black/Mexican-American Project Report*, 26–27; L. Clifford Davis interview.

119. *Black/Mexican-American Project Report*, 46.

120. "La Raza vs. the School Board," *PC*, September 26–October 9, 1970.

121. "Vatos' Views on School Zoning," *PC*, August 8, 1970.

122. "La Raza vs. the School Board," *PC*, September 26–October 9, 1970; *Black/Mexican-American Project Report*, 26–49.

123. *Black/Mexican-American Project Report*, 47.

124. "Everett Split with Mexican-Americans," *HFT*, September 19, 1970. See also "Desegregation Plan Still Goes," *HI*, February 14, 1970.

125. *Black/Mexican-American Project Report*, 26–27; San Miguel, *Brown, Not White*, 102–3, 106.

126. "Houston Attorney Urges Appeal of Connally's School Ruling," *HP*, May 26, 1971.

127. Castillo admitted that more needed to be done to combat the racism endemic in the Huelga Schools. See *Black/Mexican-American Project Report*, 27, and San Miguel, *Brown, Not White*, 103.

128. "Browns and Blacks Meet to Discuss Education," *PC*, July 29, 1971.

129. "Panel to Protest Protection Racket," *DMN*, June 27, 1969.

130. "Anglo Named as Tri-Ethnic Panel Leader," *DMN*, July 12, 1973.

131. "Negro-Latin Talk Demand Renewed," *DTH*, October 28, 1970.

132. "Black Student Union," *Space City!*, n.d., Salazar Papers, HMRC.

133. "Should Chicanos Assimilate?," *PC*, August 12, 1971.

134. See Phillips, *White Metropolis*, 166; McMillan interview; and Salas interview.

135. "The Latins' Story," *DTH*, September 22, 1968.

136. "Should Chicanos Assimilate?," *PC*, August 12, 1971.

137. "Conservatives, Liberals All the Same," *PC*, February 20, 1971.

138. Graves, "Together, a New Society," April 3, 1971, Graves Papers, TSU.

139. "Black and Brown Coalition Flyer," by Tomas García, ca. May 4, 1972, Huelga Schools Collection, HMRC. The BBC attempted to push the University of Houston to adopt Black and Chicano Studies programs in 1972. See also "The Introduction of Appropriate Black and Chicano Content into a Social Work Curriculum" by the BBC, January 31, 1972, Raul de Anda to Leonel J. Castillo, February 8, 1972, and de Anda to Castillo, February 20, 1972, Castillo Papers, HMRC.

140. "Blacks and Chicanos in Houston Mobilize against Racist Education," *Militant*, March 17, 1972.

141. *Black/Mexican-American Project Report*, 35, 41.

142. Ibid., 48; "The Black/Mexican-American Relations Project," *HCHR Newsletter*, November 1972; "Study of Intergroup Tensions between Blacks and Chicanos," n.d., HCHR Papers, HMRC.

Conclusion

1. In this section I frequently use the more all-inclusive "Hispanic" or "Latino/a" to describe persons of Latin American descent. The black/brown divide in Texas, and indeed in the United States generally, has grown to include not only Mexican Americans but also other groups as more immigrants have arrived from Central and South America. However, the examples I cite primarily come from conflicts between African Americans and Mexican Americans. See "2001, The Race for City Hall," *HC*, September 9, 2001; "Election 2001," *HC*, November 8, 2001; "Grassroots Effort Put Brown over Top," *HC*, December 3, 2001 "Chitlins and Chile Can Mix in Houston," *HC*, December 17, 2001; and "Lee's Way," *HC*, December 29, 2001.

2. L. Clifford Davis interview. See also Duncantell interview.

3. Sherman interview. See also Bryant interview and Ada Anderson interview, 22.

4. C. Anderson Davis interview, 32. See also Williams interview.

5. Earl Allen interview. See also C. Anderson Davis interview, 32–33.

6. L. Clifford Davis interview.

7. Duncantell interview; Peter Johnson interview.

8. Griffin interview; Goldberg, "Racial Change," 373.

9. Duncantell interview.

10. Peter Johnson interview.

11. Orozco interview.

12. Cruz interview.

13. Mindiola interview.

14. Gutiérrez interview by author. See also Solís interview.

15. Burns interview, 13.

16. Goldberg, "Racial Change," 362.

17. Calderón interview. See also Gloria De León interview and Bonilla interview, 37–38.

18. Mindiola interview.

19. Ibid. See also Dávila interview and Guerra interview.

20. McMillan interview.

21. Williams interview, 5.

22. Butts interview, 34.

23. José Angel Gutiérrez interview, July 22, 1984 (videocassette), Gutiérrez Papers, UTSA.

24. Salas interview.

25. See Dittmer, *Local People*; Chafe, *Civilities and Civil Rights*; Charles M. Payne, *I've Got the Light of Freedom*; and Fairclough, *Race and Democracy*.

26. See Navarro, *La Raza Unida Party*; Ernesto Chávez, "*¡Mi raza primero!*"; Mariscal, *Brown-eyed Children*; and Vigil, *Crusade for Justice*.

27. "What Went Wrong with the Voting Rights Act?," *Washington Monthly*, November 1987; "Brown Like Me?," *Nation*, March 8, 2004; Kamasaki and Yzaguirre, "Black-Hispanic Tensions," 17–40; Vaca, *Presumed Alliance*, 9.

28. See David Jacobson, *Immigration Reader*.

29. "Missing Link," *Color Lines*, issue 13 (Summer 2001), ⟨http://www.colorlines.com/printerfriendly.php?ID=122⟩ (May 22, 2008).

30. Vaca, *Presumed Alliance*, 4–6; "Race Relations: Browns vs. Blacks," *Time* magazine, July 29, 1991.

31. "Black-Brown Divide Saps Political Clout," *USA Today*, March 28, 2008; "Polls Don't Capture Blacks' Intense Debate over Immigration," *New American Media*, April 18, 2008, ⟨http://news.newamericamedia.org/news/view_article.html?article_id=fb23de948687c6c 2be106ea5e6f0e1da⟩ (May 13, 2008).

32. "Who's Rebuilding New Orleans?," *St. Petersburg Times*, October 23, 2005; "USHCC [United States Hispanic Chamber of Commerce] Deplores Remarks by New Orleans Mayor Ray Nagin regarding Mexicans and the Rebuilding of New Orleans," *Hispanic Business Journal*, October 28, 2005; "New Spice in the Gumbo," *Newsweek*, December 5, 2005.

33. "Nagin Calls for Rebuilding 'Chocolate' New Orleans," CNN.com, January 17, 2006; "Race Injects Itself into New Orleans Runoff," *USA Today*, April 24, 2006.

34. "Who's Rebuilding New Orleans?," *St. Petersburg Times*, October 23, 2005 (quota-

tions); "In New Orleans, No Easy Work for Willing Latinos," *Washington Post*, December 18, 2005.

35. "Who's Rebuilding New Orleans?," *St. Petersburg Times*, October 23, 2005.

36. Arturo's last name was withheld. See "In New Orleans, No Easy Work for Willing Latinos," *Washington Post*, December 18, 2005, and "Racial Divisions Highlighted in Aftermath of Storm," *DMN*, December 4, 2005.

37. See "Race Relations: Browns vs. Blacks," *Time* magazine, July 29, 1991; "The Rift," *Southern Poverty Law Center Intelligence Report*, no. 118 (Summer 2005); "L.A. Blackout," *Southern Poverty Law Center Intelligence Report*, no. 124 (Winter 2006); "Roots of Latino/Black Anger," *Los Angeles Times*, January 7, 2007; "Gang Mayhem Grips LA," *Observer*, March 18, 2007; "Simple as Black vs. Brown," *Los Angeles CityBeat*, March 19, 2008; "The Rainbow Coalition Evaporates," *City Journal* 18, no. 1 (Winter 2008); and "Fear of a Black-Brown Race War in Los Angeles," *Final Call*, April 3, 2008, ⟨http://www.finalcall.com/artman/publish/article_4526.shtml⟩ (May 13, 2008).

38. "The Rift," *Southern Poverty Law Center Intelligence Report*, no. 118 (Summer 2005); "Blacks, Latinos in the South: Cooperation or Confrontation?," *USA Today*, November 4, 2006.

39. "Deep Divisions, Shared Destiny—A Poll of Black, Hispanic, and Asian Americans on Race Relations," *New American Media*, December 12, 2007, ⟨http://media.new americamedia.org/images/polls/race/exec_summary.pdf⟩ (May 13, 2008).

40. "The Black-Brown Divide," *Time* magazine, January 26, 2008.

41. "Black-Brown Divide," *Newsweek*, January 26, 2008; "Facts Don't Back Black, Brown Divide in Texas," *Chicago Sun-Times*, March 4, 2008.

42. See, e.g., "Hispanics' Reluctance on Obama Highlights Black-Brown Divide," *New York Sun*, February 11, 2008, and "The Black-Brown Divide," *Esquire*, May 21, 2008.

43. "Hispanics Give Clinton Crucial Win," Pew Hispanic Center, Pew Research Center Publication, March 7, 2008, ⟨http://pewresearch.org/pubs/759/hispanics-give-clinton-crucial-wins⟩ (March 13, 2008); "The Latino Vote Is Pro-Clinton, Not Anti-Obama," *Los Angeles Times*, February 7, 2008; "Can Obama Connect with Hispanic Voters?," *HC*, February 10, 2008; "Latinas Held Key to Clinton's Texas Victory," Womensenews.com, March 4, 2008, ⟨http://www.womensenews.org/article.cfm?aid=3515⟩ (March 13, 2008).

44. Vaca, *Presumed Alliance*, 2.

45. "How Hispanics Voted in the 2008 Election," Pew Hispanic Center, Pew Research Center Publications, November 5, 2008, ⟨http://pewresearch.org/pubs/1024/exit-poll-analysis-hispanics⟩ (November 13, 2009); "A Permanent Democratic Majority?," Salon.com, November 13, 2008.

46. "Deep Divisions, Shared Destiny—A Poll of Black, Hispanic, and Asian Americans on Race Relations," *New American Media*, December 12, 2007, ⟨http://media.new americamedia.org/images/polls/race/exec_summary.pdf⟩ (May 13, 2007).

47. Coretta Scott King to Mario Obledo, May 3, 1986, Obledo Papers, UCD; "Obledo to Chair 'Rainbow Coalition,'" *El Hispano*, December 30, 1987; "Jackson, Latino Activists Hope to Form 'Black-Brown Coalition,'" *Chicago Tribune*, April 5, 2008.

48. Muñoz and Henry, "Rainbow Coalitions," 602–8.

49. "The Rift," *Southern Poverty Law Center Intelligence Report*, no. 118 (Summer 2005).

50. "Rep. Sheila Jackson Lee: Immigration Is the Civil Rights Issue of Our Time," April 4,

2006, ⟨http://www.democracynow.org/2006/4/4/rep_sheila_jackson_lee_immigration_is⟩ (November 13, 2009).

51. McMillan interview. See also Duncantell interview and L. Clifford Davis interview.

52. Gutiérrez interview by author. See also Gómez interview, Guadarrama interview, and Santos interview.

53. Peter Johnson interview. See also "A Call for Unity, Not Segregation," *Los Angeles Times*, June 16, 2009, ⟨http://articles.latimes.com/2009/jun/16/local/me-tobar16⟩ (November 13, 2009).

54. See "Overview of Race and Hispanic Origin: Census 2000 Brief," March 2001, ⟨http://www.census.gov/prod/2001pubs/c2kbr01-1.pdf⟩ (November 13, 2009). Issues relating to the 2010 census and race have also been controversial. See "Are Latinos White?," March 3, 2010, ⟨http://www.truthout.org/are-latinos-white-census-confusion-sparks-debate-over-racial-identity57472⟩ (April 14, 2010).

55. Whitaker, *Race Work*, 206.

Bibliography

Manuscript Collections

Arlington, Texas
  University of Texas, Arlington, Special Collections
    Pancho Medrano Papers
    Migrant Farm Workers Organizing Movement Collection
Austin, Texas
  Austin History Center, Austin Public Library
    African American Miscellaneous Vertical File
    Clipping Files
    PASO Folder
  Nettie Lee Benson Latin American Collection, University of Texas, Austin
    Paul Andow Collection
    William Flores Collection
    Louis Gayton Collection
    José Angel Gutiérrez Papers
    Eduardo Idar Jr. Papers
    Raza Unida Party Papers
    Jacob I. Rodriguez Collection
    Julian Samora Papers
    George I. Sánchez Collection
  Dolph Briscoe Center for American History, University of Texas, Austin
    Richard Morehead Papers
    State of Texas v. NAACP Case Records, 1911, 1945–61
  Lyndon Baines Johnson Presidential Library
    Administrative History Office of Economic Opportunity
    Texas Governor John Connally Papers
    Barefoot Sanders Personal Papers
    White House Central Files
    White House Confidential Files

Texas State Library and Archives Commission
John Ben Shepperd Speeches
Texas Education Agency Papers
J. W. Edgar Correspondence
Texas Good Neighbor Commission Papers
Corpus Christi, Texas
Special Collections and Archives, Texas A&M University, Corpus Christi, Bell Library
Clipping Files
Dr. Hector P. García Papers
Dallas, Texas
Texas/Dallas History and Archives Division, Dallas Public Library
Clipping Files
Juanita Craft Collection
Anita Martinez Collection
Davis, California
Special Collections Department, Peter J. Shields Library, University of California, Davis
Mario G. Obledo Papers
Fort Worth, Texas
Genealogy, History, and Archives, Fort Worth Public Library
City Managers Office Papers
Clipping Files
Bertha Collins Collection
Samuel Garcia Papers
Houston, Texas
Department of Special Collections, Robert J. Terry Library, Texas Southern University
Curtis Graves Papers
Texas Southern University Riot Papers
Houston Metropolitan Research Center, Houston Public Library
Afro-American Miscellaneous Collection
Brode Family Collection
Luis Cano Papers
John E. Castillo Papers
Leonel J. Castillo Collection
Civil Rights Microfiche
Clipping Files
Carmen Cortes Collection
Ernest Eguia Collection
Alfred J. Hernández Papers
John J. Herrera Papers
Houston Council on Human Relations Papers
Huelga Schools Collection
Moses LeRoy Collection
LULAC Council #60 Collection
Miscellaneous Files

Guadalupe Quintanilla Papers
Political Association of Spanish-Speaking Organizations Collection
Reverend Moses L. Price Collection
Raza Unida Party Convention Papers
Gregory Salazar Papers
Reverend Lee H. Simpson Papers
Felix Tijerina Sr. Family Papers
VISTA Collection
Special Collections, University of Houston Libraries
Thomas R. Cole Desegregation Papers
Jan De Hartog Collection
Liberty, Texas
Texas State Library and Archives Commission, Sam Houston Regional Library and
    Research Center
Texas Attorney General Price Daniel Records
Texas Governor Price Daniel Records
U.S. Senator Price Daniel Papers
Lubbock, Texas
Southwest Collection/Special Collections Library, Texas Tech University
Ecumenical Council on Social Concerns Papers
Texas Governor E. Preston Smith Papers
San Antonio, Texas
Institute of Texan Cultures
Clipping Files
Oral History Collection
Special Collections, University of Texas, San Antonio
José Angel Gutiérrez Papers
Judge Albert A. Peña Papers
Mario Marcel Salas Papers
Texana/Genealogy Collection, San Antonio Public Library
Chicano File
Clipping Files
PASO File
Rio Grande Valley Strike File

Microfilmed Collections

NAACP Branch Department Files, Geographical File Houston, Texas, 1956–65
NAACP Campaign for Educational Equality, 1956–65, NAACP Papers
NAACP Texas State Conference Papers

Legal Cases

Bell v. Rippy, 133 F.Supp. 811 (1955)
Bell v. Rippy, 146 F.Supp. 485 (1956)

Borders v. Rippy, 184 F.Supp. 402 (1960)

Borders v. Rippy, 195 F.Supp. 732 (1961)

Brown v. Board of Education, 347 U.S. 483 (1954)

Brown v. Board of Education (II), 349 U.S. 294 (1955)

Cisneros v. Corpus Christi Independent School District, 324 F.Supp. 599 (S.D. Tex. 1970)

Delgado v. Bastrop ISD, No. 388 Civil, Final Judgment (1984)

Del Rio Independent School District v. Salvatierra, 33 S.W. 2d 790 (1930)

Demetrio P. Rodriguez et al. v. San Antonio ISD et al., CA No. 68-175-SA (1971)

Edgewood ISD v. Kirby, 777 S.W. 2d 391 (1989)

Flax v. Potts, 204 F.Supp. 458 (N.D. Tex. 1962)

Grovey v. Townsend, 295 U.S. 45 (1935)

Hernandez v. Driscoll CISD, Civil Action No. 1384 (S.D. Tex. 1957)

In re Rodriguez, 81 F. 337 (1897)

Johnson v. State of Texas, 467 S.W. 2d 247 (1971)

Johnson v. State of Texas, 404 U.S. 951, 92 S.Ct. 273 (1971)

Keyes v. School District No. 1, 413 U.S. 189 (1973)

Morales v. Shannon, 516 F.2d 411 (CA5 1975)

Nixon v. Condon, 286 U.S. 73 (1932)

Nixon v. Herndon, 273 U.S. 536 (1927)

Pete Hernandez v. Texas, 347 U.S. 475 (1954)

Potts v. Flax, 313 F.2d 284 (1962)

Rodriguez v. San Antonio I.S.D., 411 U.S. 1, 93 S.Ct. 1278 (1973)

Ross v. Eckels, 317 F.Supp. 512 (S.D. Tex. 1970)

Ross v. Eckels, 434 F.2d 1140 (5th Cir. 1970)

Smith v. Allwright, 321 U.S. 649 (1944)

State of Texas v. NAACP, No. 56-469 (S.D. Tex. 1957)

Sweatt v. Painter, 339 U.S. 629 (1950)

Tasby v. Estes, CA-3-4211-C (July 1971)

Tasby v. Estes, 342 F.Supp. 945, 947 (1971)

Oral History Interviews

Earl Allen, interview by author, November 10, 2009.

George Allen, interview by Yvonne Johnson, March 29, 1985, Dallas Public Library.

————, interview by Gerald Saxon, March 13, 1981, Dallas Public Library.

Ada Anderson, interview by Cheri Wolfe, November 17, 1993, Institute of Texan Cultures.

Gonzalo Barrientos, interview by José Angel Gutiérrez, 1996, CMAS No. 93, University of Texas, Arlington.

Reverend Claude William Black Jr., interview by Syreeta Sweeny, April 11, 2006, University of Texas, San Antonio.

————, interview by Cheri Wolfe, March 14, 1994, Institute of Texan Cultures.

Ruben Bonilla, interview by José Angel Gutiérrez, 1998, CMAS No. 8, University of Texas, Arlington.

Thelma Scott Bryant, interview by author, March 6, 2000.

Harry Burns, interview by Cheri Wolfe, November 16, 1993, August 9, 1994, Institute of Texan Cultures.

Pansy Burtis, interview by author, November 3, 2009.

Ernesto Calderón, interview by José Angel Gutiérrez, 1998, CMAS No. 125, University of Texas, Arlington.

Alma Canales, interview by José Angel Gutiérrez, 1997, CMAS No. 131, University of Texas, Arlington.

Leonel Castillo, interview by José Angel Gutiérrez, 1998, CMAS No. 59, University of Texas, Arlington.

Emmett Conrad, interview by Alan Mason, November 18, 1980, Dallas Public Library.

Juan Cornejo, interview by José Angel Gutiérrez, 2000, CMAS No. 149, University of Texas, Arlington.

Juanita Craft, interview by John Egerton, Civil Rights Documentation Project, June 10, 1968, Dallas Public Library.

———, interview by David Stricklin and Gail Tomlinson, February 5, 20, March 20, 29, April 24, 1979, Institute of Texan Cultures.

Lauro Cruz, interview by José Angel Gutiérrez, 1998, CMAS No. 67, University of Texas, Arlington.

Diana Dávila, interview by José Angel Gutiérrez, 1998, CMAS No. 94, University of Texas, Arlington.

Reverend C. Anderson Davis, interview by Cheri Wolfe, December 15, 1993, Institute of Texan Cultures.

L. Clifford Davis, interview by author, October 22, 2009.

Gloria De León, interview by José Angel Gutiérrez, 1998, CMAS No. 110, University of Texas, Arlington.

Luís Diaz de León, interview by José Angel Gutiérrez, 1999, CMAS No. 135, University of Texas, Arlington.

Ovide Duncantell, interview by author, October 23, 2009.

James Farmer, oral history interview II, July 20, 1971, by Paige Mulhollan, Internet Copy, Lyndon Baines Johnson Presidential Library, 〈http://www.lbjlib.utexas.edu/johnson/archives.hom/oralhistory.hom/Farmer/farmer2.pdf〉. June 15, 2007.

Charles "Boko" Freeman, e-mail responses to e-mailed questions, November 10, 2009.

———, interview by author, November 3, 2009.

———, interview by D. Savetill of Indymedia, 〈http://radio.indymedia.org/uploads/SavetillD10Boko_0.mp3〉. November 20, 2009.

Margaret Gómez, interview by José Angel Gutiérrez, 1998, CMAS No. 95, University of Texas, Arlington.

Marvin C. Griffin, interview by author, March 25, 2004.

Cesareo Guadarrama, interview by José Angel Gutiérrez, 1997, CMAS No. 42, University of Texas, Arlington.

René Guerra, interview by José Angel Gutiérrez, 1998, CMAS No. 73, University of Texas, Arlington.

José Angel Gutiérrez, interview by author, October 30, 2009.

Aaron Henry, oral history interview I, September 12, 1970, by T. H. Baker, Internet Copy, Lyndon Baines Johnson Presidential Library, ⟨http://www.lbjlib.utexas.edu/johnson/ archives.hom/oralhistory.hom/Henry-A/Henry01.PDF⟩. June 15, 2007.

Peter Johnson, interview by author, November 19, 2009.

Dr. Isidore J. Lamothe, interview by Cheri Wolfe, October 18, 1993, Institute of Texan Cultures.

Severita Lara, interview by José Angel Gutiérrez, 1996, CMAS No. 13, University of Texas, Arlington.

William Lawson, interview by author, November 3, 2009.

Moses LeRoy, interview by George Green, August 19, 1971, Labor Interview #20, University of Texas, Arlington.

Ernest McMillan, e-mail responses to e-mailed questions, November 12, 2009.

———, interview by author, November 4, 2009.

Francisco "Pancho" Medrano, interview by George Green and Carr Winn, November 1971, University of Texas, Arlington.

Tatcho Mindiola, interview by José Angel Gutiérrez, 1999, CMAS No. 143b, University of Texas, Arlington.

Diana Orozco, interview by José Angel Gutiérrez, 1998, CMAS No. 88, University of Texas, Arlington.

Judge Albert Peña Jr., interview by José Angel Gutiérrez, 1996, CMAS No. 15, University of Texas, Arlington.

———, interview by Francis B. Roser, May 13, 1991, San Antonio Public Library.

Mario Salas, interview by author, November 20, 2009.

Ofelia Santos, interview by José Angel Gutiérrez, 1998, CMAS No. 83, University of Texas, Arlington.

Carol B. Sherman, interview by author, July 20, 2000.

James "Skip" Shockley, interview by William Cordova, June 5, 2008, ⟨http://www.its abouttimebpp.com/Media/Audio/Interview_with_James_Skip_Shockley-Black_ Panther_Party-Dallas_Chapter.mp3⟩. November 12, 2009.

Sherrill Smith, interview by author, October 20, 2009.

———, interview by Jan H. Cohen, March 2, 1972, Labor Interview #24, University of Texas, Arlington.

Eliseo Solís, interview by José Angel Gutiérrez, 1997, CMAS No. 61, University of Texas, Arlington.

Victor Treviño, interview by José Angel Gutiérrez, 1998, CMAS No. 38, University of Texas, Arlington.

Carlos Truan, interview by José Angel Gutiérrez, 1998, CMAS No. 84, University of Texas, Arlington.

Darrell Vines, interview by author, November 2, 2009.

Mary Vines, interview by author, November 2, 2009.

Dr. David Williams, interview by Cheri Wolfe, October 21, 1993, Institute of Texan Cultures.

Newspapers, Magazines, and Newsletters

AFL-CIO News
Austin American
Austin American-Statesman
Austin Statesman
Beaumont Enterprise
Black Panther
Brownsville Herald
Capital City Argus
Chicago Sun-Times
Chicago Tribune
Compass
Corpus Christi Caller
Corpus Christi Caller-Times
Daily Texan
Dallas Americano
Dallas Express
Dallas Morning News
Dallas News
Dallas Notes
Dallas Observer
Dallas Post Tribune
Dallas Times Herald
East Austin Times
Echo
El Deguello
El Hispano
El Informador
El Malcriado
El Paso Herald-Post
El Paso Times
El Sol (Houston)
El Sol de Texas (Dallas)
Esquire
Fort Worth Press
Fort Worth Star-Telegram
Forum (Austin NAACP branch
    newsletter)
Forumeer (American G.I. Forum
    newspaper)
Free Lee Otis
HCHR Newsletter
Hispanic Business Journal
Houston Chronicle

Houston Forward Times
Houston Informer
Houston Post
Houston Press
Houston Tribune
Iconoclast
International Socialist Review
Involvement Committee Newsletter
La Crónica
Lake Como Weekly
La Prensa
La Raza
La Vida Latina en Houston
Look
Los Angeles CityBeat
Los Angeles Times
Lubbock Avalanche-Journal
LULAC News
MALDEF Newsletter
Militant
Muhammad Speaks
Nation
New Republic
News Bulletin (American G.I. Forum
    newsletter)
Newsweek
New Yorker
New York Sun
Observer
Old Mole
Papel Chicano
People's World
Petal Paper
Por Mientras (RUP newsletter)
St. Petersburg Times
San Antonio Express
San Antonio Express and News
San Antonio Light
San Antonio News
San Antonio Register
Saturday Evening Post
Sentinel
Sepia

SNCC Newsletter
Southern Education Reporter
Southern Poverty Law Center Intelligence
  Report
Southern School News
Space City!
Student Voice (SNCC newsletter)
Sun (supplement of San Antonio News)
Tejano News
Texas Almanac (supplement of Dallas
  Morning News)
Texas Observer

Time
UAW News
UAW Washington Report
USA Today
Valley Evening Monitor
Valley Morning Star
Voice of HOPE
Wall Street Journal
Washington Monthly
Washington Post
West Texas Times

Published Reports, Government Documents, Electronic Documents, and Other Public Papers

Annals of Congress: The Debates and Proceedings in the Congress of the United States. "History of Congress." 42 vols. Washington, D.C.: Gales and Seaton, 1834–56.

"Article 1, Section 8, Clause 4 (Citizenship)." The Founders' Constitution Webpage, ⟨http://press-pubs.uchicago.edu/founders/print_documents/a1_8_4_citizenships8 .html⟩. November 13, 2009.

Badillo, David A. MALDEF and the Evolution of Latino Civil Rights. Notre Dame: Institute for Latino Studies, University of Notre Dame, 2005.

Berman, David, director. The Strange Demise of Jim Crow. Galveston, 1997. Videocassette.

"The Black/Mexican-American Project Report." Report of the Houston Council on Human Relations. July 1972.

"Black Panther Gets 30 Years for One Joint," ⟨http://www.hippy.com/php/article-156 .html⟩. May 15, 2008.

Block, Robinson. "A History of People's Party II: Houston's Black Panther Party," ⟨http:// houston.indymedia.org/news/2009/02/66654.php⟩. October 29, 2009.

"The Bracero Program." The Farmworkers' Website, ⟨http://www.farmworkers.org/ bracerop.html⟩. January 15, 2007.

Carmack, William R., and Theodore Freedmen, Dallas, TX: Factors Affecting School Desegregation. New York: Anti-Defamation League, B'Nai B'rith, 1963.

Daniel, Price. Opinion No. V-128. Digest of Opinions of the Attorney General of Texas. Austin, 1947.

———. "Supreme Court Decisions on Separate Schools: Speech of Hon. Price Daniel of Texas." Congressional Record, 83rd Cong., 2nd sess., 1954.

"Deep Divisions, Shared Destiny—A Poll of Black, Hispanic, and Asian Americans on Race Relations." New American Media, December 12, 2007, ⟨http://media.new americamedia.org/images/polls/race/exec_summary.pdf⟩. May 13, 2008.

"Ethnic Isolation of Mexican Americans in the Public Schools of the Southwest." Report I, U.S. Commission on Civil Rights. April 1971.

"Everywhere It's Raining Bags of Groceries." [?] The Black Panther, ca. July 1971,

⟨http://www.itsabouttimebpp.com/Chapter_History/Houston_Chapter_2.html⟩. November 9, 2009.

"The Excluded Student: Educational Practices Affecting Mexican Americans in the Southwest." Report III, U.S. Commission on Civil Rights. May 1972.

Ferg-Cadina, James A. "Black, White, and Brown: Latino School Desegregation Efforts in the Pre- and Post- *Brown v. Board of Education* Decision." Mexican American Legal Defense and Education Fund, May 2004.

Freeman, Charles "Boko." "The Police Assassination of Carl Hampton," ⟨http://www.itsabouttimebpp.com/Chapter_History/Police_Assassination_of_Carl_Hampton.html⟩. August 12, 2009.

General and Special Laws of the State of Texas, Passed by the Regular Session of the Forty-Eighth Legislature, Austin, Convened January 1943 and Adjourned May 1943. Austin: State of Texas, 1943.

Griffin, John Howard, and Theodore Freedman. *What Happened in Mansfield?: A Report on the Crisis Situation in Mansfield, Texas, Resulting from Efforts to Desegregate Its School System.* New York: Anti-Defamation League of B'Nai B'rith, 1957.

"Hispanics Give Clinton Crucial Win." Pew Hispanic Center, Pew Research Center Publication, March 7, 2008, ⟨http://pewresearch.org/pubs/759/hispanics-give-clinton-crucial-wins⟩. March 13, 2008.

"History of SER-Jobs for Progress." LULAC webpage, ⟨http://www.lulac.org/programs/economic/ser_jobs/index.html⟩. June 11, 2010.

"How Hispanics Voted in the 2008 Election." Pew Hispanic Center, Pew Research Center Publications, November 5, 2008, ⟨http://pewresearch.org/pubs/1024/exit-poll-analysis-hispanics⟩. November 13, 2009.

"It's Not the Distance, 'It's the Niggers': Comments on the Controversy over School Busing." New York: Division of Legal Information and Community Service, NAACP Legal Defense and Education Fund, Inc., May 1972.

Kuhlman, Martin. "Booker T. Bonner: Texas Civil Rights Activist." Unpublished essay, part of Bonner's ITC interview.

"The Legacy of Eleuterio Escobar." Benson Latin American Collection webpage, ⟨http://www.lib.utexas.edu/benson/escobar/escobar11.html⟩. August 10, 2009.

"The Mexican American: A New Focus on Opportunity." Report to the President, June 9, 1967.

"Mexican Americans and the Administration of Justice in the Southwest." Report of the U.S. Commission on Civil Rights, March 1970.

Morland, J. Kenneth. "Lunch-Counter Desegregation in Corpus Christi, Galveston, and San Antonio, Texas." Southern Regional Council Special Report, May 10, 1960.

Muse, Benjamin. *Special Report, Memphis.* Southern Regional Council publication, 1964.

"Overview of Race and Hispanic Origin: Census 2000 Brief," March 2001, ⟨http://www.census.gov/prod/2001pubs/c2kbr01-1.pdf⟩. November 13, 2009.

"People's Party II Rally to Protest Conner's Murder." [probably *Voice of Hope*, n.d.], ⟨http://www.itsabouttimebpp.com/Chapter_History/pdf/Houston/Houston_12.pdf⟩. May 15, 2009.

"Polls Don't Capture Blacks' Intense Debate over Immigration." *New American Media*,

April 18, 2008, ⟨http://news.newamericamedia.org/news/view_article.html?article_id=fb23de948687c6c2be106ea5e6f0e1da⟩. May 13, 2008.

"Report of the Legal and Legislative Subcommittee of the Texas Advisory Committee on Segregation in the Public Schools," September 1, 1956.

"Rep. Sheila Jackson Lee: Immigration Is the Civil Rights Issue of Our Time," April 4, 2006, ⟨http://www.democracynow.org/2006/4/4/rep_sheila_jackson_lee_immigration_is⟩. November 13, 2009.

"Riots, Civil and Criminal Disorders." Hearings before the Permanent Subcommittee on Investigations of the Committee on Government Operations, U.S. Senate, 90th Cong., 1st sess., Parts I, III.

Rochin, Refugio I., and Lionel Fernandez. "U.S. Latino Patriots: From the American Revolution to Afghanistan: An Overview," ⟨http://pewhispanic.org/files/reports/17.3.pdf⟩. June 6, 2011.

Rodríguez, Jake. "What Price Education? What Is It Worth? Where Does It Begin? Who Does It Benefit? What Can We Do about It?" Report of the Little School of 400, 1962.

Schott, Richard L., research project director. "Ethnic and Race Relations in Austin: A Report by the Policy Research Project on Ethnic and Race Relations in Austin," Austin History Center, 2000.

Skelton, Daniel. "A Summary of School Desegregation Court Cases, 1896–1975." Greater Dallas Community Relations Commission, ca. 1975.

"Texas." Report to the U.S. Commission on Civil Rights from the State Advisory Committee. 1961.

"The Texas Front—1967 . . . In the Nation's War on Poverty." Annual Report of the Texas Office of Economic Opportunity, September 30, 1967.

"Toward Quality Education for Mexican Americans: Mexican American Education Survey." Report IV of the U.S. Commission on Civil Rights, February 1974.

"Transcript of Treaty of Guadalupe Hidalgo." Our Documents webpage, ⟨http://www.ourdocuments.gov/doc.php?doc=26&page=transcript⟩. November 10, 2009.

"The Unfinished Education: Mexican American Educational Series." Report II of the U.S. Commission on Civil Rights, October 1971.

What Price Wetbacks? Report of the American G.I. Forum of Texas and the Texas State Federation of Labor. Austin, 1953.

Dissertations and Theses

Araiza, Lauren Ashley. "For Freedom of Other Men: Civil Rights, Black Power, and the United Farm Workers, 1965–1973." PhD diss., University of California, Berkeley, 2006.

Barrera, Baldemar James. "'We Want Better Education!': The Chicano Student Movement for Educational Reform in South Texas, 1968–1970." PhD diss., University of New Mexico, 2007.

Behnken, Brian D. "On Parallel Tracks: A Comparison of the African-American and Latino Civil Rights Movements in Houston." MA thesis, University of Houston, 2001.

———. "Fighting Their Own Battles: Blacks, Mexican Americans, and the Struggle for Civil Rights in Texas." PhD diss., University of California, Davis, 2007.

Brilliant, Mark. "Color Lines: Civil Rights Struggles on America's 'Racial Frontier,' 1945–1975." PhD diss., Stanford University, 2002.

Clayson, William. "Texas Poverty and Liberal Politics: The Office of Economic Opportunity and the War on Poverty in Texas." PhD diss., Texas Tech University, 2001.

Gillette, Michael L. "The NAACP in Texas, 1937–1957." PhD diss., University of Texas, 1984.

Gilliam, Stephanie. "Mama, Activist, and Friend: African-American Women in the Civil Rights Movement in Dallas, Texas, 1945–1998." MA thesis, Oklahoma State University, 1998.

González, Gabriela. "Two Flags Entwined: Transborder Activists and the Politics of Race, Ethnicity, Class, and Gender in South Texas, 1900–1950." PhD diss., Stanford University, 2004.

Houston, Ramona Allaniz. "African Americans, Mexican Americans, and Anglo Americans and the Desegregation of Texas, 1946–1957." PhD diss.: University of Texas, 2000.

Johnson, Yvonne. "Desegregating Dallas, 1936–1961." MA thesis, University of Texas Dallas, 1985.

Kuhlman, Martin. "The Civil Rights Movement in Texas: Desegregation of Public Accommodations, 1950–1964." PhD diss., Texas Tech University, 1994.

Mantler, Gordon. "Black, Brown, and Poor: Martin Luther King Jr., the Poor People's Campaign, and Its Legacies." PhD diss., Duke University, 2008.

Montes, Rebecca Ann. "Working for American Rights: Black, White, and Mexican American Dockworkers in Texas during the Great Depression." PhD diss., University of Texas, Austin, 2005.

Orozco, Cynthia E. "The Origins of the League of United Latin American Citizens (LULAC) and the Mexican American Civil Rights Movement in Texas with an Analysis of Women's Political Participation in a Gendered Context, 1910–1929." PhD diss., University of California, Los Angeles, 1992.

Quintanilla, Guadalupe. "The Little School of the 400 and Its Impact on Education for Spanish Dominant Bilingual Children of Texas." PhD diss., University of Houston, 1976.

Quiroz, Ann Dee. "Black, White, and Brown: The Houston Council on Human Relations and Tri-Racial Relations in Houston." MA thesis, University of Houston, 1998.

Prewitt, Steven W. "'We Didn't Ask to Come to This Party': Self Determination Collides with the Federal Government in the Public Schools of Del Rio, Texas, 1890–1971." PhD diss., University of Houston, 2000.

Seals, Donald. "The Wiley-Bishop Student Movement: A Case Study of the 1960 Civil Rights Sit-Ins." MA thesis, Baylor University, 2001.

Articles in Journals, in Books, and Online

Aguirre, Frederick P. "*Mendez v. Westminster School District*: How It Affected *Brown v. Board of Education*." *Journal of Hispanic Higher Education* 4, no. 4 (October 2005): 321–32.

Arias, Beatriz M. "The Impact of *Brown* on Latinos: A Study of Transformation of Policy Intentions." *Teachers College Record* 107, no. 9 (September 2005): 1974–98.

Arriola, Christopher. "Knocking on the Schoolhouse Door: *Mendez v. Westminster*, Equal Protection and Mexican Americans in the 1940s." *La Raza Law Journal* 8, no. 2 (1995): 166–207.

Avila, Eric R., Karen Mary Davalos, Chela Sandoval, and Rafael Pérez-Torres. "Roundtable on the State of Chicana/o Studies." *Aztlán* 27, no. 2 (Fall 2002): 141–52.

Bailey, Richard. "The Starr County Strike." *Red River Valley Historical Review* 4, no. 1 (Winter 1979): 42–61.

Barrera, B. James. "The 1968 Edcouch-Elsa High School Walkout: Chicano Student Activism in a South Texas Community." *Aztlán* 29, no. 2 (Fall 2004): 93–122.

Beck, William W., Glenn M. Linden, and Michael E. Siegel. "Identifying School Desegregation Leadership Styles." *Journal of Negro Education* 49, no. 2 (Spring 1980): 115–33.

Behnken, Brian D. "'Count on Me': Reverend M. L. Price of Texas: A Case Study in Civil Rights Leadership." *Journal of American Ethnic History* 25, no. 1 (Fall 2005): 61–84.

———. "'The Dallas Way': Protest, Response, and the Civil Rights Experience in Big D and Beyond." *Southwestern Historical Quarterly* 111, no. 1 (July 2007): 1–29.

———. "'We Want Justice!': Police Murder, Mexican American Community Response, and the Chicano Movement." In *The Hidden 1970s: Histories of Radicalism*, ed. Dan Berger. Piscataway, N.J.: Rutgers University Press, 2010.

Blanton, Carlos Kevin. "The Citizenship Sacrifice: Mexican Americans, the Saunders-Leonard Report, and the Politics of Immigration, 1951–1952." *Western Historical Quarterly* 40, no. 3 (Autumn 2009): 299–320.

———. "George I. Sánchez, Ideology, and Whiteness in the Making of the Mexican American Civil Rights Movement, 1930–1960." *Journal of Southern History* 72, no. 3 (August 2006): 569–604.

Brophy, William. "Active Acceptance–Active Containment: The Dallas Story." In *Southern Businessmen and Desegregation*, ed. Elizabeth Jacoway and David R. Colburn. Baton Rouge: Louisiana State University Press, 1982.

Brown, Olive D., and Michael R. Heintze. "Mary Branch: Private College Educator." In *Black Leaders: Texans for Their Times*, ed. Alwyn Barr and Robert A. Calvert. Austin: Texas State Historical Association, 1985.

Carrigan, William D., and Clive Webb. "The Lynching of Persons of Mexican Origin or Descent in the United States, 1848 to 1928." *Journal of Social History* 37, no. 2 (Winter 2003): 411–38.

———. "Muerto por Unos Desconocidos (Killed by Persons Unknown): Mob Violence Against Blacks and Mexicans." In *Beyond Black and White: Race, Ethnicity, and Gender in the U.S. South and Southwest*, ed. Stephanie Cole, Alison M. Parker, and Laura F. Edwards. College Station: Texas A&M University Press, 2003.

Castro, Tony. "La Raza Unida: A Third Party Is Born." *Race Relations Reporter* 4, no. 1 (January 1973): 13–17.

Chávez, Alicia. "Dolores Huerta and the United Farm Workers." In *Latina Legacies: Identity, Biography, and Community*, ed. Vicki L. Ruiz and Virginia Sánchez Korrol. New York: Oxford University Press, 2005.

Chicanas Speak Out. New York: Pathfinder Press, a Merit pamphlet, 1971.

Clayson, William. "'The Barrios and the Ghettos Have Organized!': Community Action, Political Acrimony, and the War on Poverty in San Antonio." *Journal of Urban History* 28, no. 2 (January 2002): 158–83.

———. "The War on Poverty and the Fear of Urban Violence in Houston, 1965–1968." *Gulf South Historical Review* 18, no. 2 (Spring 2003): 38–59.

Contreras, A. Reynaldo, and Leonard A. Valverde. "The Impact of *Brown* on the Education of Latinos." *Journal of Negro Education* 63, no. 3 (Summer 1994): 470–81.

Dailey, Jane. "Sex, Segregation, and the Sacred after *Brown*." *Journal of American History* 91, no. 1 (June 2004): 119–44.

Day, Barbara Thompson. "The Heart of Houston: The Early History of the Houston Council on Human Relations, 1958–1972." *Houston Review* 8, no. 1 (1986): 1–32.

Dressman, Frances. "'Yes, We Have No Jitneys!': Transportation Issues in Houston's Black Community, 1914–1924." In *Black Dixie: Afro-Texan History and Culture in Houston*, ed. Howard Beeth and Cary D. Wintz. College Station: Texas A&M University Press, 1992.

Dulaney, W. Marvin. "The Progressive Voters League—A Political Voice for African Americans in Dallas." *Legacies: A History Journal for Dallas and North Central Texas* (Spring 1991): 27–35.

———. "Whatever Happened to the Civil Rights Movement in Dallas, Texas?" In *Essays on the American Civil Rights Movement*, ed. W. Marvin Dulaney and Kathleen Underwood. College Station: Texas A&M University Press, 1993.

Durham, Kenneth R. "The Longview Race Riot of 1919." *East Texas Historical Journal* 18, no. 2 (1980): 13–24.

Enstam, Elizabeth York. "The Dallas Equal Suffrage Association, Political Style, and Popular Culture: Grassroots Strategies of the Woman Suffrage Movement, 1913–1919." *Journal of Southern History* 68, no. 4 (November 2002): 817–48.

Fisher, Robert. "The Urban Sunbelt in Comparative Perspective: Houston in Context." In *Essays on Sunbelt Cities and Recent Urban America*, ed. Robert B. Fairbanks and Kathleen Underwood. College Station: Texas A&M University Press, 1990.

Foley, Neil. "Becoming Hispanic: Mexican Americans and the Faustian Bargain with Whiteness." *Reflexiones* (1997): 53–70.

———. "Partly Colored or Other White: Mexican Americans and Their Problems with the Color Line." In *Beyond Black and White: Race, Ethnicity, and Gender in the U.S. South and Southwest*, ed. Stephanie Cole, Allison Parker, and Laura F. Edwards. College Station: Texas A&M University Press, 2003.

———. "Straddling the Color Line: The Legal Construction of Hispanic Identity in Texas." In *Not Just Black and White: Historical and Contemporary Perspectives on Immigration, Race, and Ethnicity in the United States*, ed. Nancy Foner and George Frederickson. New York: Russell Sage Foundation, 2005.

García, Mario T. "Mexican Americans and the Politics of Citizenship: The Case of El Paso, 1936." *New Mexico Historical Review* 59, no. 2 (April 1984): 187–204.

Goldberg, Robert A. "Racial Change on the Southern Periphery: The Case of San Antonio, Texas, 1960–1965." *Journal of Southern History* 49, issue 3 (August 1983): 349–74.

González, Gabriela. "Carolina Munguía and Emma Tenayuca: The Politics of Benevolence and Radical Reform." *Frontiers: A Journal of Women Studies* 24 nos. 2, 3 (2003): 200–229.

Graham, Richard. Introduction to *The Idea of Race in Latin America: 1870–1940*, ed. Richard Graham. Austin: University of Texas Press, 1990.

Guajardo, Miguel A., and Francisco J. Guajardo. "The Impact of *Brown* on the Brown of South Texas: A Micropolitical Perspective on the Education of Mexican Americans in a South Texas Community." *American Educational Research Journal* 41, no. 3 (Fall 2004): 501–26.

Guglielmo, Thomas A. "Fighting for Caucasian Rights: Mexicans, Mexican Americans, and the Transnational Struggle for Civil Rights in World War II Texas." *Journal of American History* 92, no. 4 (March 2006): 1212–37.

Gutiérrez, David G. "Migration, Emergent Ethnicity, and the 'Third Space': The Shifting Politics of Nationalism in Greater Mexico." *Journal of American History* 86, no. 2 (September 1999): 481–517.

Hall, Jacquelyn Dowd. "The Long Civil Rights Movement and the Political Uses of the Past." *Journal of American History* 91, no. 4 (March 2005): 1233–63.

Haney López, Ian F. "Retaining Race: LatCrit Theory and Mexican American Identity in *Hernandez v. Texas*." *Harvard Latino Law Review* 2 (1997): 279–96.

Harrison, Cecille E., and Alice K. Laine. "Operation Breadbasket in Houston, 1966–1978." In *Black Dixie: Afro-Texan History and Culture in Houston*, ed. Howard Beeth and Cary D. Wintz. College Station: Texas A&M University Press, 1992.

Haynes, Robert V. "Black Houstonians and the White Democratic Primary, 1920–1945." In *Black Dixie: Afro-Texan History and Culture in Houston*, ed. Howard Beeth and Cary D. Wintz. College Station: Texas A&M University Press, 1992.

Hine, Darlene Clark. "Blacks and the Destruction of the Democratic White Primary, 1935–1944." *Journal of Negro History* 62, no. 1 (January 1977): 43–59.

Hurtado, Aída, and Carlos H. Arce. "Mexicans, Chicanos, Mexican Americans, or Pochos . . . ¿Qué Somos? The Impact of Language and Nativity on Ethnic Labeling." *Aztlán* 17, no. 1 (Spring 1986): 103–30.

Jensen, F. Kenneth. "The Houston Sit-In Movement of 1960–1961." In *Black Dixie: Afro-Texan History and Culture in Houston*, ed. Howard Beeth and Cary D. Wintz. College Station: Texas A&M University Press, 1992.

Kamasaki, Charles, and Raul Yzaguirre. "Black-Hispanic Tensions: One Perspective." *Journal of Intergroup Relations* 21, no. 4 (Winter 1994–95): 17–40.

Kaplowitz, Craig A. "A Distinct Minority: LULAC, Mexican American Identity, and Presidential Policymaking, 1965–1972." *Journal of Policy History* 15, no. 2 (2003): 192–222.

Knight, Alan. "Racism, Revolution, and *Indigenismo*: Mexico, 1910–1940." In *The Idea of Race in Latin America, 1870–1940*, ed. Richard Graham. Austin: University of Texas Press, 1990.

Kocka, Jürgen. "Comparison and Beyond." *History and Theory* 42 (February 2003): 39–44.

Kuhlman, Martin. "The Civil Rights March on Austin, Texas, 1963." In *Bricks without*

Straw: A Comprehensive History of African Americans in Texas, ed. David A. Williams. Austin: Eakin Press, 1997.

La Raza Unida Party in Texas. New York: Pathfinder Press, a Merit pamphlet, 1970.

Lawson, Steven F. "From Sit-In to Race Riot: Businessmen, Blacks, and the Pursuit of Moderation in Tampa, 1960–1967." In Southern Businessmen and Desegregation, ed. Elizabeth Jacoway and David R. Colburn. Baton Rouge: Louisiana State University Press, 1982.

Lofton, Paul S. "Calm and Exemplary: Desegregation in Columbia, South Carolina." In Southern Businessmen and Desegregation, ed. Elizabeth Jacoway and David R. Colburn. Baton Rouge: Louisiana State University Press, 1982.

Martín Alcoff, Linda. "Latino vs. Hispanic: The Politics of Ethnic Names." Philosophy & Social Criticism 31, no. 4 (2005): 395–407.

Martínez, George A. "African-Americans, Latinos, and the Construction of Race: Toward an Epistemic Coalition." Chicano-Latino Law Review 19 (Spring 1998): 1–11.

Melosi, Martin V. "Dallas-Fort Worth: Marketing the Metroplex." In Sunbelt Cities: Politics and Growth since World War II, ed. Richard M. Bernhard and Bradley R. Rice. Austin: University of Texas Press, 1983.

Minna Stern, Alexandra. "From Mestizophilia to Biotypology: Racialization and Science in Mexico, 1920–1960." In Race and Nation in Modern Latin America, ed. Nancy P. Applebaum, Anne S. Macpherson, and Karin Alejandra Rosemblatt. Chapel Hill: University of North Carolina Press, 2007.

Montoya, Margaret E. "A Brief History of Chicana/o School Segregation: One Rationale for Affirmative Action." La Raza Law Journal 12, no. 2 (2001): 159–70.

Muñoz, Carlos Jr., and Charles Henry. "Rainbow Coalitions in Four Big Cities: San Antonio, Denver, Chicago, and Philadelphia." PS 19, no. 3 (Summer 1986): 598–609.

Olguín, B. V. "Sangre Mexicana/Corazón Americano: Identity, Ambiguity, and Critique in Mexican-American War Narratives." American Literary History 14, no. 1 (2002): 83–114.

Oliver, Bonnie J. "The Life and Time of Barbara Jordan: A Twentieth-Century Baptist and Political Pioneer." Baptist History and Heritage 41, no. 3 (Summer–Fall 2006): 66–78.

Ramos, Lisa Y. "Dismantling Segregation Together: Interconnections between the Méndez v. Westminster (1946) and Brown v. Board of Education (1954) School Segregation Cases." Equity and Excellence in Education 37, no. 3, (September 2004): 247–54.

Rhinehart, Marilyn, and Thomas Kreneck. "The Minimum Wage March of 1966." Houston Review 11, no. 1 (1989): 27–44.

Rivas-Rodriguez, Maggie. "Framing Racism: Newspaper Coverage of the Three Rivers Incident." In Mexican Americans and World War II, ed. Maggie Rivas-Rodriguez. Austin: University of Texas Press, 2005.

Rivera, George, Jr. "Nosotros Venceremos: Chicano Consciousness and Change Strategies." Journal of Applied Behavioral Science 8, no. 7 (1972): 56–71.

Robinson, Toni, and Greg Robinson. "The Limits of Interracial Coalitions: Méndez v. Westminster Reexamined." In Racial Transformations: Latinos and Asians Remaking *the United States*, ed. Nicholas De Genova. Durham, N.C.: Duke University Press, 2006.

Rodriguez, Marc Simon. "Cristaleño Consciousness: Mexican-American Activism between Crystal City, Texas, and Wisconsin, 1963–1980." In *Oppositional Consciousness: The Subjective Roots of Social Protest*, ed. Jane J. Mansbridge and Aldon Morris. Illinois: University of Chicago Press, 2001.

———. "A Movement Made of 'Young Mexican Americans Seeking Change': Critical Citizenship, Migration, and the Chicano Movement in Texas and Wisconsin, 1960–1975." *Western Historical Quarterly* 34, no. 3 (Autumn 2003): 275–300.

Ruiz, Vicki L. "Morena/o, blanca/o y café con leche: Racial Constructions in Chicana/o Historiography." *Mexican Studies/Estudios Mexicanos* 20, issue 2 (Summer 2004): 343–59.

———. "South By Southwest: Mexican Americans and Segregated Schooling." *OAH Magazine of History* 15, no. 2 (Winter 2001): 23–27.

———. "We Always Tell Our Children They Are Americans: *Mendez v. Westminster*." *Brown Quarterly* 6, no. 3 (Fall 2004): 1–10.

Salinas, Guadalupe. "Mexican-Americans and the Desegregation of Schools in the Southwest." *Houston Law Review* 8 (1971): 946–66.

San Miguel, Guadalupe. "'The Community Is Beginning to Rumble': The Origins of Chicano Educational Protest in Houston, 1965–1970." *Houston Review* 13, no. 3 (1991): 127–47.

———. "The Struggle against Separate and Unequal Schools: Middle Class Mexican Americans and the Desegregation Campaign in Texas, 1929–1957." *History of Education Quarterly* 23, no. 3 (Fall 1983): 343–59.

Sheridan, Clare. "'Another White Race': Mexican Americans and the Paradox of Whiteness in Jury Selection." *Law and History Review* 21, no. 1 (Spring 2003): 109–44.

SoRelle, James M. "The Emergence of Black Business in Houston, Texas: A Study of Race and Ideology, 1919–1945." In *Black Dixie: Afro-Texan History and Culture in Houston*, ed. Howard Beeth and Cary D. Wintz. College Station: Texas A&M University Press, 1992.

Urrutia, Liliana. "An Offspring of Discontent: The Asociación Nacional México-Americana, 1949–1954." *Aztlán* 15 (Spring 1984): 177–84.

Ware, Gilbert. "The NAACP-Inc. Fund Alliance: Its Strategy, Power, and Destruction." *Journal of Negro Education* 63, no. 3 (1994): 323–35.

Watson, Jon. "Crossing the Colour Lines in the City of Angels: The NAACP and the Zoot-Suit Riot of 1943." *University of Sussex Journal of Contemporary History*, issue 4 (2002): 1–11.

Wilson, Steven H. "*Brown* over 'Other White': Mexican Americans' Legal Arguments and Litigation Strategy in School Desegregation Lawsuits." *Law and History Review* 21, no. 1 (Spring 2003): 145–94.

Wintz, Cary D. "Blacks." In *The Ethnic Groups of Houston*, ed. Fred R. von der Mehden. Houston: Rice University Studies, 1984.

Books

Achor, Shirley. *Mexican Americans in a Dallas Barrio*. Tucson: University of Arizona Press, 1978.

Almaguer, Tomás. *Racial Fault Lines: The Historical Origins of White Supremacy in California*. Berkeley: University of California Press, 1994.

Anderson, James D. *The Education of Blacks in the South, 1860–1935*. Chapel Hill: University of North Carolina Press, 1988.

Anderson, Stephen C. *J. W. Edgar: Educator for Texas*. Austin: Eakin Press, 1984.

Arsenault, Raymond. *Freedom Riders: 1961 and the Struggle for Racial Justice*. New York: Oxford University Press, 2006.

Austin, Curtis J. *Up against the Wall: Violence in the Making and Unmaking of the Black Panther Party*. Fayetteville: University of Arkansas Press, 2006.

Balderama, Francisco E., and Raymond Rodriguez. *Decade of Betrayal: Mexican Repatriation in the 1930s*. Albuquerque: University of New Mexico Press, 2006.

Ball, Howard. *A Defiant Life: Thurgood Marshall and the Persistence of Racism in America*. New York: Crown Publishers, 1998.

Barr, Alwyn. *Black Texans: A History of African Americans in Texas, 1528–1995*. Norman: University of Oklahoma Press, 1996.

Barr, Alwyn, and Robert A. Calvert, eds. *Black Leaders: Texans for Their Times*. Austin: Texas State Historical Association, 1981.

Barrera, Mario. *Race and Class in the Southwest: A Theory of Racial Inequality*. Notre Dame: University of Notre Dame Press, 1980.

Bartley, Numan V. *The Rise of Massive Resistance: Race and Politics in the South during the 1950s*. Baton Rouge: Louisiana State University Press, 1997.

Bauman, Robert. *Race and the War on Poverty: From Watts to East L.A.* Norman: University of Oklahoma Press, 2008.

Bayor, Ronald H., ed. *The Columbia Documentary History of Race and Ethnicity in America*. New York: Columbia University Press, 2004.

Beeth, Howard, and Cary D. Wintz, eds. *Black Dixie: Afro-Texan History and Culture in Houston*. College Station: Texas A&M University Press, 1992.

Belknap, Michael R. *Urban Race Riots*. New York: Garland, 1991.

Bell, Derrick. *Silent Covenants*: Brown v. Board of Education *and the Unfulfilled Hopes for Racial Reform*. New York: Oxford University Press, 2005.

Berg, Manfred. *The Ticket to Freedom: The NAACP and the Struggle for Black Political Integration*. Gainesville: University Press of Florida, 2005.

Bernstein, Patricia. *The First Waco Horror: The Lynching of Jesse Washington and the Rise of the NAACP*. College Station: Texas A&M University Press, 2006.

Blanton, Carlos Kevin. *The Strange Career of Bilingual Education in Texas, 1836–1981*. College Station: Texas A&M University Press, 2004.

Boff, Leonardo, and Clodovis Boff. *Introducing Liberation Theology*. Maryknoll, N.Y.: Orbis Books, 1987.

Borstelman, Thomas. *The Cold War and the Color Line: American Race Relations in the Global Arena*. Cambridge: Harvard University Press, 2001.

Boxill, Bernard R. *Blacks and Social Justice*. Lanham: Rowman and Littlefield, 1992.

Branch, Taylor. *At Canaan's Edge: America in the King Years, 1965–1968*. New York: Simon and Schuster, 2006.

———. *Parting the Waters: America in the King Years, 1954–1963*. New York: Simon and Schuster, 1988.

———. *Pillar of Fire: America in the King Years, 1963–1965*. New York: Simon and Schuster, 1998.

Brodkin, Karen. *How the Jews Became White Folks and What That Says about Race*. New Brunswick, N.J.: Rutgers University Press, 1998.

Bronder, Saul E. *Social Justice and Church Authority: The Public Life of Archbishop Robert E. Lucey*. Philadelphia: Temple University Press, 1982.

Brown, Norman D. *Hood, Bonnet, and Little Brown Jug: Texas Politics, 1921–1928*. College Station: Texas A&M University Press, 1984.

Bryson, Conrey. *Dr. Lawrence A. Nixon and the White Primary*. El Paso: Texas Western Press, 1974.

Buitron, Richard, Jr. *The Search for Tejano Identity in San Antonio, Texas, 1913–2000*. New York: Routledge, 2004.

Carleton, Don E. *Red Scare!: Right-Wing Hysteria, Fifties Fanaticism, and Their Legacy in Texas*. Austin: Texas Monthly Press, 1985.

Caro, Robert A. *Master of the Senate: The Years of Lyndon Johnson*. New York: Knopf, 2002.

Carrigan, William D. *The Making of a Lynching Culture: Violence and Vigilantism in Central Texas, 1836–1916*. Chicago: University of Illinois Press, 2006.

Carroll, Patrick J. *Felix Longoria's Wake: Bereavement, Racism, and the Rise of Mexican American Activism*. Austin: University of Texas Press, 2003.

Carson, Clayborne. *In Struggle: SNCC and the Black Awakening of the 1960s*. Cambridge: Harvard University Press, 1995.

Chafe, William H. *Civilities and Civil Rights: Greensboro, North Carolina, and the Black Struggle for Freedom*. New York: Oxford University Press, 1981.

Chappell, David L. *A Stone of Hope: Prophetic Religion and the Death of Jim Crow*. Chapel Hill: University of North Carolina Press, 2004.

Chávez, Ernesto. *"¡Mi raza primero!": Nationalism, Identity, and Insurgency in the Chicano Movement in Los Angeles, 1966–1978*. Berkeley: University of California Press, 2002.

Cleaver, Kathleen, and George Katsiaficas. *Liberation, Imagination, and the Black Panther Party: A New Look at the Panthers and Their Legacy*. New York: Routledge, 2001.

Cole, Thomas. *No Color Is My Kind: The Life of Eldrewey Stearns and the Integration of Houston*. Austin: University of Texas Press, 1997.

Collier-Thomas, Bettye. *Sisters in the Struggle: African-American Women in the Civil Rights–Black Power Movement*. New York: New York University Press, 2001.

Countryman, Matthew J. *Up South: Civil Rights and Black Power in Philadelphia*. Philadelphia: University of Pennsylvania Press, 2006.

Cox, Patrick L. *Ralph W. Yarborough: The People's Senator*. Austin: University of Texas Press, 2002.

Craig, Richard B. *The Bracero Program: Interest Groups and Foreign Policy*. Austin: University of Texas Press, 1971.

Davidson, Chandler. *Biracial Politics: Conflict and Coalition in the Metropolitan South.* Baton Rouge: Louisiana State University Press, 1972.

Davis, Matthew D. *Exposing a Culture of Neglect: Herschel T. Manuel and Mexican American Schooling.* Greenwich, Conn.: Information Age Publishing, 2005.

De Genova, Nicholas. *Racial Transformations: Latinos and Asians Remaking the United States.* Durham, N.C.: Duke University Press, 2006.

de la Luz Sáenz, José. *Los México-Americanos en la Gran Guerra y Su Contingente en Pro de la Democracia, la Humanidad, y la Justicia.* San Antonio: Artes Gráficas, 1933.

De León, Arnoldo. *Ethnicity in the Sunbelt: A History of Mexican-Americans in Houston.* College Station: Texas A&M University Press, 2001.

———. *Mexican Americans in Texas: A Brief History.* Wheeling, W.Va.: Harland Davidson, Inc., 1999.

———. *They Called Them Greasers: Anglo Attitudes toward Mexicans in Texas, 1821–1900.* Austin: University of Texas Press, 1983.

Dittmer, John. *Local People: The Struggle for Civil Rights in Mississippi.* Chicago: University of Illinois Press, 1994.

Donato, Rubén. *The Other Struggle for Equal Schools: Mexican Americans during the Civil Rights Movement.* New York: State University of New York Press, 1997.

Douglas, Davison M., ed. *School Busing: Constitutional and Political Developments.* New York: Garland, 1994.

Du Bois, W. E. B. *Black Reconstruction in America: An Essay toward a History of the Past Which Black Folk Played in the Attempt to Reconstruct Democracy in America, 1860–1880.* 1935. Reprint, New York: Free Press, 1999.

Dudziak, Mary L. *Cold War Civil Rights: Race and the Image of American Democracy.* Princeton: Princeton University Press, 2000.

Edsall, Thomas B., and Mary D. Edsall, *Chain Reaction: The Impact of Race, Rights, and Taxes on American Politics.* New York: Norton, 1991.

Eskew, Glenn T. *But for Birmingham: The Local and National Movements in the Civil Rights Struggle.* Chapel Hill: University of North Carolina Press, 1997.

Espinosa, Gastón, Virgilio Elizondo, and Jesse Miranda, eds. *Latino Religions and Civic Activism in the United States.* New York: Oxford University Press, 2005.

Fairclough, Adam. *Race and Democracy: The Civil Rights Struggle in Louisiana.* Athens: University of Georgia Press, 1995.

———. *To Redeem the Soul of America: The Southern Christian Leadership Conference and Martin Luther King, Jr.* Athens: University of Georgia Press, 1987.

Farmer, James. *Lay Bare the Heart: An Autobiography of the Civil Rights Movement.* Fort Worth: Texas Christian University Press, 1998.

Fine, Sidney. *Violence in the Model City: The Cavanagh Administration, Race Relations, and the Detroit Riot of 1967.* Ann Arbor: University of Michigan Press, 1989.

Flynn, Jean. *Henry B. Gonzalez: Rebel with a Cause.* Austin: Eakin Press, 2004.

Foley, Neil. *Quest for Equality: The Failed Promise of Black-Brown Solidarity.* Cambridge: Harvard University Press, 2010.

———. *The White Scourge: Mexicans, Blacks, and Poor Whites in Texas Cotton Culture.* Los Angeles: University of California Press, 1999.

Foner, Philip S., ed. *The Black Panthers Speak.* New York: Da Capo Press, 1995.

Frederickson, George M. *The Black Image in the White Mind: The Debate on Afro American Character and Destiny, 1817–1914*. Middletown, Conn.: Wesleyan University Press, 1987.

———. *The Comparative Imagination: On the History of Racism, Nationalism, and Social Movements*. Los Angeles: University of California Press, 2000.

———. *Racism: A Short History*. Princeton: Princeton University Press, 2003.

Gaillard, Frye. *Cradle of Freedom: Alabama and the Movement That Changed America*. Tuscaloosa: University of Alabama Press, 2006.

García, Ignacio M. *Chicanismo: The Forging of a Militant Ethos among Mexican Americans*. Tucson: University of Arizona Press, 1997.

———. *Hector P. García: In Relentless Pursuit of Justice*. Houston: Arte Público Press, 2002.

———. *United We Win: The Rise and Fall of La Raza Unida Party*. Tucson: University of Arizona Press, 1989.

———. *Viva Kennedy: Mexican Americans in Search of Camelot*. College Station: Texas A&M University Press, 2000.

———. *White but Not Equal: Mexican Americans, Jury Discrimination, and the Supreme Court*. Tucson: University of Arizona Press, 2009.

García, Juan Ramon. *Operation Wetback: The Mass Deportation of Mexican Undocumented Workers in 1954*. Westport, Conn.: Greenwood Press, 1980.

García, Mario T. *Católicos: Resistance and Affirmation in Chicano Catholic History*. Austin: University of Texas Press, 2008.

———. *Desert Immigrants: The Mexicans of El Paso, 1880–1920*. New Haven: Yale University Press, 1982.

———. *Mexican Americans: Leadership, Ideology, and Identity, 1930–1960*. New Haven: Yale University Press, 1989.

Garrow, David J. *Bearing the Cross: Martin Luther King, Jr., and the Southern Christian Leadership Conference*. New York: Vintage Books, 1988.

Glaude, Eddie S., Jr. *Is It Nation Time?: Contemporary Essays on Black Power and Black Nationalism*. Chicago: University of Chicago Press, 2002.

Gómez, Laura E. *Manifest Destinies: The Making of the Mexican American Race*. New York: New York University Press, 2007.

Gómez-Quiñones, Juan. *Chicano Politics: Reality and Promise, 1940–1990*. Albuquerque: University of New Mexico Press, 1990.

Gonzales, Manuel G. *Mexicanos: A History of Mexicans in the United States*. Bloomington: Indiana University Press, 2000.

González, Gilbert. *Chicano Education in the Era of Segregation*. Philadelphia: Balch Institute Press, 1990.

Govenar, Alan B. *The Early Years of Rhythm and Blues*. Atglen, Pa.: Schiffer Publishing, 2004.

Govenar, Alan B., and Jay F. Brakefield. *Deep Ellum and Central Track: Where the Black and White Worlds of Dallas Converged*. Denton: University of North Texas Press, 1998.

Green, George Norris. *The Establishment of Texas Politics: The Primitive Years, 1938–1957*. Westport, Conn.: Greenwood Press, 1979.

Griswold del Castillo, Richard. *The Treaty of Guadalupe Hidalgo: A Legacy of Conflict.* Norman: University of Oklahoma Press, 1990.

Griswold del Castillo, Richard, and Richard A. Garcia. *César Chávez: A Triumph of Spirit.* Norman: University of Oklahoma Press, 1997.

Gross, Ariela J. *What Blood Won't Tell: A History of Race on Trial in America.* Cambridge: Harvard University Press, 2008.

Grossman, James R. *Land of Hope: Chicago, Black Southerners, and the Great Migration.* Chicago: University of Chicago Press, 1989.

Gutiérrez, David G. *Walls and Mirrors: Mexican Americans, Mexican Immigrants, and the Politics of Ethnicity.* Berkeley: University of California Press, 1995.

Gutiérrez, Gustavo. *A Theology of Liberation: History, Politics, and Salvation.* Maryknoll, N.Y.: Orbis Books, 1988.

Gutiérrez, José Angel. *The Making of a Chicano Militant: Lessons from Cristal.* Madison: University of Wisconsin Press, 1998.

———. *We Won't Back Down: Severita Lara's Rise from Student Leader to Mayor.* Houston: Piñata Books, 2005.

Hall, Jacquelyn Dowd. *Revolt against Chivalry: Jessie Daniel Ames and the Women's Campaign against Lynching.* New York: Columbia University Press, 1979.

Hammerback, John C., Richard J. Jensen, and José Angel Gutiérrez. *A War of Words: Chicano Protest in the 1960s and 1970s.* Westport, Conn.: Greenwood Press, 1985.

Haney López, Ian F. *White by Law: The Legal Construction of Race.* New York: New York University Press, 1996.

Harley, Sharon, ed. *Sister Circle: Black Women and Work.* New Brunswick, N.J.: Rutgers University Press, 2002.

Harley, Sharon, and Rosalyn Terborg-Penn, eds. *The Afro-American Woman: Struggles and Images.* Baltimore: Black Classic Press, 1997.

Haynes, Robert V. *A Night of Violence: The Houston Riot of 1917.* Baton Rouge: Louisiana State University Press, 1976.

Heintze, Michael R. *Private Black Colleges in Texas, 1865–1954.* College Station: Texas A&M University Press, 1985.

Henry, Aaron. *Aaron Henry: The Fire Ever Burning.* Jackson: University Press of Mississippi, 2000.

Herman, Max Arthur. *Fighting in the Streets: Ethnic Succession and Urban Unrest in Twentieth-Century America.* New York: Peter Lang Publishing, 2005.

Herzog, Stephen J. *Minority Group Politics: A Reader.* New York: Holt, Rinehart and Winston, 1971.

Hill, Lance. *The Deacons for Defense: Armed Resistance and the Civil Rights Movement.* Chapel Hill: University of North Carolina Press, 2004.

Hine, Darlene Clark. *Black Victory: The Rise and Fall of the White Primary in Texas.* Millwood, N.Y.: KTO Press, 1979.

———. *Hine Sight: Black Women and the Re-Construction of American History.* Bloomington: Indiana University Press, 1997.

Hodgson, Godfrey. *The World Turned Right Side Up: A History of the Conservative Ascendance in America.* Boston: Houghton Mifflin, 1996.

Ignatiev, Noel. *How the Irish Became White*. New York: Routledge, 1996.

Irons, Peter H. *Jim Crow's Children: The Broken Promise of the* Brown *Decision*. New York: Viking Books, 2002.

Jacobson, David, ed. *The Immigration Reader: America in a Multidisciplinary Perspective*. Malden, Mass.: Wiley-Blackwell, 1998.

Jacobson, Matthew Frye. *Whiteness of a Different Color: European Immigrants and the Alchemy of Race*. Cambridge: Harvard University Press, 1998.

Jeffries, Judson L. *Huey P. Newton: The Radical Theorist*. Jackson: University Press of Mississippi, 2002.

Jonas, Gilbert. *Freedom's Sword: The NAACP and the Struggle against Racism in America*. New York: Routledge, 2005.

Jones, Charles E., ed. *The Black Panther Party Reconsidered*. Baltimore: Black Classic Press, 1998.

Jordan, Barbara. *Barbara Jordan: Speaking the Truth with Eloquent Thunder*. Austin: University of Texas Press, 2007.

Joseph, Peniel E. *Waiting 'Til the Midnight Hour: A Narrative History of Black Power in America*. New York: Henry Holt, 2006.

———, ed. *The Black Power Movement: Rethinking the Civil Rights–Black Power Era*. New York: Routledge, 2006.

Justice, Blair. *Violence in the City*. Fort Worth: Texas Christian University Press, 1969.

Kaplowitz, Craig A. *LULAC, Mexican Americans, and National Policy*. College Station: Texas A&M University Press, 2005.

Kellar, William Henry. *Make Haste Slowly: Moderates, Conservatives, and School Desegregation in Houston*. College Station: Texas A&M University Press, 1999.

Kells, Michele Hall. *Héctor P. García: Everyday Rhetoric and Mexican American Civil Rights*. Carbondale: Southern Illinois University Press, 2006.

Kennedy, Randall. *Nigger: The Strange Career of a Troublesome Word*. New York: Vintage Book, 2002.

Kluger, Richard. *Simple Justice: The History of* Brown v. Board of Education *and Black America's Struggle for Equality*. New York: Vintage Books, 2004.

Kozol, Jonathan. *The Shame of the Nation: The Restoration of Apartheid Schooling in America*. New York: Crown, 2005.

Kreneck, Thomas H. *Mexican American Odyssey: Felix Tijerina, Entrepreneur and Civic Leader, 1905–1965*. College Station: Texas A&M University Press, 2001.

La Botz, Dan. *César Chávez and La Causa*. New York: Pearson Longman, 2006.

Ladino, Robin Duff. *Desegregating Texas Schools: Eisenhower, Shivers, and the Crisis at Mansfield High*. Austin: University of Texas Press, 1996.

Lamb, Matthew L., and Matthew Levering, eds. *Vatican II: Renewal within Tradition*. New York: Oxford University Press, 2008.

Lewis, David L. *King: A Biography*. Chicago: University of Illinois Press, 1978.

Linden, Glenn M. *Desegregating Schools in Dallas: Four Decades in the Federal Courts*. Dallas: Three Forks Press, 1995.

Lipsitz, George. *The Possessive Investment in Whiteness: How People Profit from Identity Politics*. Philadelphia: Temple University Press, 1998.

Manis, Andrew. *A Fire You Can't Put Out: The Civil Rights Life of Birmingham's Reverend Fred Shuttlesworth*. Tuscaloosa: University of Alabama Press, 1999.

Mariscal, George. *Brown-eyed Children of the Sun: Lessons from the Chicano Movement, 1965–1975*. Albuquerque: University of New Mexico Press, 2005.

Márquez, Benjamin. *LULAC: The Evolution of a Mexican-American Political Organization*. Austin: University of Texas Press, 1993.

Martinez, Richard Edward. *PADRES: The National Chicano Priest Movement*. Austin: University of Texas Press, 2005.

Marx, Anthony W. *Making Race and Nation: A Comparison of South Africa, the United States, and Brazil*. Cambridge: Cambridge University Press, 1997.

Mason, Kenneth. *African Americans and Race Relations in San Antonio, Texas, 1867–1937*. New York: Garland, 1998.

Matovina, Timothy. *Guadalupe and Her Faithful: Latino Catholics in San Antonio, from Colonial Origins to the Present*. Baltimore: Johns Hopkins University Press, 2005.

McGirr, Lisa. *Suburban Warriors: The Origins of the New American Right*. Princeton: Princeton University Press, 2001.

McKnight, Gerald. *The Last Crusade: Martin Luther King Jr., the FBI, and the Poor People's Campaign*. Boulder: Westview Press, 1998.

McMillen, Neil R. *The Citizens' Council: Organized Resistance to the Second Reconstruction, 1954–1964*. Chicago: University of Illinois Press, 1994.

McWhorter, Diane. *Carry Me Home: Birmingham, Alabama: The Climactic Battle of the Civil Rights Revolution*. New York: Touchstone, 2002.

Mease, Quentin R. *On Equal Footing: A Memoir*. Austin: Eakin Press, 2001.

Medina, Lara. *Las Hermanas: Chicana/Latina Religious-Political Activism in the U.S. Catholic Church*. Philadelphia: Temple University Press, 2005.

Meier, August, and Elliott Rudwick. *CORE: A Study in the Civil Rights Movement, 1942–1968*. New York: Oxford University Press, 1973.

Meier, Matt S., and Feliciano Ribera. *Mexican Americans/American Mexicans: From Conquistadors to Chicanos*. New York: Hill and Wang, 1993.

Melosi, Martin V. *Garbage in the Cities: Refuse, Reform, and the Environment*. Pittsburg: University of Pittsburg Press, 2005.

Menchaca, Martha. *Recovering History, Constructing Race: The Indian, Black, and White Roots of Mexican Americans*. Austin: University of Texas Press, 2002.

Miller, Marilyn Grace. *Rise and Fall of the Cosmic Race: The Cult of Mestizaje in Latin America*. Austin: University of Texas Press, 2004.

Mindiola, Tatcho, Yolanda Flores Nieman, and Nestor Rodriguez. *Black-Brown: Relations and Stereotypes*. Austin: University of Texas Press, 2002.

Montejano, David. *Anglos and Mexicans in the Making of Texas, 1836–1986*. Austin: University of Texas Press, 1987.

Morris, Aldon. *The Origins of the Civil Rights Movement: Black Communities Organizing for Change*. New York: Free Press, 1984.

Muñoz, Carlos. *Youth, Identity, Power: The Chicano Movement*. New York: Verso, 1989.

Navarro, Armando. *The Cristal Experiment: A Chicano Struggle for Community Control*. Madison: University of Wisconsin Press, 1998.

———. *La Raza Unida Party: A Chicano Challenge to the U.S. Two-Party Dictatorship.* Philadelphia: Temple University Press, 2000.

———. *Mexican American Youth Organization: Avant-Garde of the Chicano Movement in Texas.* Austin: University of Texas Press, 1995.

Nevels, Cynthia Skove. *Lynching to Belong: Claiming Whiteness through Racial Violence.* College Station: Texas A&M University Press, 2007.

Newman, Mark. *The Civil Rights Movement.* Westport, Conn.: Greenwood Press, 2004.

———. *Divine Agitators: The Delta Ministry and Civil Rights in Mississippi.* Athens: University of Georgia Press, 2004.

Ogbar, Jeffrey O. G. *Black Power: Radical Politics and African American Identity.* Baltimore: Johns Hopkins University Press, 2004.

Olivas, Michael A., ed. *Colored Men and Hombres Aquí:* Hernandez v. Texas *and the Emergence of Mexican American Lawyering.* Houston: Arte Público Press, 2006.

Oppenheimer, Martin. *The Sit-In Movement of 1960.* Brooklyn: Carlson Publishing, 1989.

Oropeza, Lorena. *¡Raza Sí! ¡Guerra No!: Chicano Protest and Patriotism during the Viet Nam War Era.* Los Angeles: University of California Press, 2005.

Overton, Volma. *Volma . . . My Journey: One Man's Impact on the Civil Rights Movement in Austin, Texas.* Austin: Eakin Press, 1998.

Packard, Jerrold M. *American Nightmare: The History of Jim Crow.* New York: St. Martins Press, 2002.

Paredes, Américo. *"With His Pistol in His Hand": A Border Ballad and Its Hero.* Austin: University of Texas Press, 1958.

———, ed. *Humanidad: Essays in Honor of George I. Sánchez.* Los Angeles: Chicano Studies Center Publications, University of California, Los Angeles, 1977.

Parks, Katie. *Remember When? A History of African Americans in Lubbock, Texas.* Lubbock: PrinTech Printers, 1999.

Payne, Charles M. *I've Got the Light of Freedom: The Organizing Tradition and the Mississippi Freedom Struggle.* Los Angeles: University of California Press, 1995.

Payne, Darwin. *Big D: Triumphs and Troubles of an American Supercity in the 20th Century.* Dallas: Three Forks Press, 2000.

———. *Quest for Justice: Louis A. Bedford Jr. and the Struggle for Equal Rights in Texas.* Dallas: Southern Methodist University Press, 2009.

Peake, Thomas R. *Keeping the Dream Alive: A History of the Southern Christian Leadership Conference from King to the Nineteen-Eighties.* New York: Peter Lang Publishing, 1987.

Perales, Alonso S. *Are We Good Neighbors?* San Antonio: Artes Gráficas, 1948.

Phillips, Michael. *White Metropolis: Race, Ethnicity, and Religion in Dallas, 1841–2001.* Austin: University of Texas Press, 2006.

Piatt, Bill. *Black and Brown in America: The Case for Cooperation.* New York: New York University Press, 1997.

Pitre, Merline. *In Struggle against Jim Crow: Lulu B. White and the NAACP, 1900–1957.* College Station: Texas A&M University Press, 1999.

Pycior, Julie Leininger. *LBJ and Mexican Americans: The Paradox of Power.* Austin: University of Texas Press, 1997.

Quiroz, Anthony. *Claiming Citizenship: Mexican Americans in Victoria, Texas.* College Station: Texas A&M University Press, 2005.

Ransby, Barbara. *Ella Baker and the Black Freedom Struggle: A Radical Democratic Vision.* Chapel Hill: University of North Carolina Press, 2003.

Reston, James, Jr. *Lone Star: The Life of John Connally.* New York: Random House Valu Publishing, 1991.

Rhoads, Joseph J. *Advancing the Cause of Democracy in Education.* Marshall: Texas Commission on Democracy and Education, 1951.

Rivas-Rodriguez, Maggie, ed. *Mexican Americans and World War II.* Austin: University of Texas Press, 2005.

Rodriguez, Eugene, Jr. *Henry B. Gonzalez: A Political Profile.* New York: Arno Press, 1976.

Roediger, David R. *The Wages of Whiteness: Race and the Making of the American Working Class.* New York: Verso, 1999.

Rogers, Mary Beth. *Barbara Jordan: American Hero.* New York: Bantam Books, 1998.

Rojas, Fabio. *From Black Power to Black Studies: How a Radical Social Movement Became an Academic Discipline.* Baltimore: Johns Hopkins University Press, 2007.

Romo, Harriett D., ed. *Latinos and Blacks in the Cities: Policies for the 1990s.* Austin: University of Texas Press, 1990.

Rosales, F. Arturo. *Chicano!: The History of the Mexican American Civil Rights Movement.* Houston: Arte Público Press, 1997.

Rosales, Rodolfo. *The Illusion of Inclusion: The Untold Political Story of San Antonio.* Austin: University of Texas Press, 2000.

Rosenbaum, Robert J. *Mexicano Resistance in the Southwest.* Dallas: Southern Methodist University Press, 1998.

Rowan, Carl Thomas. *Dream Makers, Dream Breakers: The World of Justice Thurgood Marshall.* Boston: Little, Brown, 1993.

Rubio, Abel G. *Stolen Heritage: A Mexican-American's Rediscovery of His Family's Lost Land Grant.* Austin: Eakin Press, 1986.

Samora, Julian, Joe Bernal, and Albert Peña. *Gunpowder Justice: A Reassessment of the Texas Rangers.* Notre Dame: University of Notre Dame Press, 1979.

Sánchez, George J. *Becoming Mexican American: Ethnicity, Culture, and Identity in Chicano Los Angeles, 1900–1945.* New York: Oxford University Press, 1995.

San Miguel, Guadalupe. *Brown, Not White: School Integration and the Chicano Movement in Houston.* College Station: Texas A&M University Press, 2001.

———. *Contested Policy: The Rise and Fall of Federal Bilingual Education in the United States, 1960–2001.* Denton: University of North Texas Press, 2004.

———. *"Let All of Them Take Heed": Mexican-Americans and the Campaign for Educational Equality in Texas, 1910–1981.* Austin: University of Texas Press, 1987.

Schmidt, Henry C. *The Roots of Lo Mexicano: Self and Society in Mexican Thought, 1900–1934.* College Station: Texas A&M University Press, 1978.

Schutze, Jim. *The Accommodation: The Politics of Race in an American City.* Secaucus, N.J.: Citadel Press, 1986.

Self, Robert O. *American Babylon: Race and the Struggle for Postwar Oakland.* Princeton: Princeton University Press, 2003.

Sepúlveda, Juan. *The Life and Times of Willie Velásquez: Su Voto es Su Voz*. Houston: Arte Público Press, 2003.

Shabazz, Amilcar. *Advancing Democracy: African Americans and the Struggle for Access and Equity in Higher Education in Texas*. Chapel Hill: University of North Carolina Press, 2004.

Sherry, Matthew. *A Brief History of Vatican II*. Maryknoll, N.Y.: Orbis Books, 2006.

Shockley, John Staples. *Chicano Revolt in a Texas Town*. Notre Dame: University of Notre Dame Press, 1974.

Shogan, Robert, and Tom Craig. *The Detroit Race Riot: A Study in Violence*. New York: Da Capo Press, 1976.

Singh, Nikhil Pal. *Black Is a Country: Race and the Unfinished Struggle for Democracy*. Cambridge: Harvard University Press, 2004.

Sloane, Todd A. *Gonzalez of Texas: A Congressman for the People*. Evanston, Ill.: John Gordon Burke Publishing, 1996.

Soltero, Carlos R. *Latinos and American Law: Landmark Supreme Court Cases*. Austin: University of Texas Press, 2006.

Sracic, Paul A. *San Antonio v. Rodriguez and the Pursuit of Equal Education: The Debate over Discrimination and School Funding*. Lawrence: University Press of Kansas, 2006.

Strain, Christopher B. *Pure Fire: Self-Defense as Activism in the Civil Rights Era*. Athens: University of Georgia Press 2005.

Strum, Philippa. *Mendez v. Westminster: School Desegregation and Mexican-American Rights*. Lawrence: University of Kansas Press, 2010.

Thornton, J. Mills, III. *Dividing Lines: Municipal Politics and the Struggle for Civil Rights in Montgomery, Birmingham, and Selma*. Tuscaloosa: University of Alabama Press, 2002.

Tijerina, Andrés. *History of Mexican Americans in Lubbock County, Texas*. Lubbock: Texas Tech Press, 1979.

Treviño, Roberto R. *The Church in the Barrio: Mexican American Ethno-Catholicism in Houston*. Chapel Hill: University of North Carolina Press, 2006.

Tuck, Stephen G. N. *Beyond Atlanta: The Struggle for Racial Equality in Georgia, 1940–1980*. Athens: University of Georgia Press, 2001.

Tushnet, Mark V. *Making Constitutional Law: Thurgood Marshall and the Supreme Court, 1961–1991*. New York: Oxford University Press, 1997.

———. *The NAACP's Legal Strategy against Segregated Education, 1925–1950*. Chapel Hill: University of North Carolina Press, 2005.

Tuttle, William M., Jr. *Race Riot: Chicago in the Red Summer of 1919*. Chicago: University of Illinois Press, 1994.

Tyson, Timothy B. *Radio Free Dixie: Robert F. Williams and the Roots of Black Power*. Chapel Hill: University of North Carolina Press, 2001.

Vaca, Nicolás C. *The Presumed Alliance: The Unspoken Conflict between Latinos and Blacks and What It Means for America*. New York: Rayo, 2004.

Van Deburg, William L. *New Day in Babylon: The Black Power Movement and American Culture, 1965–1975*. Chicago: University of Chicago Press, 1992.

Vargas, Zaragosa. *Labor Rights Are Civil Rights: Mexican American Workers in Twentieth-Century America*. Princeton: Princeton University Press, 2004.

Vasconselos, José. *La Raza Cósmica*. Mexico D.F.: Espasa Calpe, S.A., 1948.

Vigil, Ernesto B. *The Crusade for Justice: Chicano Militancy and the Government's War on Dissent*. Madison: University of Wisconsin Press, 1985.

Vinovskis, Maris A. *The Birth of Head Start: Preschool Education Policies in the Kennedy and Johnson Administrations*. Chicago: University of Chicago Press, 2005.

von der Mehden, Fred R., ed. *The Ethnic Groups of Houston*. Houston: Rice University Studies, 1984.

Watson, Dwight. *Race and the Houston Police Department, 1930–1990: A Change Did Come*. College Station: Texas A&M University Press, 2006.

Wendt, Simon. *The Spirit and the Shotgun: Armed Resistance and the Struggle for Civil Rights*. Gainesville: University Press of Florida, 2007.

Whitaker, Matthew. *Race Work: The Rise of Civil Rights in the American West*. Lincoln: University of Nebraska Press, 2005.

Wilhoit, Francis M. *The Politics of Massive Resistance*. New York: G. Braziller Books, 1973.

Williams, Juan. *Thurgood Marshall: American Revolutionary*. New York: Times Books, 1998.

Williams, Yohuru. *Black Politics/White Power: Civil Rights, Black Power, and the Black Panthers in New Haven*. St. James, N.Y.: Brandywine Press, 2000.

Wilson, Steven Harmon. *The Rise of Judicial Management in the U.S. District Court, Southern District of Texas, 1955–2000*. Athens: University of Georgia Press, 2003.

Wilson, William H. *Hamilton Park: A Planned Black Community in Dallas*. Baltimore: Johns Hopkins University Press, 1998.

Woodard, Komozi. *A Nation within a Nation: Amiri Baraka (LeRoi Jones) and Black Power Politics*. Chapel Hill: University of North Carolina Press, 1999.

Woodward, C. Vann. *The Comparative Approach to American History*. New York: Oxford University Press, 1997.

———. *The Strange Career of Jim Crow*. Commemorative ed. New York: Oxford University Press, 2002.

Zamora, Emilio. *Claiming Rights and Righting Wrongs in Texas: Mexican Workers and Job Politics during World War II*. College Station: Texas A&M University Press, 2009.

———. *The World of the Mexican Worker in Texas*. College Station: Texas A&M University Press, 1993.

Index

Aaron, James, 163, 164

Abernathy, Ralph David, 142, 151, 189

Adair, Christia V., 19, 55

Advocating Rights for Mexican-American Students (ARMAS), 199–200, 295 (n. 26)

African American/Mexican American conflict: racism and, 1–2, 8, 11, 13–14, 37–38, 62–63, 65–68, 72–73, 127, 195, 215–18, 227–28; demographics and, 4, 229, 232, 238; segregation as dividing force in, 6, 68–69, 77, 195–96, 216; geographic distance and, 6–7, 11, 97–98, 127–28, 227, 230; perceptions of cultural and social dissimilarity in, 7, 11, 126, 191, 226–27, 229; racial issues and, 8–9, 10, 40, 56–57, 69–70, 93–96, 98, 188, 189, 191, 238–39; Mexican American whiteness and, 8–9, 14, 35–36, 37–38, 56–57, 70, 103, 127–28, 189, 227–28; intergroup jealousies and, 9, 10, 96, 215, 238; political competition and, 9, 98–100, 113, 191, 224, 228–29, 232, 233, 235–36, 238; violence in, 10, 13–14, 37–38, 188, 218, 226, 234; rhetoric of unity and rhetorical tactlessness and, 10, 56–57, 72–73, 94–96, 100–101, 126, 219–20; over government resources, 10, 101, 112–13, 126–27, 191, 227, 229–30, 238; in Black/Brown Power movement, 10, 187–94, 215–16, 226; Mexican American brownness and, 10, 189–90, 215, 226; cultural nationalism and, 10, 193, 218–19, 230; class biases and tensions and, 11, 226; regional differences and, 11, 226; parallel organizations and, 35, 68–69, 99, 188–89, 191; differing levels of government support as cause of, 36, 38, 40, 68–69, 99–100, 191, 229; tactical differences and, 36–37, 55, 69–70, 72–73, 95, 99, 116, 192–93; fear and indifference and, 38, 64, 77, 191; Mexican American disapproval of black protests and, 76–77, 93–97, 225; lack of familiarity and, 93, 191, 230; comparisons of victimization, 100–101, 109–10, 112, 126, 219–20; ethno-racial self-interest or essentialism and, 97, 101, 126, 127–28, 185–86, 188–89, 191–92, 218–19, 238, 267 (n. 153); Mexican American perceptions that blacks monopolized government aid, 109–11, 112–13, 126; Mexican-American Ad Hoc Committee on Equal Employment Opportunity, 112–13, 126–27; in tri-ethnic committees, 123, 185–86, 217; Poor People's Campaign and, 151–52; Huelga Schools and, 195, 215–17; cross-racial meetings that grew out of Huelga Schools and, 217; *The Black/Mexican-American Project Report* and, 221–22; over jobs, 227, 229, 232–33, 238; burden of history and, 230; renewal of Voting Rights Act and, 232; over immigration reform, 232–33; after Hurricane Katrina, 233–34; gang warfare and, 234, 236; over housing, 234, 238; *New American Media* poll on, 234–35; in 2008 Democratic Party primary election, 235–36

African American/Mexican American cooperation: in Black/Brown Power movement, 10, 11, 164, 174–75, 185–87, 191, 219, 220, 226; in school integration, 11, 34, 41, 220–21; in labor movement, 11, 108, 124–

333

26; in Rainbow Coalition, 11, 164, 185–86; political, 11, 186; coalition-building, 55–56, 58–60, 95–97, 123, 164, 185–87, 220–21, 226, 232, 238; in Bexar County Coalition, 100, 123; in Rio Grande Valley strike and Minimum Wage March, 108, 124–26; in Alabama Sympathy Marches, 118, 123; Southwest Conference for Political Unity, 123; and ecumenism, 130–32, 148, 152–53; Ecumenical Fellowship and, 130–37; Project Equality, 137–41; Southern Christian Leadership Conference and, 142–45; Ecumenical Council on Social Concerns and, 145–47; Poor People's Campaign and, 150–52; in Santos Rodríguez protest, 174–75; anti–Vietnam War movement and, 186–87; in tri-ethnic committees, 191, 200; in Huelga Schools, 203, 215; borrowing of movement tactics and, 219; Black and Brown Coalition and, 220–21; "Manifesto on Behalf of Black Children" and, 221; *The Black/Mexican-American Project Report* and, 223–24; *New American Media* poll and, 236–37; political, 236–37; in 2008 presidential election, 236; Henry Cisneros election and, 237; Martin Luther King, Jr. holiday and, 237; National Rainbow Coalition and, 237; Federico Peña election and, 237; Antonio Villaraigosa election and, 237; Sheila Jackson Lee and, 237–38

African Americans: civil rights movement tactics and/or goals, 2, 14, 17, 18, 35–36, 225, 249 (n. 2); racism toward Mexican Americans, 9, 56, 97, 127, 188, 217, 218, 232–33; community development, 15–18, 23, 225; leadership, 16–17; struggle for voting rights, 19–21, 23; fight for education equality, 21–23, 207–15, 225; Mexican Americans allies, 34, 60–61, 64–65, 96–97; opponents in state/national government, 51–55; allies in state/national government, 57–60, 87, 98–99; protests, 72, 73–83, 116–17, 120–22; Mexican American opponents, 76–77, 93–96; response to President Kennedy's assassination, 116–17; elections and, 118–20, 123; antipoverty efforts, 122–23; police abuse of, 156, 157–59, 162–63, 164. *See also* Sit-in movement

Alabama Sympathy March, 118, 123, 138
Albuquerque Walkout, 110–11
Alcozar, Alex, 111
All-American Community, 145–46, 152
Allee, Alfred Y. (A. Y.), 89–90, 114, 125, 173. *See also* Texas Ranger(s)
Allee, Tom, 90
Allen, Earl, 16, 127, 136, 147, 161; protests in Houston, 76; protests in Dallas, 80, 117; on African American/Mexican American relations, 97, 227; ecumenical activism, 132, 147–48; TSU disturbance and, 158–59; Senate testimony, 161
Allen, George, 120
Allred, James, 46
All-White Democratic Primary, 19–21
American Civil Liberties Union (ACLU), 42, 186
American G.I. Forum, 24, 35, 42, 57, 62, 86, 95, 123, 149; development of, 31; opposition to Mexican American segregation, 31–32; whiteness strategy, 32, 65–66, 85, 98, 111, 189, 293–94 (n. 11); antipoverty and, 104–5; in Ad Hoc Committee, 112–13. *See also* Avila, Manuel; Calderon, Carlos I.; García, Hector P.; Idar, Eduardo, Jr.
Andow, Paul, 93–94, 95
Anglos/Anglo Americans. *See* Whites
Antibusing campaign. *See* Busing
Anti–Vietnam War movement, 186–87
Armendariz, Albert, 30, 56–57
Arnold, Roy, 174
Arredondo, Frances, 204
Arredondo, Jesus, 188
Arturo, 234
Asociación Nacional México-Americana (ANMA), 33–34, 35
Atwell, William, 52, 202, 209; *Bell* case, 52–53; *Borders* case, 53–54
Austin, 6, 79, 83, 103, 122, 286–87 (n. 105); segregation in, 6; civil rights demonstrations in, 78, 118; government response to protests, 78; anti–Vietnam War movement and, 186–87
Author, The, 172–73
Avila, Manuel, 62, 65–66, 69, 70. *See also* American G.I. Forum
Aztlán, 171

Massive resistance movement, 38, 50–55, 68–69

Mathis, 45, 93, 173

Maxey, Thomas, 25

McAllister, Walter W., 83, 167

McBrayer, O. A., 145

McCain, John, 236

McCamant, J. T., 26

McCormick, Paul, 41

McDowell, Cleve, 161

McMahon, J. A., 162–63

McMillan, Marion Ernest "Ernie," 97, 165–67, 188; on sit-ins in Dallas, 97; formation of Dallas SNCC, 165; protests in Dallas, 165–66; on anti–Vietnam War movement, 187; dismissal of Jesus Arredondo, 188; on ethno-racial essentialism, 188, 192; on African American/Mexican American relations, 188, 192, 230, 238; on ethnic nationalism, 188, 193

Mease, Quentin, 74, 78, 160

Medrano, Francisco "Pancho," 95, 124–26, 144, 174, 226, 232; as critic of conservative Mexican American leaders, 95; formation of Brown Berets, 174

Melba Theater, 49–50

Méndez, Gonzalo and Felícitas, 41

Mendez v. Westminster School District, 3, 41, 48, 249 (n. 5)

Mendoza, Reynaldo, 88

Mexican-American Ad Hoc Committee on Equal Employment Opportunity, 112–14

Mexican American Conference on Civil Rights, 113, 114, 177

Mexican American Education Council (MAEC), 201, 216, 296–97 (n. 53); formation of, 201; Huelga Schools, 201–4; African American/Mexican American relations and, 216–17, 220

Mexican American Legal Defense and Education Fund (MALDEF), 190, 217; brownness strategy, 190, 196, 197–98; organization of, 196–97; legal battles, 196–98, 200–201, 202–3

Mexican Americans: movement tactics, 3, 14, 23–24, 44, 73, 85, 87, 225; whiteness and, 4, 7, 24, 25, 42, 44–45, 85, 225; racism toward African Americans, 7–9, 13–14,

62–64, 65–68, 216; bifurcation of leadership of, 8–9, 40–41, 63–65, 73, 86–87, 109–10, 171–73, 184–85; community development, 23–24, 225; citizenship, 24–25; school desegregation and, 27–28, 39–40, 196–99, 225; allies in state/national government, 28–29, 35–35, 42–43, 56, 68–69; African American allies, 56–57, 60, 200, 221; disapproval of black protests, 72–73, 76–77, 190, 225; transition of leadership and tactics in the 1960s, 83–84, 93, 102–3, 109–10, 184, 225–26; response to President Kennedy's assassination, 86; labor activism, 105–9; police abuse of, 164, 173, 175; school boycotts, 198–205. *See also* Brownness strategy; Whiteness strategy

Mexican American War, 24

Mexican American Youth Organization (MAYO), 148, 154, 163, 164, 173, 177, 188; Rainbow Coalition, 164, 185; protests, 173–74, 176–79, 198–99; organization of, 176–77; in Houston, 177–79, 287 (n. 110); "Manifesto of the People," 178; disbanding, 180; exclusion of African Americans, 188; brownness strategy, 188, 190, 197–98

Mexican Mafia, 234

Mexican schools. *See* Education: segregated Mexican schools

Miller, Tom, 78

Mindiola, Tatcho, 229–30

Minimum Wage March (1966), 98, 106–9, 124, 127, 131, 138, 226, 268 (n. 15)

Minority Mobilization (MM), 148

Missionary Baptist General Convention (MBGC), 16

Molina, Arthur, 98

Montalbo, Phillip, 41, 63, 64, 172

Montejano, David, 5, 93

Moody Park riot, 165

Moore, Joan, 191

Moorehead, Michael, 174

Moreno, Luisa, 33

Muñiz, Ramsey, 181, 189; 1972 gubernatorial campaign, 181; 1974 gubernatorial campaign, 183–84; drug arrests of, 184, 289 (n. 137); ethno-racial essentialism of, 189, 192

Mutualistas, 32–33

Vaca, Nicolás C., 236
Vancronkhite, John, 32
Varela, Maria, 188
Vargas, Zaragosa, 34
Vázquez, Alfonso, 85
Velázquez, William, 176
Verver, Isabel, 46–47
Vigil, Ernesto, 231
Villaraigosa, Antonio, 237
Vines, Darrell, 145, 146
Vines, Mary, 145
Vinson, Fred M., 22
"Viva Kennedy" club(s), 3, 85–86
Volunteers in Service to America (VISTA), 104, 133–34, 161, 206; elimination of, 135–36, 148–50, 155
Voting Rights Act of 1965, 103, 118, 120, 130, 155; renewal of in 1975, 232

Waller, Douglas, 161
Warden, Ben, 29
War on Poverty, 103–4, 105, 122–23
Warren, Earl, 45
Webb, Clive, 6
Weingarten's Supermarket, 74
Welch, Louis, 156–57, 160, 165
Wesley, Carter, 20, 61
Western Hemisphere Act, 232
"What Price Education?," 84
Wheeler Street, 157
Whitaker, Matthew, 238
White, Hattie Mae, 207–8
White, Lulu, 16, 18, 19, 20, 21, 50
White, Macel, 208
White flight, 213, 299–300 (n. 104)
White House Conference on Civil Rights, 111, 113, 128
Whiteness strategy, 7–8, 36–37, 62–63, 65–66, 116, 189, 223, 227–28, 238, 293–94 (n. 11); development, 8–9, 24, 43, 225, 246 (n. 49); as contradictory strategy, 8–9, 37, 43, 48–49, 70; African American response to, 9, 37–38, 127, 227; census data forms and, 26, 27, 32, 111–12; health/medical forms and, 26, 30–31, 32, 98–99, 111; city directories and, 27; "other white" strategy and, 27; school desegregation and, 27–28, 42, 189; government response to, 28–29, 68, 84; poll tax receipts and, 32; "class apart" theory and, 44–45, 46, 250 (n. 22); appeals to white allies, 56–57; traffic tickets, 85; as anti-integration tool, 200, 203, 204–5. See also *In re Rodriguez*
Whites: segregationist views of, 5–6, 14; government leaders and, 40, 45, 50–51, 52–55, 56–57, 68–69, 88–89, 180; ecumenical leaders and, 130–42, 145–47; reaction to Black/Brown Power, 155–56, 164, 170, 204, 213–14
Wickliff, Aloysius M., 76, 77
Wiley College, 16, 22, 81
Williams, David, 230
Williams, Harrison, 115
Williams, Lee G., 105
"Winter Garden Project," 179
Woods, L. A., 27, 42, 57, 68
Woodward, C. Vann, 5
Woolworth's, 74, 79, 81
World War I, 17–18, 28
World War II, 2, 3, 17, 28

Ximenes, Vicente, 114

Yarborough, Don, 87, 98
Yarborough, Ralph, 107, 108
Youth Opportunity Centers, 104